MCITP: Windows Server 2008
Server Administrator Study Guide

Exam 70-646

OBJECTIVE	CHAPTER
Planning for Server Deployment	
Plan server installations and upgrades. *May include but is not limited to: Windows Server 2008 edition selection, rollback planning, BitLocker implementation requirements*	1, 2, 8
Plan for automated server deployment. *May include but is not limited to: standard server image, automation and scheduling of server deployments*	2
Plan infrastructure services server roles. *May include but is not limited to: address assignment, name resolution, network access control, directory services, application services, certificate services*	4, 5, 6, 7
Plan application servers and services. *May include but is not limited to: virtualization server planning, availability, resilience, and accessibility*	2, 9
Plan file and print server roles. *May include but is not limited to: access permissions, storage quotas, replication, indexing, file storage policy, availability, printer publishing*	6
Planning for Server Management	
Plan server management strategies. *May include but is not limited to: remote administration, remote desktop, server management technologies, Server Manager and ServerManagerCMD, delegation policies and procedures*	1, 2, 3, 5
Plan for delegated administration. *May include but is not limited to: delegate authority, delegate Active Directory objects, application management*	5
Plan and implement Group Policy strategy. *May include but is not limited to: GPO management, GPO backup and recovery, Group Policy troubleshooting, Group Policy planning*	5

Sybex®
An Imprint of
WILEY

OBJECTIVE	CHAPTER
Monitoring and Maintaining Servers	
Implement patch management strategy. *May include but is not limited to: operating system patch level maintenance, Windows Server Update Services (WSUS), application patch level maintenance*	3
Monitor servers for performance evaluation and optimization. *May include but is not limited to: server and service monitoring, optimization, event management, trending and baseline analysis*	3
Monitor and maintain security and policies. *May include but is not limited to: remote access, monitor and maintain NPAS, network access, server security, firewall rules and policies, authentication and authorization, data security, auditing*	4, 8
Planning Application and Data Provisioning	
Provision applications. *May include but is not limited to: presentation virtualization, terminal server infrastructure, resource allocation, application virtualization alternatives, application deployment, System Center Configuration Manager*	2, 3, 5, 7
Provision data. *May include but is not limited to: shared resources, offline data access*	6, 7
Planning for Business Continuity and High Availability	
Plan storage. *May include but is not limited to: storage solutions, storage management*	9
Plan high availability. *May include but is not limited to: service redundancy, service availability*	9
Plan for backup and recovery. *May include but is not limited to: data recovery strategy, server recovery strategy, directory service recovery strategy, object level recovery*	5, 9

Exam objectives are subject to change at any time without prior notice and at Microsoft's sole discretion. Please visit Microsoft's website (www.microsoft.com/learning) for the most current listing of exam objectives.

Sybex®
An Imprint of
WILEY

MCITP
Windows Server® 2008
Server Administrator
Study Guide

MCITP
Windows Server® 2008
Server Administrator
Study Guide

Darril Gibson

WILEY

Wiley Publishing, Inc.

Acquisitions Editor: Jeff Kellum
Development Editor: Candace English
Technical Editor: Stuart Ami
Production Editor: Eric Charbonneau
Copy Editor: Kim Wimpsett
Production Manager: Tim Tate
Vice President and Executive Group Publisher: Richard Swadley
Vice President and Executive Publisher: Joseph B. Wikert
Vice President and Publisher: Neil Edde
Media Project Supervisor: Laura Moss
Media Development Specialist: Shawn Patrick
Media Quality Assurance: Josh Frank
Book Designer: Judy Fung
Compositor: Craig Woods, Happenstance Type-O-Rama
Proofreaders: Nancy Bell and Robert Shimonski
Indexer: Nancy Guenther
Cover Designer: Ryan Sneed

Copyright © 2008 by Wiley Publishing, Inc., Indianapolis, Indiana

Published simultaneously in Canada

ISBN: 978-0-470-29315-7

For general information on our other products and services or to obtain technical support, please contact our Customer Care Department within the U.S. at (800) 762-2974, outside the U.S. at (317) 572-3993 or fax (317) 572-4002.

Wiley also publishes its books in a variety of electronic formats. Some content that appears in print may not be available in electronic books.

Library of Congress Cataloging-in-Publication Data:
Gibson, Darril.
   MCITP : Windows server 2008 server administrator study guide (Exam 70-646) / Darril Gibson. — 1st ed.
      p. cm.
   ISBN 978-0-470-29315-7 (paper/cd-rom)
   1. Electronic data processing personnel—Certification. 2. Microsoft software—Examinations—Study guides.
   3. Microsoft Windows server. I. Title.
   QA76.3.G5263 2008
   005.4'476—dc22
                                        2008027402

10 9 8 7 6 5 4 3

Dear Reader,

Thank you for choosing *MCITP: Windows Server 2008 Server Administrator Study Guide (70-646).* This book is part of a family of premium quality Sybex books, all written by outstanding authors who combine practical experience with a gift for teaching.

Sybex was founded in 1976. More than thirty years later, we're still committed to producing consistently exceptional books. With each of our titles we're working hard to set a new standard for the industry. From the paper we print on, to the authors we work with, our goal is to bring you the best books available.

I hope you see all that reflected in these pages. I'd be very interested to hear your comments and get your feedback on how we're doing. Feel free to let me know what you think about this or any other Sybex book by sending me an email at nedde@wiley.com, or if you think you've found a technical error in this book, please visit http://sybex.custhelp.com. Customer feedback is critical to our efforts at Sybex.

Best regards,

Neil Edde
Vice President and Publisher
Sybex, an Imprint of Wiley

To my loving wife of more than 16 years, who continues to provide me love and encouragement even when I don't deserve it.

Acknowledgments

No book is written alone. Instead, there is a wealth of people working behind the scenes to help make a book the best possible. I'm grateful for the hard work put in behind the scenes by several people. Stuart Ami, the technical editor; Candace English, the development editor; Eric Charbonneau, the production editor; and Kim Wimpsett, the copy editor, all provided a significant amount of work that helped produce this book. I'm grateful to each of them.

I'm also grateful to my agent, Carole McClendon, for helping open up so many opportunities for me, including this one, and to Jeff Kellum, the acquisitions editor, for having the faith in me to take on this project.

About the Author

Darril Gibson has been teaching Microsoft networking concepts since the NT 4.0 days and has been teaching a myriad of other topics since many years before then. He's been a Microsoft Certified Trainer (MCT) since 1999 and holds many other certifications, including MCSE (NT 4.0, 2000, 2003), MCDBA (SQL Server 7.0 and 2000), MCTS (Vista, Server 2008 Active Directory, Server 2008 Applications Infrastructure, Server 2008 Network Infrastructure and SQL Server 2005), MCITP (Server 2008 Server Administrator, Vista Enterprise Support Technician, SQL Server 2005 Database Administrator and SQL Server 2005 Database Developer), MCAD (.NET), and MCSD (VB 6, .NET).

Darril has developed several video training courses for KeyStone Learning Systems and has written and co-authored several other technical books. He has a passion for teaching and enjoys sharing knowledge in the classroom as much as he does through books.

He currently works full-time on a government contract providing a wide array of technical training to military and government personnel in support of a network operations support center (NOSC). The NOSC supports over 100,000 users and provides a great environment to see current technologies in action. He moonlights as an adjunct professor at a local college (ECPI College of Technology) teaching system engineer courses.

Darril lives with his wife and two dogs in Virginia Beach, Virginia, but on most weekends they can be found playing on about 24 acres of land in Halifax County. He's been learning the power of water as he's tried to create a pond on this land. He's found that configuring networks is a piece of cake compared to building a good pond, but he hasn't given up yet.

Contents at a Glance

Contents

Table of Exercises

Introduction

Microsoft has recently changed its certification program to contain three primary series: Technology, Professional, and Architect. The Technology Series of certifications are intended to allow candidates to target specific technologies and are the basis for obtaining the Professional Series and Architect Series of certifications. The certifications contained within the Technology Series consist of one to three exams, focus on a specific technology, and do not include job-role skills. By contrast, the Professional Series of certifications focus on a job role and are not necessarily focused on a single technology but rather a comprehensive set of skills for performing the job role being tested. The Architect Series of certifications offered by Microsoft are premier certifications that consist of passing a review board consisting of previously certified architects. To apply for the Architect Series of certifications, you must have a minimum of 10 years of industry experience.

When obtaining a Technology Series certification, you are recognized as a Microsoft Certified Technology Specialist (MCTS) on the specific technology or technologies that you have been tested on. The Professional Series certifications include Microsoft Certified IT Professional (MCITP) and Microsoft Certified Professional Developer (MCPD). Passing the review board for an Architect Series certification will allow you to become a Microsoft Certified Architect (MCA).

This book has been developed to give you the critical skills and knowledge you need to prepare for the PRO: Windows Server 2008 Server Administrator exam (exam 70-646).

The Microsoft Certified Professional Program

Since the inception of its certification program, Microsoft has certified more than 2 million people. As the computer network industry continues to increase in both size and complexity, this number is sure to grow—and the need for *proven* ability will also increase. Certifications can help companies verify the skills of prospective employees and contractors.

Microsoft has developed its Microsoft Certified Professional (MCP) program to give you credentials that verify your ability to work with Microsoft products effectively and professionally. Several levels of certification are available based on specific suites of exams. Microsoft has recently created a new generation of certification programs:

Microsoft Certified Technology Specialist (MCTS)   The MCTS can be considered the entry-level certification for the new generation of Microsoft certifications. The MCTS certification program targets specific technologies instead of specific job roles. You must take and pass one to three exams.

Microsoft Certified IT Professional (MCITP)   The MCITP certification is a Professional Series certification that tests network and systems administrators on job roles, rather than only on a specific technology. The MCITP generally consists of passing one to three exams, in addition to obtaining an MCTS-level certification.

Microsoft Certified Master   The Microsoft Certified Master certification is a step above the Professional Series certification and is currently offered for Windows Server 2008, SQL Server 2008, and Exchange Server 2007. Qualified MCITPs attend advanced training specific to the certification track, must successfully complete in-class written and lab exams, and then complete a separate qualification lab exam.

Microsoft Certified Professional Developer (MCPD)   The MCPD certification is a Professional Series certification for application developers. Similar to the MCITP, the MCPD is focused on a job role rather than on a single technology. The MCPD generally consists of passing one to three exams, in addition to obtaining an MCTS-level certification.

Microsoft Certified Architect (MCA)   The MCA is Microsoft's premier certification series. Obtaining the MCA requires a minimum of 10 years of experience and requires the candidate to pass a review board consisting of peer architects.

How Do You Become Certified as a Windows Server 2008 Server Administrator?

Attaining a Microsoft certification has always been a challenge. In the past, students have been able to acquire detailed exam information—even most of the exam questions—from online "brain dumps" and third-party "cram" books or software products. For the new generation of exams, this is simply not the case.

Microsoft has taken strong steps to protect the security and integrity of its new certification tracks. Now prospective candidates must complete a course of study that develops detailed knowledge about a wide range of topics. It supplies them with the true skills needed, derived from working with the technology being tested.

The new generations of Microsoft certification programs are heavily weighted toward hands-on skills and experience. It is recommended that candidates have troubleshooting skills acquired through hands-on experience and working knowledge.

Fortunately, if you are willing to dedicate the time and effort to learn Windows Server 2008 Active Directory, you can prepare yourself well for the exam by using the proper tools. By working through this book, you can successfully meet the exam requirements to pass the Windows Server 2008 Active Directory exam.

This book is part of a complete series of Microsoft certification study guides, published by Sybex Inc., that together cover the new MCTS, MCITP, and MCPD exams, as well as the core MCSA and MCSE operating system requirements. Please visit the Sybex website at www.sybex.com for complete program and product details.

MCITP Requirements

Candidates for MCITP Server Administrator certification on Windows Server 2008 must pass three Windows Server 2008 exams: 70-640 (Windows Server 2008 Active Directory Configuration), 70-642 (Windows Server 2008 Network Infrastructure Configuration), and 70-646 (Windows Server 2008 Server Administrator). For a more detailed description of the Microsoft certification programs, including a list of all the exams, visit the Microsoft Learning website at www.microsoft.com/learning/mcp.

The Windows Server 2008 Server Administrator Exam

The Windows Server 2008 Server Administrator exam covers concepts and skills related to planning, configuring, troubleshooting, and managing Windows Server 2008 servers.

 Microsoft provides exam objectives to give you a general overview of possible areas of coverage on the Microsoft exams. Keep in mind, however, that exam objectives are subject to change at any time without prior notice and at Microsoft's sole discretion. Please visit the Microsoft Learning website (www.microsoft.com/learning/mcp) for the most current listing of exam objectives.

Types of Exam Questions

In an effort to both refine the testing process and protect the quality of its certifications, Microsoft has focused its newer certification exams on real experience and hands-on proficiency. There is a greater emphasis on your past working environments and responsibilities and less emphasis on how well you can memorize. In fact, Microsoft says that certification candidates should have hands-on experience before attempting to pass any certification exams.

 Microsoft will accomplish its goal of protecting the exams' integrity by regularly adding and removing exam questions, limiting the number of questions that any individual sees in a beta exam, limiting the number of questions delivered to an individual by using adaptive testing, and adding new exam elements.

Exam questions may be in a variety of formats: depending on which exam you take, you'll see multiple-choice questions, as well as select-and-place and prioritize-a-list questions. Simulations and case study–based formats are included as well. You may also find yourself taking what's called an *adaptive format exam*. Let's take a look at the types of exam questions and examine the adaptive testing technique, so you'll be prepared for all the possibilities.

 With the release of Windows 2000, Microsoft stopped providing a detailed score breakdown. This is mostly because of the various and complex question formats. Previously, each question focused on one objective. Recent exams, such as the Windows Server 2008 Active Directory exam, however, contain questions that may be tied to one or more objectives from one or more objective sets. Therefore, grading by objective is almost impossible. Also, Microsoft no longer offers a score. Now you will be told only whether you pass or fail.

Multiple-Choice Questions

Multiple-choice questions come in two main forms. One is a straightforward question followed by several possible answers, of which one or more is correct. The other type of multiple-choice question is more complex and based on a specific scenario. The scenario may focus on several areas or objectives.

Select-and-Place Questions

Select-and-place exam questions involve graphical elements that you must manipulate to successfully answer the question. For example, you might see a diagram of a computer network, as shown in the following graphic taken from the select-and-place demo downloaded from Microsoft's website:

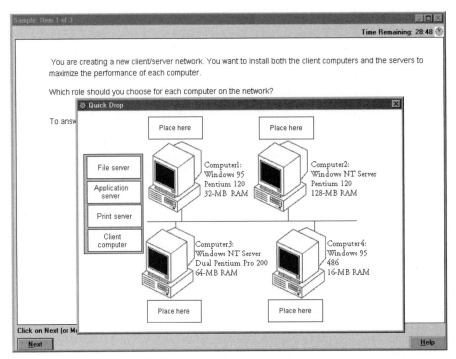

A typical diagram will show computers and other components next to boxes that contain the text "Place here." The labels for the boxes represent various computer roles on a network, such as a print server and a file server. Based on information given for each computer, you are asked to select each label and place it in the correct box. You need to place *all* of the labels correctly. No credit is given for the question if you correctly label only some of the boxes.

In another select-and-place problem, you might be asked to put a series of steps in order by dragging items from boxes on the left to boxes on the right and placing them in the correct order. One other type requires that you drag an item from the left and place it under an item in a column on the right.

For more information on the various exam question types, go to
www.microsoft.com/learning/mcpexams/policies/innovations.asp.

Simulations

Simulations are the kinds of questions that most closely represent actual situations and test
the skills you use while working with Microsoft software interfaces. These exam questions
include a mock interface on which you are asked to perform certain actions according to a
given scenario. The simulated interfaces look nearly identical to what you see in the actual
product, as shown in this example:

Because of the number of possible errors that can be made on simulations, be sure to
consider the following recommendations from Microsoft:

- Do not change any simulation settings that don't pertain to the solution directly.

- When related information has not been provided, assume that the default settings
  are used.

- Make sure that your entries are spelled correctly.

- Close all the simulation application windows after completing the set of tasks in the
  simulation.

The best way to prepare for simulation questions is to spend time working with the graphical interface of the product on which you will be tested.

Case Study–Based Questions

Case study–based questions first appeared in the MCSD program. These questions present a scenario with a range of requirements. Based on the information provided, you answer a series of multiple-choice and select-and-place questions. The interface for case study–based questions has a number of tabs, each of which contains information about the scenario. Currently, this type of question appears only in most of the Design exams.

 Microsoft will regularly add and remove questions from the exams. This is called *item seeding*. It is part of the effort to make it more difficult for individuals to merely memorize exam questions that were passed along by previous test-takers.

Tips for Taking the PRO: Windows Server 2008 Server Administrator Exam

Here are some general tips for achieving success on your certification exam:

- Arrive early at the exam center so you can relax and review your study materials. During this final review, you can look over tables and lists of exam-related information.

- Read the questions carefully. Don't be tempted to jump to an early conclusion. Make sure you know *exactly* what the question is asking.

- Answer all questions. If you are unsure about a question, then mark the question for review and come back to the question at a later time.

- On simulations, do not change settings that are not directly related to the question. Also, assume default settings if the question does not specify or imply which settings are used.

- For questions you're not sure about, use a process of elimination to get rid of the obviously incorrect answers first. This improves your odds of selecting the correct answer when you need to make an educated guess.

Exam Registration

You can take the Microsoft exams at any of more than 1,000 Authorized Prometric Testing Centers (APTCs) around the world. For the location of a testing center near you, call Prometric at 800-755-EXAM (755-3926). Outside the United States and Canada, contact your local Prometric registration center.

Find out the number of the exam you want to take and then register with the Prometric registration center nearest to you. At this point, you will be asked for advance payment for the exam. The exams are $125 each, and you must take them within one year of payment.

You can schedule exams up to six weeks in advance or as late as one working day prior to the date of the exam. You can cancel or reschedule your exam if you contact the center at least two working days prior to the exam. Same-day registration is available in some locations, subject to space availability. Where same-day registration is available, you must register a minimum of two hours before test time.

 You may also register for your exams online at www.prometric.com.

When you schedule the exam, you will be provided with instructions regarding appointment and cancellation procedures, ID requirements, and information about the testing center location. In addition, you will receive a registration and payment confirmation letter from Prometric.

Microsoft requires certification candidates to accept the terms of a nondisclosure agreement before taking certification exams.

Is This Book for You?

If you want to achieve the MCITP Windows Server 2008 Server Administrator certification and your goal is to prepare for the exam by learning how to use and manage the operating system, this book is for you. You'll find clear explanations of the fundamental concepts you need to grasp and plenty of help to achieve the high level of professional competency you need to succeed in your chosen field.

However, if you just want to attempt to pass the exam without really understanding Windows Server 2008, this study guide is *not* for you. It is written for people who want to acquire hands-on skills and in-depth knowledge of Windows Server 2008.

What's in the Book?

What makes a Sybex study guide the book of choice for hundreds of thousands of MCPs? We took into account not only what you need to know to pass the exam, but what you need to know to take what you've learned and apply it in the real world. Each book contains the following:

Objective-by-objective coverage of the topics you need to know   Each chapter lists the objectives covered in that chapter.

The topics covered in this study guide map directly to Microsoft's official exam objectives. Each exam objective is covered completely.

Assessment test   Directly following this introduction is an assessment test that you should take. It is designed to help you determine how much you already know about Windows Server 2008 Active Directory. Each question is tied to a topic discussed in the book. Using the results of the assessment test, you can figure out the areas where you need to focus your study. Of course, we do recommend you read the entire book.

Exam essentials   To highlight what you learn, you'll find a list of exam essentials at the end of each chapter. The "Exam Essentials" section briefly highlights the topics that need your particular attention as you prepare for the exam.

Glossary   Throughout each chapter, you will be introduced to important terms and concepts that you will need to know for the exam. These terms appear in italic within the chapters, and at the end of the book, a detailed glossary gives definitions for these terms, as well as other general terms you should know.

Review questions, complete with detailed explanations   Each chapter is followed by a set of review questions that test what you learned in the chapter. The questions are written with the exam in mind, meaning that they are designed to have the same look and feel as what you'll see on the exam. Question types are just like the exam, including multiple-choice, exhibits, and select-and-place.

Hands-on exercises   In each chapter you'll find exercises designed to give you the important hands-on experience that is critical for your exam preparation. The exercises support the topics of the chapter, and they walk you through the steps necessary to perform a particular function.

Real-world scenarios   Because reading a book isn't enough for you to learn how to apply these topics in your everyday duties, we have provided real-world scenarios in special sidebars. These explain when and why a particular solution would make sense, in a working environment you'd actually encounter.

Interactive CD   Every Sybex study guide comes with a CD complete with additional questions, flashcards for use with an interactive device, and the book in electronic format. Details are in the following section.

What's on the CD?

With this new member of our best-selling Study Guide series, we are including quite an array of training resources. The CD offers bonus exams and flashcards to help you study for the exam. We have also included the complete contents of the study guide in electronic form. The CD's resources are described here:

The Sybex e-book for Windows Server 2008 Server Administrator   Many people like the convenience of being able to carry their whole study guide on a CD. They also like being able to search the text via computer to find specific information quickly and easily. For these reasons, the entire contents of this study guide are supplied on the CD in PDF. We've also included Adobe Acrobat Reader, which provides the interface for the PDF contents as well as the search capabilities.

The Sybex test engine   This is a collection of multiple-choice questions that will help you prepare for your exam. There are four sets of questions:

- Two bonus exams designed to simulate the actual live exam.
- All the questions from the study guide, presented in a test engine for your review. You can review questions by chapter, or you can take a random test.
- The assessment test.

Here is a sample screen from the Sybex test engine:

Sybex flashcards for PCs and handheld devices   The "flashcard" style of question offers an effective way to quickly and efficiently test your understanding of the fundamental concepts covered in the exam. The Sybex flashcards set consists of 100 questions presented in a special engine developed specifically for the Study Guide series. Here's what the Sybex flashcards interface looks like:

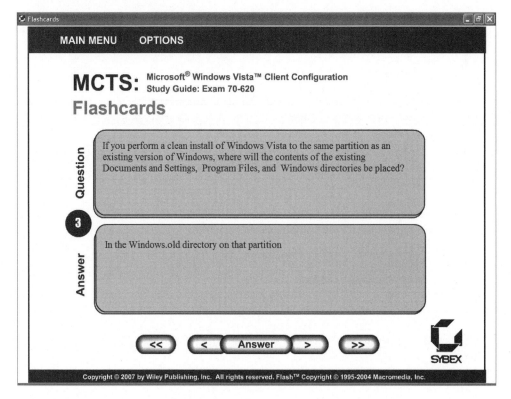

Because of the high demand for a product that will run on handheld devices, we have also developed, in conjunction with Land-J Technologies, a version of the flashcard questions that you can take with you on your Palm OS PDA.

Hardware and Software Requirements

You should verify that your computer meets the minimum requirements for installing Windows Server 2008 as listed in Chapter 1, "Introducing Windows Server 2008." You can install Windows Server 2008 on a separate system or as a Virtual PC image on an existing operating system. Either way, you need to ensure that your computer or virtual PC environment meets or exceeds the recommended requirements for a more enjoyable experience. Exercises in Chapter 1 will lead you through this process.

The remaining exercises in this book assume that you have installed Windows Server 2008.

 You can download a demo copy of Windows Server 2008 from www.microsoft.com/windowsserver2008/en/us/trial-software.aspx.

Contacts and Resources

To find out more about Microsoft Education and Certification materials and programs, to register with Prometric, or to obtain other useful certification information and additional study resources, check the following resources:

Microsoft Learning Home Page

www.microsoft.com/learning

This website provides information about the MCP program and exams. You can also order the latest Microsoft Roadmap to Education and Certification.

Microsoft TechNet Technical Information Network

www.microsoft.com/technet

800-344-2121

Use this website or phone number to contact support professionals and system administrators. Outside the United States and Canada, contact your local Microsoft subsidiary for information.

Prometric

www.prometric.com

800-755-3936

Contact Prometric to register to take an exam at any of more than 800 Prometric Testing Centers around the world.

MCP Magazine Online

www.mcpmag.com

Microsoft Certified Professional Magazine is a well-respected publication that focuses on Windows certification. This site hosts chats and discussion forums and tracks news related to the MCTS and MCITP program. Some of the services cost a fee, but they are well worth it.

WindowsITPro Magazine

www.windowsITPro.com

You can subscribe to this magazine or read free articles at the website. The study resource provides general information on Windows Vista, Server, and .NET Server.

MCITP Success

www.mcitpsuccess.com

This is one of my websites. I welcome feedback from you about this book or about books you'd like to see from me in the future. I especially love to hear from readers who have passed exams after using one of my books. You can reach me by writing to darrilgibson@mcitpsuccess.com.

Assessment Test

1. How many virtual servers are supported on the Windows Server 2008 Enterprise edition with Hyper-V?

    A. 1

    B. 2

    C. 3

    D. 4

2. A fellow administrator is trying to create a read-only domain controller within an existing domain but has been unsuccessful. What might you suggest he verify?

    A. Verify DCPromo is installed.

    B. Verify the PDC Emulator role is a Windows Server 2008 server.

    C. Verify that DNS is running on the network.

    D. Verify the Write Protect capability is set in Active Directory.

3. What Microsoft tool can be used to remotely install Windows Vista and Windows Server 2008 images onto computers?

    A. Ghost

    B. WDS

    C. WSUS

    D. WSv

4. You want to use Windows Deployment Services to deploy Windows Server 2008 to seven servers. Some of the servers are 32-bit, and some of the servers are 64-bit. How many images are needed on the Windows Deployment Services server?

    A. 1

    B. 2

    C. 3

    D. 7

5. You have deployed a Windows Server 2008 server using Server Core. You want to manage the server remotely using Remote Desktop Connection (RDC). How should you prepare the server to enable RDC?

    A. Run the `WinRM` command

    B. Run the `WinRS` command

    C. Run the `scregedit` command.

    D. Run the `netsh` command.
    `Cscript scregedit.wsf /AR 0`

6. You have configured a server for remote access as shown in the following dialog box.

However, you find you can't access the server from a computer running Windows XP SP1. Without sacrificing security and minimizing costs, what can you do to resolve the problem?

A. Upgrade the computer to Windows Vista.

B. Install SP2 on the Windows XP computer.

C. Install SP2 and the Remote Desktop Client 6.0 upgrade on the computer.

D. Select the setting Allow Connections from Computers Running Any Version of Remote Desktop.

7. You are an administrator of a growing branch location in a large enterprise. WSUS is used throughout the organization, and you have a WSUS server at your location. Updates approved at the main office have adversely impacted a line-of-business application run at your location, and you have just been given authority to configure WSUS so that you can approve and deploy updates from your WSUS server. What mode should you select for your WSUS server to allow you to manage the updates while still reporting summary status to the WSUS server at headquarters?

A. Independent mode

B. Stand-alone mode

C. Replica mode

D. Autonomous mode

8. You are one of several administrators in a large enterprise. You are tasked with identifying a solution that will allow you to deploy software based on a schedule and provide detailed reports. What tool should you recommend?

A. GO

B. WSUS

C. SCCM

D. WSRM

9. You are managing a network composed of two subnets. DHCP is configured to issue IP addresses to each subnet. The first subnet is using the following scope: 172.16.0.1 through 172.16.31.254 with a subnet mask of 255.255.0.0. You have run out of addresses on the first subnet. No other problems are present. What should be done?

   A. Modify the scope to include the full range of IP addresses in the subnet.

   B. Create another scope to include the remaining IP addresses in the subnet.

   C. Create a new subnet, and add a scope to serve clients in that subnet.

   D. Move the clients in the second subnet to the first subnet.

10. Salespeople are issued laptops and frequently access the network using a VPN. In the past, salespeople have connected with laptops that are infected with a virus and have released it within your network. What could you implement that could protect you against this in the future?

   A. Install antivirus software on the VPN server, and scan the client before granting access.

   B. Tell salespeople to use antivirus software on their laptops.

   C. Use SCCM to deploy antivirus software to the clients.

   D. Install a NAP solution using VPN enforcement.

11. You administer a large enterprise with several remote offices. Recently, a read-only domain controller (RODC) was placed in the Hampton, Virginia, location. You want to ensure that passwords of the ITAdmins group are not cached on this server, even if a member of the group logs onto the system. You don't want to affect any other RODCs. What should you do?

   A. Use Group Policy to manage the ITAdmins group with the Restricted Groups Group Policy settings.

   B. At the RODC in Hampton, Virginia, add the ITAdmins group to the Denied RODC Password Replication Group.

   C. At any writable domain controller, add the ITAdmins group to the Denied RODC Password Replication Group.

   D. Add the ITAdmins group to the Password Replication Policy of the RODC located in Hampton, Virginia.

12. You have deployed a public key infrastructure (PKI) and want to build a Certificate Services server that will answer queries on the status of certificates, instead of forwarding an entire certificate revocation list. What protocol will this server support?

   A. OCSP

   B. ORP

   C. TLS

   D. CRL

13. Your company has just purchased the SalesTracker program, and it needs to be available to all the salespeople in your company. It should be available to all the salespeople via the Start menu. Salespeople's accounts are located in the Sales OU. How should you accomplish this?

    A. Use Group Policy to assign the SalesTracker package to users. Link the GPO to the Sales OU.

    B. Use Group Policy to publish the SalesTracker package to users. Link the GPO to the Sales OU.

    C. Use Group Policy to publish the SalesTracker package to computers. Link the GPO to the Sales OU.

    D. Use Group Policy to assign the SalesTracker package to users. Link the GPO to the domain.

14. You manage a small domain that includes two domain controllers. One domain controller was installed with Windows Server 2008, and you just upgraded the second domain controller to Windows Server 2008 from Windows Server 2003. You've read about using Distributed File System (DFS) for replication of the sysvol folder, and you want to use it. What should you do, if anything?

    A. Raise the domain functional level to Windows Server 2008 and nothing else.

    B. Raise the forest functional level to Windows Server 2008, and migrate FRS to DFS.

    C. Raise the domain functional level to Windows Server 2008, and migrate FRS to DFS.

    D. Nothing needs to be done. Once all domain controllers are running Windows Server 2008, the sysvol folder is replicated using DFS.

15. You want to add DFS to a Windows Server 2008 server. What must you add first?

    A. FRS

    B. WSRM

    C. Directory Services

    D. File Services

16. You manage a file server named Srv1. Multiple shares exist on this server, but you need to restrict the amount of data that users can store in a share named Public. What can you install to help with this task?

    A. DFS

    B. FSRM

    C. WSRM

    D. NTFS

17. You are planning to create a server farm of several Terminal Services terminal servers. You want to ensure that each server is used equally. What Terminal Services service should you include in the server farm?

    A. TS Load Balancing

    B. TS RemoteApp

    C. TS Session Broker

    D. TS Gateway

18. You manage several Windows Server 2008 servers on your network. Occasionally, you are called at home to troubleshoot a problem. You want administrators to be able to remotely administer a server via the Internet. What should you install?

A. Add the TS Gateway service to your network.

B. Add the TS Session Broker service to your network.

C. Place all your servers external to the company firewall with public IP addresses.

D. Place all your servers in a DMZ.

19. Several users in your network are using Outlook 2003. Outlook 2003 includes a company-purchased add-in that isn't compatible with Outlook 2007. The company wants to upgrade all users to Outlook 2007. What should you do?

A. Install Outlook 2007 side-by-side with Outlook 2003 on each user's system.

B. Install Outlook 2007 on a terminal server, and grant users access to the terminal server to run Outlook 2007.

C. Give each user two computers. One can run Outlook 2003, and the other can run Outlook 2007.

D. Install Outlook 2007 in compatibility mode so that Outlook 2003 and Outlook 2007 can run on the same system.

20. You have taken over the management of a Windows Server 2008 server in a remote office. The drive is protected by BitLocker. You are tasked with implementing multifactor authentication to add a layer of protection to BitLocker. What two methods can be used? (Choose two.)

A. Require a user to enter a password when the computer starts.

B. Require a user to insert a USB flash drive with the recovery key.

C. Require a user to enter a PIN when the computer starts.

D. Require the user to insert a USB flash drive with the startup key.

21. You are implementing a VPN solution and want to choose a tunneling protocol that will provide the highest level of confidentiality, integrity, and authentication. All the clients will run Windows Vista SP1 or greater. Your VPN server is located behind a NAT. What would you choose?

A. PPP

B. PPTP

C. L2TP

D. SSTP

22. Your company is planning on deploying Microsoft SQL Server to support an online application. SQL Server must remain operational even if a single server fails, and costs should be minimized. What should you recommend to support the SQL Server installation?

A. Install Windows Server Standard edition on two servers. Implement a failover cluster.

B. Install Windows Server Enterprise edition on two servers. Implement a failover cluster.

C. Install Windows Server Standard edition on two servers. Implement an NLB cluster.

D. Install Windows Server Enterprise edition on two servers. Implement an NLB cluster.

23. You are planning on deploying several file servers on Windows Server 2008 servers. You need to develop a plan that will provide fault tolerance if a single server fails. Additionally, the storage solution must minimize costs. The existing network infrastructure can handle additional load. What would you recommend?

   A. Implement a failover cluster, and use iSCSI for the storage solution.

   B. Implement a failover cluster, and use FC for the storage solution.

   C. Implement an NLB cluster, and use iSCSI for the storage solution.

   D. Implement an NLB cluster, and use FC for the storage solution.

Answers to Assessment Test

1. **D.**   Three editions of Windows Server 2008 support virtualization: Windows Server 2008 Standard edition with Hyper-V (supports one virtual server), Windows Server 2008 Enterprise edition with Hyper-V (supports four virtual servers), and Windows Server 2008 Datacenter edition with Hyper-V (supports an unlimited number of virtual servers). For more information, see Chapter 1, "Introducing Windows Server 2008."

2. **B.**   To support read-only domain controllers, the domain controller hosting the PDC Emulator FSMO role must be running Windows Server 2008. For more information, see Chapter 1, "Introducing Windows Server 2008."

3. **B.**   Windows Deployment Services (WDS) is used to deploy images onto computers. Ghost is a product of Symantec (not Microsoft). Windows Software Update Services (WSUS) is used to deploy updates to computers, not entire operating systems. Three editions of Windows Server 2008 support virtualization, and Windows Server Virtualization (WSv) allows a single server to host multiple servers virtually. For more information, see Chapter 2, "Planning Server Installs and Upgrades."

4. **C.**   Windows Deployment Services (WDS) includes both boot and install images. A single boot image can be used for all servers regardless of whether the server is using 32-bit or 64-bit architecture. However, a 32-bit server needs a 32-bit install image, and a 64-bit server needs a 64-bit image. For more information, see Chapter 2, "Planning Server Installs and Upgrades."

5. **D.**   The following `scregedit` Windows script file command would be used to enable the Server Core server to be administered remotely using RDC:

    `Cscript scregedit.wsf /AR 0`

    The `WinRM` command is used to prepare Server Core to respond to Windows Remote Shell commands using the `WinRS` command. `WinRS` would be issued from other computers, not the Server Core server. The NetShell (`netsh`) command would be used to configure the firewall to allow the Server Core server to be managed remotely using any MMC. For more information, see Chapter 2, "Planning Server Installs and Upgrades."

6. **C.**   After installing Service Pack 2 onto Windows XP, you can install the Remote Desktop Client 6.0 upgrade, which includes network-level authentication. Upgrading the computer to Windows Vista needlessly adds costs. Just adding Service Pack 2 wouldn't be enough. Changing the setting would sacrifice security. For more information, see Chapter 3, "Using Windows Server 2003 Management Tools."

7. **D.**   Autonomous mode allows you to control updates at your WSUS server while still reporting summary information to the primary server. Replica mode forces your WSUS server to act as a downstream server and accept all approved updates from the upstream server at headquarters. Independent and stand-alone modes aren't selection modes for a WSUS server. For more information, see Chapter 3, "Using Windows Server 2003 Management Tools."

8. C.   System Center Configuration Manager (SCCM) can be used to deploy applications based on a schedule and provide detailed reports. Group Policy object (GPO) can also be used to deploy applications, but it doesn't have the sophisticated abilities of SCCM (such as scheduling the deployment or providing reports). Windows Server Update Services (WSUS) can be used to deploy updates, but not entire applications. Windows System Resource Manager (WSRM) can be used control the amount of resources granted to individual applications or individual users, but it cannot deploy software. For more information, see Chapter 3, "Using Windows Server 2003 Management Tools."

9. A.   You should modify the scope to include the full range of IP addresses (172.16.0.1 through 172.16.255.254 with a subnet mask of 255.255.0.0). It is not possible to add a second scope with the same network ID (172.16.0.0). It is not necessary (and would add substantial more work) to add a new subnet. Moving the clients from the second subnet to the first would add to the problem, not help it. For more information, see Chapter 4, "Monitoring and Maintaining Network Infrastructure Servers."

10. D.   Network Access Protection (NAP) can be used. VPN clients can be checked to ensure they are healthy, and if not, they would not be issued a health certificate. Without a health certificate, the clients can be restricted to limited access within the network. It's not possible to scan the client from the VPN server. Asking users to keep their computers protected with anti-virus software is a good first step but needs to be enforced technically. System Center Configuration Manager (SCCM) can be used to deploy software and updates, but not to clients that are outside the network until a NAP solution is implemented. For more information, see Chapter 4, "Monitoring and Maintaining Network Infrastructure Servers."

11. D.   Since you want to affect only the RODC in Hampton and not affect any other RODCs, you must modify the Password Replication Policy, which can be accessed by selecting the properties of the RODC object in Active Directory Users and Computers. Restricted Groups can't be used to manage a single RODC and isn't even recommended for all RODCs. The Denied RODC Password Replication Group will affect all RODCs in the domain so wouldn't meet the needs of the question. For more information, see Chapter 5, "Monitoring and Maintaining Active Directory."

12. A.   The Online Certificate Status Protocol (OCSP) is used to check the status of a certificate as an alternative to checking the certificate revocation list (CRL). An online responder is the server that answers the OCSP requests, but there isn't an ORP protocol. Transport Layer Security (TLS) is used for encryption and authentication purposes but not with certificates. The CRL is not a protocol. For more information, see Chapter 5, "Monitoring and Maintaining Active Directory."

13. A.   By assigning an application package, you cause it to appear on the Start menu for users who receive the package. Since you want it to be assigned to users in the Sales OU, you would link the GPO to the Sales OU. Publishing the GPO would cause it to be available through the Control Panel, but not on the Start menu. Publishing it to computers wouldn't guarantee that salespeople would have access to the program if they logged onto a computer that wasn't in the Sales OU. Linking the GPO to the domain would cause all users to receive the application, instead of just the users in the Sales OU. For more information, see Chapter 5, "Monitoring and Maintaining Active Directory."

14. C.   To use DFS, you must be in Windows Server 2008 domain functional level. If sysvol folder replication was originally done with File Replication Service (FRS), then you must migrate FRS to DFS. Since one of the domain controllers was just upgraded from Windows Server 2003, the domain functional level could not be Windows Server 2008. This also means that replication is currently being done with FRS. You would need to raise the domain functional level to Windows Server 2008 and migrate FRS to DFS. The forest functional level does not matter. Switching from FRS to DFS is not automatic. For more information, see Chapter 6, "Monitoring and Maintaining Print and File Servers."

15. D.   The File Services role must be added to a server before the Distributed File System (DFS) services can be added. DFS is a replacement for the File Replication Service (FRS), and FRS is not required to be installed before DFS. The Windows System Resource Manager (WSRM) is used to limit the amount of CPU and memory resources that an application is using. Directory Services is part of Active Directory. Although a domain-based DFS requires Active Directory Domain Services, a stand-alone based DFS server doesn't require Active Directory Domain Services. For more information, see Chapter 6, "Monitoring and Maintaining Print and File Servers."

16. B.   The File Server Resource Manager allows you to implement quotas on both a folder and a volume (or partition) basis. The Distributed File System (DFS) can be used to organize data in a namespace or replicate data but doesn't include quotas. The Windows System Resource Manager (WSRM) is used to limit the amount of CPU and memory resources that an application is using. Although you can implement quotas on a volume basis with any NTFS volume, you cannot implement quotas on a per-share or per-folder basis using just NTFS. For more information, see Chapter 6, "Monitoring and Maintaining Print and File Servers."

17. C.   TS Session Broker provides load balancing (and session state management). Each new session is directed to the terminal server with the fewest connections. There isn't a service known as TS Load Balancing. TS RemoteApp allows users to run a single program via a terminal server. TS Gateway allows users to access terminal servers via the Internet. For more information, see Chapter 7, "Planning Terminal Services Servers."

18. A.   The Terminal Services (TS) Gateway will allow you to connect to internal resources via the Internet. TS Gateway uses IIS to accept RDP over SSL connections and translates them into Terminal Services connections. TS Session Broker is used to manage session state and provide load balancing in a terminal server farm. It isn't necessary, nor would it be very safe, to place all your servers on the Internet or a DMZ. For more information, see Chapter 7, "Planning Terminal Services Servers."

19. B.   Outlook 2003 and Outlook 2007 aren't compatible on the same system. However, if one application is run in a Terminal Services session and the other application is run on the client's computer, both applications can run. It's not necessary to build two separate client systems, and it's not possible to install both versions side-by-side on the same system in any mode. For more information, see Chapter 7, "Planning Terminal Services Servers."

20. C, D.   Multifactor authentication can be added to BitLocker either by requiring a user to enter a PIN when the computer starts or by requiring the user to insert a USB with the startup key. A recovery password or a USB flash drive with a recovery key is used to recover a locked BitLocker drive using the BitLocker recovery console. For more information, see Chapter 8, "Planning Windows Server 2008 Security."

21. D.   The Secure Socket Tunneling Protocol (SSTP) uses Secure Sockets Layer (SSL) and passes through port 443. It provides all the security requirements and can pass through a NAT. Point-to-Point Protocol is a dial-up protocol, not a tunneling protocol. Point-to-Point Tunneling Protocol (PPTP) does not provide integrity or authentication. Layer 2 Tunneling Protocol (L2TP) will meet the security requirements if used with IPSec, but IPSec cannot pass through a NAT. For more information, see Chapter 8, "Planning Windows Server 2008 Security."

22. B.   A failover cluster will provide the required server fault tolerance. Windows Server 2008 Enterprise edition supports failover clusters. Windows Server 2008 Standard edition does not support failover clusters. An NLB cluster won't provide fault tolerance for SQL Server. For more information, see Chapter 9, "Planning Business Continuity and High Availability."

23. A.   A failover cluster will provide fault tolerance if a single server fails. Internet Small Computer System Interface (iSCSI) will utilize existing network infrastructure and therefore will minimize costs. Fibre Channel (FC) uses specialized hardware and connections and will substantially increase the cost of the storage solution. A network load balancing (NLB) cluster will not provide fault tolerance if a single server fails but can provide high availability; the difference is that a failover cluster uses shared disk storage (the files on the file server), but an NLB cluster doesn't share a common data source. For more information, see Chapter 9, "Planning Business Continuity and High Availability."

Chapter 1

Introducing Windows Server 2008

MICROSOFT EXAM OBJECTIVES COVERED IN THIS CHAPTER:

✓ **Planning for Server Deployment**

- Plan Server Installations and Upgrades. May include but is not limited to: Windows Server 2008 edition selection, rollback planning, Bitlocker implementation requirements.

✓ **Planning for Server Management**

- Plan Server Management Strategies. May include but is not limited to: remote administration, remote desktop, server management technologies, Server Manager and ServerManagerCMD, delegation policies and procedures.

This chapter is designed to give you a short overview of many of the features of Windows Server 2008, especially as they relate to the 70-646 exam. Future chapters will delve a little deeper into the topics, but first we'll start with a foundation.

I fully expect you to want to install a copy of Windows Server 2008 on a system. After all, it's hard to learn something that you haven't seen and played with. One of the primary sections of this chapter will walk you through the steps of installing Server 2008 and configuring it as a domain controller.

You'll notice in the list of objectives that rollback planning, Bitlocker implementation requirements, remote administration, remote desktop, and delegation policies and procedures are listed. Rollback planning is covered in Chapter 2, "Planning Server Deployments." Remote administration and remote desktop are covered in Chapter 3, "Using Windows Server 2008 Server Management Tools." Chapter 5, "Monitoring and Maintaining Active Directory" covers delegation policies and procedures. Bitlocker implementation requirements are covered in Chapter 8, "Planning Windows Server 2008 Security."

Windows Server 2008 Editions

Microsoft has released multiple editions of Windows Server 2008. Most editions come in both 32-bit and 64-bit editions except for the Itanium edition, which comes only in the 64-bit edition.

Three include virtualization capabilities using the Hyper-V virtualization technology. Hyper-V is the virtual machine technology that allows multiple operating systems to run concurrently on the same system. Virtualization can be used for server consolidation where multiple servers can be combined onto a single server or to consolidate testing or development environments. Hyper-V will work only on 64-bit systems.

The editions that include Hyper-V are as follows. The most significant differences between these editions are related to how many virtual servers each edition can host.

Windows Server 2008 Standard with Hyper-V   The Standard with Hyper-V edition is for small to medium-sized businesses. It includes support for a single virtual server.

Windows Server 2008 Enterprise with Hyper-V   The Enterprise edition is for larger organizations and can support up to four virtual servers. It also includes support for clustering and hot-add memory capabilities.

Windows Server 2008 Datacenter with Hyper-V   The Datacenter edition is for high-end applications and large-scale virtualization. It adds to the features of the Enterprise edition, including hot-add processor capabilities. An unlimited number of virtual servers can be hosted on the Datacenter edition.

> The Enterprise and Datacenter editions both support hot-add capabilities. *Hot-add means you can add* physical processors or physical memory without shutting down the system. The system hardware must also support this capability.

The same three editions exist without Hyper-V:

Windows Server 2008 Standard without Hyper-V   The Standard with Hyper-V edition is for small to medium-sized businesses.

Windows Server 2008 Enterprise without Hyper-V   The Enterprise edition is for larger organizations.

Windows Server 2008 Datacenter without Hyper-V   The Datacenter edition is for high-end applications, including very large databases.

Additionally, two editions are designed for specific workloads:

Windows Web Server 2008   This edition is designed to be a dedicated web server and hosts Internet Information Services (IIS) edition 7.0 and all the associated components such as ASP.NET and the Microsoft .NET Framework.

Windows Server 2008 for Itanium-based systems   This is designed to work on systems using the high-end 64-bit Itanium processors. It is optimized for large databases.

🌐 Real World Scenario

Choosing the Correct Operating System

Consider this scenario: You are working as a network administrator, and the company is considering consolidating several servers onto a single server using Windows Virtualization. It will host three virtual servers. Which operating system would you use?

First, you would use one of the editions that includes Hyper-V. These are the Standard, Enterprise, and Datacenter editions. Second, you would need to choose an edition that supports five virtual servers. Standard supports one virtual server, Enterprise supports up to four virtual servers, and Datacenter supports an unlimited number of servers. Windows Server 2008 Enterprise edition with Hyper-V will meet your needs.

Table 1.1, Table 1.2, and Table 1.3 show the different server roles matched to the available Windows Server 2008 editions.

TABLE 1.1 Specialized Server Roles

Server Role	Web	Itanium	Standard	Enterprise	Datacenter
Web Services (IIS)	Yes	Yes	Yes	Yes	Yes
Application Server	No	Yes	Yes	Yes	Yes
Print Services	No	No	Yes	Yes	Yes
Hyper-V	No	No	Yes	Yes	Yes

Notice that the Web edition supports the Web Services role running IIS and nothing else. The Itanium edition supports high-end application server applications such as Microsoft's SQL Server with very large databases or Microsoft Exchange Server with a large number of users and mailboxes.

TABLE 1.2 Active Directory (AD) Server Roles

Server Role	Web	Itanium	Standard	Enterprise	Datacenter
AD Domain Services	No	No	Yes	Yes	Yes
AD Lightweight Directory Services	No	No	Yes	Yes	Yes
AD Rights Management Services	No	No	Yes	Yes	Yes
AD Certificate Services	No	No	Partial	Yes	Yes
AD Federation Services	No	No	No	Yes	Yes

The Standard edition supports creating certificate authorities but doesn't support all of the functionality of certificate services.

TABLE 1.3   Network Infrastructure and General Server Roles

Server Role	Web	Itanium	Standard	Enterprise	Datacenter
DHCP Server	No	No	Yes	Yes	Yes
DNS Server	No	No	Yes	Yes	Yes
Fax Server	No	No	Yes	Yes	Yes
UDDI Services	No	No	Yes	Yes	Yes
Windows Deployment Services	No	No	Yes	Yes	Yes
File Services	No	No	Partial	Yes	Yes
Network Policy and Access Services	No	No	Partial	Yes	Yes
Terminal Services	No	No	Partial	Yes	Yes

The Standard edition has limited support for some of these roles. For File Services, only one Distributed File System (DFS) root is supported. For Network Policy and Access Services, it is limited to 250 RRAS connections, 50 IAS connections, and 2 IAS Server Groups. For Terminal Services, it is limited to 250 connections.

Key Benefits of Windows Server 2008

When weighing the costs of upgrading from your current operating system to Windows Server 2008, IT professionals must consider what the benefits are and then determine whether the benefits are worth the costs.

Although the following benefits are extensive, they make a difference only if your environment will use the added benefits. Expect Microsoft to stress the benefits of new features in every way possible—including in exams.

IIS 7 and the .NET Framework

The Windows Server 2008 Web edition has been expressly created to support the Web role. It hosts IIS 7 and includes support for ASP.NET and the current versions of the .NET Framework. When released, the .NET Framework 3.0 was included. However, the .NET Framework 3.5 can be downloaded and installed if your web developers need it for their web applications.

As background, the most widely used web server on the Internet is Apache, which is a free product that can run on Unix—or one of the Unix derivatives (such as Linux)—which is also free. Microsoft has been steadily breaking into this market with its Web edition product in Windows Server 2003 and IIS 6. Windows Server 2008 offers additional capabilities with the Web edition and IIS 7.

However, IIS is not only for the Internet. Many companies use IIS on their intranet to serve Internet technologies to internal employees. IIS 7 supports web pages, websites, web applications, and web services. While the Web edition provides dedicated support for IIS 7, any edition can run IIS 7.

Microsoft has improved the security of IIS by ensuring that separate web applications are isolated from each other in a "sandboxed" configuration. Of significant value to server administrators, the IIS administration tool has been improved for many of the common administrative tasks.

Chapter 7, "Planning Terminal Services Servers," will cover the maintenance of IIS 7 in more depth.

Virtualization

The Windows Server virtualization role is one of the biggest additions in Windows Server 2008 and, arguably, one of the most exciting.

For years, there has been an ongoing trend of server consolidation. For example, instead of having one DHCP server, one file server, and one IIS server, it's possible to have one server running all of these roles. Individually, each of the servers might be using only 5 to 10 percent of the available processing power. With all of the roles on a single server, the server's resources are more fully being utilized. From a management perspective, spending $20,000 or so on a single server and using only about 5 percent of it just doesn't make fiscal sense.

However, consolidating roles onto a single server does have drawbacks. As a simple example, a patch applied for one service may have an unwanted side effect on another service. However, if each server is running within the host as an isolated system, then changes to one system do not affect another system.

Consider Figure 1.1. If you're running Windows Server 2008 Enterprise edition, you can have as many as four virtual servers. In the figure, three virtual servers are running: one is running Windows 2008, one is running Linux (Novell SUSE Linux Enterprise Server), and one is running Windows Server 2003. Each of these virtual servers is completely isolated from the others, but they are sharing the host's network interface card (NIC) and other hardware resources.

 At this writing, the only Linux version supported in Hyper-V is Novell SUSE Linux Enterprise Server.

From the network perspective, the four servers (the host and the three virtual servers) would appear as shown in Figure 1.2. Even though the virtual servers are hosted within a single Windows Server 2008 system, they appear as separate individual servers. They have their own hostnames and their own IP addresses.

Virtualization solves many of the problems that occurred with traditional server consolidation. It allows multiple servers to be consolidated onto a single server, while still allowing each server to remain isolated from other servers hosted on the same machine.

FIGURE 1.1   Virtual server within a host

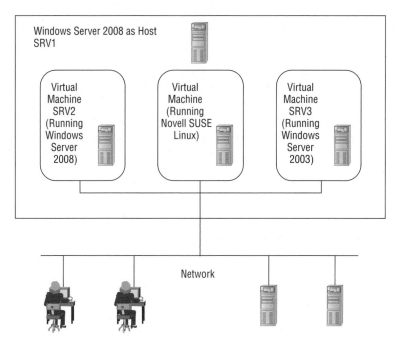

FIGURE 1.2   Virtual servers on a network

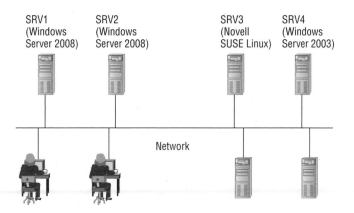

When planning for a Windows Server 2008 virtualization solution, remember a few key points:

- The host must be running a 64-bit edition of Windows Server 2008. (Virtual machines can run either 32-bit or 64-bit editions).

- Windows Server 2008 Standard edition supports one virtual server.

- Windows Server 2008 Enterprise edition supports as many as four virtual servers.

- Windows Server 2008 Datacenter edition supports an unlimited number of virtual servers.

- Hardware requirements of the host depend on the hardware requirements of the individual virtual machines. It wouldn't be uncommon to see a host designed to support many virtual servers with as many as 32 or more processors and 64GB or more of RAM.

Chapter 2, "Planning Server Deployments," will cover Windows Server virtualization in more depth.

Security

Security is intertwined in all aspects of the operating system. Since before the release of Windows XP SP2, Microsoft has developed products with the mantra of SD^3+C (Secure by Design, Secure by Default, Secure in Deployment and Communications).

In other words, security is considered in the entire life cycle of any of Microsoft's products. It wasn't always that way. In the past, Microsoft had usability as the most important aspect of the products, and the security was implemented toward the end of the development process. Inevitably, this caused problems.

Some of the security improvements include the following:

BitLocker Drive Encryption   BitLocker Drive Encryption available on Server 2008 is the same feature available in Vista Enterprise and Vista Ultimate. It allows entire data volumes (any non-OS volume) to be protected with encryption. If a system is stolen, BitLocker makes it significantly more difficult to boot from another added volume and then access existing data. This can protect regular data and also operating system data such as the Active Directory database on a domain controller.

Network Access Protection (NAP)   When clients access the network remotely (via dial-up or VPN remote access technologies), there is the risk that they aren't healthy. For example, they could be infected with viruses or not have the most recent updates and patches. NAP allows the system to check the health of these clients before they are allowed access. Unhealthy clients can be quarantined until the health problems are addressed.

Improved Security Log   Many of the events recorded in the security log have been improved. For example, when audited data is changed, not only is the event listed, but also new and old values are included. Additional events have been added to show permission changes and IPSec activity.

Chapter 8, "Planning Windows Server 2008 Security," has a section dedicated to security, but you can expect security topics to come up throughout the book.

Interaction with Vista

Windows Server 2008 and Windows Vista are designed to work best together. Some of the features that are available when Windows Vista and Server 2008 are used on the same network are as follows:

Improved Group Policy   Many additional Group Policy management settings are available to manage Vista clients. As one example, Group Policy can be used to limit bandwidth usage by individual applications.

Event subscription   This allows you to configure computers to monitor for specific events and forward them to other computers. With event subscription, you can more easily centrally monitor computers on your network.

NAP features   When Vista clients access a network access server (using either dial-in or VPN technologies), NAP features built into both Vista and Server 2008 protect the network. NAP will check the client to ensure it is compliant with predefined security requirements. If not, NAP can restrict the client from accessing the network until the security issues are addressed.

IPv6 support   Both Vista and Server 2008 support the use of both of both IPv4 and IPv6. IPv6 is installed and active by default.

Windows XP and Windows Server 2003

What Microsoft did with Windows Vista and Windows Server 2008 is similar to how it released Windows XP and Windows Server 2003.

First, the desktop operating system was released. While consumers started trying the new operating system, the final development on the Server product was being finished.

I remember that when Windows XP came out, people were complaining about it. However, once Server 2003 came out and administrators realized how well Windows XP and Windows Server 2003 worked together, the migration to Windows XP began in earnest.

When Windows Vista was released, people were complaining about it. I fully expect that once administrators begin migrating to Windows Server 2008 and realize how well Windows Vista and Windows Server 2008 work together, the migration to Windows Vista will move into full swing.

History repeats itself. Even in the IT world.

New Features of Windows Server 2008

If you're coming to Windows Server 2008 from a Windows Server 2003 background, you're probably very interested in learning what's new. There's a lot that's similar, which will reduce your learning curve. There's also a lot that's new.

Server Manager

Server Manager is a new console designed to streamline the management of a Windows Server 2008 server. As an administrator, expect to use Server Manager for many different purposes.

The first time you looked at Event Viewer in an operating system, it was new and different. However, in time, Event Viewer became a common tool you used often that was very simple to use. Expect Server Manager to be as common to you as Event Viewer. As a matter of fact, it even includes some of Event Viewer's data.

Figure 1.3 shows Server Manager. It's actually a Microsoft Management Console (MMC) with several useful snap-ins added.

FIGURE 1.3   Server Manager

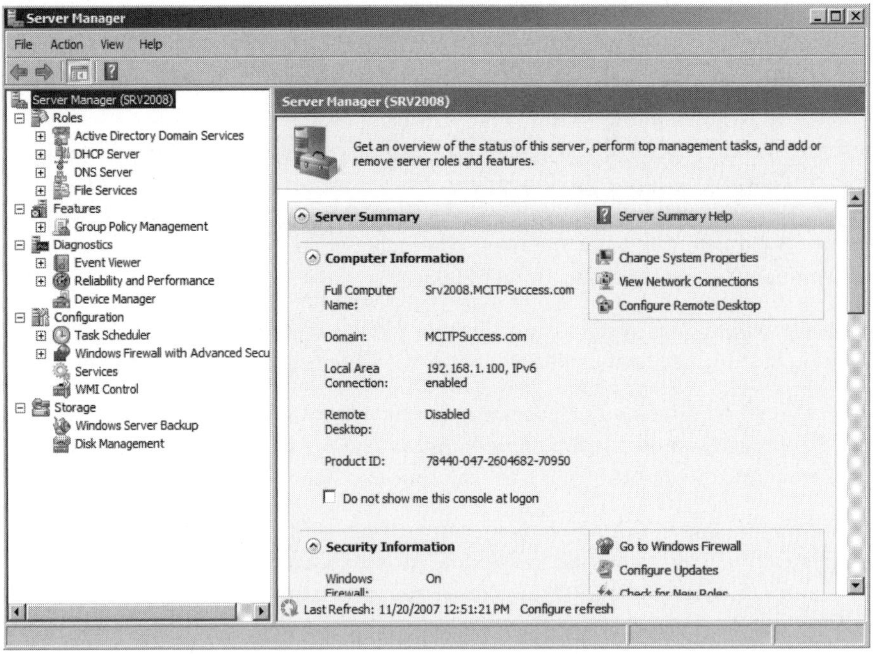

Server Manager includes many tools that can be used to do the following:

Manage a server's identity   Here you can find basic computer information such the computer name, workgroup or domain name, local area connection data, and whether remote desktop is enabled. It also includes a link to system properties, so many of these items can be modified.

Display the current status of the server   Server Manager queries the system logs and identifies the types of messages that have been listed. If warnings or errors are found in the logs for the role, an icon appears indicating the health of the server.

Easily identify problems with any installed roles   Each role has a summary page that shows events for the role. This is a filtered view showing only the events for this role. The actual number of informational messages, warnings, and errors are listed, and you can double-click any of the events to view the message.

Manage server roles, including adding and removing roles   As many as 17 roles can be installed on the server, and by clicking the Roles selection, each of the installed roles is listed. You can add roles by clicking the Add Roles link, which will launch the Add Roles Wizard. Similarly, you can remove roles by clicking the Remove Roles link.

Add and remove features   Features (such as Windows PowerShell or BitLocker Encryption) can be added or removed using Server Manager.

Perform diagnostics   Access to Event Viewer, the Reliability and Performance Monitor tools, and Device Manager are accessible here. These tools allow you to do some basic investigations when troubleshooting server problems.

Configure the server   Four snap-ins are included: Task Scheduler, Windows Firewall, Services, and WMI Control.

Configure backups and disk store   Windows Server Backup and Disk Management tools are included here.

You'll use the Server Manager tool in maintenance and management tasks covered throughout this book.

To launch Server Manager, you can select Start ➤ Administrative Tools ➤ Server Manager. Also, you can right-click Computer in the Start menu and select Manage.

Server Manager has a related command-line tool named `ServerManagerCmd.exe`. Many of the same tasks performed through the Server Manager GUI can be performed via the command-line tool.

The strength of any command-line tool is the ability to script the tasks required and then, when necessary, simply rerun the script. You no longer need to wade through the screens and hope you're remembering exactly what you clicked last time. Instead, you simply run your verified script, and you're done. Additionally, you can schedule scripts to run at some future time.

You'll be using Server Manager throughout the book.

Server Core

Server Core is a completely new feature in Windows Server 2008. It allows you to install only what's needed on the server to support the specific role the server will assume.

For example, if you're planning on creating a server that will be a DHCP server and only a DHCP server, you can use Server Core. Instead of installing the full Windows Server 2008 operating system, Server Core will install only a subset of the executable files and supporting dynamic link libraries (DLLs) needed for the Role you select.

A significant difference between Server Core and the full operating system is that Server Core does not have a graphical user interface (GUI). Instead, all interaction with Server Core takes place through the command line.

Server Core provides several benefits:

- It requires less software so uses less disk space. Only about 1GB is used for the install.
- Since it is less software, it requires fewer updates.
- It minimizes the attack surface since fewer ports are opened by default.
- It's easier to manage.

Server Core cannot be used for all possible server roles, but it can be used with many. The following server roles are supported on Server Core:

- Active Directory Domain Services
- Active Directory Lightweight Directory Services (AD LDS)
- DHCP Server
- DNS Server
- File Services
- Print Services
- Web Services
- Hyper-V

Server Core does not include all the features available on other Server installations. For example, it does not include the .NET Framework or Internet Explorer.

Server Core will be explored in greater depth in Chapter 2, "Planning Server Deployments."

PowerShell

The difference between a good administrator and a great administrator is often determined by their ability to script.

PowerShell is scripting on steroids—in a good way. It combines the command-line shell with a scripting language and adds more than 130 command-line tools (called *cmdlets*).

As an administrator, expect to use PowerShell quite frequently for many administrative and management tasks. Currently, you can use PowerShell with the following:

- Exchange Server
- SQL Server
- Internet Information Services
- Terminal Services
- Active Directory Domain Services
- Managing services, processes, and the registry

Windows PowerShell isn't installed by default. However, you can easily install it using the Server Manager's Add Features selection.

Windows Deployment Services

One of the most time-consuming tasks involved with computers can be setting up new systems. To install the operating system alone, it may take 30 minutes. Add the time it takes to install current patches, updates, and additional applications, as well as set up baseline security, and your time for a single system can be three or more hours. And that's just one box!

If you have 20 computers to set up, it can take one-and-a-half workweeks (60 hours). In short, this is unacceptable.

Historically, administrators have used imaging technologies (such as Symantec's Ghost) to capture an image and then deploy this image to multiple computers.

Remote Installation Services (RIS) was Microsoft's previous foray into automating the installation of systems. Unfortunately, it had some issues that prevented it from becoming popular with a lot of administrators. Windows Deployment Services (WDS) is a significant redesign of RIS.

Windows Deployment Services uses the Windows Image (WIM) format. A significant improvement with WIM over RIS images is that it is file-based and works well across many different hardware platforms. Further, tools are available that allow the images to be modified without having to completely rebuild the image.

WDS includes three primary component categories:

Server components   The server components provide a method for a client to be able to boot with network access and load the operating system. It includes a Preboot Execution Environment (PXE, often called "pixie") server and Trivial File Transfer Protocol (TFTP) server. The server includes a shared folder with images and other files used to load an image onto a remote computer.

Client components   The client components include a Windows Pre-Installation Environment (Windows PE) that allow the client to boot into a graphical user interface and select an appropriate image from the server.

Management components   WDS includes tools used to manage server, images, and client computer accounts. For example, Sysprep is used to remove computer unique information (such as SIDs) before capturing images, and the WDS Capture utility is used to capture images and store them in the WIM format.

Figure 1.4 shows how WDS would work. The WDS server holds the images. PXE clients would boot and then connect to the WDS server. A Windows PE image would be downloaded to the client. This image includes a graphical user interface that could be used with user interaction or scripted to automate the process.

FIGURE 1.4   Windows Deployment Services

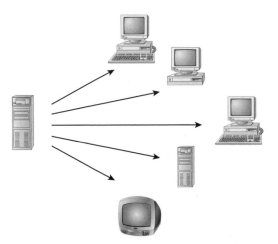

You'll explore Windows Deployment Services in greater depth in Chapter 2.

New Functionality in Terminal Services

Terminal Services provides two distinct capabilities:

For the administrator   Allows the administrator to remotely administer systems using Remote Desktop Connection or Remote Desktops. With Windows Server 2008, Remote Desktop Connection 6.0 is available, which provides some security improvements, but generally, the remote desktop functionality is similar in Windows Server 2008 as it was in Windows Server 2003.

For end users   Allows end users to run programs from Terminal Services servers. The significant change in Windows Server 2008 is the ability for multiple users to run programs centrally from a single server. From the user's perspective, it appears as though the programs are actually running on their system. Additionally, Terminal Services applications can more easily traverse firewalls allowing applications to be accessed without the need to create VPN connections.

You'll explore Windows Terminal Services in greater depth in Chapter 7.

Network Access Protection

Network Access Protection (NAP) is an added feature that can help protect your network from remote access clients. Yes, you read that correctly. NAP helps you protect the *network* from the *clients*.

Within a local area network (LAN), you can control client computers to ensure they're safe and healthy. You can use Group Policy to ensure that it's locked down from a security perspective and that it's getting the required updates. Antivirus and spyware software can be pushed out, regularly updated and run on clients. You can run scripts to ensure that all the corporate policies remain in place.

However, you can't control a client accessing your network from a hotel or someone's home. It's entirely possible for a virus-ridden computer to connect to your network and cause significant problems.

The solution is NAP, which is a set of technologies that can be used to check the health of a client. If the client is healthy, it's allowed access to the network. If unhealthy, it's quarantined and allowed access to remediation servers that can be used to bring the client into compliance with the requirements.

Health policies are determined and set by the administrator (that's you). For example, you may choose to require that all current and approved updates are installed on clients. In the network you use Windows Software Update Services (WSUS) to approve and install the updates on clients. Since the VPN client isn't in the network, they might not have the required updates. The client would be quarantined, and a WSUS server could be used as a remediation server to push the updates to the client. Once the updates are installed, the client could be rechecked and issued a health certificate and then granted access to the network.

You'll explore NAP in greater depth in Chapter 4, "Monitoring and Maintaining Network Infrastructure Servers."

Read-Only Domain Controllers

A *read-only domain controller* (RODC) hosts a read-only copy of the Active Directory database. This is somewhat of a misnomer, because changes *can* be made to the database. However, the changes can come only from other domain controllers, and the entire database isn't replicated; instead, only a few select objects are replicated.

Usually, domain controllers are considered peers where they are all equal (with a few exceptions). Any objects can be added or modified (such as adding a user or a user changing their password) on any domain controller. These changes are then replicated to other domain controllers. However, with RODCs, changes to the domain controller can come only from other domain controllers. Moreover, the changes are severely restricted to only a few select objects.

The huge benefit of the RODC is that credentials of all users and computers in Active Directory are not replicated to the RODC. This significantly improves the security of domain controllers that are placed at remote locations. If stolen, they hold the credentials of only a few objects.

As an example, when Sally logs on for the first time at the remote office, the RODC contacts a regular domain controller at the main office to verify the credentials of Sally. In addition to verifying the credentials, the domain controller can replicate the credentials to the RODC; Sally's credentials are then cached on the RODC. The next time Sally logs on, the RODC checks her credentials against the cached credentials.

If the RODC is somehow stolen, the entire Active Directory database isn't compromised since the RODC would hold only a minimum number of accounts.

The one requirement to support read-only domain controllers is that the domain controller hosting the PDC Emulator FSMO role must be running Windows Server 2008.

FSMO roles (including the PDC Emulator) are covered in the "Review of Active Directory" section later in this chapter.

🌐 Real World Scenario

Authentication at a Remote Office

Consider a remote office connected that has only 10 users and little physical security. The office is connected to the main office via a low-bandwidth wide area network (WAN) link. The challenge you face is allowing the users to log in and authenticate.

In past versions, you had one of two choices: place a domain controller (DC) in the remote office or allow the users to authenticate over the WAN link to a DC at the main office.

With little physical security, the DC could get stolen, and suddenly your entire domain could be compromised. Remember, the DC holds information for all users and computers. A solution would be to implement physical security, but with only 10 users, it's likely that you don't have the budget or staff to do this for a single server.

If the bandwidth is low (say a demand-dial 56K connection), then authentication could be very time-consuming for users. Additionally, depending on the usage of the connection, it may already be close to maximum usage or, worse, unreliable.

With Windows Server 2008, you have a third option. Place an RODC at the remote location. Users can log on to the DC using credentials cached on the RODC. This allows the users to quickly log on even if the WAN connection is slow or unreliable. If the DC is stolen, you still have some problems to deal with, but you won't need to consider rebuilding your entire domain. Instead, you need to deal only with the accounts at the remote office.

Improvements in Failover Clustering

Before discussing the improvements in failover clustering, let's review the big picture of clustering.

In Figure 1.5, the client connects to a virtual server (named Server1) that is configured as part of a two-node cluster. The nodes are SrvClust1 and SrvClust2. Both the cluster nodes have connections to the network, to each other, and to a shared quorum disk. Only one node is active in a cluster at a time.

FIGURE 1.5   A two-node failover cluster

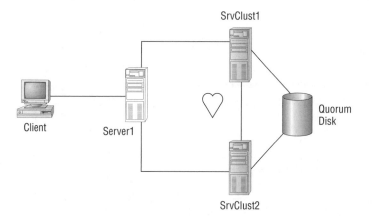

As an example, you could be running SQL Server 2008 on both servers within a cluster configuration. SrvClust1 would be active, and SrvClust2 would be inactive. In other words, even though both servers are running, only SrvClust1 is responding to requests. SrvClust2's primary job at this point is to monitor the heartbeat of SrvClust1. If SrvClust1 goes down or services stop running, SrvClust2 recognizes the failure and is able to cover the load. From the client's perspective, there may be a momentary delay, but the actual outage is significantly limited.

Not all Windows Server 2008 editions support clustering. The only editions that do support clustering are these three:

- Windows Server 2008 Enterprise edition

- Windows Server 2008 Datacenter edition

- Windows Server 2008 Itanium edition

The two editions that do *not* support clustering are Windows Server 2008 Standard edition and Web edition.

Some of the improvements that Windows Server 2008 brings to failover clustering are as follows:

- Eliminates the quorum disk as a single point of failure with a new quorum model.

- Provides a tool for validating your hardware for cluster support before it's deployed.

- Provides enhanced support for storage area networks.

- Provides improved management tools that make setting up clusters easier.

- The quorum disk is now referred to as a *witness disk*.

Failover clustering will be covered in more depth in Chapter 9, "Planning Business Continuity and High Availability."

Installing Windows Server 2008

If you don't have an instance of Windows Server 2008 installed, you'll want to do that as quickly as possible. Server administration is a participation sport. You can't hope to get good at this without digging in and getting your hands into the operating system.

In this section, you'll learn how to get a free evaluation copy of Windows Server 2008 (if you don't already have one) and how to install it on Virtual PC. This will allow you to do your regular work on Windows Vista or Windows XP and then, when desired, launch Windows Server 2008 on the same system.

Hardware Requirements

Table 1.4 lists the basic system requirements for Windows Server 2008 editions.

TABLE 1.4   Hardware Requirements for Windows Server 2008 Editions

	Standard	Enterprise	Datacenter
Processor (min)	1GHz (x86) 1.4GHz (x64)	1GHz (x86 1.4GHz (x64)	1GHz (x86) 1.4GHz (x64)
Processor (recommended)	2GHz or faster	2GHz or faster	2GHz or faster
Memory (min)	512MB	512MB	512MB
Memory (recommended)	2GB or more	2GB or more	2GB or more
Memory (max)	4GB (32 bit) 32GB (64 bit)	64GB (32 bit) 2TB (64 bit)	64GB (32 bit) 2TB (64 bit)
Disk space (min)	10GB	10GB	10GB
Disk space (recommended)	40GB	40GB	40GB

Hardware resources would need to be increased for any systems using Hyper-V technology and running virtual machines. For example, if you're running three virtual servers within a Windows Server 2008 Enterprise edition, you would need additional processing power, more memory, and more disk space.

Running Windows Server 2008 on Your System

To get the most out of the book and your studies, it's best to have a Windows Server 2008 operating system installed. This allows you to see and apply the concepts. I strongly encourage you to get a copy of Windows Server 2008 and install it on a system that you can access regularly.

In the sidebar "How to Obtain a Copy of Windows Server 2008," I explain how you can get evaluation copies of Windows Server 2008. If your budget allows, you might consider investing in a subscription to TechNet (http://technet.microsoft.com). In addition to providing you with copies of all the current operating systems and current applications (such as Microsoft Office and Visio), it also provides you with a wealth of technical resources such as videos and TechNet articles.

How to Obtain a Copy of Windows Server 2008

It's common for Microsoft to provide free evaluation copies of Server operating systems for your use. Currently, you can download Windows Server 2008 30-day and 180-day evaluation editions free of charges here:

http://www.microsoft.com/windowsserver2008/en/us/trial-software.aspx

Beware, though. These files are quite large. If you're using a slower dial-up link, you might want to see whether Microsoft is currently offering an evaluation DVD via regular mail. Purchasing an evaluation DVD isn't an available option at this writing, but Microsoft has often included this as an option with other Server products. There's a nominal cost involved with this option, but it's better than trying to download more than 2GB at 56KB.

The download is an .iso image of the actual DVD. Search with your favorite search engine for *Download Windows Server 2008,* and you'll find the link.

Once you download the .iso image, you can burn it to a DVD. If you don't have the software needed to burn it to DVD, you can use one of the many freeware utilities (such as ImgBurn) to burn the .iso image to your DVD.

Using Virtual PC 2007

Virtual PC is an excellent tool that will allow you to install multiple instances of Windows Server 2008 on a single operating system. For example, you may be running Windows XP or Windows Vista on your primary computer. Instead of making this system a dual-boot or multiboot operating system, you can use Virtual PC to install all of these operating systems and make them easily accessible within your primary operating system.

Exercise 1.1 will show you how you can download and install Virtual PC and begin installing any operating system within Virtual PC.

EXERCISE 1.1

Installing Virtual PC 2007

1. Use your favorite search engine, and enter Download Virtual PC. At this writing, the current version is Virtual PC 2007, and you can find information on it at http://www.microsoft.com/windows/products/winfamily/virtualpc/default.mspx.

2. Save the file to somewhere on your hard drive (such as c:\downloads).

3. Once the download completes, click Run to run the Setup file. Click Run or Continue (on Windows Vista) again in the Security Warning box.

4. Follow the installation wizard to finish installing Virtual PC.

5. Click Start ➢ All Programs ➢ Microsoft Virtual PC to launch Virtual PC.

6. On the Welcome to the New Virtual Machine Wizard page, click Next.

   If you already have at least one virtual machine installed on Virtual PC, the New Virtual Machine Wizard won't start automatically. Instead, you need to click the New button in Virtual PC to launch the wizard.

7. On the Options page, ensure that Create a Virtual Machine is selected, as shown in the following graphic. Click Next.

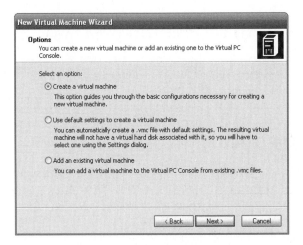

8. On the Virtual Machine Name and Location page, enter Server2008 in the Name and Location box. Click Browse. Notice that this defaults to the My Documents\My Virtual Machines location. You can leave this as the default or browse to another location if desired. Click Next.

9. On the Operating System page, select Windows Vista. This will select a memory size of 512MB and a virtual disk size of 65GB. Click Next.

10. On the Memory page, accept the default of Using the Recommended RAM, and click Next.

11. On the Virtual Hard Disk Options page, select A New Virtual Hard Disk, and click Next.

12. On the Virtual hard Disk Location, accept the defaults, and click Next.

13. On the Completing the New Virtual Machine Wizard page, click Finish. The Virtual PC Console will open with the new virtual PC, as shown in the following graphic.

Note that while you've created the virtual PC instance, it's just an empty shell at this point. Windows Server 2008 still needs to be installed.

14. With the virtual machine selected, click Start in the Virtual PC Console to launch it.

15. Select the CD menu, and select Capture ISO Image. On the Select CD Image to Capture page, browse to where your ISO image is located, select it, and click Open.

    Alternatively, you can insert the Windows Server 2008 operating system DVD into your system DVD player. If the AutoPlay feature starts the DVD on the host operating system, close the window. Within Virtual PC, on the CD Menu, select Use Physical Drive X:\, where X: is the drive.

16. With the bootable DVD image captured, you can reset your Virtual PC either by selecting the Action menu and clicking Reset or by pressing Right Alt+Del keys to force a reboot to the DVD. At this point, the installation of Windows Server 2008 will start.

From this point on, the installation will work the same whether it is on Virtual PC or on a clean system. If you did Exercise 1.1 ("Installing Virtual PC 2007"), continue from step 2 in Exercise 1.2. If you chose not to use Virtual PC, begin Exercise 1.2 at step 1.

In Exercise 1.2, you will install Windows Server 2008.

EXERCISE 1.2

Installing Windows Server 2008

1. Insert the Windows Server 2008 operating system DVD. If the AutoPlay feature doesn't start the installation, use Windows Explorer to browse to the DVD drive, and double-click Setup.

2. If the Language Choice screen appears, accept the default language, time, currency, and keyboard. Click Next.

3. On the installation screen, click Install Now.

4. On the Product Key page, enter the product key. Click Next.

5. On the Select the Operating System page, select Windows Server 2008 (Full Installation), as shown in the following graphic. I'll cover how to install the Server Core installation in Chapter 2. Click Next.

6. On the License Terms page, review the license terms, and click the I Accept the License Terms box. Click Next.

7. On the Type of Installation page, click Custom (Advanced).

8. On the Where Do You Want to Install Windows page, click Drive Options (Advanced). Click New. Change the size to 40,000MB, as shown in the following graphic. Click Apply.

9. Select Disk 0 Partition 1, and click Next. The partition will be formatted with NTFS as part of the installation. At this point, take a break. The installation will continue on its own.

10. When complete, the Password Change screen will complete. Click OK.

11. Enter a new password in the two text boxes. I enter P@ssw0rd on test installations. It meets complexity requirements and doesn't require me to remember multiple passwords. I don't recommend using this password on a production server. Hit Enter after the passwords are entered.

12. Once the password has been changed, the screen indicates success. Click OK.

13. If you've installed this on Virtual PC, follow the remaining steps to finalize the installation:

    a. Install the Virtual Machine Additions by selecting the Action menu and then clicking Install or Update Virtual Machine Additions. In the dialog box that appears, click Continue.

    b. In the AutoPlay dialog box, click Run setup.exe.

    c. On the Welcome page, click Next.

    d. On the Setup Completed page, click Finish. When the Virtual Machine Additions completes the installation, it will indicate you must restart the computer. Click Yes.

    e. Once it reboots, select Action, and then click Close. Select Save State. This will save all the changes you've made to the installation and close the Virtual PC.

What I've done when learning Windows Server 2008 is to make a copy of the virtual hard drive image after I've activated it and use it as a baseline. Then if anything goes wrong, I simply make another copy of the baseline and start over.

 When working with Virtual PC, the Right Alt key (the Alt key to the right of the spacebar) is referred to as the Host key. To log on, instead of pressing Ctrl+Alt+Del, press the Right Alt+Del keys. To change the display to full-screen mode, press Right Alt+Enter. When in full-screen mode, press Right Alt+Enter to change back to Windows mode. If the cursor ever seems to be "stuck" in Virtual PC, press the Right Alt key to allow you to move it out of the Virtual PC window. Last, when turning off Virtual PC, you will be prompted to save your changes. This commits all the changes you've made during the session to the virtual hard disk. If you choose not to save your changes, the next time you reboot, none of your changes will apply.

Activating Windows Server 2008

Just as any Windows operating system today, Windows Server 2008 must be activated. Typically a computer will connect with a Microsoft server over the Internet. Data is transferred and back and forth and the computer is activated. You may have computers that connect with the Internet but still need to be activated. This can be done with the Key Management Service (KMS)

If a computer can't be activated, you'll lose all functionality when the activation period expires. The only thing the computer can do is access the tools used to activate it.

In larger companies, volume license keys are purchased for multiple servers instead of purchasing licenses individually. When using volume license keys you have two choices of how to activate your servers: Multiple Activation Key (MAK) and Key Management Service (KMS).

Multiple Activation Key   With a Multiple Activation Key (MAK), a company purchases a fixed number of licenses and any servers installed with this key can be activated over the Internet with Microsoft. If the computers have Internet access, this is an automated process. It's also possible to activate a MAK by phone for systems without Internet access.

Key Management Service   The Key Management Service (KMS) can be used instead of MAK if you want to eliminate the need to connect directly to Microsoft computers. For example, you may have servers in a secure network without Internet access. Instead of manually activating each server over the phone, you can use the KMS.

First, you would install the KMS on a server and activate it using traditional means (via the Internet or phone). The KMS can then be used to activate other systems within your network.

Systems activated by the KMS must contact the KMS at least once every 6 months to renew their activation. All contact with the KMS is automated without any user intervention.

Review of Active Directory

Active Directory is Microsoft's implementation of a directory service. A *directory service* holds information about resources within the domain. Resources are stored as objects and include users, computers, groups, printers, and more.

In Windows Server 2008, five different server roles support Active Directory:

- Active Directory Domain Services
- Active Directory Certificate Services
- Active Directory Federation Services
- Active Directory Lightweight Directory Services
- Active Directory Rights Management Services

The primary role is Active Directory Domain Services. The other roles add to the capabilities of Active Directory.

Objects include users, computers, groups, and more. The Active Directory database is stored only on servers holding the role of domain controllers.

A significant benefit of using Active Directory Domain Services is that it enables you as an administrator to manage desktops, network servers, and applications all from a centralized location.

Active Directory Elements

Active Directory can spread beyond a single domain, though. Take a look at Figure 1.6. This figure shows the logical structure of Active Directory in a multiple-domain, multiple-tree forest.

Active Directory has several elements you should know for the exam:

Root domain The MCITPSuccess.com domain (labeled 1) is the root domain. The root domain is the very first domain created in a forest. This domain would also be considered a parent domain to both the Consulting.MCITPSuccess.com domain (labeled 2) and the Training.MCITPSuccess.com domain (labeled 3).

FIGURE 1.6 Logical structure of Active Directory

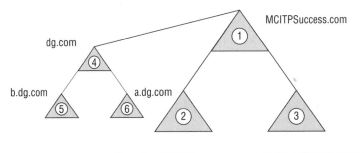

If nothing were added other than the root domain, the root domain would also be called a *tree* and a *forest*.

Child domain Both the Consulting.MCITPSuccess.com and Training.MCITPSuccess.com domains are considered child domains of the MCITPSuccess.com. A child domain has the same namespace (in this case MCITPSuccess.com) as the parent.

Tree A tree is a group of domains that share the same namespace. In the figure, there are two trees. The domains labeled 1, 2, and 3 all share the same namespace of MCITPSuccess.com and so compose one tree. The second tree is composed of the domains labeled 4, 5, and 6; these domains share the same namespace of dg.com. Even though the second tree has a different namespace, it is associated with the first namespace, as shown with the connecting line.

Forest A forest is all of the domains in all the trees in the same logical structure as the root domain. In other words, all the trees in the world aren't part of a single forest. Instead, only trees created off the root domain are part of the forest to which the root domain belongs.

Trusts Each of these domains is connected with a line with another domain in the forest. The line implies a two-way trust. A trust allows users in one domain to be able to access resources in another domain (if permissions are granted). Two-way means that users in domain 1 can access resources in domain 2, and users in domain 2 can access resources in domain 1.

Additionally, trusts within a forest are transitive. Since domain 2 trusts domain 1, and domain 1 trusts domain 3, then domain 1 also trusts domain 3.

Active Directory Domain Services Schema   The Active Directory Domain Services schema contains definitions of all the objects that can be contained in Active Directory Domain Services and also lists the attributes or properties of those objects.

A real-world example of the schema is the white pages of a phone book. No matter what city you're in, you expect to find names, addresses, and phone numbers in the white pages. The schema of the white pages defines a single object (a phone listing) with three attributes or properties (name, address, and phone number). Of course, a phone book would have multiple listings. If I called up the phone company and asked them to publish my birthday in their next phone book, they'd probably laugh. Or a tech geek might tell me, "Sorry, that property is not in our schema."

In Active Directory Domain Services, you can add objects such as users, computers, groups, and more. You can't add a kitchen sink object because it's not in the schema. Further, you can't add birthday attributes to the user object because it's not in the schema.

There is only one Active Directory Domain Services schema for the entire forest. Other schemas exist for other Active Directory roles. For example, the Active Directory Lightweight Directory Services role contains its own schema.

Global catalog   The global catalog is a listing of all objects in the forest. It holds a full listing (including all attributes) of objects in the domain and a partial (only some of the attributes) read-only copy of the objects from other domains. The global catalog is held on a domain controller configured as a global catalog server. The first domain controller in a domain is automatically configured as a global catalog server, and replica domain controllers can be configured as global catalog servers if desired.

Many processes and applications regularly use the global catalog to identify objects and attributes. For example, when a user logs on, the global catalog is queried to identify the Universal Group membership.

Consider a forest of six domains. The global catalog could be quite huge if it held all the attributes of all the objects. To make the size of the global catalog more manageable in large forests, the global catalog includes only some of the more often used attributes of objects. For example, a user object may have as many as 100 different attributes such as name, user logon name, universal principal name, SAM account name, password, street address, post office box, city, state, ZIP, and much more. Clearly some of these attributes are more important than others. The schema defines which attributes are replicated to the global catalog.

FSMO roles   In a Windows Server 2008, domain controllers can hold additional flexible single master operations (FSMO) roles. Five FSMO roles exist. Two (the Schema Master and the Domain Naming Master) are unique to the forest. The other three (RID Master, PDC Emulator, and Infrastructure Master) are contained in each domain in the forest.

It's common for all of the roles to exist on a single domain controller, but it isn't required. In a two-domain forest, the first domain controller in the root domain would hold all five roles by default. The first domain controller in the child domain would hold the three domain roles. These roles can be transferred to other domain controllers if desired or seized if the domain controller holding the role is no longer operational.

Schema Master   The Schema Master role holds the only writable copy of the schema. If the schema needs to be modified (such as when installing Microsoft Exchange for the first time), the Schema Master must be on line and reachable. Only one server in the entire forest holds the role of Schema Master.

Domain Naming Master   The Domain Naming Master role is the sole role used to manage the creation of new domains within the forest. It ensures that domains are not created with duplicate names. Only one server in the entire forest holds the role of Domain Naming Master.

RID Master   The RID Master is used to create new unique security identifiers (SIDs). While you and I refer to users and computers based on their names, resources refer to this objects based on their SIDs. When granting permissions to resources, the SID is added to the access control list. SIDs must be unique—one of kind, never to be repeated. If you have duplicate SIDs on your network, you end up with a painful assortment of problems that become quite challenging to troubleshoot.

A SID is created by a domain SID and relative identifiers (RIDs) issued by the RID Master role. The RID Master role issues RIDS to other domain controllers. It keeps track of what RIDs have been issued, ensuring no duplicate SIDs exist on your network. One server in each domain within a forest holds the role of RID Master.

PDC Emulator   The PDC Emulator role is the miscellaneous role. It fulfills a variety of purposes in the domain.

In NT 4.0 (yes, a long, long time ago), there was one Primary Domain Controller (PDC) and multiple Backup Domain Controllers (BDCs). The PDC held the only writable copy of the domain database. When changes occurred, the BDC had to contact the PDC to make the change. When Windows 2000 was introduced, domain controllers were created as multiple masters with loose convergence. In other words, all held writable copies of Active Directory, and given enough time, the database would converge and all copies would be identical. However, it was unlikely that all domain controllers would be upgraded to Windows 2000 immediately. Instead, the PDC was upgraded first, and it held the role of PDC Emulator. All BDCs contacted the PDC Emulator just as if it were the PDC.

Let me ask you a question: Are you running NT 4.0 today? No, I see. The designers of the FSMO roles peered into their crystal balls and predicted this. They gave the PDC other jobs.

It is the time synchronizer for the domain. You can synchronize the PDC emulator with a third-party time source to ensure it's accurate. All domain controllers in the domain get their time from the PDC Emulator. All client computers get their time from the domain controller they authenticate with when they start. This ensures that all computers within the domain have the same time. This is critical for the support of Kerberos; if computers are more than five minutes off, they are locked out of the domain.

The PDC Emulator is the point of contact for managing password changes. When a user changes their password, it is recorded with the PDC Emulator. Ultimately, Active Directory Domain Services will replicate the new password to all domain controllers, but there will be a short period of time when the change hasn't been replicated to all. If the user tries to log in shortly after changing their password and contacts a different domain controller before the password is replicated, they could be denied access even though they've given the correct password. Instead, the logon services queries the PDC Emulator to see whether the user has recently changed their password.

New to Windows Server 2008 is support for read-only domain controllers. To support read-only domain controllers, the server holding the role of PDC Emulator must be running Windows Server 2008.

One server in each domain within a forest holds the role of PDC Emulator.

Infrastructure Master   The Infrastructure Master role is useful only in a multiple domain forest. It keeps track of changes in group membership in other domains that affect a group in its domain.

For example, consider a domain local group named DL_ColorPrinter in DomainA. It could have a global group from DomainB named G_Managers as a member. If the group membership in DomainB changes, DomainA wouldn't be aware of the changes since the change occurred in another domain. To resolve this issue, the Infrastructure Master role periodically queries the global catalog to identify any changes.

The one restriction on the Infrastructure Master role is that it won't function as desired if it is also holding the role of the global catalog server. In a multiple domain forest, the Infrastructure Master should not be a global catalog server. If it's a single domain forest, it doesn't matter.

One server in each domain within a forest holds the role of Infrastructure Master.

Promoting a Server to a Domain Controller

Most Windows Server 2008 servers can be promoted to the role of a domain controller. The exception is Server 2008 Web edition and Itanium edition.

By promoting a server to a domain controller, you are installing Active Directory Domain Services on the server (and the other necessary pieces) for Active Directory Domain Services to work.

The tool used to promote a server is DCPromo. It can be run from the command line or the Run box.

To support Active Directory Domain Services, Domain Name System (DNS) must be running on the network. If it is not installed and available, DCPromo will identify the omission, and you'll be prompted to install DNS as part of the promotion process.

When running DCPromo, you will be asked what function the new domain controller will fulfill. The choices are as follows:

- First domain controller in the forest
- First domain controller in a new domain within an existing tree within an existing forest
- First domain controller in a new domain in a new tree within an existing forest
- Replica domain controller in an existing domain

If this is the first domain controller in a new domain or the first domain controller in the forest, you'll also be asked to choose the domain functional level and the forest functional level. The choice is guided by what version of Windows is running on all the domain controllers.

The choices for domain functional level are as follows:

- Windows Server 2000 native
- Windows Server 2003
- Windows Server 2008

Once all the domain controllers are Windows Server 2003 or Windows Server 2008, then the domain functional level can be raised to the higher level. The domain functional level is raised using Active Directory Users and Computers. At higher levels, additional features and functionality are available.

The choices for forest functional level are as follows:

- Windows Server 2000 native
- Windows Server 2003
- Windows Server 2008

Once all domains are at a given domain functional level, the forest functional level can be raised to that level. The forest functional level is raised using Active Directory Domains and Trusts.

Another requirement for promoting a server to a domain controller is that the IP addresses should be static. If you have dynamically assigned IP addresses (either IPv4 or IPv6), a warning will appear indicating you should assign static IP addresses for both IPv4 and IPv6.

Promoting a server to a domain controller involves two distinct steps:

1. Add the Active Directory Domain Services role using Server Manager.
2. Run the DCPromo wizard to install Active Directory Domain Services.

Exercise 1.3 and Exercise 1.4 walk you through the necessary steps to promote a server to a domain controller.

Domain Functional Level and Forest Functional Level

The domain functional level and forest functional level identify features available within your domain and forest. If all **DOMAIN CONTROLLERS** are Windows Server 2008, the domain functional level could be raised to Windows 2008. Once all domains are raised to Windows Server 2008, the forest functional level can be raised to Windows 2008.

Notice how I've bolded and capitalized **DOMAIN CONTROLLERS**? The editors really don't like it, but there's an important reason for this: a quirk I've noticed in the classroom is that students often change this definition in their heads. Instead of remembering that all **DOMAIN CONTROLLERS** must be Windows Server 2008 to raise the functional level to 2008, students often change this definition to all servers must be Windows Server 2008. However, a domain can be in the domain functional level of 2008 with Windows Server 2000 servers, Windows Server 2003 servers, and Windows Server 2008 servers. The difference is that all **DOMAIN CONTROLLERS** must be Windows Server 2008 to be able to raise the domain functional level to 2008.

EXERCISE 1.3

Adding the Active Directory Domain Services Role

1. Launch Server Manager. Click Start ➢ Administrator Tools ➢ Server Manager.

2. In Server Manager, select Roles.

3. Select Add Roles.

4. On the Before You Begin page, review the requirements, and click Next.

5. On the Select Server Roles page, select the check box next to Active Directory Domain Services, and click Next.

6. On the Active Directory Domain Services page, review the information, and click Next.

7. On the Confirm Installation Selections page, click Install.

8. On the Installation Results page, review the information. Note that you must still run the Active Directory Domain Services Installation Wizard (DCPromo) to make the server a fully functional domain controller. Click Close.

EXERCISE 1.4

Installing Active Directory Domain Services

1. Boot into a Windows Server 2008 server.

2. Click Start ➢ Run. At the Run line, enter DCPromo, and click OK.

3. On the Welcome screen, click Next.

4. On the Operating System Compatibility screen, review the information, and click Next.

5. On the Choose a Deployment Configuration page, select Create a New Domain in a New Forest. Your display will look similar to the following graphic. Click Next.

If your computer were part of an existing forest, you could create a replica domain controller within an existing domain. However, this exercise is assuming your server will be the first domain controller in the forest.

6. On the Name the Forest Root Domain page, enter MCITPSuccess.com as the fully qualified domain name. Click Next.

7. If the Domain NetBIOS Name page appears, accept the default of MCITPSUCESS.

8. On the Set Forest Functional Level page, accept the Forest functional level of Windows 2000. Click Next.

9. On the Set Forest Functional Level page, accept the default of Windows 2000. Click Next.

10. On the Set Domain Functional Level page, accept the default of Windows 2000 Native. Click Next.

11. On the Additional Domain Controller Options page, note that both the DNS server and the global catalog are selected as options. Active Directory Domain Services requires DNS, and if not available on the network, DCPromo will give you the option of installing it. Additionally, the first domain controller within a domain is a global catalog server. Click Next.

    If you have dynamically assigned addresses assigned, a warning will appear indicating you must assign static IP addresses for both IPv4 and IPv6. Either assign static IP addresses or click Yes; the computer will use a dynamically assigned IP address and configure static IP addresses later. As a best practice, domain controllers should use statically assigned IP addresses.

12. If this server is on an isolated network without other DNS servers, a warning dialog box will appear indicating that a delegation for this DNS server can't be created and other hosts may not be able to communicate with your domain from outside the domain. This is normal when installing DNS for the first domain controller in a forest. Click Yes to continue.

13. On the Location for Database, Log Files, and SYSVOL page, accept the defaults, and click Next.

14. On the Directory Services Restore Mode Administrator Password page, enter P@ssw0rd in both the Password and Confirm password boxes. This password is needed if you need to restore Active Directory Domain Services. On a production domain controller, a more secure password would be required. Click Next.

15. On the Summary page, review your selections, and click Next. Active Directory Domain Services will be installed.

16. After a few minutes, the wizard will complete. On the Completion page, click Finish.

17. On the Active Directory Domain Services dialog box, click Restart Now. Once your system reboots, Active Directory Domain Services will be installed.

Active Directory Domain Services Tools

When Active Directory Domain Services is installed, several tools are installed with it. These tools are used to manage and maintain Active Directory Domain Services and are as follows:

- Active Directory Users and Computers
- Active Directory Sites and Services
- Active Directory Domains and Trusts

- DSADD
- DSDButil
- DSGet
- DSMGMT
- DSMod
- DSMove
- DSQuery
- DSRM
- GPFixup
- Ksetup
- LDP
- NetDOM
- NLtest
- NSlookup
- Repadmin
- W32tm

Summary

Windows Server 2008 brings a lot of new features and benefits that will drive a lot of migrations to the new operating system. This chapter presented many of these new additions.

One of the significant benefits of Windows Server 2008 is virtualization. Three editions (Windows Server 2008 Standard with Hyper-V, Windows Server 2008 Enterprise with Hyper-V, and Windows Server 2008 Datacenter with Hyper-V) support virtualization. Each edition can be purchased with or without Hyper-V, which is the technology that supports virtualization. The Standard edition supports one virtual server, the Enterprise edition supports as many as four virtual servers, and the Datacenter edition supports an unlimited number of virtual servers. Virtualization is supported on only 64-bit operating systems.

In this chapter, you learned about many of the new features of Windows Server 2008. These included Server Manager, Server Core, PowerShell, Windows Deployment Services, and read-only domain controllers.

Exercises led you through the process of installing Windows Server 2008 on a Virtual PC. After reviewing many of the basics of Active Directory Domain Services, you learned how to promote the server to a domain controller.

Exam Essentials

Know the different Windows Server editions and the capabilities of each.   You should know which edition to use for a strictly IIS deployment and which editions support virtualization, including how many virtual servers are supported in the different editions. You should also know which editions support clustering.

Know the different ways Windows Server 2008 can be activated.   You should know the differences between the Multiple Activation Key (MAK) and the Key Management Service (KMS) both used within corporate networks to activate. KMS is used when multiple computers don't have access to the Internet.

Know the impact of adding multiple virtual servers to a Windows Server 2008 server. Remember that each virtual server has its own hardware requirements. Adding virtual servers may require adding additional processing, disk, memory, and/or network capabilities.

Know how to launch and use Server Manager.   Server Manager is the primary tool used to manage and maintain server roles. You should be very familiar with this GUI.

Know how to promote a server to a domain controller.   Know that promoting a domain controller is a two-step process. First you use Server Manager to add the role to the server, and second you run DCPromo to promote the server.

Review Questions

1. Which of the following Windows Server 2008 editions support Active Directory Domain Services? (Choose all that apply.)

    A.   Web edition

    B.   Itanium edition

    C.   Standard edition

    D.   Enterprise edition

    E.   Datacenter edition

2. You need to create a DHCP server. Which editions of Windows Server 2008 will support this role? (Choose all that apply.)

    A.   Web edition

    B.   Itanium edition

    C.   Standard edition

    D.   Enterprise edition

    E.   Datacenter edition

3. Your company is consolidating servers and has decided to use the virtualization features in Windows Server 2008. A single server will be used to support five virtual servers. What editions support this? (Choose all that apply.)

    A.   Web edition with Hyper-V

    B.   Itanium edition with Hyper-V

    C.   Standard edition with Hyper-V

    D.   Enterprise edition with Hyper-V

    E.   Datacenter edition with Hyper-V

4. What command-line tool can you use to configure a server role?

    A.   Server Manager

    B.   Initial Configuration Tasks

    C.   `ServerManagerCmd.exe`

    D.   `RoleConfig.exe`

5. A fellow administrator is trying to create a read-only domain controller within an existing domain but has been unsuccessful. What might you suggest he do?

    A.   Verify DCPromo is installed.

    B.   Verify that PDC Emulator is a Windows Server 2008 server.

    C.   Verify that DNS is running on the network.

    D.   Verify the Write Protect feature is enabled for Active Directory Domain Services.

6. You help manage a seven-domain forest with two trees. How many schemas exist in this forest?

   A. 1

   B. 2

   C. 4

   D. 7

7. You help manage a seven-domain forest with two trees. How many Domain Naming Masters exist in this forest?

   A. 1

   B. 2

   C. 4

   D. 7

8. You help manage a seven-domain forest with two trees. How many RID Master roles exist in this forest?

   A. 1

   B. 2

   C. 4

   D. 7

9. Users in the research and development department use laptops, and often these laptops hold proprietary information. Management wants to protect the data on these laptops. What technology would you implement?

   A. NTFS permissions

   B. Server Core

   C. NAP

   D. BitLocker Drive Encryption

10. You manage a server that has been used as a file server. Management has decided to have this server host IIS as well. What should you do to support this additional functionality?

    A. Use Server Manager to add a feature.

    B. Use Server Manager to add a role.

    C. Install Windows Server 2008 Web edition.

    D. Add BitLocker Drive Encryption.

11. You are running a Windows Server 2008 Enterprise edition server. It is currently hosting two virtual servers, and you are planning on adding a virtual server. What should you do or check before you add the virtual server?

    A. Upgrade the server to the Datacenter edition.

    B. Ensure the hardware resources are adequate.

    C. Remove one of the virtual servers.

    D. Add Hyper-V to the server.

12. You've decided to consolidate two servers onto an existing 32-bit Windows Server 2008 Enterprise edition server with 4GB of RAM. However, you are unable to get virtualization running on this server. What's a likely problem?

    A. The server must be running the 64-bit operating system.

    B. Not enough memory is installed.

    C. The Enterprise edition doesn't support virtualization.

    D. The Enterprise edition supports only one virtual server.

13. You boot into a Windows Server 2008 server, and instead of a GUI, you get only a command line. What's the reason for this behavior?

    A. The server is booted into safe mode.

    B. Server Core is installed.

    C. Server Manager is not installed.

    D. `ServerManagerCmd.exe` is running on startup.

14. Before raising the domain functional level to Windows Server 2008, what must exist in your domain?

    A. All servers must be running Windows Server 2008.

    B. PDC Emulator must be running Windows Server 2008.

    C. All domain controllers must be running Windows Server 2008.

    D. The global catalog server must be installed on the Infrastructure Master.

15. You manage a two-domain forest. Each domain hosts two domain controllers. All domain controllers are global catalog servers. What should be done to optimize this configuration?

    A. Remove one of the global catalog servers in the root domain.

    B. Remove one of the global catalog servers in each domain.

    C. Add a redundant domain controller to each of the domains.

    D. Move the PDC emulator to a different domain controller in each of the domains.

16. You are an administrator for a multiple-site company. A remote office has 10 users with little physical security. They are complaining that it takes too long to log in. They do not have a domain controller at the remote location. What can you do to resolve the problem?

   A. Add a domain controller.

   B. Add a read-only domain controller.

   C. Reduce the bandwidth of the link between the remote office and headquarters.

   D. Add a global catalog server to the remote office.

17. A fellow administrator created a PowerShell script. She has shared it with you, and you try to run it on your system but are unsuccessful. What do you need to do to run a PowerShell script?

   A. You must be a member of the Enterprise Admins group.

   B. You must be a member of the Domain Admins group.

   C. The server role of PowerShell must be added using Server Manager.

   D. The server feature of PowerShell must be added using Server Manager.

18. Your company has purchased 50 new computers that will be deployed to employees with Windows Vista and several applications. What Microsoft technology can you use to streamline this deployment?

   A. Use Ghost to create images and cast the images to the systems.

   B. Run Sysprep on all the computers before installing the operating system.

   C. Use Windows Software Update Services.

   D. Use Windows Deployment Services.

19. Clients access your network remotely via a virtual private network (VPN) that is hosted on a Windows Server 2003 server. Recently, clients infected by viruses have accessed the network and caused significant problems before the problem was identified and contained. What can you do to prevent this in the future?

   A. Upgrade the server to Windows Server 2008, and add Windows Deployment Services.

   B. Upgrade the server to Windows Server 2008, and implement Network Access Protection.

   C. Upgrade the server to Windows Server 2008, and add read-only domain controllers.

   D. Upgrade the server to Windows Server 2008, and implement BitLocker Drive Encryption.

20. You are planning on deploying 15 Windows Server 2008 servers in a secure network. These servers must have very limited access to the main network and may not connect with the Internet. You need to plan a method to automate the activation of these servers. What should you do?

   A. Implement MAK in the secure network.

   B. Implement MAK in the main network.

   C. Implement KMS in the secure network.

   D. Implement MAK in the secure network.

Answers to Review Questions

1. C, D, E.   The Enterprise and Datacenter editions support all elements of Active Directory. The Standard edition supports most elements of Active Directory (including Active Directory Domain Services). Neither Web edition nor Itanium edition supports the installation of any Active Directory services on them; they can be members of an Active Directory Domain Services domain.

2. C, D, E.   The Standard, Enterprise, and Datacenter editions support any of the standard roles (including DHCP). The Web edition supports only the Web Services role running IIS. The Itanium edition is targeted to high-end applications.

3. E.   Only the Datacenter edition supports more than four virtual servers. The Enterprise edition supports four virtual servers. Standard supports one virtual server. Neither the Web edition nor the Itanium edition supports virtual servers.

4. C.   The `ServerManagerCmd.exe` command-line tool allows you to do many of the same tasks via the command-line that you can do using the Server Manger GUI. Initial Configuration Tasks is a GUI that automatically launches when you start the server. There is no such program as `RoleConfig.exe`.

5. B.   To support read-only domain controllers, the domain controller hosting the PDC Emulator FSMO role must be running Windows Server 2008. DCPromo is a tool used to promote a server to a domain controller. DNS is a core requirement for a Windows domain. If the domain is running, then DNS must already be running. There is no such thing as a Write Protect feature for Active Directory Domain Services.

6. A.   Only one schema exists in a forest. It is hosted on the server holding the Flexible Single Master Operations (FSMO) role of the Schema Master role.

7. A.   The Domain Naming Master is one of the FSMO roles that is unique in the forest. Only one Domain Naming Master exists in a forest.

8. D.   The RID Master is one of the FSMO roles. One RID Master exists in every domain in the forest, and since the forest holds seven domains, there must be seven RID masters.

9. D.   BitLocker Drive Encryption allows entire volumes to be encrypted. If the laptop is lost or stolen, the data protected by BitLocker Drive Encryption would be significantly harder to access. Using NTFS permissions would only marginally protect a system; if the local administrator password is cracked, NTFS permissions can be changed. Neither Server Core nor Network Access Protection provides any protection to a lost or stolen laptop.

10. B.   Server Manager can be used to add features and roles. The Web Server (IIS) is a role and would be added with Server Manager. Since the server is currently being used as a file server, the operating system should not be reinstalled with Web Server edition. BitLocker will protect drives, but this isn't necessary for IIS.

11. B.   You need to ensure that the server has enough hardware resources (CPU, memory, disk, and NIC bandwidth) to support the new virtual server. The Enterprise edition supports as many as four virtual servers, and only two are currently running; adding one will make it three, so there's no need to upgrade the edition or remove a virtual server. Since virtual servers are already running, Hyper-V must be running.

12. A.   A core requirement to support virtualization is the host operating system must be running the 64-bit edition of the operating system. Without knowing how much memory the servers are currently using, it's difficult to determine whether 4GB would be enough. The Enterprise edition supports as many as four virtual servers (when the edition includes Hyper-V).

13. B.   Server Core boots into the command line only. It doesn't have a graphical user interface (GUI). Safe mode has a GUI. Server Manager is an application and wouldn't affect the functionality of the operating system. `ServerManagerCmd.exe` is a command-line alternative to Server Manager, but it wouldn't cause the operating system to show only the command line.

14. C.   Once all domain controllers are running Windows Server 2008, the domain can be raised to domain functional level of Windows Server 2008. It doesn't matter what operating system servers are running, only what operating system the domain controllers are running. Raising the domain functional level is not dependent on PDC Emulator or global catalog servers.

15. B.   In a multiple domain forest, the domain controller holding the Infrastructure Master role should *not* also be hosting the global catalog. Since only four domain controllers exist and each of these is also a global catalog server, this requirement isn't being met, so the Infrastructure Master role won't function. With two domain controllers in each domain, you already have redundancy. There are no restrictions on the PDC Emulator role related to the global catalog server.

16. B.   With little physical security, a real threat is the loss of any domain controller placed in the remote site. A read-only domain controller would hold only minimal data from the domain and is an ideal solution for this situation. Adding a domain controller would be too risky. A global catalog server is a domain controller first with the additional functionality of holding the global catalog, but since you don't have adequate physical security, you should not add any domain controller. Reducing the bandwidth would make the problem of slow logons worse since less bandwidth would be available.

17. D.   PowerShell is not enabled by default. It can be enabled by using Server Manager and adding a feature. It is a feature, not a role. PowerShell does not require Domain Admins or Enterprise Admins permissions to run. These elevated permissions may be required depending on the script contents, but the actual script isn't explained.

18. D.   Windows Deployment Services is Microsoft's solution to automate the process of deploying multiple computers quickly. After a single computer is installed as desired, an image can be captured and deployed to as many other computers as desired. Ghost is a popular imaging program, but it is owned by Symantec, not Microsoft. Sysprep is run on a computer immediately prior to capturing the image, not prior to installing the operating system. Windows Software Update Services is used to deploy approved Windows updates to client computers within a domain, not entire operating systems.

19. B.   Network Access Protection is a set of technologies that can be used to check the health of VPN clients and quarantine them or restrict their access if unhealthy. Windows Deployment Services is used to automate the deployment of new workstations. Read-only domain controllers are used for remote offices and include only a few objects from the domain. BitLocker Drive Encryption is used to encrypt drives but wouldn't protect the clients from viruses.

20. C.   You can the Key Management Service (KMS) in the secure network to automate the activation of these servers. Traffic to the main network must be minimized according to the scenario so any method that adds traffic to the main network is unacceptable. Multiple Activation Key (MAK) requires Internet access.

Chapter
2

Planning Server Deployments

MICROSOFT EXAM OBJECTIVES COVERED IN THIS CHAPTER:

✓ **Planning for Server Deployment**

- Plan Server Installations and Upgrades. May include but is not limited to: Windows Server 2008 edition selection, rollback planning, Bitlocker implementation requirements.

- Plan for Automated Server Deployment. May include but is not limited to: standard server image, automation and scheduling of server deployments.

- Plan Application Servers and Services. May include but is not limited to: virtualization server planning, availability, resilience, and accessibility.

✓ **Planning for Server Management**

- Plan Server Management Strategies. May include but is not limited to: remote administration, remote desktop, server management technologies, Server Manager and ServerManagerCMD, delegation policies and procedures.

✓ **Planning Application and Data Provisioning**

- Provision Applications. May include but is not limited to: presentation virtualization, terminal server infrastructure, resource allocation, application virtualization alternatives, application deployment, System Center Configuration Manager.

When planning server deployments, you need to consider several elements. Will you manually install the servers or automate the installations with Windows Deployment Services? Will you install the full operating system or use Server Core for some of the roles? If you do use Server Core, will you configure the servers for remote management?

One of the features of Windows Server 2008 that has so many IT departments and administrators excited is virtualization. Before you even purchase your hardware, you need to consider whether you want to use Microsoft's Hyper-V technology and virtualize some of your servers. You'll need to know which editions support virtualization and how many licenses are provided with your Windows Server 2008 edition.

I'll answer all of these questions and more in this chapter.

You'll notice in the list of objectives that Windows Server 2008 Edition Selection, Bitlocker implementation requirements, availability, resilience, remote administration, remote desktop, delegation policies and procedures, terminal server infrastructure, resource allocation, and System Center Configuration Manager are listed. Windows Server 2008 Edition Selection was covered in Chapter 1, "Introducing Windows Server 2008." Remote administration, remote desktop, resource allocation and System Center Configuration Manager are covered in Chapter 3, "Using Windows Server 2008 Server Management Tools." Chapter 5, "Monitoring and Maintaining Active Directory" covers delegation policies and procedures. Chapter 7, "Planning Terminal Services Servers," covers terminal server infrastructure. Bitlocker implementation requirements are covered in Chapter 8, "Planning Windows Server 2008 Security." Chapter 9, "Planning Business Continuity and High Availability" covers availability and resilience.

Introducing Windows Deployment Services

The primary purpose of Windows Deployment Services (WDS) is to provide a simplified method of rapidly deploying Windows operating systems over the network.

You can use Windows Deployment Services to install and configure Microsoft Windows operating systems remotely on computers that are Preboot Execution Environment (PXE, pronounced "pixie") enabled. A PXE client computer may not have an operating system, but it has the capability to boot to the network.

After booting to the network, the client can access the WDS server to install one of the following operating systems:

- Windows Server 2008
- Windows Vista
- Windows Server 2003
- Windows XP

Many types of installation images exist, and they can easily be confused. The two broad categories are boot images and install images, and each category has different types of images.

Although it's similar, the version of Windows Deployment Services that was available in Windows Server 2003 is *not* the same as the Windows Deployment Services available in Windows Server 2008.

The Big Picture of WDS

The overall steps needed to set up Windows Deployment Services are as follows:

1. **Ensure network requirements are met.** DHCP must be running on the network. Only one DHCP server is needed as long as routers are 1542 compliant (the routers pass BOOTP broadcasts which are used by DHCP servers and DHCP clients). The server holding the WDS role must be a member of a domain. Since a domain must be running, DNS must be running to support Active Directory Domain Services.

> BOOTP (also known as Bootstrap Protocol) is a protocol used by clients to obtain IP addresses automatically. BOOTP is a special broadcast that uses UDP ports 67 and 68. Although routers don't pass broadcasts in general, a RFC 1542–compliant router will pass BOOTP broadcasts through UDP ports 67 and 68.

2. **Add the WDS role using Server Manager.** This adds the Deployment Server and Transport Server services, which are used to capture and deploy images.

3. **Configure the WDS server.** Launch the Configure Server Wizard from within Server Manager. The biggest consideration is if the WDS server is also the DHCP server. If so, you need to configure special settings so DHCP and WDS can work properly together.

4. **Add boot and install images to the WDS server.** Basic images (see the "Install Images" section of this chapter) are available from the operating system installation DVD in the Sources directory. You can add more images after you've added the basic images.

   You can use a single WDS server for both 32-bit and 64-bit images.

5. **Manipulate permissions for image groups.** The permissions allow you to manage who has access to which images. For example, you could create a server image that you want only IT administrators to access. By granting the appropriate permissions, other users won't have access to this image.

Once you've created and configured WDS, you can deploy images to PXE-enabled clients:

1. **Reboot the PXE client, and press F12.** The PXE client will receive TCP/IP configuration from the DHCP server and then connect to the WDS server.

2. **When prompted, press F12 again.** The install program is launched from the WDS server.

3. **Select the desired image from the install program menu.** The Windows Boot Manager menu (a command-line program) will display boot images that can be used if more than one boot image is added to WDS. If only a single boot image is available, it will automatically be selected. After an image is selected, the files will be downloaded to the computer, and the boot program will start.

4. **Log in.** Based on the user you log in as, you will see images that can be downloaded. By default, the Authenticated Users group has access to all images, but the security settings can be changed.

5. **Pick an image.** The available images can be standard (operating system only) or custom (including applications, service packs and updates, security settings, and more).

   Follow the wizard to complete the installation. The required files will be downloaded to the computer and installed.

WDS has replaced Remote Installation Services (RIS), which was released with Windows 2000. The purpose of RIS (and the purpose of WDS) is to reduce the time needed to deploy computers. The execution of RIS in a real-world environment fell far short.

Will WDS take over third-party imaging tools as the choice for IT professionals to deploy operating systems? Only time will tell, but just as RIS was tested in MCSE Server 2000 and MCSE Server 2003 certifications, expect WDS to be tested in MCITP Server 2008 certifications.

Boot Images

Boot images are those used to boot up a system for the sole purpose of connecting to the WDS server:

Generic boot images   A generic boot image (or just boot image) is used to connect to the WDS server to download an install image. The boot image downloads a mini–operating system that provides a graphical user interface (GUI). The user can then use the GUI to pick the specific install image desired.

Both basic install images and custom (standard) install images can be chosen once a client boots from the boot image. The boot image is available on the installation DVD in the Sources directory as boot.wim.

The boot image is a 16-bit real-mode program that will boot into both 32-bit and 64-bit systems. In other words, only one boot image is needed for both 32-bit and 64-bit systems.

RIS vs. WDS

Microsoft is touting the strengths of Windows Deployment Services, and you can bet you'll see it on the exam. However, you may find that WDS is not what you use on the job.

WDS is intended to replace the functionality of RIS that came out in Windows 2000 and that was supported in Windows 2003.

On the job, RIS just didn't meet the needs of most companies. In one large enterprise where I worked, RIS was tried with painful consequences. We ultimately returned to using Symantec's Ghost since Ghost worked universally with all systems, while new RIS images needed to be used for each different computer model we used. For a company using a single computer brand and model, RIS worked fine.

The promise and the vision of RIS looked great back then, which is why we gave it a try. The promise and vision of WDS looks great today, and it includes many improvements over RIS. However, Symantec has not stood still, and today's Ghost is also much improved over previous versions.

If I weren't writing this book, I doubt I would have looked at WDS as closely as I did. The old saying "Fool me once, I'm blaming you. Fool me twice, they'll blame me" goes through my head. (Is that the way the saying goes?) Many IT administrators may think the same thing. They invested time and energy into trying RIS, only to return where they started. They may not be willing to do the same thing with WDS, the replacement for RIS.

All that said, though, I can say I was pleasantly surprised with the ease of use and functionality of WDS. Having mastered the learning curve, it would be something I would try in a real-world environment instead of forking over the money for Ghost.

Either way, remember that you can fully expect Microsoft to test your knowledge of WDS on the exam.

However, the 64-bit editions of Windows Server 2008 include a 64-bit boot image. The 64-bit boot image should be used only for 64-bit systems. One of the differences is that the 64-bit boot image shows (and allows you to choose) only 64-bit install images.

You can tell which version of the boot image has been installed in WDS by checking the Architecture column in the boot images display of WDS; 32-bit images are labeled as "x86" and 64-bit images are labeled as "X64."

Capture images   A capture image is used to capture an image from a reference computer. A capture image is created within WDS by modifying a standard boot image.

The difference between a boot image and a capture image is that a boot image is used to download an image from WDS to a destination computer. A capture image is used to allow the destination computer to create an image of itself.

Discover images   A discover image is used by clients that aren't PXE enabled. The discover image is created within WDS, converted to an .iso image, and then burned to a CD or DVD. Non-PXE clients can boot to the media and then connect to the WDS server to select the desired install image.

A discover image is created from a boot image (boot.wim) within WDS. The challenge is converting the .wim file to an .iso image file. WDS does not include tools to do this, but downloadable tools are available.

Install Images

Install images are those used to install an image onto a computer. The two types of install images are basic images and custom images:

Basic images   A basic image includes the operating system only. It is built from the install.wim file that can be found on the installation DVD in the Sources directory.

Two different install images are used for 32-bit and 64-bit systems.

Custom images   A custom image can also include applications, service packs and updates, security baseline settings, configuration settings, and anything else you want to add to the image.

After the custom image is created, unique information is removed with Sysprep. After rebooting, the computer PXE boots to the WDS server, and a capture image program is run, capturing the image of the configured computer. The captured image can then be deployed to other computers.

You can also think of a custom image as a baseline or standard image. By creating a standard image and deploying new servers from this standard image, you are assured that your servers are being deployed following a standard.

What's the difference between custom images and standard images? Nothing. In most of the WDS documentation, you'll see custom images referred to as images that you customize by adding applications and settings. However, in the exam objectives, these images are referred to as *standard images. Standard* in this context refers to an image that has been standardized.

Custom images provide the most flexibility. You can capture images of fully configured computers and then deploy identical images to many computers. For example, you may be setting up a web server farm of 10 Internet Information Services (IIS) servers. You could set up and fully configure one server, capture the image, and then deploy the image to the other nine servers.

Capturing and deploying images will take significantly less time than setting up each server individually. From management's perspective, less time is saved money. From an IT administrator's perspective, less time on a single project is less frustration.

> ### Real World Scenario
>
> #### Creating Images with Symantec's Ghost
>
> The tool I've used most often to deploy many computers has been Symantec's Ghost, which has been around since the NT 4.0 days and continues to improve.
>
> With Ghost, I am able to create an image of a single system that includes the operating system, applications, patches, and baseline security settings. Using Microsoft's Sysprep, I remove unique computer information (such as the security identifier) and then save that image to a Ghost server or even onto a bootable CD or DVD.
>
> Now, whenever I need a new computer configured, I boot to the Ghost application and "cast" the image to the new machine. With bootable DVDs I've used in the classroom, I've had images that I can cast onto computers in about eight minutes.
>
> In one large organization I worked in, a standard desktop configuration was created and saved as a Ghost image. The organization passed the Ghost image to HP, and HP put it on every computer purchased by the organization. Now IT people take the computer out of the box, plug it in, and then follow a short setup wizard to install a full operating system including applications and default security settings. It takes less than 3 minutes of interaction by a technician and less than a total of 30 minutes for a full installation to complete. Once the installation is complete, the technician adds the computer to the domain and adds some final configuration changes.
>
> This has significantly reduced the total cost of ownership and has helped to standardize installations for all users across the organization. The WDS custom (or standard) image can be used similar to a Ghost image.

WDS Requirements

Before installing WDS on your network, you need to meet some requirements. The requirements are on the network, on the WDS server, and on the clients and are as follows:

Network requirements   The following services must exist on the network to support WDS:

- Active Directory Domain Services
- Dynamic Host Configuration Protocol (DHCP)
- Domain Name Services (DNS)

Server component requirements   Windows Deployment Services must be installed on the server. This includes the Deployment Server service and the Transport Server service. The server must be a member of a domain. The server must have an NTFS partition where images are stored. At least one boot image and one install image needs to be added to the WDS server image store.

Client component requirements   The client components include a Windows Preinstallation Environment (Windows PE) that allows the client to boot from the LAN (typically by pressing F12) and to select an appropriate image from the WDS server. Clients must be PXE clients or must use the Windows Server 2008 version of Windows PE. Additionally, the user starting the client must have a domain account to log into the domain.

WDS is *not* dependent on any domain functional level or forest functional level.

WDSUtil

You can use the Windows Deployment Services command-line utility (WDSUtil) in place of the GUI for WDS. As a matter of fact, don't be surprised if you see WDSUtil on the test.

As with any command-line utility, WDSUtil can be scripted. In other words, you create the scripts once and don't have to re-create them. These aren't fancy scripts but instead are simple batch files.

For example, you could create a batch file named createwds.bat that has all the configuration commands for WDS. If WDS crashes and you need to rebuild it from scratch, you'd install WDS and then run your batch file to complete the configuration.

The basic syntax of WDSUtil is as follows:

WDSUtil [Options] <Command> [Command Parameters]

Of course, the devil is in the details. There are many different commands, and each command can have different parameters. The commands are accessed by using a backslash (/). In this context, commands are often referred to as *switches*. A command (or switch) modifies how the command-line utility runs.

For any command, you can add the options shown in Table 2.1.

TABLE 2.1   Modifying Any WDSUtil Command with a Switch

Switch	Description
/? or /Help	Displays help for the specified command. For example, to get help on the /Add command, you could use this: WDSUtil /Add /?
/Verbose	Displays verbose output for the specified command. Think of verbose as "wordy." If the default output doesn't give you enough information, try the verbose output.
/Progress	Displays progress while the command is being executed.

Tables 2.2 through 2.5 list the commands available for WDSUtil.

Specifically, Table 2.2 shows the commands that can be used to configure a WDS server. Table 2.3 lists the commands that manipulate WDS . You can manipulate images with the commands in Table 2.4. Table 2.5 shows commands that you can use to manage devices. In this context, a device is a computer that is accessing WDS.

TABLE 2.2   WDS Server Configuration Commands

Command	Description
/Initialize	Used for the initial configuration of a WDS server
/Uninitialize	Used to revert changes made during server initialization
/Update	Used to update a server resource from a known good source

TABLE 2.3   WDS Service Commands

Command	Description
/Stop	Used to stop all WDS services.
/Start	Used to start all WDS services. Also starts multicast transmissions and namespaces.
/Disable	Used to disable all WDS services.
/Enable	Used to enable all WDS services.

TABLE 2.4   Image Commands

Command	Description
/New	Used to create new capture/discover images. Also used to create multicast transmissions/namespaces.
/Copy	Used to copy images within the image store.
/Export	Used to export images from the image store to a WIM file.
/Add	Used to add images, image groups, and devices.
/Convert	Used to convert an existing RIS RIPrep image to a WIM image.
/Remove	Used to remove images or image groups. Also used to remove multicast transmissions and namespaces
/Replace	Used to replace images with new versions.

TABLE 2.5   Table Device Commands

Command	Description
/Approve	Used to approve auto-add devices
/Reject	Used to reject auto-add devices
/Delete	Used to delete records from the auto-add device database

In the following sections, I'll present the full syntax for some of these commands.

Installing Windows Deployment Services

Once you are certain that you have the required network services running on your network (Active Directory Domain Services, DHCP, and DNS), you can add the Windows Deployment Services role to a server by using Server Manager.

WDS includes two core services:

Deployment Server service   The Deployment Server service is the primary service used by WDS. It is used to configure and install Windows operating systems remotely.

Transport Server service   The Transport Server service includes the core networking elements that are used to transmit data using multicasting. It can be installed by itself to support multicasting but must be installed if WDS is being installed.

The following exercises that set up and configure Windows Deployment Services assume that you are running a domain, the server is a member of the domain, and DHCP is also running on the network. For a test environment, it is completely acceptable to have a single server hosting all the necessary roles. Your computer will be a domain controller hosting Active Directory Domain Services, will be running DNS to support Active Directory Domain Sevices, and will be configured as a DHCP server with at least one scope.

Exercise 2.1 shows how to add the Windows Deployment Services role to a server.

EXERCISE 2.1

Installing Windows Deployment Services

1.   Launch Server Manager by clicking Start ➢ Administrator Tools ➢ Server Manager.

2.   In Server Manager, select Roles.

3.   Select Add Roles.

4. On the Before You Begin page, review the requirements, and click Next.

5. On the Select Server Roles page, select the check box next to Windows Deployment Services. Your display will look similar to the following graphic. Click Next.

6. On the Overview of Windows Deployment Services page, review the notes, and click Next.

7. On the Select Role Services page, verify that Deployment Server and Transport Server are selected, and click Next.

8. On the Confirm Installation Selections page, review your selections, and click Install.

9. After the installation completes, the Installation Results page appears. Review the information, and click Close.

Once WDS is installed, you need to configure it. Exercise 2.2 shows how to add the Windows Deployment Services role to a server.

Configuring Windows Deployment Services

1. Launch Windows Deployment Services by clicking Start ➢ Administrator Tools ➢ Windows Deployment Services.

2. In Windows Deployment Services, select Servers. Select your server. At this point, your server has a yellow icon with an exclamation mark indicating that it hasn't been configured yet.

3. Right-click your server, and select Configure Server.

4. On the wizard's welcome page, review the information, and click Next.

5. On the Remote Installation Folder Location page, either select a different path or accept the default of `C:\RemoteInstall`. Ideally, you would select a partition that is not the same as the operating system, but for a test environment, it's OK to use the same partition. Click Next.

If you chose the same partition as the operating system, you will receive a system volume warning. Read the warning, and click Yes.

If the DHCP Option 60 page does not appear in the following step, double-check to ensure you have DHCP installed as mentioned in the tip before Exercise 2.1. If you're not sure how to install DHCP, you can use Exercise 4.1 in Chapter 4, "Monitoring and Maintaining Network Infrastructure Servers."

6. On the DHCP Option 60 page, review the information. Since your server is also holding the role of a DHCP server, select both check boxes, as shown in the following graphic. Click Next.

The DHCP option 60 is used to notify a booting PXE client that there is a listening PXE server on the network. Selecting the Do Not Listen on Port 67 option tells WDS not to listen on port 67 since the DHCP server is listening on this port. This is necessary so that booting clients can find the DHCP server on the network.

7. On the PXE Server Initial Settings page, select Respond to All (Known and Unknown) Client Computers.

Note that you would often choose the first option (Do Not Respond to Any Client Computer) in a production environment until you have configured the server. The second option (Respond to Only Known Client Computers) can be used if you pre-stage client computers. *Prestaging* a client computer is done by creating a computer account in Active Directory with the computer's GUID.

8. Click Finish.

9. After a moment, the configuration will complete. Uncheck the Add Images to the Windows Deployment Server box, and click Finish.

It's also possible to configure the WDS server from the command line using WDSUtil. You could use the following three commands. The first command initializes the server with the default settings and identifies the folder that will hold the images and be shared. If the folder does not exist, WDSUtil will create it.

```
WDSUtil /initialize-server /reminst:" <driveletter>\<foldername>"
```

For example, if you plan on placing images in the RemoteInstall folder on the D: drive, you can use the following command:

```
WDSUtil /initialize-server /reminst:c:\RemoteInstall
```

If DHCP is installed on the same server as WDS, you can use the following command to configure the DHCP settings:

```
WDSUtil /Set-Server /UseDHCPPorts:no /DHCPoption60:yes
```

After the server is initialized, you can configure the server to respond to clients. For example, to respond to all clients (known and unknown), you can use the following command:

```
WDSUtil /Set-Server /AnswerClients:all
```

If you are running DHCP on the same server as WDS, you may find that the DHCP server has stopped working after installing WDS. Return to the properties of the server (in WDS), and click the DHCP tab. Verify both Do Not Listen on Port 67 and Configure DHCP Option 60 to PXE Client are selected.

Once WDS is configured, you need to add two primary types of images at this point: boot images and install images. You can obtain both images from the Sources directory of the installation DVD: Exercise 2.3 shows how to add image groups and images to the Windows Deployment Services server. Note that at this point, only the default boot and install images are added. Once the default images are added, you can add special-purpose images.

Adding Image Groups and Images to WDS

1. Launch Windows Explorer by selecting Start ➢ Computer. Browse to the C: drive, and add a folder named Images.

2. Using your Windows Server 2008 installation DVD, copy the boot.wim and install. wim files from the Sources directory of the DVD into the C:\Images directory.

3. If not already launched, launch Windows Deployment Services by clicking Start ➢ Administrator Tools ➢ Windows Deployment Services.

4. Select the Install Images folder under your server. Right-click the folder, and select Add Image Group. Enter **Marketing**, and click OK. This creates a folder that you can add images to and use permissions to restrict who can access the images.

5. On the Image File page, click Browse. Browse to the C:\Images directory. Select the install.wim file, and click Open. Click Next.

6. On the List of Available Images page, review the images available. Ensure all images are selected, and click Next.

7. On the Summary page, click Next. When the wizard completes, click Finish.

8. In WDS, right-click the Boot Images folder. Select Add Boot Image.

9. On the Image File page, browse to the C:\Images folder, and add the boot.wim file. Click Open. Click Next.

10. On the Image Metadata page, accept the default name and description, and click Next.

11. On the Summary page, click Next. When complete, click Finish.

This will add the images to the image store. Your Windows Deployment Services Server should look similar to the following graphic.

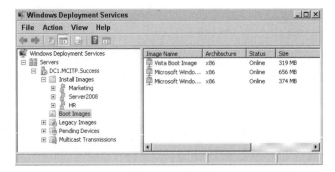

At this point, you could boot a PXE client and press F12 to boot using the NIC. When prompted to press F12 for network service boot, press F12 again. This will access the WDS server, and you can select one of the boot images.

You will then be prompted to log in. Based on the permissions assigned to the user account that logs in, you will be able to choose from a list of install images.

While the previous exercise showed how to add images using the GUI, it's also possible to add images using the WDSUtil command.

To add a boot image named boot.wim that exists in the C:\bootimage directory, you can use the following command:

```
WDSUtil /Add-Image: c:\bootimage\boot.wim /ImageType: boot
```

To add an install image named install.wim that exists in the C:\installimage directory, you can use the following command:

```
WDSUtil /Add-Image: c:\installimage\install.wim /ImageType:install
/ImageGroup:IIS
```

Creating a Standard Server Image

If you were configuring a single computer, you'd need to do the following:

1. Install the operating system.
2. Install applications.
3. Install current updates, services packs, and patches.
4. Implement security requirements.

To complete a single computer, it could easily take a few hours. If you had to deploy 30 computers, it could take you more than 90 hours. From a total cost of ownership (TCO) perspective, this is simply too long.

By creating a custom image, you can install all these elements on a single computer (referred to as a *reference computer*) and then deploy the custom image to as many computers as desired.

For example, you may be tasked with building a web farm of 10 IIS servers. Instead of building 10 servers from scratch, you build 1, create an image, and then deploy the image to the other 9 computers.

Building a Reference Computer

To build a reference computer, you start with a clean installation of the operating system. This can be deployed from WDS or installed from a DVD.

After the operating system is installed, you ensure it has all the current service packs, updates, security patches, and anything else the operating system needs to make it up-to-date.

Next, you install any needed applications. As an example, if this is one of ten IIS servers that will make up a web farm, you add the IIS role. If all IIS servers were to host the same application, you could install and configure the web application to be hosted on the web farm.

For end-user computers, you could add Office applications, antivirus and anti-spyware software, and any other applications needed by the users.

When you think the computer is set up as you need it, test it. This will save yourself some time.

You can also think of this reference computer as your standard computer. In other words, you have created this computer with all the standard settings. If it's a server image, when you need another server deployed instead of creating one from scratch, you use the standard image to create another server.

Running Sysprep

When the operating system is installed, there are several unique elements created specifically for the computer on which it's installed. For example, the computer is identified with a unique security identifier (SID). What does unique mean? One of a kind. Never to be repeated.

If you created an image of a computer with a unique, one-of-a-kind SID and deployed that image to 100 computers, you'd have 100 computers with the same SID. Many other settings such as the computer name would be the same that should be unique.

Supposedly unique settings that aren't unique will create a lot of problems that just don't make sense and have caused a few too many IT administrators to sit alone in a room repeatedly banging their head against a wall asking "Why, why, why?"

To avoid the needless head banging, you simply have to run one program—Sysprep. Sysprep "sanitizes" your computer. Any settings that should be unique are reset and will be re-created the next time the computer reboots.

WARNING When using Sysprep, you need to ensure that the version you are using matches the operating system. In other words, don't try to use Sysprep from Windows XP on a Server 2008 system. Instead, find the Sysprep file on the Windows Server 2008 operating system when creating a Windows Server 2008 image.

Sysprep is located in the `%systemroot%\system32\sysprep` directory. You can launch it from the command line or from the GUI. You could enter the following command:

```
%systemroot%\system32\sysprep\sysprep /oobe /generalize /reboot
```

Or you could just run Sysprep without any switches, and the GUI will launch. Select the System Cleanup Action as Enter System Out-of-Box Experience (OOBE), and select the Generalize check box. Accept the default of Reboot for the Shutdown Options. Your display will look similar to Figure 2.1.

WARNING If Sysprep is not run to properly prepare the computer, WDS will not recognize the drive when you try to capture the image. Since the drive can't be recognized, WDS simply can't create an image of your reference computer.

FIGURE 2.1 Running Sysprep

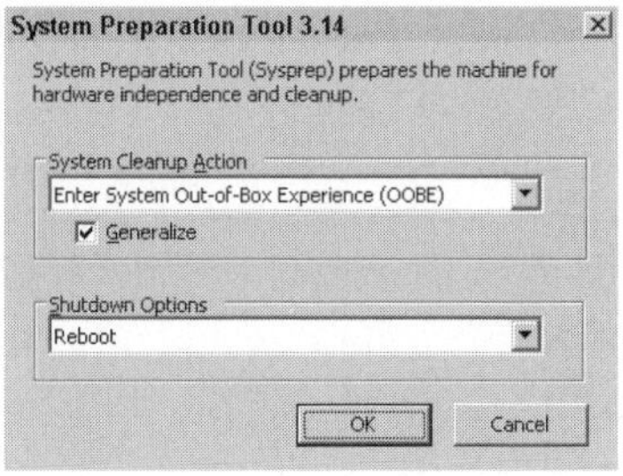

Sysprep will sanitize the computer and then reboot. Remember, the purpose of running Sysprep is to capture the image. Don't let the computer reboot into the operating system, but instead, press F12 to boot into WDS to capture the image.

Exercise 2.4 shows how to create and capture a custom image.

EXERCISE 2.4

Creating and Capturing a Custom Image

1. If not already launched, launch Windows Deployment Services by clicking Start ➢ Administrator Tools ➢ Windows Deployment Services.

2. Browse to the Boot Images container. Select a boot image from this container. Right-click the image, and select Create Capture Boot Image.

3. On the Capture Image Metadata page, change the image name to Capture Image. Change the image description to Use This to Capture an Image from a Reference Computer. Click Browse, and browse to a location to store the image. Name the image **Capture Image**. Click Next.

4. The image WIM file will be created from the basic boot image. Once the process completes, click Finish.

5. To add the capture image to the Boot Images container, right-click Boot Images, and select Add Boot Image. Follow the wizard to add the capture image you just created. Your display should look similar to the following graphic.

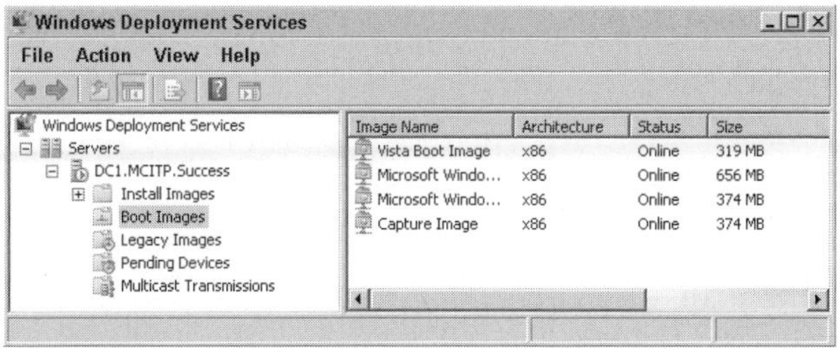

EXERCISE 2.4 *(continued)*

6. Create a custom reference computer. This can be customized in any way you desire. For test purposes, the content of the computer isn't as important as the process of capturing it.

7. Run Sysprep by entering the following command at the command line:

   %systemroot%\system32\sysprep\sysprep /oobe /generalize /reboot

   Alternately, you could launch Sysprep and select the three settings of Enter System Out-of-Box Experience (OOBE), Generalize, and Reboot.

8. When the computer reboots, press F12 to start a network boot. The computer will obtain TCP/IP information from DHCP.

9. When prompted, press F12 again. This will launch the Windows Boot Manager menu and display any boot images available on the WDS server.

   If desired, you can modify the Windows Boot Manager menu by using the Boot Configuration Data Editor (bcdedit) program available at the command prompt.

10. Select the image named Capture Image that you created earlier in this exercise.

    The capture image program will be downloaded to the reference computer and allow you to capture the reference computer's system. Depending on the speed of your NICs and network traffic, this may take some time.

11. On the Welcome to the Image Capture Wizard page, click Next.

12 On the Image Capture Source page, select C:\ as the volume to capture.

    If a volume doesn't show, it indicates that Sysprep wasn't run (or wasn't run with the correct switches or selections). You'll need to reboot into the system and rerun Sysprep. Ensure that OOBE and Generalize are selected.

13. Still on the Image Capture Source page, enter **IISFarm** as the image name, and enter **IIS Server configured for Web Farm** as the description. Click Next.

14. On the Image Capture Destination page, click the Browse button. Browse to a location of your choosing, and enter **IISimage** as the name. Leave the file type blank. Click Save.

15. Still on the Image Capture Destination page, leave the Upload to WDS Server check box unchecked. Click Next.

16. The image capture program will begin. Be patient. This may take hours to capture the image.

17. After the image has been captured, copy it to a folder on the WDS server. This can be over the network or copied to a USB drive and copied to the server.

18. If it's not already launched, launch Windows Deployment Services by clicking Start ➤ Administrator Tools ➤ Windows Deployment Services.

19. Right-click Install Images, and select Add Image Group. In the Add Image Group dialog box, enter **IISServers**, and click OK.

20. Right-click the ISSServers Image group, and select Add Install Image.

21. In the Image File dialog box, click Browse, and browse to where you copied the captured image. Select your image, and click Open. Click Next.

22. On the List of Available Images page, verify your image is selected, and click Next.

23. On the Summary page, click Next. WDS will check the integrity of the image, and once done, it will add it as an image that can be deployed.

It's also possible to create and add a new capture image using the WDSUtil command-line program. For example, to create the capture image from the boot image (stored in C:\Boot) and store it in the C:\Capture directory, use the following command:

```
WDSUtil /New-CaptureImage /Image: C:\boot\install.wim /Architecture:x86
/Filepath: c:\Capture\capture.wim
```

Once the image is created, you can add it to the image store with the following command:

```
WDSUtil /Add-Image /ImageFile: C:\Capture\capture.wim /ImageType:boot
```

Configuring Windows Deployment Services

You can perform the majority of the management of WDS through the Windows Deployment Services GUI or the command-line tool WDSUtil.

If you look at the GUI, you'll see only five containers:

Install Images   The Install Images container holds the install images that have been added to the image store. Install images can be the basic install images (install.wim from the Sources directory of installation DVDs) or custom images. By manipulating permissions of install images, you can control who can receive which images.

Boot Images   The Boot Images container holds the boot images that have been added to WDS. It can include the boot.wim image included from the Windows Server 2008 or Windows Vista installation DVD in the Sources directory. It can also include capture images and discover images.

Legacy Images   If your WDS server was upgraded from an RIS server, the Legacy Images container holds RIPrep images that were used with RIS. RIPrep images can be converted to WIM images using either the GUI or the command-line tool WSDUtil.

Pending Devices   The Pending Devices container is meaningful only if you configure the PXE Response Settings (in the properties of the WDS server) to notify administrators of unknown clients. When set, after an unknown client connects to the WDS server, the client will appear in the Pending Devices container, and the administrator can approve the client. Once approved, the client can then log in and select the desired image.

Multicast Transmission   The Multicast Transmission container allows you to create multicast sessions. Multicast sessions can be either auto-cast or scheduled-cast. An auto-cast session starts as soon as the first client connects and allows other clients to join the transmission in progress. A scheduled-cast can be begin after a specified number of clients connect or at a specific day and time.

Additionally, the server has several properties pages that you can manipulate. You can access these by right-clicking the server and selecting Properties.

Exercise 2.5 will show you how to change the permissions for image groups. As a reminder, image groups hold install images, and by manipulating the permissions, you can control which images are available to different users. Users will be offered only those images that they have permissions to download and use.

EXERCISE 2.5

Changing Permissions for Image Groups

1. Launch Active Directory Users and Computers by clicking Start ➤ Administrator Tools ➤ Active Directory Users and Computers.

2. Right-click the domain, and select New ➤ Organizational Unit.

3. In the New Organizational Unit dialog box, enter **ITGurus** as the OU name. Click OK.

4. Right-click the ITGurus OU, and select New ➤ Group.

5. In the New Group dialog box, enter **G_ITAdmins** as the group name. Ensure that both Global and Security are checked. Your display should look similar to the following graphic. Click OK.

6. Right-click the ITGurus OU, and select New ➤ User.

7. Enter **Peter** as the first name. Enter **Parker** as the last name. Enter **PeterParker** as the logon name. Your display should look similar to the following graphic. Click Next.

8. Enter **P@ssw0rd** in the Password and Confirm password boxes. Deselect User Must Change Password at Next Logon. Click Next. Review the information you've entered, and click Finish.

9. Double-click the Peter Parker account to open the properties page. Select the Member Of tab. Click Add.

10. In the Select Groups dialog box, enter **G_ITAdmins**. This is the group you created earlier in this exercise. Click OK. On the properties page, click OK again.

   At this point, you have created an account and added that account to the G_ITAdmins group. Any permissions granted to the G_ITAdmins group will be granted to the Peter Parker user account. Your display should look similar to the following graphic.

11. If it's not already launched, launch Windows Deployment Services by clicking Start ➤ Administrator Tools ➤ Windows Deployment Services.

12. Within WDS, browse to the Install Images ➤ IISServers container.

13. Right-click the IISServers Image group, and select Security. Your goal is to remove the Authenticated Users group from accessing the ISSServers Image group. However, these permissions are inherited, so you must first disable inheritance.

14. Click Advanced. Deselect the Include Inheritable Permissions from This Object's Parent check box. In the Windows Security dialog box, review the information, and click Copy. This will copy all the inherited permissions to this object but allow them to be manipulated. Click OK.

Modifying the inherited permissions works the same way in Active Directory Users and Computers (as we're doing in this step) as it does in NTFS. As a matter of fact, the dialog boxes are identical. Inherited permissions can't be modified unless you change their behavior. The three choices are as follows:

- Copy (changes the permissions from inherited to applied so that they can be modified)

- Remove (removes all inherited permissions)

- Cancel (makes no changes)

15. Select the Authenticated Users group, and click Remove. Click OK. Removing the Authenticated Users group will prevent any user from accessing the images in the IISServers Image group.

16. Click Add, enter **G_ITAdmins**, and click OK. By default, the Read & Execute, List Folder Contents, and Read permissions are granted. This will be enough to allow users in the G_ITAdmins group to access and deploy images through WDS. Your display should look similar to the following graphic. Click OK.

At this point, only users in the G_ITAdmins group will be able to see and pick images located in the IISServers Image group.

Deploying a Computer Image

With images created, you now need to deploy the image. Remember, the destination computer must be a PXE client (meaning it can boot from the NIC to the LAN).

WDS does not provide any capability to partition a hard drive. If partitions are desired, you can use DiskPart to partition the hard drive before the installation.

The PXE client will first locate the DHCP server and receive TCP/IP configuration information such as the IP address and subnet mask, and then it will contact the WDS server. Once WDS is contacted, the computer's identity will be checked. The computer could be known or unknown, and depending on how the WDS server is configured, the WDS server could answer the computer or ignore it. A computer is known if it is prestaged in Active Directory Domain Services with its GUID. You'll see how to do this in the next section.

Additionally, WDS can be configured so that an administrator is notified when an unknown computer connects. The computer will be listed as a pending device, and the administrator can then approve or reject the computer, either allowing or disallowing the computer to download an image.

If WDS answers the computer, the user will be presented with a list of possible boot images that can be chosen from a command-line menu. These images will download and install only the boot program, which provides a GUI interface.

Once the boot program and the GUI are launched, the user will be able to log in to the domain. The user will then be given a choice of install images from which to choose. Only images that the user has permissions to install will appear.

Prestaging Computers

A prestaged computer has been created in Active Directory before the PXE-boot session is started. WDS identifies prestaged computers by using a globally unique identifier (GUID).

PXE clients include GUIDs. These are sometimes included on a sticker on the case of the computer, sometimes inside the case, and sometimes in the BIOS. It is a 32-character hexadecimal code. Once you locate the GUID, you can create the account in Active Directory and use it to prestage the computer.

To prestage the computer, launch Active Directory Users and Computers. Right-click the container or organizational unit you want to add the computer to and select New ➢ Computer. Enter the computer name, and click Next.

In the Managed dialog box, select This Is a Managed Computer, and enter the computer's GUID. Figure 2.2 shows a computer being added with the GUID entered.

Managing Devices

When configuring the WDS server to respond to clients, you have three choices:

- Do not respond to any clients.
- Respond only to known clients.
- Respond to all (known and unknown) client computers.

You can also select the option to allow administrators to approve unknown clients. Figure 2.3 shows these choices.

FIGURE 2.2 Creating a prestaged computer in ADUC

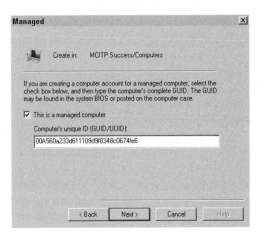

FIGURE 2.3 Configuring the WDS server to respond to clients

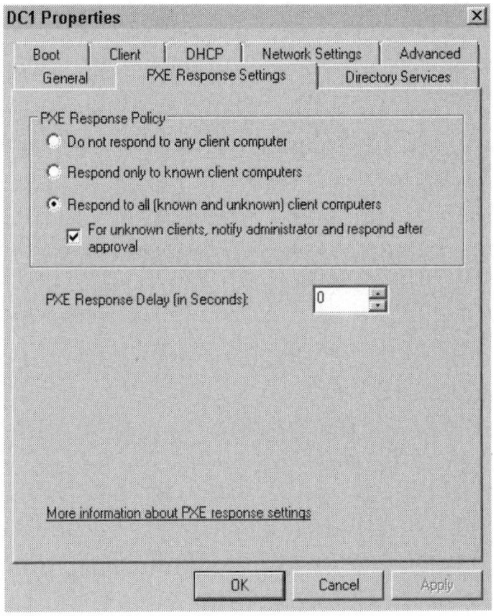

Before you have fully configured WDS, it's a good idea to set it so that it does not respond to any clients. If set this way, the WDS server won't respond to the client at all. You'll never get to the menu that allows you to press F12 the second time.

Known clients are those that have been prestaged in Active Directory, as demonstrated in the previous section. If properly prestaged, everything works without any other action.

If you've selected the option to allow administrators to approve unknown clients, then after pressing F12 the first time, the WDS server will answer. However, instead of downloading the boot image, it will indicate that it's waiting for a response from the administrator.

The unknown client will appear in the Pending Devices container within WDS, as shown in Figure 2.4. The administrator can then right-click the client and approve it. It's also possible for the administrator to select Name and Approve, which creates a computer account in Active Directory based on the name the administrator chooses.

FIGURE 2.4   Approving an unknown client

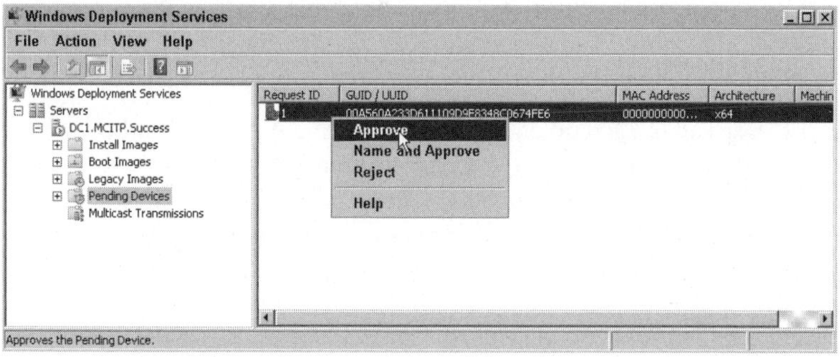

As soon as the client is approved, the client will be prompted to press F12 again to start the download of the boot image. From here on, the deployment of the image is as usual.

Exercise 2.6 shows how to deploy an image to a client computer.

EXERCISE 2.6

Deploying an Image

1. Boot a PXE-enabled computer, and press F12 to start a network boot. The computer will obtain TCP/IP information from DHCP.

   Note that if your PXE client boots to an installed operating system instead of the NIC, you'll need to enter the BIOS to change the boot order.

2. When prompted, press F12 again. This will launch the Windows Boot Manager menu and display any boot images available on the WDS server.

3. If prompted, select a boot image from the menu. This will launch the boot program, which is a graphical user interface.

4. On the Windows Deployment Services menu, select your locale and keyboard or input method, and click Next.

5. On the login screen, enter the username and password of a user. The permissions and group membership of this user will determine which images are viewable.

6. Enter **MCITP\PeterParker** as the username. If your domain is something different from MCITP, then enter your domain name followed by a slash and then PeterParker (the user created earlier and added to the G_ITAdmins group).

7. Enter the password of **P@ssw0rd**, and click OK.

8. Accept the defaults, and click Next.

9. On the Operating System page, you will be presented with a listing of images from which you can choose. Select one of the operating systems, and click Next.

If you had saved the IIS server image, you would be able to choose it from this menu.

Note that the user you logged on as is a member of the Authenticated Users group. The default permissions for image groups grant access to authenticated users. Unless this was changed in other groups, the user will be able to see all images in all image groups. The difference at this point is that users who are *not* in the G_ITAdmins group will not be able to see images in the IISServers Image group since the permissions in this group have been changed.

10. On the Where Do You Want to Install Windows page, choose a partition, and click Next. On the warning screen, click OK. Your computer will connect with the WDS server and download the image.

Multicast Transmissions

Deploying an image to one or many computers can take a lot of bandwidth. Depending on what else is going on in your network, the extra bandwidth taken up by WDS may be unacceptable.

Using a multicast transmission allows you to send only one transmission that is received by multiple computers at the same time. The destination computers need to join a multicast group, and then when the multicast transmission begins, the image will be sent to all computers in the group.

When configuring multicast transmissions, you need to consider your network layout. For example, some routers won't pass multicast transmissions automatically. Additionally, doing a multicast transmission in some segments of your network may significantly load down the network.

Two choices for multicast transmissions are automatic (auto-cast) and scheduled (scheduled-cast).

Automatic Multicast (Auto-Cast) Transmissions

An automatic multicast transmission will automatically begin after the first client has connected. Then as additional clients connect, they join the transmission that has already started. Even though a client may have missed part of the transmission, they will still get the full transmission. You can think of auto-cast as an "always-on" transmission, though it will transmit only when clients are connected.

A significant benefit of auto-cast is that even though multiple clients may be connected, the server is sending only one stream that takes less bandwidth. Compare this to five different clients connecting to WDS to download an install image; the WDS server will actually be sending five different transmissions in the second example.

Scheduled Multicast (Scheduled-Cast) Transmissions

Scheduled multicast transmissions can be done based on two criteria: how many clients connect or the time of day.

By specifying a threshold of connected clients, you can tell the server when to start the multicast transmission. For example, you may have nine servers that need a copy of an image. You set up the multicast transmission and specify 9 as the threshold. When the ninth client connects, the multicast begins.

Scheduled transmissions can be very useful when WDS is in one location and the clients are located elsewhere. You can set up WDS and then go to the clients. After all the clients have connected, the transmission will start automatically. You don't have to return to the WDS server to start the process.

Once the client connects to the server (before the threshold is reached), it will display a message saying it's waiting for the server. This might look like it's not working, but it's actually normal. It has connected to the server and is waiting for the multicast transmission to begin.

To verify the client has actually connected to the server, you can refresh the server to show the clients currently connected.

Figure 2.5 shows a multicast transmission with one client connected. Deploy IIS Servers is the name of the multicast transmission. The details pane shows one client connected.

FIGURE 2.5   Verifying a client has connected

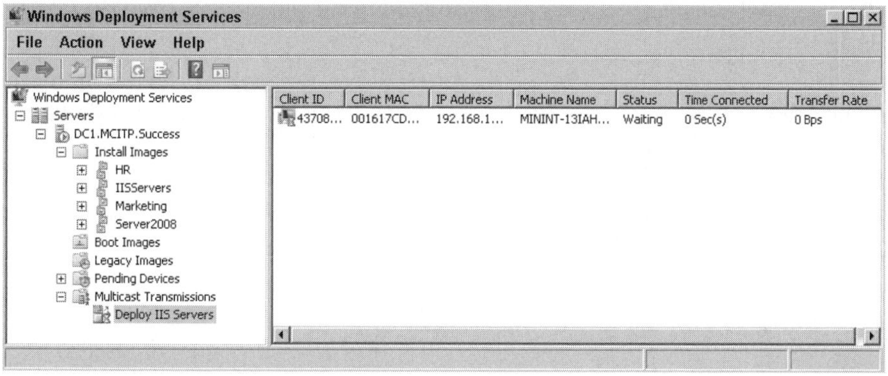

The second scheduled-cast capability is based on the time. You can specify what day and what time to start the multicast session.

As an example, say you have created your standard server and now need to deploy nine more using the same settings. However, you may realize that you'd significantly slow down the network if you did it in the middle of the day.

You can configure a multicast transmission to occur in the middle of the night:

1. Within WDS, right-click the image you want to deploy.

2. Select Create Multicast Transmission.

3. Enter a friendly name for your transmission such as **Deploy IIS Servers**.

4. Select Scheduled Cast.

5. Select Start Automatically at a Later Time, and enter the date and time when you want the multicast transmission to begin. Your display will look similar to the following graphic. Click Next, and click Finish.

Before you leave for the night, make sure your destination computers have connected to the WDS server to accept this transmission. Specifically, boot the client into WDS by pressing F12 to boot to the LAN and then pressing F12 to boot to WDS. Select a boot image. After the boot image has loaded, you can then follow the wizard to select the multicast transmission using the friendly name.

If you change your mind about starting the multicast transmission later and want to start it immediately for a client, you can right-click the client within the multicast transmission container and select Bypass Multicast. The transmission will start immediately.

You can also start the session immediately for all connected clients. Simply right-click the session, and select Start. All connected clients will begin to receive the transmission.

Introducing Server Core

Server Core is an installation of Windows Server 2008 that installs only what is necessary to support the installed services. Instead of a full GUI, only the command line is available for configuration. You can think of Server Core as "Windows without windows."

Although you can do a lot via the command line, expect to do most of the administration of Server Core remotely. Because of this, configuring Server Core for remote administration becomes very important.

Many IT departments and administrators will see two primary benefits of Server Core: increased security due to a reduced attack surface and a simpler installation due to fewer drivers and services being installed:

Reduced attack surface   Since Server Core installs only what is necessary, there is less to attack. This follows a long-standing security principle of eliminating unneeded services and protocols.

For example, if IIS is not needed on a server, you simply don't install it. If it's not installed, you don't need to worry about any IIS attacks on this server. This might seem rather obvious, but I remember when IIS was installed by default on Windows Server 2000 and subsequently became the victim of the rather nasty Nimda virus.

Server Core takes this a step further and eliminates many of the underlying core services and files. A new installation installs only about 40 services. While a full Server installation installs close to 6GB of files, Server Core installs only about 1GB.

Security is not sacrificed. Server Core includes Windows Firewall, IPSec, and Windows File Protection. It also includes Event Log, Performance Monitor counters, and outgoing HTTP support.

Simpler installation   A simple but direct benefit of Server Core is that there are fewer moving parts and therefore fewer things to go wrong. I'm reminded of the old KISS phrase ("Keep It Simple, Silly"). The simpler things are, the less that can go wrong.

In a full installation when things go wrong, Microsoft releases patches and hotfixes. With fewer files installed on a Server Core installation, expect to do less patching.

Additionally, with less running on a Server Core installation, less maintenance is required, and less disk space is required.

Installing Server Core is relatively easy. Whether you're installing from a CD, over the network, or via WDS, it works the same way up to the point of choosing the version. When you choose a Server Core installation, it simply installs significantly fewer files. Because of this, expect the installation to complete much more quickly.

Although the Server Core interface shows only the command line by default, the mouse still works, and you can access Task Manager by pressing Ctrl+Shift+Esc.

Of course, any standard command-line commands work in a Server Core installation. For example, if you want to stop and start DNS that has been installed in a Server Core installation, you could use the Service Control Manager to issue `stop` and `start` commands as follows:

```
sc stop dns
```

```
sc start dns
```

For a list of commands available from the Server Core installation, enter `Help` at the command line.

Server Core can host the following server roles:

- The DNS role
- The DHCP role
- The File Services role
- The Print Services role
- The Active Directory Domain Services role
- The Active Directory Lightweight Directory Services role
- The Internet Information Services role
- The Streaming Media Services role
- Hyper-V

Managing Server Core Remotely

One of the first things you'll want to do after installing Server Core is to configure it for remote administration. (Well, maybe you'll rename it with `wmic` since you don't have the choice to set the name during the install, then set the IP address with `netsh` if it's not a DHCP client, and finally configure it for remote administration.) Three primary methods of remote administration are possible:

Using Remote Desktop Connection   Configure using the `scregedit.wsf` Windows script file.

Managing remotely using an MMC snap-in   Configure using the NetShell (`netsh`) command to manipulate the firewall settings.

Using Windows Remote Shell   Configure using the `WinRm` command to create a WinRM listener.

Using Remote Desktop Connection

Remote Desktop Connection (RDC) allows you to remotely connect to a server and administer it as if you were standing in front of it. Almost anything you could do while physically at the server, you'll find you can do remotely via RDC.

You can access RDC via Start ➤ All Programs ➤ Accessories ➤ Remote Desktop Connection. If you click the Options button to expand the options, your display will look like Figure 2.6.

To enable the ability to access a Server Core installation remotely using RDC, you can use the `scregedit.wsf` script. You'll explore `scregedit.wsf` more fully later in this chapter, but for now here's what you need to do:

1. Log on to your Server Core installation.

2. At the command prompt, enter the following command:

    Cscript c:\windows\system32\scregedit.wsf /AR 0

FIGURE 2.6   Launching Remote Desktop Connection

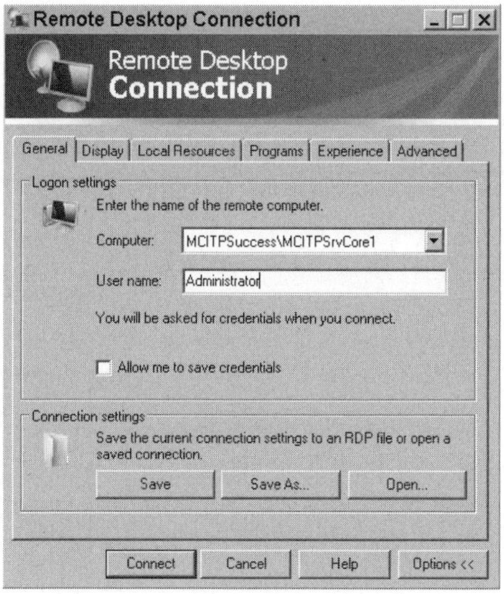

The CSCRIPT C:\WINDOWS\SYSTEM32\SCREGEDIT.WSF /AR 0 command is all you need to enter to use Remote Desktop Connection to remotely manage a Server Core installation of Windows Server 2008. No other commands or configurations are necessary.

You will now be able to use RDC to remotely administer your Server Core installation. Remember, though, whether you access the Server Core installation locally or remotely via RDC, you'll have access only to the command prompt.

Remotely Manage Server Core Using an MMC Snap-In

You may want to remotely manage different Server Core elements using an MMC snap-in. As a simple example, you may want to view events on a remote computer running Server Core.

Although the Event Viewer administrative tool is not available on a Server Core installation, the events are still being recorded. Once you properly configure Server Core, you can launch Event Viewer from another server and simply connect to the computer running Server Core.

Figure 2.7 shows Event Viewer. You can either right-click Event Viewer (Local) and select Connect to Another Computer or select the Connect to Another Computer action in the far-right pane.

However, by default Server Core will not allow these connections. You must first configure the firewall on Server Core to allow these connections.

FIGURE 2.7   Connecting Event Viewer to a remote computer

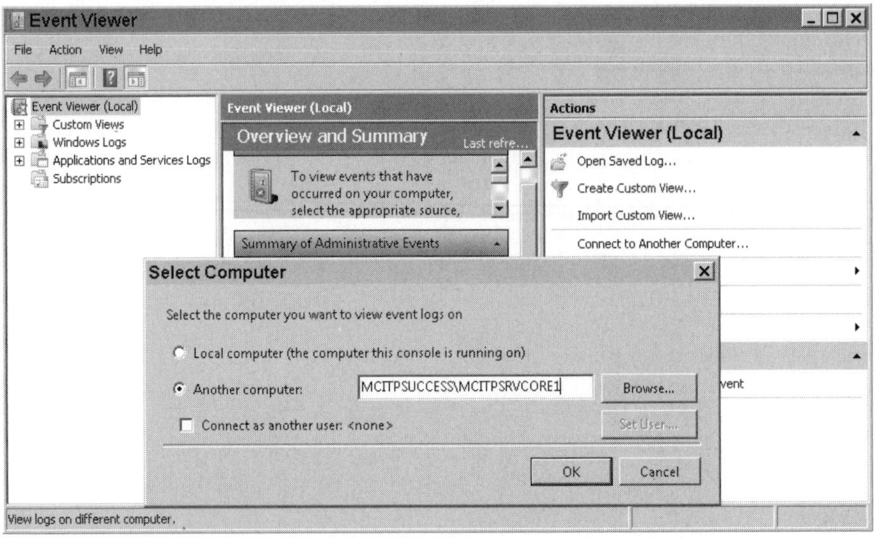

To enable remote administration from any MMC snap-in, enter the following command at the command-line prompt on your Server Core installation. Note that although the command spans two lines in the following sample, you should enter it as only a single command at the command prompt.

```
Netsh advfirewall firewall set rule group = "Remote Administration" new
enable = yes
```

When entered successfully, the result is as follows:

```
Updated 3 rule(s).
```

```
Ok.
```

Using Windows Remote Shell

You may also want to enter command-line tools and scripts from one computer to query a Server Core installation. Once configured on the Server Core server with the WinRM command, the Windows Remote Shell program allows you to issue commands from another server with the WinRS command.

When using Windows Remote Shell, keep in mind that you have a client and a server (even though both systems may be running a Windows Server product):

Server side   In the context of this section, the server side is the server running Server Core. You configure the server with a WS-Management listener to listen for Windows Remote Shell requests and respond with the appropriate data. The WinRM command is run on the server to configure the listener as follows:

```
WinRM quickconfig
```

When the previous command is entered on a Server Core installation, it prompts you to set up a WinRM listener on HTTP://* to accept WS-Man requests to any IP on the system and to enable the WinRM firewall exception. If you press Y for yes, it will make the changes.

Client side   The client is where you run the Remote Shell command (WinRS). The WinRS command queries the server and returns the appropriate data. Again, the client doesn't mean you're running a client operating system such as Windows Vista but instead means you're the client requesting data from the WS-Management listener on the server side.

Once configured, you can then enter client-side commands to query the server. Commands are entered from the client-side command line in the following format:

```
Winrs -r:computername command
```

For example, to run a WMIC command to get time zone data on a remote server named MCITPSrvCore1, you could use the following command:

```
Winrs -r:MCITPSrvCore1 WMIC timezone
```

The Windows Management Instrumentation Control (WMIC) is used to query and configure Windows Management Interface (WMI) settings on computers. The previous example queried for time zone data. WMIC is frequently used to manipulate services such as setting a specific service to disabled or starting and stopping services.

Server Core Registry Editor

Microsoft has included a script file named scregedit.wsf within the server that allows you to configure many settings. I think of this as the Server Core (sc) Registry Editor (regedit) Windows script file (wsf). Using this script, you can modify the following registry settings:

- Enable remote desktop connections
- Enable Terminal Server clients on previous versions of Windows to connect to a Server Core installation
- Enable automatic updates
- Configure DNS SRV records
- Manage IPSec Monitor remotely

Since scregedit.wsf is a script file, you need to preface it with the cscript command, which is a command-line version of the Windows Scripting Host (WSH). You can use cscript to run scripts by typing **cscript** and the name of the scripting file (**scregedit.wsf** for the Server Core Registry Editor scripting file) and adding any switches if the script supports them.

As with most Server Core files, the scregedit.wsf script file is located in the C:\Windows\System32 directory of a default installation. You could either change the directory using the CD (change directory) command or include the full path of the script file.

For example, to change the directory and then run the command, you use the following code:

```
CD C:\Windows\System32
```

```
Cscript scregedit.wsf /AR /v
```

To run the script without changing the directory, you use this code:

```
Cscript c:\windows\system32\scregedit.wsf /AR /v
```

The following paragraphs show the available switches available using `scregedit.wsf` including the syntax:

Enable remote desktop connections   This allows remote administration connections using Terminal Services so that administrators can remotely administer a Server Core installation. Within the script file, this is listed as Allow Remote Administration Connections (Terminal Services).

The switches used to enable remote desktop connections or view the current settings are as follows:

```
/AR [/v][value]
```

The possible values of `/AR` are as follows:

    0 = Enabled

    1 = Disabled

The `/v` switch is used to view the Remote Terminal Services Connection setting.

Just looking at the switch, you may think that 1 would enable the setting and 0 would disable it since 1 typically implies True or On while 0 typically implies False or Off. However, using the `/v` switch, you can see that the actual registry setting is `fDenyTSConnections`. Understanding this, using 0 to disable the setting and 1 to enable the setting makes more sense.

Setting a Deny setting to False (with 0 for the `/AR` setting) gives you two negatives; two negatives give a positive. On the other hand, setting a Deny setting to True (with 1 for the `/AR` setting) tells the system to deny the access.

As an example, the following command will show the current setting of remote administration connections:

```
Cscript c:\windows\system32\scregedit.wsf /AR /v
```

The next command will enable remote administration connections by setting the value to 0:

```
Cscript c:\windows\system32\scregedit.wsf /AR 0
```

Allow connections from previous versions of Windows (Terminal Services)   Ideally, any connections to a Windows Server 2008 installation will be from clients running Windows Vista or newer operating systems. If using older operating systems (such as Windows XP or Server 2003), you can configure the CredSSP-based user authentication for Terminal Services connections to allow pre–Windows Vista versions of Windows to connect remotely.

The Credential Security Support Provider (CredSSP) is a more secure protocol that is supported by Windows Vista, Server 2008, and new operating systems. It requires fewer remote computer resources initially and allows network-level authentication.

The switches used to enable connections from previous versions of Windows or view the current settings are as follows:

```
/CS [/v][value]
```

The possible values of /CS are as follows:

   0 = Allow previous versions

   1 = Require CredSSP

The /v switch is used to view the Terminal Services CredSSP setting.

As an example, the following command will show the current setting of allowing previous versions of Windows to use remote administration connections:

```
Cscript c:\windows\system32\scregedit.wsf /CS /v
```

The next command will enable previous versions of Windows to use remote administration connections by setting the value to 0:

```
Cscript c:\windows\system32\scregedit.wsf /CS 0
```

Manage automatic updates (AU)   These settings can be used to configure how automatic updates are applied to the Windows system. It includes the ability to disable automatic updates and to set the installation schedule.

```
/AU [/v][value]
```

The possible values of /AU are as follows:

   4 = Enable Automatic Updates

   1 = Disable Automatic Updates

The /v switch is used to view the current Automatic Update setting.

As an example, the following command will show the current setting of automatic updates:

```
Cscript c:\windows\system32\scregedit.wsf /AU /v
```

The next command will enable automatic updates by setting the value to 4:

```
Cscript c:\windows\system32\scregedit.wsf /AU 4
```

IP Security (IPSec) Monitor remote management This setting configures the server to allow the IP Security (IPSec) Monitor to be able to remotely manage IPSec.

```
/IM [/v][value]
```

The possible values of /IM are as follows:

   0 = Do not allow

   1 = Allow remote management

The /v switch is used to view the current IPSec Monitor setting.

As an example, the following command will show the current setting of allowing remote management using the IPSec Monitor:

```
Cscript c:\windows\system32\scregedit.wsf /IM /v
```

The next command will enable remote management using the IPSec Monitor by setting the value to 1:

```
Cscript c:\windows\system32\scregedit.wsf /IM 1
```

DNS SRV priority   This setting configures the priority for DNS SRV records and is useful only on domain controllers.

```
/DP [/v][value]
```

The possible values of /DP are as follows:

> 0 through 65535
>
> The recommended value is 200.

The /v switch is used to view the current DNS SRV priority setting value.

DNS SRV weight   This setting configures the weight for DNS SRV records and is useful only on domain controllers.

```
/DW [/v][value]
```

The possible values of /DW are as follows:

> 0 through 65535
>
> The recommended value is 50.

The /v switch is used to view the current DNS SRV weight setting value.

Command-line reference   This setting displays a list of common tasks and how to perform them from the command line within Server Core.

```
/CLI
```

As an example, you would enter the command as follows:

```
Cscript c:\windows\system32\scregedit.wsf /CLI
```

Creating a Rollback Plan

When you're performing any type of upgrade, you need to have a rollback plan. A rollback plan will allow you to get back to square one in case things go wrong with an upgrade.

When upgrading a single user's system, if things go wrong, only one user is impacted. However, when upgrading a single server, you have the potential of impacting multiple users. Depending on how big your enterprise is, this could be tens, hundreds, or even thousands of users.

Often when I'm working with computers and am ready to make a significant change such as an upgrade, I ask this simple question: "What's the worst that could happen?" This is what I need to plan and prepare for.

As a twist on an old saying, "Expect the best things in life, but prepare for the occasional outage in the server room."

Two primary actions can help you with your rollback plan:

Creating backups   This could be a backup of the data or the entire server.

Enabling another server When updating a server, identify another server to take over the upgraded server's role.

Creating Backups

Often, the most valuable information we have on a server is the data. For example, if a server is an application server or a file server, we can fully expect the server to be housing a significant amount of data. It could be large databases, users' home folders, archived data, websites, or any other type of important data.

Your environment already has some type of backup plan in place (at least it should), but you may want to double-check.

I remember working in one enterprise where the intranet was heavily used. Each department had its own intranet web pages and someone with some basic skills to update the data. IIS was used to serve the web pages.

The group responsible for IIS administration upgraded the IIS version. They fully expected a smooth upgrade, but something went wrong. Ultimately they had to rebuild the server from scratch.

No problem, they thought. We have backups.

Unfortunately, they didn't have any recent backups. The backups were never tested with test restores, and the backup results weren't monitored. The password on the account used to do the backups expired, so all of the recent backups failed.

The lesson from this is, don't assume that the backups are valid. Before starting an upgrade, you may want to do a test restore.

Additionally, backups may be occurring on a weekly schedule such as every Sunday. If you do the upgrade on Wednesday, and things go wrong, will you lose three days of data? Is this acceptable? There's nothing wrong with creating a backup just prior to the start of your upgrade.

If the server you are upgrading doesn't have much data but instead has the value in the configuration, you may want to consider creating an image.

For example, you may be preparing to upgrade a DNS server. The configuration of DNS can be quite detailed. If you have an effective change management plan in place, all of the current configuration changes may be available, but it still may take hours to build and configure a DNS server.

> If you've built up some scripting skills, you can also use scripting to cap-
> ture all the settings of a server. You can then use scripting to reconfigure
> another server from scratch. Windows PowerShell, NetShell, AppCmd, and
> WDSUtil are a few of the scripting tools you can use to re-create a server
> configuration.

Instead, you could create an image of the DNS server just prior to the upgrade. If the upgrade fails, you could then easily just re-create the server from this image.

While you would end the day no further than where you started, at least your day will end. You wouldn't be in front of the DNS server until the wee hours of the morning trying to get it back into service.

WDS allows you to easily create an image of any server. In the event of a failure in the upgrade, you can just reimage the machine, and you are back to square one.

Enabling Another Server

Another rollback plan could include creating or enabling another server to fulfill the role of the upgraded server in the event of upgrade catastrophe.

In other words, if you're upgrading a server such as a DHCP server, you could have a second DHCP server ready to put into action in case the upgrade fails. When you realize you need to roll back the upgrade, you plug in and enable the second DHCP server, and your network continues to hum.

Of course, it's also possible that you have two DHCP servers on your network already. The second DHCP server may have been created specifically as a redundant DHCP server.

In this case, a failed upgrade may not impact the network because the second DHCP server can handle the load of both DHCP servers. You would need to verify only that the second DHCP server is configured to service all of the same scopes as the first DHCP server.

Utilizing Virtualization

Windows Server virtualization, or Hyper-V, is one of the most talked about additions to Server 2008. A single physical server can host an almost unlimited number of virtual servers. I say "almost" because you are limited to only the hardware capabilities.

Virtual servers hosted on a single physical server appear and behave as if they were actu-ally physical servers on the network. If you'll forgive the pun, from a client perspective, there is virtually no difference.

Consider Figures 2.8 and 2.9. Figure 2.8 shows three virtual servers (DC1, DNS1, and DHCP1) hosted on a single physical server with two of the servers running Server Core.

Provisioning

Provisioning within IT is loosely defined as supplying or providing computing services or resources. It's worth defining this because of the fourth major objective of the 70-646 exam: "Planning Application and Data Provisioning."

When studying for application provisioning, you want to understand the benefits of virtualization. Application provisioning can also be achieved with Terminal Services (covered in Chapter 7, "Planning Terminal Services Servers").

Data provisioning is where the computing resources (such as data) are provided. Data provisioning will be covered in more depth in Chapter 6, "Monitoring and Maintaining Print and File Servers."

FIGURE 2.8 Three virtual servers within one physical server

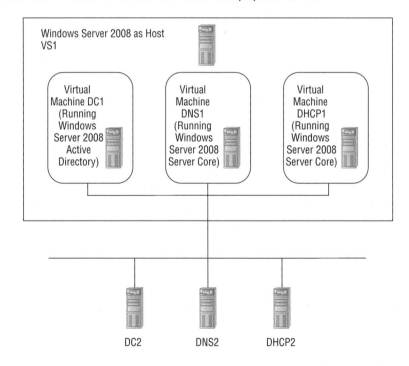

Figure 2.9 shows how the virtual servers appear on the network. Each virtual server will have an individual server name and IP address. Even though the traffic is going through VS1, the redirection is transparent on the network.

FIGURE 2.9   Virtual servers' appearance on the network

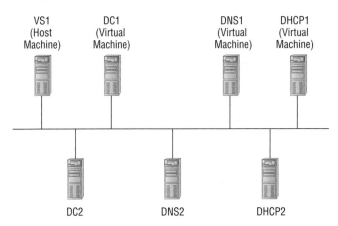

The primary reason that companies are excited about virtualization is because of the ability to save money. By using virtual servers, companies have the potential to save money in three key areas:

Hardware   Let's state the obvious: one physical server costs less than 10 physical servers. Admittedly, you need to beef up the core resources (processors, memory, disk, and network interface) of this single server. But still, the overall cost will be significantly less.

Power   The cost of power continues to rise. Although you and I see it most predominantly at the gasoline pump, companies feel the pinch when the electric bill comes. It's estimated that for every watt reduced on the electric bill, power expenses are reduced by more than $3 per year. Additionally, some companies want to reduce power for environmental reasons—it makes sense to be "green" for public relations, especially when it improves the bottom line by reducing energy costs.

Licensing   The Windows Server 2008 Enterprise edition with Hyper-V includes licenses for four virtual servers, and the Windows Server 2008 Datacenter edition includes licenses for an unlimited number of servers. By running multiple virtual servers on single physical server, you can significantly reduce licensing costs.

Virtual Server Uses

When thinking about converting your servers to virtual servers, you might want to consider the Ferrari rule. If you had a Ferrari, you could get out onto the highway and drive 180 miles per hour almost everywhere you go. However, just because you can does not mean it's a good idea to do so.

The same goes for virtualizing your servers. Sometimes it makes sense, and the following are a few instances where virtual servers are used to solve problems:

- Hosting applications
- Consolidating servers
- Creating a test bed

Hosting Applications

It's not uncommon for legacy line-of-business applications to need to be hosted on a separate server. A variety of incompatibility issues can crop up.

For example, applications that worked well on Windows Server 2000 or Windows Server 2003 may not work well on Windows Server 2008. You can create a virtual system hosting the older application on an older operating system, and your problem is solved.

You may remember one of the goals of kindergarten was to teach us to play well with others. Unfortunately, not everyone learned that lesson.

Server applications should also be able to get along with each other, but some are just not compatible with others. In a perfect world, as long as you have enough hardware resources such as processing power, memory, and disk space, all the applications will be able to coexist with each other. Unfortunately, all server applications haven't learned this lesson either. Some applications don't play well with others.

As an example, in early versions of Microsoft SQL Server and Microsoft Exchange Server they just didn't get along well. Both assumed they were the only application, and both attempted to take all the memory. Ultimately, one of the applications lost. Although this problem has long been solved for SQL and Exchange, it hasn't been solved for all server applications.

By hosting an unfriendly application on a separate virtual server, you can isolate it from other applications.

These applications aren't typically mainstream applications (such as SQL and Exchange) but are often homegrown line-of-business (LOB) applications. An obvious solution would be to upgrade the application, but that often isn't an easy (or inexpensive) option. Virtualization can be both easy and cheap.

You can also host 32-bit and 64-bit operating systems on a single server. For example, you may have one server running an application on 32-bit Windows Server 2003 and another server running an application on a 64-bit Windows Server 2003. Hyper-V can be used to host both applications within two virtual machines on the same server.

Consolidating Servers

One of the obvious reasons to use virtual servers is to consolidate many servers onto a single box. For some servers using powerful processors, it's possible that the actual percent of processing power rarely exceeds 5 percent. You have all this processing power, but it's just sitting there, unused.

What might your company do if an employee worked only about 5 percent of the time that they were clocked in? No, no, they wouldn't promote this person.... In most companies, the employee would be given better direction, or they may be invited to find employment elsewhere.

If you have several underutilized servers, you can consolidate them onto a single server, and the resources will be more fully utilized. Not only does this provide better utilization of the resources, but it's also easier to maintain and manage a single server with multiple virtual servers.

Test Bed

Virtual servers can be used to host a test bed. A *test bed* is an isolated computer (or computers) used to perform different testing. The testing could be compatibility testing, performance testing, or simply just to learn concepts in a new product.

In Chapter 6, I'll cover Group Policy in detail. When developing and deploying Group Policy objects, the importance of testing can't be overstressed.

However, there's a conflict. You want to test your group policies in a realistic environment, but you don't want to deploy untested group policies into the live environment.

Take a look at Figure 2.10. You can create a virtual domain. You'd first create your domain controller. By using a recent backup of system state from one of your live domain controllers, you could create an exact replica of the live domain. Add some network support with DNS and DHCP hosted on a server, and then add your clients.

FIGURE 2.10   Creating a virtual domain for GPO testing

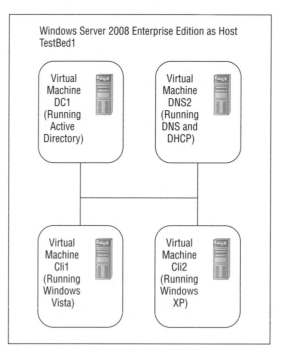

You would want your test bed isolated from the live environment. Otherwise, you could run into some significant problems such as the group policies you are testing being replicated to live domain controllers.

With your virtual domain set up this way, you can create the group policies you want to test, move the computer objects to any desired OU, and log on as any user. You will then be able to see the exact impact of your new or modified group policies.

Admittedly, you can also use the Group Policy Management Console (GPMC). The GPMC includes Group Policy Results (and the Group Policy Results Wizard), which will tell you the resulting group policies for specific users logging onto a specific computer. However, in a highly managed environment (one with many Group Policy settings), it's easy to get overwhelmed and miss a setting.

By testing the actual policies, you have a much better chance of seeing exactly what happens with changed or added group policies.

Virtual Server Licensing

When planning to deploy servers, it's important to understand the licensing requirements of virtual servers. The licensing requirements of the three editions of Windows Server 2008 are as follows:

Windows Server 2008 Standard with Hyper-V   The Standard with Hyper-V editions includes support for a single virtual server. A single virtual instance license is included.

Windows Server 2008 Enterprise with Hyper-V   The Enterprise editions can support up to four virtual servers. Licensing for the four virtual servers is included as part of the license with the Enterprise edition.

Windows Server 2008 Datacenter with Hyper-V   An unlimited number of virtual servers can be hosted on the Datacenter editions. Licensing for unlimited number of virtual servers is included with the single Datacenter license of the host machine.

Summary

When deploying servers, WDS can streamline the process for you and save you a significant amount of time. The network must have at least one DHCP server, DNS, and Active Directory Domain Services running to support WDS. A single WDS server can then be used to deploy both 32-bit and 64-bit editions of Windows Server 2008 operating systems.

WDS can use a single boot image (for the initial boot of a server using the NIC) for both 32-bit and 64-bit systems. Install images can then be selected from the WDS server. Systems with 32-bit architecture require a 32-bit image, and systems with 64-bit architecture require a 64-bit image.

It's also possible to create custom or standard images. Once you install the operating system, you can fully configure it and then capture the image using WDS. This image can then be deployed to other servers using the same settings. Before the image is captured, the Sysprep program must be run on the server to remove unique settings such as the security ID (SID).

Some server roles can be installed on a Windows Server Core installation to provide added security and stability. When this is done, you will likely want to manage the server remotely and must configure the remote management at the server. The three tools used to prepare the server for remote management are the `scregedit.wsf` Windows script file, `WinRM quickconfig` to enable remote `WinRS` commands, and the NetShell (`netsh`) program to configure the firewall.

Last, you learned some of Server 2008's Hyper-V virtualization capabilities including both the benefits and the licensing model basics. The Windows Server 2008 Standard edition includes a free license for a single virtual server, Enterprise includes four licenses, and Datacenter includes unlimited licenses.

Exam Essentials

Know how to install and configure WDS.   This includes knowing the requirements for WDS and how to use the WDS GUI and the `WDSUtil` command-line tool. The Transport Server feature is installed to support multicasting images.

Know what clients are supported by WDS.   You should know that a single WDS server can support both 32-bit and 64-bit operating systems. Images for 32-bit and 64-bit systems can be held and deployed from the same WDS server.

Know the different image types and how to capture and add images to WDS.   Know the difference between boot and install images and between basic and standard (custom) images. Be familiar with the process of creating a standard (custom) image, including the use of Sysprep.

Know how to deploy images using WDS.   This includes the process of booting a single PXE client and selecting an image and also using multicast transmissions to deploy an image to multiple clients at the same time. You should also know how to schedule a deployment.

Know how to configure Server Core for remote management.   You should know how to configure Server Core for remote desktop connections with WinRM, how to configure Server Core to be managed by any MMC, and how to configure Server Core to be managed remotely using the `WinRS` command. You should be familiar with all the switches in the `scregedit.wsf` Windows script file.

Know the capabilities of Windows virtualization.   This includes knowing the benefits of virtualization and some basic scenarios when it would be used. Additionally, you should know the specific licensing of each edition of Windows Server 2008 with Hyper-V.

Review Questions

1. You want to use Windows Deployment Services (WDS) to deploy basic server images to 20 computers. Eight of the computers have one motherboard type using a 32-bit processor. Nine of the computers are using another 32-bit motherboard. The last three servers are using 64-bit processors. How many WDS servers are needed?

    A. 1

    B. 2

    C. 3

    D. 20

2. You are using Windows Deployment Services (WDS) to deploy Windows Server 2008 onto several new servers. The WDS server is set up to respond only to known computers. None of the new servers can connect to the WDS server. What should be done?

    A. Run Sysprep on each of the servers before booting.

    B. Prestage each of the computers in WDS.

    C. Prestage each of the computers in Active Directory.

    D. Log onto the new servers using an account with administrative privileges.

3. You need to deploy seven 64-bit Windows Server 2008 servers that will all be used for File Services roles. You build the first server (named FS1) and plan to use Windows Deployment Services (WDS) to deploy the rest. You've added a capture image from a generic 32-bit boot image and then boot FS1 by pressing the F12 key. You successfully connect to WDS and launch the capture image. However, WDS does not allow you to select any local drives to image. What is the problem?

    A. Sysprep has not been run on the WDS server.

    B. Sysprep has not been run on FS1.

    C. The capture image must be built from a 64-bit boot image.

    D. FS1 needs to be fully booted (not from the F12 key).

4. You are using Windows Deployment Services (WDS) to deploy Windows Server 2008 images. You want to create a capture image from the command line. What command would you use?

    A. `WinRM`

    B. `scregedit.wsf`

    C. `WDSImage`

    D. `WDSUtil`

    ```
    WDSUtil /New-CaptureImage /Image: C:\boot\install.wim /Architecture:x86
    /Filepath: c:\Capture\capture.wim
    ```

5. You want to deploy an install image of Windows Server 2008 to nine new servers using Windows Deployment Services (WDS). What would be the best way?

   A. Multicast the image to all servers simultaneously.

   B. Deploy the image to each server individually.

   C. Deploy the image to one server, run Sysprep on it, and then deploy the image to the rest of the servers.

   D. Deploy the image to no more than three servers at a time.

6. Which Windows Deployment Services (WDS) image type can be used to deploy an image to a non-PXE client?

   A. Capture image

   B. Boot image

   C. Install image

   D. Discover image

7. You are an administrator in a company where users work only a single shift. You are using Windows Deployment Services (WDS) to deploy images to several servers in your environment where users are also transferring large volumes of video files over the network. While deploying an image to a server, several users complained that the network was performing slowly, and you suspect it was because of the bandwidth used by WDS. What can you do to prevent these problems?

   A. Start the deployment of the images just before the users log on.

   B. Don't deploy the images over the network.

   C. Run WDS in quiet mode.

   D. Schedule the deployment of the images for sometime after-hours.

8. You want to use Windows Deployment Services (WDS) to deploy basic server images to 20 computers. Eight of the computers have one motherboard type using a 32-bit processor. Nine of the computers are using another 32-bit motherboard. The last three servers are using 64-bit processors. How many images are needed?

   A. 1

   B. 2

   C. 3

   D. 4

9. You want to use Windows Deployment Services (WDS) to deploy basic server images to 20 computers. You will be deploying as many as 20 images to servers located on three separate subnets. Routers in your network are RFC 1542 compliant. How many DHCP servers are needed?

   A. 1

   B. 2

   C. 3

   D. 20

10. You manage a network environment including many Windows Server 2008 servers running Server Core. You've been able to manage these servers remotely with Remote Desktop Connection (RDC) using your desktop PC running Windows Vista. However, you've logged on to a different PC running Windows XP and find you cannot connect to the servers running Server Core. Why not?

   A. Windows XP cannot connect to Server Core. You can connect using Windows Vista only.

   B. You need to upgrade the RDC version on Windows XP.

   C. You need to modify the CredSSP setting on the Server Core servers.

   D. You need to install SP2 on Windows XP.

11. You have built a Windows Server 2008 server hosting Active Directory Domain Services in a Server Core configuration. You want to manage the server remotely using Remote Desktop Connection (RDC). You manage servers remotely using both a desktop running Windows XP and a laptop running Windows Vista. Which of the following commands should you run on the Server Core server? (Choose all that apply.)

   A. `Cscript scregedit.wsf /AR 0`

   B. `Cscript scregedit.wsf /IM 1`

   C. `Cscript scregedit.wsf /CS 0`

   D. `Cscript scregedit.wsf /AU 4`

12. You have built a Windows Server 2008 server hosting Active Directory Domain Services in a Server Core configuration. You want to manage the server remotely using Active Directory Users and Computers (ADUC). Which of the following commands should you run on Server Core to enable the use of ADUC?

   A. `Cscript scregedit.wsf /AR 0`

   B. `Cscript scregedit.wsf /ADUC 1`

   C. `WinRM quickconfig`

   D. `Netsh advfirewall firewall set rule group = "Remote Administration" new enable = yes`

13. You have built a Windows Server 2008 server fulfilling a File Services role in a Server Core configuration. You want to manage the server remotely using WinRS commands. Which of the following commands should be run on Server Core to enable `WinRS` commands?

   A. `Cscript scregedit.wsf /AR 0`

   B. `WinRS quickconfig`

   C. `WinRM quickconfig`

   D. `Netsh advfirewall firewall set rule group = "Remote Administration" new enable = yes`

14. You have built a Windows Server 2008 server running DHCP in a Server Core configuration. You want to manage the server remotely using Remote Desktop Connection (RDC). Which of the following commands can be used to enable RDC?

    A. `Cscript scregedit.wsf /AR 0`

    B. `Cscript scregedit.wsf /AR 1`

    C. `WinRM quickconfig`

    D. `Netsh advfirewall firewall set rule group = "Remote Administration" new enable = yes`

15. You manage a DNS server hosted on Windows Server 2008 in a Server Core server configuration. You realize you need to restart the DNS service. How can you accomplish this?

    A. Use the Services applet to restart DNS.

    B. Use the `sc` command to stop and start the DNS service.

    C. Use the DNS snap-in to restart the DNS service.

    D. Restart the service using the `scregedit` script file.

16. You want to reduce the attack surface of several of your Server 2008 servers. You are considering using Server Core for as many servers as possible. Which of the following roles will support Server Core? (Choose all that apply.)

    A. Domain Name Services

    B. Dynamic Host Configuration Protocol

    C. Certificate Services

    D. Active Directory Domain Services

    E. Internet Information Services

17. You are preparing to upgrade a server from Windows Server 2003 to Windows Server 2008. What is a recommended course of action to prepare for the possibility that things may go wrong? (Choose all that apply.)

    A. Create backups of the data.

    B. Create backups of the system configuration.

    C. Create an image of the server.

    D. Ensure that another server can fulfill the role of the server you are upgrading.

18. You are planning to consolidate 20 servers onto a single server running Windows Server 2008 Datacenter with Hyper-V. How many licenses are required?

    A. 1

    B. 19

    C. 20

    D. 21

19. How many virtual server licenses are included with Windows Server 2008 Datacenter edition?

    A. 0

    B. 1

    C. 4

    D. Unlimited

20. You are planning on deploying 50 new computers running Windows Vista. Each computer is PXE compatible. You need to design a plan that will allow you to simultaneously install Windows Vista on as many 25 computers. What should you include in your plan?

    A. Use WDS with the Transport Server Feature to cast the images using unicast.

    B. Use WDS with the Transport Server Feature to cast the images using multicasting.

    C. Use WDS with the Deployment Server Feature to cast the images using unicast.

    D. Use WDS with the Deployment Server Feature to cast the images using multicasting.

Answers to Review Questions

1. **A.** A single WDS server can deploy images to systems with different hardware configurations, including both 32-bit and 64-bit systems.

2. **C.** *Prestaging* a client computer is done by creating a computer account in Active Directory with the computer's GUID. The computer is then "known," and the WDS server will respond to it. Sysprep would be done on only a custom or standard image after it has been configured and before it is captured. Computers cannot be prestaged in WDS. Since the new servers can't connect to the WDS server, you wouldn't be able to log in.

3. **B.** If Sysprep is not run on FS1 to properly prepare it, WDS will not recognize the drive when you try to capture it. Sysprep is not run on WDS. The 32-bit boot image (and the capture image created from the boot image) can be used for both 32-bit and 64-bit systems. FS1 cannot be imaged if the operating system is running; it must be booted using the F12 key.

4. **D.** WDSUtil is the command-line equivalent of the WDS GUI, and you can create a capture image using the following command (entered on the same line with no carriage returns):

   `WDSUtil /New-CaptureImage /Image: C:\boot\install.wim /Architecture:x86 /Filepath: c:\Capture\capture.wim`

   WinRM and scregedit.wsf are both used to prepare a Server Core server for remote administration. There is no such command as WDSImage.

5. **A.** By multicasting to all the servers at the same, you are using the least amount of bandwidth since the WDS server sends the data out only once; this would also be the easiest method. Deploying the image to each server individually (or even in groups of three) would take more work and more bandwidth. Since we are deploying only an install image (not a custom or standard image), Sysprep is not needed.

6. **D.** A discover image is created from a boot image. It can then be converted to an .iso image and burned to a CD. The CD can be used to boot the non-PXE client and contact the Windows Deployment Services server.

7. **D.** WDS allows you to schedule multicasting for a specific time. Since users work only a single shift, you can schedule the deployment for after-hours. It wouldn't help to set the deployment to a time just before they log on, because the users would still be impacted. WDS deploys the images only over the network. There is no quiet mode for WDS.

8. **C.** Three images are needed: the same boot image is used for both 32-bit and 64-bit systems. However, different install images are used for both 32-bit and 64-bit systems.

9. **A.** A single DHCP server can serve multiple servers on multiple subnets in support of WDS.

10. **C.** By default, the Credential Security Support Provider (CredSSP) is enabled on Windows Server 2008, which allows connections only from those clients running Windows Vista or newer. To allow Windows XP to connect, you'd need to change the setting to allow previous versions on the Server Core servers. You can do this with the scregedit /CS 0 command.

11. A, C.   The Server Core Registry Editor Windows script file (`scregedit.wsf`) is used to manipulate registry settings within a Server Core server. The first setting is /AR 0, which will enable RDC. Since you need to manage Server Core from both Windows XP and Windows Vista, you also need to change the setting of the Credential Security Support Provider (CredSSP), which is supported only by Windows Vista and newer systems. Using the /CS 0 switch, you can allow previous versions (such as Windows XP) to remotely manage the Server Core server. The /IM switch is used to enable the IPSec monitor remotely, and the /AU switch is used to configure Automatic Updates. Neither the /IM nor the /AU switch affects the remote desktop connection.

12. D.   The shown NetShell command will enable the Server Core server to be remotely managed using MMC snap-ins including Active Directory Users and Computers. The Server Core Registry Editor Windows script file (`scregedit.wsf`) is used to enable RDC. The AR switch would be set to 0 to enable RDC. The default is set to 1, which disables RDC. `WinRM quickconfig` will configure a WinRM listener on the Server Core server to allow WinRS commands to be issued remotely.

13. C.   `WinRM quickconfig` will configure a WinRM listener on the Server Core server to allow WinRS commands to be issued remotely. The Server Core Registry Editor Windows script file (`scregedit.wsf`) is used to enable RDC using the /AR 0 switch. The shown `Netsh` command will enable the Server Core server to be remotely managed using MMC snap-ins.

14. A.   The Server Core Registry Editor Windows script file (`scregedit.wsf`) is used to enable RDC. The AR switch would be set to 0 to enable RDC. The default is set to 1, which disables RDC. `WinRM quickconfig` will configure a WinRM listener on the Server Core server to allow WinRS commands to be issued remotely. The shown `Netsh` command will enable the Server Core server to be remotely managed using MMC snap-ins.

15. B.   `sc` is a command-line program used to communicate with the Service Control Manager and services. Server Core doesn't support Windows programs or applets such as Services or MMC snap-ins. The `scregedit` script file can be used to view and change configuration settings on a Server Core server, but it can't be used to stop and start services.

16. A, B, D, E.   The following roles can be supported on a Server Core server: DNS, DHCP, File Services, Print Services, Active Directory Domain Services, Active Directory Lightweight Directory Services, Internet Information Services, Hyper-V, and Streaming Media Services. Certificate Services cannot be hosted on a Server Core server.

17. A, B, C, D.   All of the answers are valid parts of a comprehensive rollback plan.

18. A.   A single license for Windows Server 2008 Datacenter with Hyper-V includes licenses for an unlimited umber of virtual servers.

19. D.   An unlimited number of virtual server licenses is included with the Datacenter edition of Windows Server 2008.

20. B.   The Windows Deployment Services (WDS) Transport Server mode can cast multiple images at the same time using multicasting. Unicast would send the images one at a time instead of simultaneously. The Deployment is needed to support WDS, but does not support multicasting without the Transport server.

Chapter

3

Using Windows Server 2008 Management Tools

MICROSOFT EXAM OBJECTIVES COVERED IN THIS CHAPTER:

✓ **Planning for Server Management**

- Plan Server Management Strategies. May include but is not limited to: remote administration, remote desktop, server management technologies, Server Manager and ServerManagerCMD, delegation policies and procedures.

✓ **Monitoring and Maintaining Servers**

- Implement Patch Management Strategy. May include but is not limited to: operating system patch level maintenance, Windows Server Update Services (WSUS), application patch level maintenance.

- Monitor Servers for Performance Evaluation and Optimization. May include but is not limited to: server and service monitoring, optimization, event management, trending and baseline analysis.

✓ **Planning Application and Data Provisioning**

- Provision Applications. May include but is not limited to: presentation virtualization, terminal server infrastructure, resource allocation, application virtualization alternatives, application deployment, System Center Configuration Manager

I recently had a watch repairman remove a link in my watch-band so that it'd fit better. After he finished, I commented to him that what he finished in just a couple of minutes would probably have taken me more than an hour to do. His response: "You could do it quickly too, if you had the right tools."

So it is with just about any task. If you have the right tools, the task is simple and can be accomplished quickly.

As an IT professional managing Windows Server 2008 servers, you have a wide range of tools available to you. Your primary job, early on, is to know what the tools are and how to use them.

In this chapter, I'll introduce some of the tools that will make your job as a system administrator easier. These include the following:

- Reliability and Performance Monitor

- Event Viewer

- Remote Management Tools

- Windows Server Update Services

- System Center Configuration Manager

You'll notice in the list of objectives that delegation policies and procedures, presentation virtualization, terminal server infrastructure, application vir-tualization alternatives, and application deployment are listed. Chapter 2, "Planning Server Deployments" covered presentation virtualization and application virtualization alternatives. Chapter 5, "Monitoring and Maintain-ing Active Directory" covers delegation policies and procedures, and applica-tion deployment.

Server-Monitoring Tools

When monitoring the performance of servers, you have two primary tools available: Reliability and Performance Monitor and Event Viewer. You can use both tools to moni-tor what's happening on the local server or configure them to monitor remote servers.

Reliability and Performance Monitor   The Reliability and Performance Monitor is similar to the Reliability and Performance tool available in Windows Vista. An administrator can use it to quickly view what is happening on a server in real time or configure it to capture data over a period of time.

A significant difference over the monitoring tools available in Windows Server 2003 is the ability to use data collector sets. When preparing for the 70-646 exam, you'll need to have a solid understanding of what data collector sets are and how you can use them to monitor a server.

Event Viewer   Event Viewer has been around in Windows Systems for many versions of Windows. As events occur, they are captured in one of several logs and made available for viewing via the Event Viewer.

Windows Server 2008 introduces a significant new feature as part of Event Viewer: event subscriptions.   *Event subscriptions* allow you to capture events on remote computers and store them on a central computer. Events are then forwarded to the receiving computer and can be viewed just as other events. Configuring event subscriptions is an important concept to fully understand when preparing for the 70-646 exam.

Both the Reliability and Performance Monitor and Event Viewer will be covered in detail in the following sections.

Reliability and Performance Monitor

The Reliability and Performance Monitor is a Microsoft Management Console (MMC) snap-in that you can use to analyze a system's performance. With Reliability and Performance Monitor, you can view data in real time, but you can also use it to capture and collect data over a period of time and store it in logs, define threshold for alerts, generate reports, and view and analyze historical metrics.

Figure 3.1 shows the Reliability and Performance Monitor on the Resource Overview page. The four primary hardware resources of any system are the CPU (processor), disk, network, and memory. When the Reliability and Performance Monitor is first launched, the Resource Overview page is shown. The left pane allows you to choose the Monitoring Tools, Data Collector Sets, and Reports nodes available in the Reliability and Performance Monitor.

Monitoring Tools   Two primary monitoring tools are included in the Reliability and Performance Monitor. The Performance Monitor shows a real-time view of performance counters. The Reliability Monitor provides a system stability index. The system stability index is a number from 1 (least stable) to 10 (most stable) derived from recent failures in both hardware and software.

Data Collector Sets   A data collector set is a group of data collection points used to review or log the performance of a system. Windows Server 2008 includes several predefined data collector sets (in the System container) that can be used to easily measure the performance of your server. You can also create your own user-defined data collector sets.

Reports   After a data collector set is run, the data is available for viewing in a report. Reports provide both summary data and detailed diagnostic results designed to allow administrators to easily identify system anomalies.

FIGURE 3.1   The Resource Overview page in the Reliability and Performance Monitor

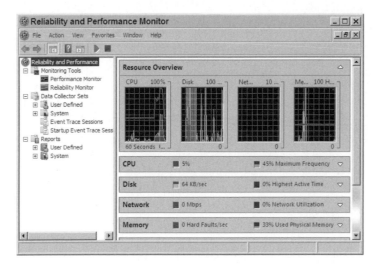

Performance Monitor

You can use the Performance Monitor to view performance data either in real time or from log files. You can display data as a graph, a histogram, or a report.

The Performance Monitor includes hundreds of counters that can be selected to measure specific performance details of a server. Counters are organized in *objects*; said another way, a Performance Monitor object is a group of counters. For example, the Processor object includes about 15 counters that can measure the details of processors within your server.

Figure 3.2 shows the Performance Monitor looking at a SQL Server machine. The main area shows a graph of the counters that have been added, with the scale at the left set to a scale of 0 to 100. Right below the graph are statistics for the selected counter in the graph. The bottom pane shows the counters that have been added.

The % Processor Time counter is selected in the bottom pane and is shown as a heavy black line in the graph. The statistics show an average of 14 percent utilization with a peak of 91 percent over a timed duration of 1 minute and 40 seconds.

> To highlight any individual counter in the Performance Monitor display, press Ctrl+H. This will change the color of the selected counter to a bold, black line. To change the selected counter, you can use the up and down arrows.

To add counters, you can either click the + icon or right-click in the graph and select Add Counters.

A report in the Performance Monitor shows the same data as a graph, but only a snapshot at a time. For example, Table 3.1 shows the same counters shown in Figure 3.2, but for only a single second.

FIGURE 3.2 The Performance Monitor

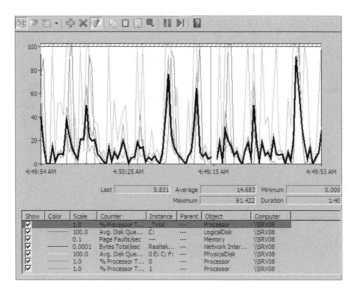

TABLE 3.1 Data from a Performance Monitor Report

Object	Counter	Value	Value	Value
Logical Disk		C:		
	Avg. Disk Queue Length	0.000		
Memory				
	Page Faults/Sec	28.248		
Network Interface		Realtek RTL8139_810x Family Fast Ethernet NIC		
	Bytes Total/Sec	0.0000		
Physical Disk				
	Avg. Disk Queue Length	0.0000		
Processor		_Total	0	1
	% Processor Time	4.624	3.836	5.413

Although Figure 3.2 shows that the total processor utilization has a range of 0 percent to 91.4 percent over a period of time, the preceding report shows the total percentage of processor time at 4.624 percent. If you watch the report over time, you can see the values change, but a single report value may not give you a full picture of the performance.

Similarly, the Avg. Disk Queue Length counter for both the logical disk (the C: partition) and the physical disk shows values of 0. This looks great—at this moment in time. For a more complete perspective, the report needs to be viewed for a while to determine what is happening.

Real World Scenario

Performance Monitor History

The Performance Monitor in the Reliability and Performance Monitor snap-in may look familiar to you. It's just about the same Performance Monitor (also known as Performance) that has been available in Windows since before Windows 2000.

It just keeps getting improved. The Reliability and Performance Monitor is just the most recent improvement. To launch Performance, you could enter `perfmon` at the Run line. That's the same command you can use to launch the Reliability and Performance Monitor.

Performance Monitor (past and present) allows administrators to view system performance metrics in real time.

In the past, I would use it to create logs by collecting data over a period of time. For example, I would create a performance baseline for a server by capturing periodic snapshots every 30 minutes of specific metrics for a week.

As time passes and the load and performance of a server changes, I could compare current performance with the baseline to determine what changed. This was (and is) referred to as *trend and baseline analysis*.

However, one of the challenges with Performance was deciding which metrics to capture. Certainly the four core resources (CPU, memory, disk, and network) would be measured, but what else? The additional metrics were dependent on the server load and also dependent on the administrator knowing what to capture.

With Windows Server 2008, the Reliability and Performance Monitor takes some of the guesswork out of deciding what objects and counters to capture. The data collector set templates start off with measurements of core resources. For example, the Active Directory Diagnostics template includes the specific counters and objects needed to accurately assess the performance of a domain controller.

As time moves on, expect more templates to appear to meet the needs of different server roles.

Reliability Monitor

The Reliability Monitor gives you an overview of a system's stability and allows you to drill into the details about events that impact system reliability. The overall stability is displayed as a stability index.

Figure 3.3 shows the Reliability Monitor on a system with a calculated stability index of 7.82. For a long period of time, the graph shows a stability index of 10 (the maximum). Then some software was installed, and a couple of application failures were encountered. These events brought down the stability index. After the second failure, the system was relatively stable, and the stability index began to creep back up.

FIGURE 3.3   The Reliability Monitor

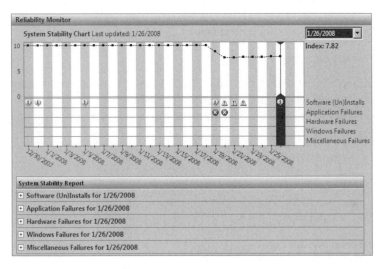

The icons in the chart are just like icons in Event Viewer (information, warning, error, and critical). You can double-click any of the icons in the System Stability Chart area to display the text of the event below the chart.

Data for the Reliability Monitor is provided by the RACAgent scheduled task. You won't find this documented anywhere (except here), but think of the RACAgent as the **R**eliability **A**nalysis **C**ollector **Agent**.

The RACAgent runs as a scheduled task by default, but if it has been disabled, you can enable it by accessing the Task Scheduler (type **taskschd.msc** at the Run line). Within the Task Scheduler, browse to Microsoft ➢ Windows ➢ RAC Container.

The RACAgent is a hidden task. To view it, you need to select View ➢ Show Hidden Tasks from the Actions pane on the right side of the Task Scheduler.

The Reliability Monitor defaults to the local system, but you can also configure it to view a remote computer. To do so, you must first enable the Remote Registry service. Once the service is enabled, you can then connect to a remote computer using the Reliability Monitor.

Exercise 3.1 shows the steps to enable the Remote Registry service and connect to a remote computer using the Reliability Monitor.

EXERCISE 3.1

Configuring Your System to Remotely Monitor a Server Using Reliability Monitor

1. Access the Run line by clicking Start ➢ Run. Enter `Services.msc` to launch the Services applet. Alternately, you can select Start ➢ Administrator Tools ➢ Services.

2. In the Services applet, browse to the Remote Registry service. Double-click the service to view the properties.

3. If the startup type is set to Disabled, change it to Manual or Automatic. When set to Automatic, the service will start automatically when Windows starts. When set to Manual, the service can be started by right-clicking the service and selecting Start within the Services applet or by clicking the Start button in the service properties.

4. If the service is not started, click the Start button. Click OK in the Remote Registry Properties page.

5. Launch the Reliability Monitor by entering `perfmon` at the Run line. Alternately, you can click Start ➢ Administrator Tools ➢ Reliability and Performance Monitor.

6. Right-click Reliability and Performance Monitor in the left pane, and select Connect to Another Computer, as shown in the following graphic.

7. Enter the name of the Remote Computer you want to monitor, and click OK.

   If you click Browse to connect to a remote computer, it uses Network Discovery to identify available remote computers. Depending on the tool you are using, clicking Browse may instead allow you to search Active Directory. As an example, the Services applet would launch the Active Directory search tool when the Browse button is clicked on a computer that is a member of a domain. Both methods allow you to enter the name of the computer directly and bypass the Browse button.

Data Collector Sets

Data dollector sets are groups of predetermined metrics that you can use to measure the performance of a system. After the data collector set is started and run, a report is available that shows the results.

You can collect three types of data in a data collector set:

Performance counters   Performance counters are used to measure system activity or the state of the system. For example, the % Processor Time counter (of the Processor object) can be used to measure the activity of the processor. The Free Megabytes counter (of the Logical Disk object) can be used to report the state of any partition in terms of how much free space is available. Most performance counters are available from the initial installation of the operating system, but as different roles and applications are added, additional counters are available. For example, Microsoft SQL Server adds counters to measure the performance of SQL Server.

Event trace data   Trace providers are built into the system (and some applications) to report when specific actions or events occur. Data collected from trace providers are combined into a trace session such as the Kernel Trace used by Resource View, which shows activity from the CPU, memory, disk, and network.

Configuration information   Configuration information is used to keep track of values of specific registry keys. Values are recorded at specific times or intervals.

Several data collector set templates are available when Server 2008 is installed. These templates can be run as they are or can be used to create user-defined data collector sets. The available templates are as follows:

Active Directory Diagnostics   This template collects Active Directory–related data that can be used to troubleshoot Active Directory performance issues. It includes registry keys, performance counters, and trace events. It is useful only when run on a server running one of the Active Directory roles.

Basic   The Basic template provides very few metrics but instead can be used to create your own template. This template includes a performance counter (measuring only the Processor object), the Kernel Trace (to show CPU, memory, disk, and network activity), and configuration information from the HKLM\Software\Microsoft\Windows NT\ CurrentVersion registry key.

System Diagnostics   The System Diagnostics template details the status of local hardware resources, system response times, and processes. The resulting report includes suggestions for ways to maximize performance and streamline system operation.

System Performance   The System Performance template provides you with a report detailing the status of local hardware resources, system response times, and processes on the local computer. It is useful when trying to identify possible cases of performance issues on a system.

Exercise 3.2 will show you how to run and view a System Performance data collector set.

Running a Data Collector Set

1. Launch the Reliability and Performance Monitor by clicking Start ➢ Administrative Tools ➢ Reliability and Performance Monitor. Alternatively, you can enter **perfmon** at the Run line.

2. Open Data Collector Sets ➢ System by either pressing the + or double-clicking each container.

3. Right-click System Performance Data Collector Set, and click Start.

   This starts the data collector set and runs it for 60 seconds, the default time length for this data collector set. You can tell the data collector set is running by the green arrow over the Data Collector Set icon. When the green arrow disappears, the data collector set has stopped.

4. After the data collector set has run, right-click it, and select Latest Report.

   If you try to view the report before it has completed, the report status will indicate the report is collecting data. Once it has completed, the report will automatically appear.

5. The System Performance report will appear in the right pane, and the report will also be selected in the left pane. The report will include summary data and diagnostics results on the CPU, Network, Disk, and Memory resources.

Although the data available from the report in the previous exercise is valuable, it shows the results for only a 60-second period. You may want to run the data collector set for a longer period of time. It's not possible to modify the system data collector set templates directly, but it is possible to create your own user-defined data collector sets from a template and modify the properties as desired.

For example, you may want to create a baseline of data for a server that you are tasked with maintaining.

A *performance baseline* is collected for a prolonged period of time (perhaps a week), with snapshots of the data taken further apart. Instead of measuring the data every second of the day, it's possible to take snapshots of the data every 30 minutes.

With a baseline collected, you now have a record of how the server was performing at a given time. Later, you can measure the performance of the server and compare it the baseline to determine whether there are any changes.

One of the uses of a baseline is to measure the performance before and after an upgrade. Imagine that you're getting ready to add a popular highly interactive website to an existing Internet Information Services (IIS) server. By creating a baseline before and after the addition, you can quantify the impact of this website addition on the overall server.

You can also do trending analysis with baselines. This goes back to an age-old question: "When do you want to know about a problem?"

The common answer: "Before it's actually a problem."

In other words, if you regularly monitor a server, you can identify trends (such as an increase in paging or a steady increase in CPU utilization). Although this increased usage doesn't degrade the performance of the system today, it may help you prevent a problem in the future.

You can identify the trend and take steps to prevent it from becoming a problem.

Real World Scenario

Trend Analysis with a Baseline

Not too long ago, I was brought into a company, and among other assignments I was managing a SQL Server machine. One of the first things I did was create a baseline on the SQL Server machine. It didn't show much because I didn't have any past data against which to compare the baseline data.

As time went on, I began to notice that the CPU utilization and the pages per second (measuring memory) counters were steadily increasing. The business was growing, and it was putting an increased load on the server.

The system had 3GB of RAM, but with the increased paging, I quickly realized it simply needed more. I was able to run some additional tests on memory utilization that proved my theory. I needed to purchase 1GB of RAM now and needed to budget for a 64-bit SQL Server in the future to get around the 4GB RAM limit of a 32-bit system.

Armed with quantifiable evidence, I was easily able to convince management of the need. I stated the following:

- Paging had increased by more than 50 percent in a four-month time frame.

- CPU and disk utilization increased by more than 10 and 25 percent, respectively, in the same time frame.

- At the current rate of growth on the database (associated with business growth), I expected the server to substantially slow down and possibly experience system crashes in the next six months without maxing the memory at 4GB.

- Further, if business continued to grow at the same rate, this server would not have been able to handle the load with only 4GB of RAM. A server with a 64-bit operating system was needed to support more RAM.

The immediate purchase of the RAM was approved, and a 64-bit server was added to the budget.

Without the quantifiable evidence, things wouldn't have gone so smoothly. Walking into management and saying you need some money to buy some RAM now and want another $10,000 to purchase a powerful server tomorrow on a hunch isn't likely to win you any support.

Even if you're correct, you need to be able to show it. Creating a baseline for trend analysis will help you show others you know what you're talking about.

Exercise 3.3 shows you how you can create a user-defined data collector set from a system template. Once the data collector set is created, you'll modify the properties so that it can be run to create a baseline.

Creating a Data Collector Set from a Template

1. Launch the Reliability and Performance Monitor by clicking Start ≻ Administrative Tools ≻ Reliability and Performance Monitor. Alternatively, you can enter **perfmon** at the Run line.

2. Open Data Collector Sets ≻ User Defined by either pressing the + or double-clicking each container.

3. Right-click User Defined Data Collector Set, and select New ≻ Data Collector Set.

4. Enter **Baseline** as the name. Ensure Create from a Template (Recommended) is selected. Click Next.

5. On the Template Data Collect Set page, select System Performance, and click Next.

6. On the Root Directory page, accept the default (`%systemdrive%\Perflogs\Admin\ Baseline`), and click Next.

   Note that system variables are identified with leading and trailing percent symbols. The `%systemdrive%` variable indicates the drive where the operating system was installed. For example, if Windows was installed on the C:\ drive, entering **%system-drive%** is the equivalent of entering **C:**. You can view this by going to the command line, changing to a different drive (such as D: by entering `D:` and pressing Enter), and then entering `%systemdrive%` and seeing that the prompt returns to C: (assuming the operating system was installed on C:).

7. On the Run As page, ensure that Save and Close is selected, and click Finish.

8. Right-click Baseline User Defined Data Collector Set, and select Properties.

   The description and keywords were entered in the System Performance template, but you can modify them here as desired. For example, you could enter **Baseline created before migration of Sales SQL Server database onto this server**.

9. Click the Directory tab.

   Your display will look similar to the following graphic. If you want to change the name or the location of the data collector set, you can do so here. The subdirectory name format shows a default yyyyMMdd\-NNNN for year, month, day, and a four-digit serial number. You can customize the subdirectory name format by clicking the > button and building the name from all the available options. You can also include the computer name in the subdirectory by selecting Prefix Subdirectory with Computer Name.

Baseline Properties   ☒

General | Directory | Security | Schedule | Stop Condition | Task |

Root directory:

%systemdrive%\PerfLogs\Admin\Baseline   Browse...

Subdirectory:

Subdirectory name format:

yyyyMMdd\-NNNN   >

☐ Prefix subdirectory with computer name

Serial number:

1   ⏶⏷

Example directory:

C:\PerfLogs\Admin\Baseline\20080127-0001

OK   Cancel   Apply   Help

10. Click the Security tab. You can change the permissions of the data collector set here. Members of the Administrators group have permissions to create, modify, and run data collector sets. Members of the Performance Log Users group can view the Performance Monitor and can create and modify data collector set when assigned the Log On as a Batch User right.

11. Click the Schedule tab. Click the Add button to add a schedule.

12. Set the beginning date to the next Sunday. For example, if today is Monday September 1, 2008, the next Sunday would be September 7.

13. Click the Expiration Date box. Change the expiration date for the Saturday seven days after the Sunday you selected. Under Launch, accept the default start time of 12:00:00 AM. Deselect all the days except Sunday.

14. Click the Stop Condition tab. Ensure the Overall Duration box is selected. Leave the duration at 1, but change Units to Weeks. Select the Stop When All Data Collectors Have Finished box.

This will allow the data collector set to run for a full week.

15. Click OK to save your baseline data collector set.

16. With the baseline data collector set selected, you'll see the NT kernel and the performance counter objects that have been added (as a part of the System Performance template). Right-click Performance Counter, and select Properties.

The performance counters that are part of the System Performance template are set to sample every second. Although this is useful if you are measuring just 60 seconds of performance data, it is overkill if you are measuring performance for a weeklong baseline. When capturing data for a period of time, it's common to change the sample interval to something less frequent. For example, for a weeklong baseline, sampling the counters every 30 minutes will give you a good enough sample to accurately assess the performance of the server.

17. With the Performance Counter Properties dialog box displayed, change the sample interval to 30 and the units to minutes. Your display will look similar to the following graphic.

    At this point, your baseline data collector set is created and ready to launch and run for seven days. Click OK.

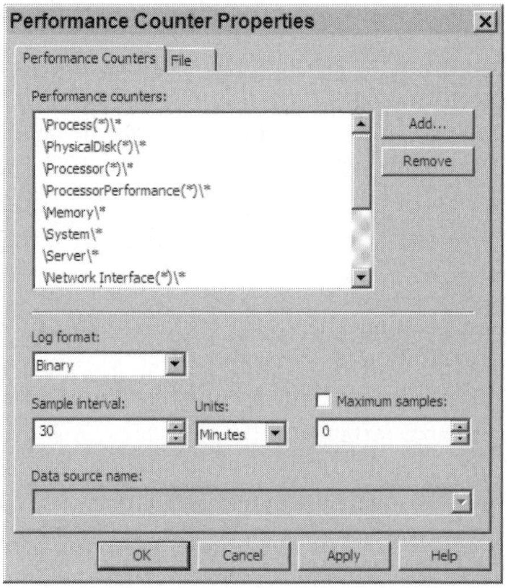

18. You can also create a template from your baseline data collector set. Right-click Baseline, and select Save Template.

19. In the Save As box, browse to where you want to save your template, enter **Baseline-Template** as the name, and click Save.

    You can now use this template just as you'd use a system template. The only difference is that your template won't appear automatically when you create a new data collector set. You must browse to where you saved the template file.

The previous exercise helps show one of the primary differences between the system data collector sets (the templates) and user-defined data collector sets. Specifically, while you can modify the properties of a user-defined data collector set, you cannot modify the properties of the system templates.

Reports: Viewing the Output of Data Collector Sets

Once you run any of the data collector sets, you can then view the results in a report. If a data collector set has never been run, a report won't be available.

Figure 3.4 shows a sample report. It starts with basics on the report such as which computer, when the report was run, and how long data was collected. The Summary section provides an overview of the collected data. The Diagnostic Results section shows details on findings.

FIGURE 3.4   Viewing a sample report

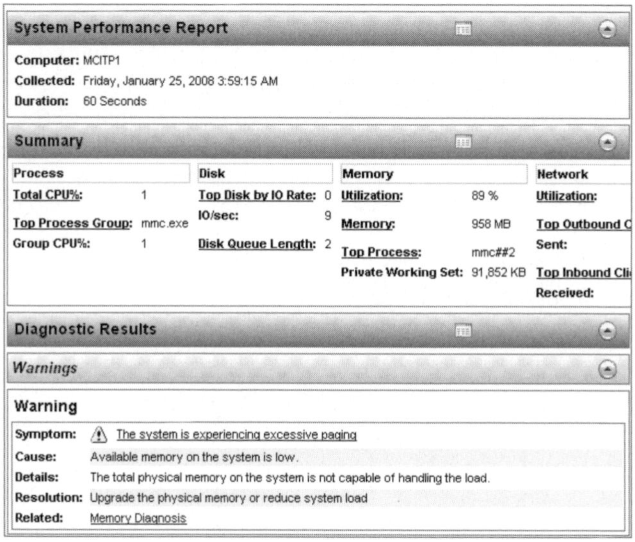

Notice that in Figure 3.4, the diagnostics recognized that excessive paging was occurring. It even gives a cause (available memory is low) and a resolution (upgrade the physical memory or reduce system load).

Figure 3.5 shows the Resource Overview section from the same report. It shows the status with colored icons. Although it can't be seen in the black-and-white figure, the icon for Memory is red, and it jumps out as something to investigate. The data shown in the Resource Overview section is derived from the trace provider Kernel Trace.

Of course, 89 percent utilization jumps out as a possible problem too. In general, anything more than 80 percent in the utilization is something to investigate. It may not be a problem today, but it certainly is a strong indicator that it may be a problem tomorrow.

FIGURE 3.5 Viewing the Resource Overview section in a report

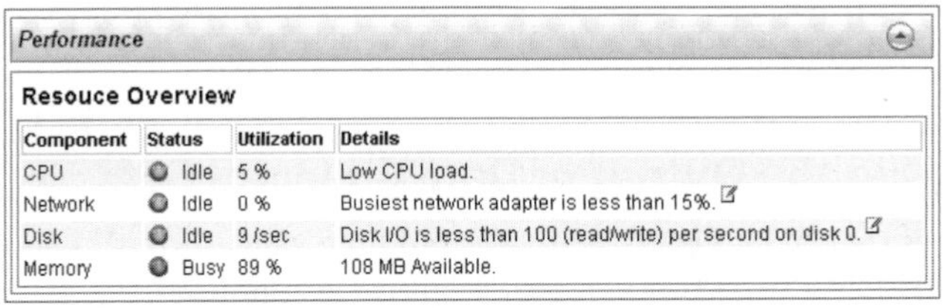

Performance

Resouce Overview

Component	Status	Utilization	Details
CPU	Idle	5 %	Low CPU load.
Network	Idle	0 %	Busiest network adapter is less than 15%.
Disk	Idle	9 /sec	Disk I/O is less than 100 (read/write) per second on disk 0.
Memory	Busy	89 %	108 MB Available.

Depending on much monitoring you do, reports can take up a lot of space. You can enable the automatic deletion of reports by right-clicking any data collector set and selecting Data Manager.

The Data Manager has three tabs:

Data Manager You can use the Data Manager tab to specify a data retention policy for your reports.

As defined in Figure 3.6, reports will be deleted when the free disk space falls to less than 200MB or the folders exceed 100. You can choose to delete the largest reports or delete the oldest reports when either of these conditions exists. To disable either of the conditions, either deselect the check box or set the condition value to 0.

FIGURE 3.6 Report's Data Manager tab for a data collector set named MCITP2

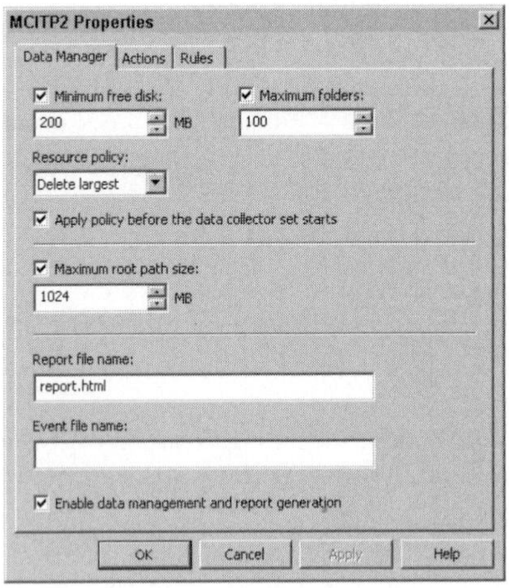

Within each report folder, an HTML file is available that can be selected directly. By default, the report name is `report.html`, but you can change this filename here.

Deselecting the Enable Data Management and Report Generation check box will prevent the `report.html` file from being created. If deselected, only the Performance Monitor data will be displayed when the report is selected from the Reports section of the Reliability and Performance Monitoring tool.

Actions   You can use the Actions tab to identify how data is archived before it is actually deleted.

For example, Figure 3.7 shows the Actions tab with an archive plan. After four weeks, a report is archived (compressed in a cabinet, or `.cab`, file), and the report data is deleted. The report can still be retrieved from the `.cab` file at this point or from the `report.html` file. Only the raw report data is deleted.

FIGURE 3.7   Report's Actions tab for MCITP2 data collector set

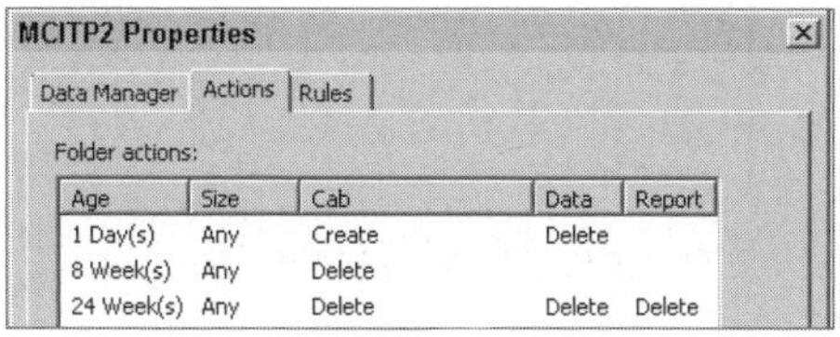

At eight weeks, the cabinet file is deleted. At this point, the data can still be viewed from the `report.html` file.

The last step of this archive plan deletes the report (`report.html`), and if somehow the cabinet file and the report data were still left over, it deletes them also.

Rules   Rules are XML files that define the Data Manager properties of the data collector set. The Rules tab lists all the rules that have been imported into the Data Manager and also can be used to export XML files.

Event Viewer

Event Viewer allows you to view events on the local system or remote computers and manage responses to those events.

Figure 3.8 shows Event Viewer in Windows Server 2008. If you used Event Viewer in past versions of Windows, you'll quickly notice that this ain't your daddy's Event Viewer. A lot of things are going on here.

Individual event logs can be selected from the left pane of Event Viewer. Of particular importance for the 70-646 exam are the subscriptions, which I'll cover in more depth later in this section.

Events and event details from the selected log appear in the middle pane.

The right pane has specific actions and properties associated with the selected log, or *log event*. A new and exciting feature is the ability to attach tasks to specific events. I'll cover this later in this section; you'll want to know about it for the 70-646 exam.

The logs are grouped together in different categories:

Custom Views   Custom Views contains logs that have been filtered. By filtering a log, you can focus the output to show only what you want to see.

FIGURE 3.8   Event Viewer

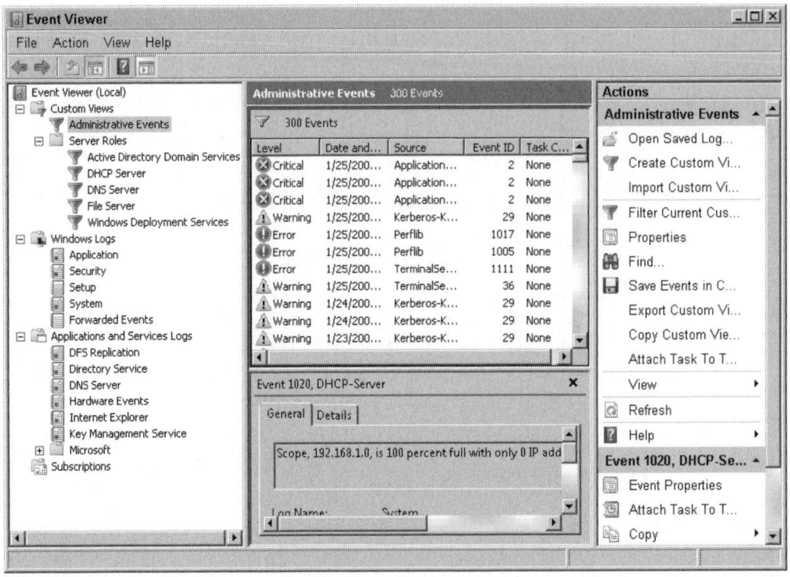

Administrative Events displays critical, warning, and error events from several different logs. The actual logs displayed differ depending on the roles that the server is filling. For example, a DNS server would include the DNS Server log.

Additional custom view logs can be created and added as desired.

Custom Views also includes the Server Roles logs. Any time a server role is added, a custom view is added to show data associated with that role. In Figure 3.8, you can see that the server is running Active Directory Domain Services, DHCP, DNS, and Windows Deployment Services, and it is configured as a file server.

Windows Logs   The Windows Logs category contains mostly the traditional Event Viewer logs. The Application log is designed to accept log entries from server applications (such as SQL Server or Exchange Server). The Security log logs security-related data such as success and failure audit entries. The Setup log is new and logs events related to application installations. System is used to log operating system and hardware-related events.

Applications and Services Logs   Applications and Services Logs stores events from a single application or component such as DFS replication or DNS. Events in these logs are focused on the topic rather than events that might have system-wide impact.

Subscriptions   Event subscriptions allow you to subscribe to events from other servers. When a subscription is created, the remote server will forward all the subscribed events to the server acting as a subscriber.

You should know the details of this topic (which we'll cover later in this section) thoroughly when preparing for the 70-646 exam.

Event Viewer supports several classification or severity levels associated with any event. The Information, Warning, Error, and Critical severity levels are available in all except the Security log. The Success and Failure audit events are found only in the Security log.

Information   As the name implies, this is just general information to indicate something has occurred. It could be as simple as logging that an operation successfully completed or that a service has started.

For example, on system startup, the event "The Event log service was started" would be logged after the log is initialized. It is displayed as a blue lowercase *i* in a white background.

Warning   This indicates that some type of issue has occurred that may result in a more serious problem if it is not addressed.

For example, if the PDC Emulator is not configured to sync with an external time source, you will receive a time-service warning indicating as much. It is displayed as a black exclamation mark (!) in a yellow triangle.

Error   This indicates a problem has occurred. The problem could impact functionality that is external to the application or component that caused the event. For example, when processing Group Policy, if a domain controller can't be located, the event will be logged as error with a suggestion to check DNS. It is displayed as a white exclamation mark (!) in a red circle.

Critical   This indicates a failure has occurred and the application or component cannot automatically recover. This is the most serious event. For example, if you're trying to install a software application that has a known incompatibility issue, the installation will fail, and the event will be logged as a critical event. It is displayed as a white *x* in a red circle.

Success Audit   This indicates that a user has successfully executed a user right. For example, a user who is granted access to the `project.doc` file opens the `project.doc` file. If audited, it will be logged as a Success Audit event.

Failure Audit   This indicates that a user has tried to execute a user right that she didn't have and failed. For example, a user who is not granted delete permission for the `project.doc` file tries to delete the file, and the deletion fails. If audited, the attempt would be logged as a Failure Audit event. The Failure Audit event is only in the Security log.

Event Subscriptions

A significant addition to Event Viewer in Windows Server 2008 is the *event subscriptions* functionality, or the ability to centrally manage events for remote computers.

Using event subscriptions, you can configure a central computer (referred to as the *collector*) to receive events from other computers (referred to as the *source*). Figure 3.9 shows the big picture of how a single collector computer could be configured to accept events from several other computers.

The primary prerequisite to create and configure subscriptions is that the Windows Event Collector service must be running and properly configured on the computer collecting the events. This service is running by default. To configure it to accept events, run the Windows Event Collector utility from the command line:

```
Wecutil qc
```

FIGURE 3.9   Event subscriptions

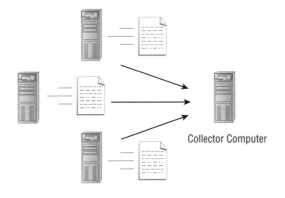

Collector Computer

Source Computers

To configure computers to forward events, you must run the following Windows Remote Management command-line tool (WinRM) on each of the computers that will forward events.

WinRM quickconfig

You have a lot of flexibility when configuring subscriptions. You can configure the subscription to include all the events from the source computer or only a select group of events. You can have the subscribed events stored in a special log called Forwarded Events, or you can merge them with other event logs on the collector computer.

Two types of event subscriptions are supported: collector initiated and source computer initiated.

Collector initiated   A collector-initiated subscription can be thought of as a pull subscription. In other words, the computer that is collecting the events periodically contacts the source computer and pulls the events off the source computer.

Collector-initiated subscriptions use the Normal delivery method. The Normal delivery method ensures the reliable delivery of events without trying to conserve bandwidth. The batch timeout is 15 minutes.

A batch timeout indicates the maximum amount of time between sending batches of events. For example, the Normal delivery mode sends batches of 5 events and uses a batch timeout of 15 minutes. This means that if fewer than 5 events occur within 15 minutes of the last batch being sent, the events will be still be sent after 15 minutes pass. If more than 5 events occur, they will be sent immediately (without waiting for the full 15 minutes to pass). The Minimize Bandwidth delivery mode will send events at least every 6 hours. The Minimize Latency delivery mode will send events at least every 30 seconds.

Source computer initiated   A source computer–initiated subscription can be thought of as a push subscription. The source computer periodically pushes the events to the collector.

Two delivery methods can be selected when using a source computer–initiated subscription. The Minimize Bandwidth delivery method limits the frequency of network connections and has a batch timeout of six hours. The Minimize Latency delivery method ensures that events are delivered within 30 seconds of the event occurrence (a batch timeout of 30 seconds).

You can view and modify the number of items in a batch by using the Windows Remote Management command-line tool (WinRM). WinRM is run from the standard command line.

To view the current value of items in a batch, use the following get command and observe the value of MaxBatchItems. Note that there are not any spaces within winrm/config.

```
WinRM get winrm/config
```

If you want to modify the value of the maximum batch items to a value of 10, you can use the following set command. Beware! The MaxBatchItems variable must be entered using the same case as shown here. You can substitute the value of 10 for any number desired.

```
WinRM set winrm/config @{MaxBatchItems="10"}
```

Exercise 3.4 shows you how you can configure computers within a domain to forward and collect events. Again, the computer that will send the events to the central computer is referred to as the *source computer*; the computer that will collect the events is referred to as the *collector*.

EXERCISE 3.4

Configuring Subscriptions

1. Log on to the source computer using an account that has administrative privileges. I am using MCITP2 as my source computer throughout this exercise.

2. Launch the command prompt by pressing Windows logo key+R, entering **cmd**, and then pressing the Enter key. The Windows logo key is to the left of the spacebar between the ALT and CTRL keys on most keyboards.

3. At the command prompt, enter the following command:

    ```
    WinRM quickconfig
    ```

4. When prompted to make these changes, press Y and then Enter.

    If you plan on configuring a pull subscription so that you can specify a delivery mode of Minimize Bandwidth or Minimize Latency, you must also run the WinRM quickconfig command on the collector computer.

5. Log on to the collector computer using an account that has administrative privileges. My collector computer is MCITP1 throughout this exercise.

6. Launch the command prompt by pressing Windows logo key+R, entering **cmd**, and then pressing the Enter key.

7. At the command prompt, enter the following command:

Wecutil qc

8. When prompted to proceed, press Y and then Enter.

9. Still at the collector computer, launch Event Viewer by clicking Start ➤ Administrative Tools ➤ Event Viewer.

10. Right-click Subscriptions, and select Create Subscription.

11. In the Subscription Properties box, enter **MCITP2 Events**, as shown in the following graphic. (You could enter the name of your source computer instead of MCITP2.) You can also access this properties dialog box after the subscription is created.

12. Accept the default destination log of Forwarded Events.

13. In the Subscription Type and Source Computers section, click Select Computers.

14. In the Computers dialog box, click the Add Domain Computers button.

15. In the Select Computer dialog box, enter the name of the computer you configured as the source computer. I am using the computer named MCITP2. Click OK.

16. In the Computers dialog box, verify your computer is identified with the fully qualified name. For example, my source computer (MCITP2) is identified as MCITP2 .mcitpsuccess.hme since it is in the domain of mcitpsuccess.hme.

17. Click Test. A dialog box should appear indicating the connectivity test succeeded. Click OK in the test dialog box, and click OK again in the Computers dialog box.

If this test fails, verify the source computer is accessible on your network and it has been configured with the `WinRM quickconfig` command.

18. Click the Select Events button.

19. Click the check boxes next to Critical, Warning, and Error. Verify By Log is selected, and click the drop-down arrow to the right of the Event Logs field. In the drop-down, check the Windows Logs box. Click OK.

This will cause all the events for all the Windows logs to be selected.

20. Click the Advanced button.

21. In the Advanced Subscription Settings dialog box, select specify user. Click the User and Password button. Enter the name of a user account with administrative permissions in the format of domain\user. Enter the user's password. Click OK in the credentials dialog box. Click OK in the Advanced Subscription Settings box.

22. In the Subscription Properties dialog box, click OK.

This will create the MCITP2 events subscription to be created.

23. Select the Forwarded Events log. You won't see events in the log immediately, but after as long as 15 minutes, you can refresh the display, and you will see events begin to appear. The following graphic shows events that have come from the server named MCITP2.

Event Tasks

Another new feature available in Windows Server 2008 is the ability to configure event
tasks. This allows you to configure your system to perform something specific in response
to specific events.

The simplest way to attach a task to an event is by right-clicking the event in Event
Viewer and selecting Attach Task to This Event, as shown in Figure 3.10. This will launch
the Create a Basic Task Wizard.

FIGURE 3.10   Attaching a task to an event

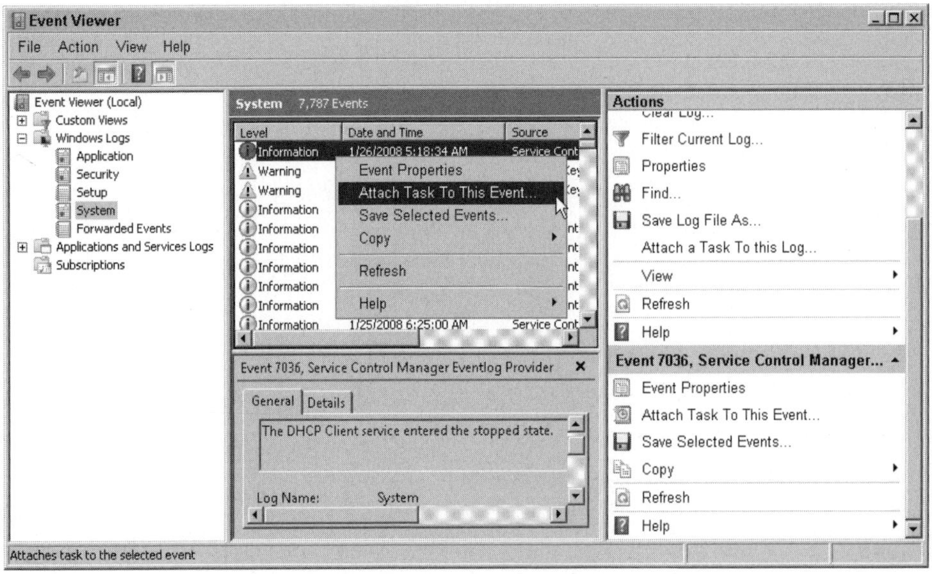

You can also attach a task by using the Actions pane located on the right. Two links are
available: Attach a Task to This Log and Attach Task to This Event.

Once created, tasks are added to the Task Scheduler. To view or modify the properties of
any task, launch the Task Scheduler (Start ➢ Administrative Tools ➢ Task Scheduler), and
select Event Viewer Tasks.

Three actions are possible when attaching tasks:

Start a program   Any executable program can be launched from here in response to the
event. This includes compiled programs (such as those with an `.exe` or `.com` extension),
batch files (`.bat`), and scripts (such as `.vbs`).

Send an email   Using the Send an Email option, you can forward an email to any SMTP
server, which will then send it to the email address identified in the To section. The email page
allows you to add a From address, a To address, a subject, the text of your email, attachments,
and the name of the SMTP server.

Display a message By selecting Display a Message, you can add the title and text of a message box that will appear when the event is triggered.

Exercise 3.5 shows you how you can schedule a task to respond when a service stops or starts. Although you can schedule a task for any event, stopping or starting a service is an event that is easy to re-create. Once configured, you will stop the service and verify your task has completed.

EXERCISE 3.5

Configuring an Event Task to Respond to an Event

1. Launch the Services applet. Select Start ➢ Administrative Tools ➢ Services.

2. Browse to the DHCP Client service.

3. Right-click the DHCP Client service, and select Stop. Leave the Services applet open.

4. Launch the Event Viewer. Select Start ➢ Administrative Tools ➢ Event Viewer.

5. Select the System log. If the System log was already selected, right-click the System log, and select Refresh.

6. Find the system event with an event ID of 7036.

   Event ID 7036 reports the stopping and starting of any service. Although this exercise focuses on the DHCP service, the event will respond with any services stopping or starting. After the event is created with the wizard, the trigger of the event can be fine-tuned to meet just about any need (such as fire only when a specific service stops, instead of when any service stops or starts).

7. Right-click the event with an event ID of 7036, and select Attach Task to This Event.

8. On the Create a Basic Task page, enter **Monitors the starting and stopping of any service** in the Description box. Click Next.

9. On the When an Event Is Logged page, review the information. Note that this information *cannot* be changed through the wizard but can be changed later by manipulating the properties of the event task. Click Next.

10. On the Action page, select Display a Message, and click Next.

11. On the Display a Message page, enter **You said you wanted to know...** in the title box. In the Message box, enter **A service has stopped or started**. Click Next.

12. Your display will look similar to the following graphic. Click Finish to create the task.

13. In the Event Viewer dialog box informing you the task has been created, click OK.

14. Return to the Services applet. Right-click the DHCP Client service, and click Start. A dialog box will appear with the title and text you specified in this exercise. The message box may not appear on top of other windows. However, if you look at the taskbar, you'll see an instance of your message box there.

While the previous exercise shows the process of displaying a message box in response to an event, don't think that's all you can do. You can get much more sophisticated in your tasks than just displaying a message box. By selecting Run a Program, you can execute a complex script that launches other programs, sends emails, and displays message boxes.

After you've completed a task, you can view and manipulate the task's properties through the Task Scheduler. To launch the Task Scheduler, select Start ➢ Administrative Tools ➢ Task Scheduler.

Task properties are shown in a smaller pane in the Task Scheduler, but you can also view them by right-clicking the task and selecting Properties. The properties of any task include six tabs.

Figure 3.11 shows the properties of a task. In the figure, the General tab is selected; it displays general properties. By selecting other tabs, you can view and manipulate other properties.

General   The General tab shows the name and description of the task and the name of the account that was used to create it.

FIGURE 3.11   Task properties

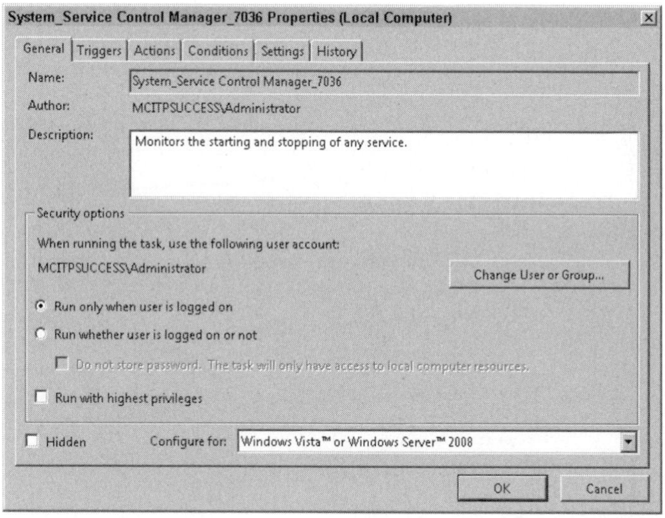

Using the Security Options section, you can change the context of how the task is run. Tasks generally need to run under the context of an account with administrator privileges. Although this task was originally created with the administrator account, you may want to change it to a service account.

The Run with Highest Privileges check box is related to User Account Control (UAC). If checked, the UAC elevated permissions will be used to run the task. If not checked, the UAC least privileges token will be used. If the task is set to run with an account in the Administrators group, ensure this box is checked.

Triggers   The Triggers tab identifies what will cause this task to run and how the task will run once it's fired. Figure 3.12 shows the Edit Trigger screen that appears when you select a trigger and click the Edit button on the Triggers tab.

By editing the trigger, you can modify the event to fire based on a different log, different source, and different event ID. Using the Custom setting, you can get pretty specific about exactly what event you're interested in and even modify the task so that it responds to multiple tasks. For example, if you want to modify a task to run any time any critical event was logged in the Forwarded Events log, you could do so on the Triggers tab.

The advanced settings allow you to modify how the task is executed. This includes delaying the execution of the task, repeating the task, stopping task after a period of time, setting activate and expiration dates, and even enabling or disabling the task.

Actions   The Actions tab defines what the event does once the trigger fires. By selecting the action and clicking Edit, you can modify what the trigger does. You may have originally had it display a message. You can use this screen to modify what the message says or change it to execute a program or send an email.

FIGURE 3.12 Modifying the task trigger

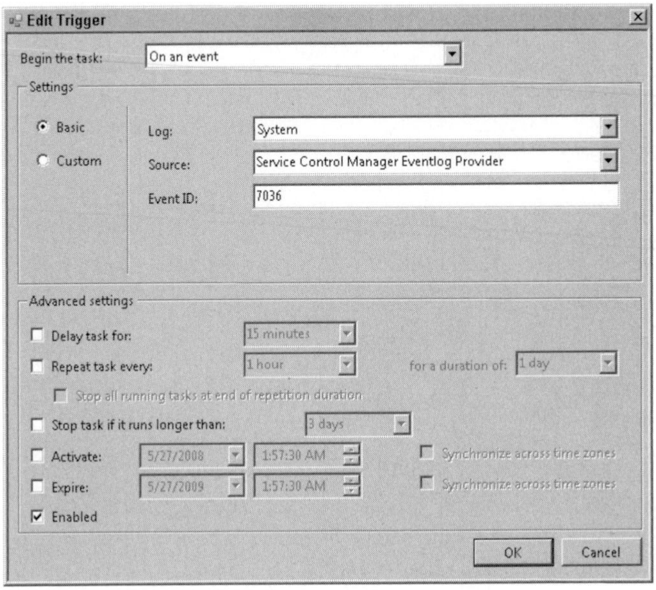

For example, when the task executes, you may want it to copy a directory tree. You can use the robocopy (Robust File Copy) command to copy a directory tree to a directory of your choice, the cscript command to execute a script, the NET command to start or stop a service, the defrag command defragment a hard drive, or just about any other program you can run normally.

Conditions The Conditions tab allows you to limit the execution of task. In other words, once the trigger fires, the conditions are examined, and as long as all the conditions are met, the task will execute. If the conditions are not met, the task will not execute (even though the trigger fired).

Figure 3.13 shows the default settings for the Conditions tab. Three categories of conditions can be selected: Idle, Power, and Network.

Settings The Settings tab allows you to specify additional settings that affect the behavior of the task such as how it can be started and how it can be stopped.

For example, you can allow the task to be run on demand (manually) and force it to be stopped if the task doesn't stop when requested.

History The History tab shows a history of the event and can be useful when troubleshooting the execution of the event. The history includes when a task is registered, when a task is triggered, when it's told to start, when the action starts, and when the action completes.

For example, you may have expected an email notification when a service was stopped, but the email didn't arrive. There could be several reasons for the failure. Checking the history log, you can verify the task was triggered and observe the results for the action. I entered the name of a nonexistent SMTP server, and the history log showed the action failed. The next step would be to examine the Action tab of the task.

FIGURE 3.13   Modifying the task conditions

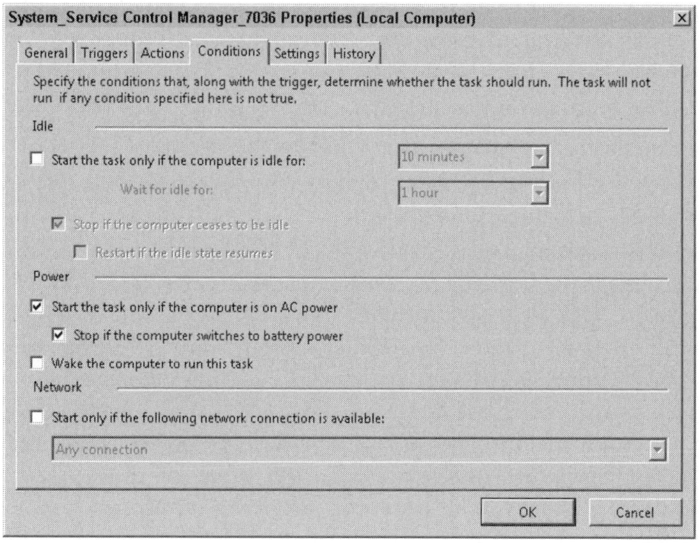

Windows System Resource Manager

The Windows System Resource Manager (WSRM) tool allows administrators to limit the amount of CPU and memory resources that any individual application is using. Additionally, WSRM can be used to manage multiple users on a single computer (such as multiple users accessing a single server using Terminal Services).

In addition to managing the total amount of CPU with WSRM, it's also possible to specify the processor affinity. Processor affinity is used to link a specific process with a specific processor.

For example, you could have a system with four processors and you want to ensure that an application uses only the fourth processor. This can get complex, so using WSRM with processor affinity should be done sparingly.

The following are some of the goals of WSRM:

Ensuring a critical application has enough resources   WSRM can be used to ensure that a single application always has enough resources at its disposal. For example, if you're running IIS as an intranet server and also using the same server as a file and print server, you may want to ensure that IIS always has enough resources.

Preventing an application from consuming excessive resources   WSRM can be used to ensure an application doesn't get greedy and try to consume too many resources. This can be useful when faced with problems such as an application with a memory leak. A memory leak in a faulty application steadily takes more and more memory until no more memory exists. By using WSRM, you can ensure that a memory leak in one application does not take memory from other applications.

Preventing a user from consuming excessive resources   When multiple users are using the same server, such as in a Terminal Services application, users can be prevented from taking more resources than allocated to them. This provides all users with an equal amount of resources.

Identifying a customer's usage   WSRM includes an accounting capability that allows you to identify specifically how many resources any individual user is consuming. Data can be fed into a Microsoft SQL Server database and be used to identify how much users are charged based on usage.

When WSRM senses that a process is exceeding its allocated resources, it first tries to change the resource usage by changing the priority of the process. If this doesn't succeed, than WSRM uses a complex algorithm to adjust the resources that the process can use.

This works similarly to how a governor works on a car. Some taxi companies want to ensure that taxi drivers don't exceed a certain speed, so a governor is installed on the car, preventing the car from exceeding the desired speed.

The difference is that while the governor prevents the car from exceeding the speed, WSRM goes into action after the threshold is exceeded. When a process or user exceeds a given threshold, WSRM takes action to throttle the process or user back to below the threshold.

Resource Allocation Policies

WSRM uses policies to manage resource allocation. The policies are applied to matched processes. In other words, the policies are applied to the specific user or specific applications that are selected by the policy. The basic policies are as follows:

Equal per process   The available CPU bandwidth is divided evenly between all the matched processes. For example, if four processes are included in the policy and the system has 100 percent of the available CPU bandwidth, WSRM will throttle down any process that exceeds 25 percent usage.

Equal per process is the default policy for managing resources. This is also referred to as process-based management.

Equal per user   The available bandwidth used for a given process is divided evenly between users. This is also referred to a user-based management.

For example, consider two users who are both running App1 on the same server and the server has a total of 100 percent of the available CPU bandwidth. If the total bandwidth used by one of the users exceeds 50 percent, then APP1 used by that user will be throttled back so that it doesn't exceed 50 percent.

Equal per session   The available bandwidth used for different users in Terminal Services sessions is divided evenly between the sessions. This also referred to as session-based management.

For example, consider two users who are both running multiple applications on the same server and the server has a total of 100 percent of the available CPU bandwidth. If the total bandwidth used by one of the users exceeds 50 percent, then individual applications by that user will be throttled back so the total doesn't exceed 50 percent.

It's also possible to create your own resource allocation policy to meet specific needs in your environment. For example, if you have a line-of-business application that needs to always have at least 50 percent of the CPU's processing capability, you can create a policy to meet that need.

Adding Windows System Resource Manager

You can add WSRM to your system using the Server Manager tool. Select Add Features, and then select the Windows System Resource Manager feature. You will be prompted to also add the Windows internal database.

After the wizard finishes installing WSRM, you may be prompted to reboot the system.

Once installed, you can access WSRM by selecting Start ➢ Administrative Tools ➢ Windows System Resource Manager. You will be prompted to connect to a computer. You can connect to the local computer or any computer in Active Directory.

Remote Management

It's highly unlikely that you work in the same place as your servers, even when you're working on the server. Instead, as an IT professional, you typically have a desk in a corner office with a beautiful view of the pond....

Well, maybe your desk isn't that glamorous, but it's highly unlikely you do all your work in the server room. The server room is usually much colder to ensure good airflow and reduce heat-related problems. Additionally, server rooms generally have much more physical security than regular office spaces.

But that doesn't mean you have to break out your winter parka each time you need to work on your server. Instead, you use one or more of the available tools that allow you to remotely manage the server.

Accessing the Desktop Remotely

Two tools allow you to access the desktop of the remote computer from somewhere else:

- Remote Desktop Connection (RDC)
- Remote Desktop

The tools have many similarities.

Both use Terminal Services   Terminal Services will be explored in greater depth in Chapter 7, "Planning Terminal Services Servers," but in short, it allows multiple users to access a remote server and run programs on the remote server. Administrators can use Terminal Services to remotely connect to servers for administration purposes, and users can use it to centrally deploy applications. When used for administration, a maximum of three administrators can connect at the same time.

Both allow only two active sessions   Whether you are using Remote Desktop Connection or Remote Desktop, or one of each, only two active sessions are allowed. This includes the console session. In other words, if one user is connected remotely and one user is connected at the server, a third session is not allowed. Similarly, if two users are connected remotely, a third session is not allowed.

For example, if both Sally and Joe connected to Srv2 via Remote Desktop and then you tried to connect to Srv2 via Remote Desktop, you would see a display similar to Figure 3.14. It informs you that too many users are logged on, but it also gives you the ability to disconnect one of the users.

FIGURE 3.14   Too many users logged on

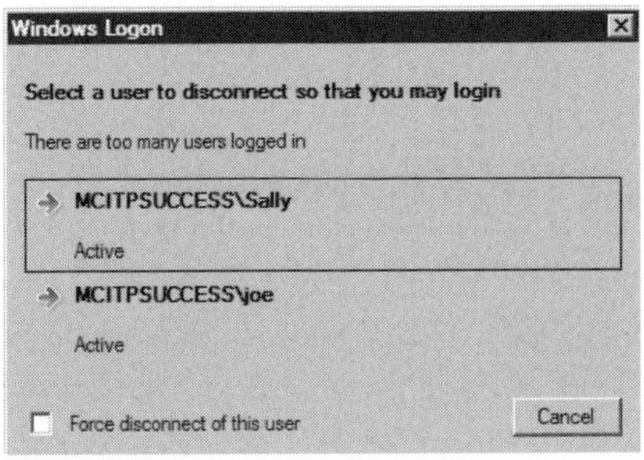

If you select one of the users (such as Joe), Joe will be sent a message saying you are trying to log on. If Joe is active, he can deny your request. However, if he isn't at the computer, the request will time out, Joe will be disconnected, and you will be able to log on.

Only users in the Administrators group will have the ability to force a user to disconnect. If you selected the check box Force Disconnect of This User, Joe would automatically be disconnected without any warning.

There's a slight technicality here. Notice that I'm not saying you can't have three sessions, only that you can't have three *active* sessions. If Joe is disconnected, his session changes from active to disconnected. If Joe logs back in later when an active session is available, Joe's original session will be just as it was when he was disconnected.

Both are enabled via System Properties   To enable Remote Desktop, click Start, right-click Computer, and select Properties. From the System Properties page, click Remote Settings. Figure 3.15 shows the System Properties page accessed from the Computer property page (after clicking Remote Settings).

FIGURE 3.15   Enabling Remote Desktop

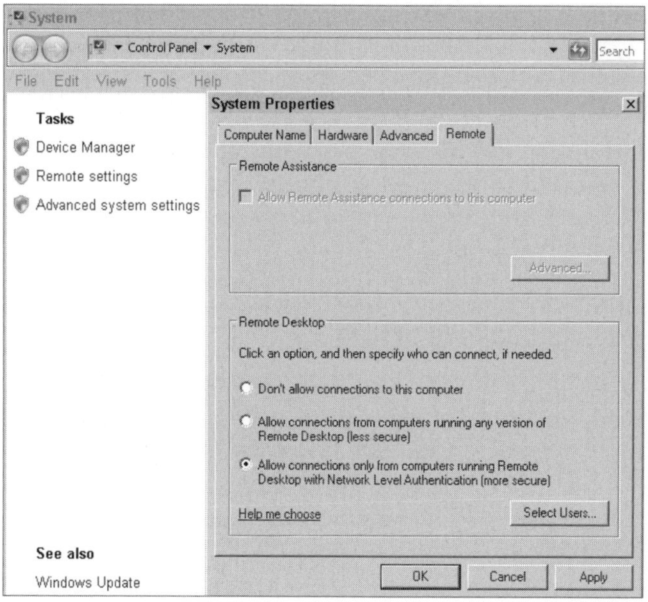

Three choices are available. The default is Don't Allow Connections to This Computer. The legacy setting (allowing versions of Remote Desktop older than Remote Desktop Connection 6.0) is for Windows XP and Windows Server 2003. The most secure setting is Network Level Authentication.

Both have compatibly issues with Windows XP and Server 2003   Security with Remote Desktop has been improved in Windows Server 2008. Network Level Authentication (NLA) is used to authenticate the user, the client machine, and the server before a Terminal Services session is even begun. NLA provides a more secure environment since a session isn't started immediately as it was in previous versions of Remote Desktop.

To support NLA, you must be using at least Windows XP with SP2 or Windows Server 2003 with SP1. With NLA support enabled, you can install the Remote Desktop Client 6.0 Upgrade. The Remote Desktop Client version 6.0 is the default installation for Windows Vista and Windows Server 2008.

> The Terminal Services features that are enabled on Server 2008 and Windows Vista are not available in the RDC client available by default on Windows XP or Windows Server 2003. To enjoy the advanced security features (such as NLA) of RDC 6.0 from Windows XP or Server 2003, you need to download and install the Remote Desktop Connection 6.0 client update. Additionally, Windows XP must have at least SP2, and Windows Server 2003 must have at least SP1 to install the client. Although not recommended, it is possible to configure the server with weakened security, allowing remote connections using the legacy RDC client.

Both have similar permission requirements   Administrators are automatically granted permissions to remotely access a server (as long as Remote Desktop has been enabled on the server). Additional users can be granted permission to access the server using a Remote Desktop connection by adding them to the Remote Desktop Users group.

Remote Desktop Connection

Remote Desktop Connection 6.0 is an application that allows you to connect to a remote computer and access the desktop just as if you were sitting in front of the remote computer.

The term *remote computer* is used loosely. In the classroom, I use RDC all the time to connect to a computer three feet away from me. You could also use it to connect to a computer in the server room three floors above you or even connect to a server at work from your computer at home. Physical distance is irrelevant.

When using Remote Desktop, you can connect to a remote server and do just about anything remotely that you could do locally. I say "just about" because the one big thing to watch out for is if a reboot causes the remote server to power down. Although it's easy to walk three feet to power up a computer, it's not so easy to press the power button on a server that may be located miles away.

To launch Remote Desktop Connection from a Windows Server 2008 computer, select Start ➤ All Programs ➤ Accessories ➤ Remote Desktop Connection. Figure 3.16 shows Remote Desktop Connection being launched.

The Remote Desktop Connection dialog box has six tabs that can be used to modify properties of your connection. The tabs are available when you click the Options button.

General   The General tab shows the computer you will connect to and the username to be used to connect. Once all the connection settings are set as you desire for a specific connection, you can save the connection settings in an RDP file (.rdp) and then use the RDP file the next time you want to connect.

Display   Using the Display tab, you can control the size and colors of the remote desktop. Remote Desktop Connection supports a resolution size of 4096×2048 if you're lucky enough to have a monitor that big.

Local Resources   You have the capability of bringing any resources on your local computer with you in your remote session and playing sounds from the remote computer to your local computer. Resources you can bring with you to the remote session include printers, the clipboard, smart cards, serial ports, drives, and any plug-and-play devices you may add to your local system.

FIGURE 3.16   Remote Desktop Connection

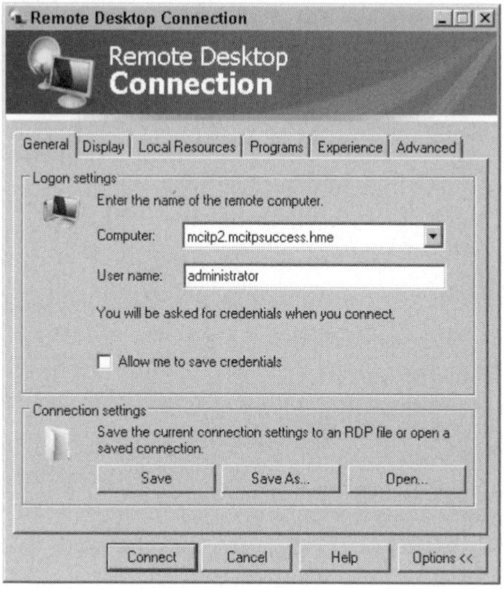

Figure 3.17 shows the choices available from the Local Resources tab. By clicking the More button, you can also include smart cards, serial ports, drives, and supported plug-and-play devices.

FIGURE 3.17   Remote Desktop Connection's Local Resources tab

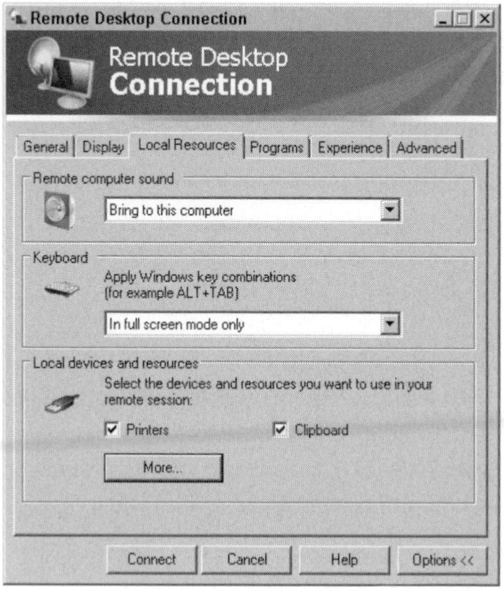

Additionally, you can identify how Windows key combinations will be interpreted. For example, when you press Ctrl+Alt+Esc, Task Manager is launched. You can select whether Task Manager will be launched on the local computer, the remote computer, or the remote computer only when you are in full-screen mode.

Programs   RDC allows you to start a program as soon as you connect. Once you select the check box to start the program, you can then give the path and filename of the program and the starting path for the application. For example, Word starts in My Documents, but you may want it to start in d:\WordDocs instead.

Experience   The user experience is directly related to the connection speed. For a LAN connection (10Mbps), you can afford to send a lot of data back and forth to enhance the user experience. However, for a modem connection of 56.6Kbps, you may want to minimize the data sent over the connection.

All of the following user experience options can be selected or deselected: Desktop Background, Font Smoothing, Desktop Composition, Show Contents of Window While Dragging, Menu and Window Animation, Themes, and Bitmap Caching. All the options are selected by default for a LAN connection.

Advanced   The Advanced tab allows you to configure both server authentication and the ability to connect from anywhere using TS Gateway.

Server authentication can be used to verify you are connected to the intended remote computer. The three options for server authentication are Connect and Don't Warn Me, Warn Me, and Do Not Connect. Windows Server 2003 SP1 or earlier servers cannot provide identification information. If using these servers, the option should be either Warn Me or Do Not Connect.

Remote Desktops

Remote Desktops is similar to Remote Desktop Connection. It uses Terminal Services and gives you access to the desktop just as if you were sitting in front of the remote server.

To launch Remote Desktops, select Start ➤ Administrative Tools ➤ Terminal Services ➤ Remote Desktops.

NOTE   Remote Desktops is available in server products (such as Windows Server 2003 and Windows Server 2008), but it is not available in desktop products (such as Windows XP and Windows Vista).

A significant difference between RDC and Remote Desktops is in how the desktops are displayed. Figure 3.18 shows Remote Desktops being used to connect to a remote server named MCITP2.

Notice that the remote server (MCITP2) is displayed in a pane of the Remote Desktops console. If I wanted to connect to the server named MCITP1, I could select it and connect to MCITP1 quite easily.

FIGURE 3.18   Remote Desktops console

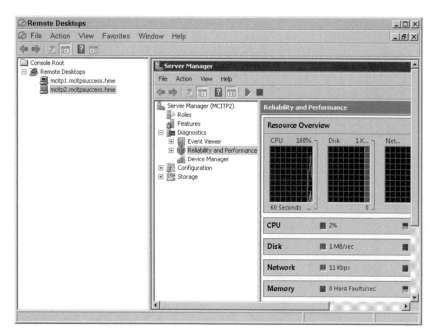

Remote Desktops is useful if you are responsible for a group of servers and want to manage them all from a single console. For example, you could be responsible for a web farm composed of five IIS servers. You could add all the IIS servers into your Remote Desktops console and easily connect to any server in the web farm.

Another difference between Remote Desktops and Remote Desktop Connection is that Remote Desktops includes the ability to connect with the /admin option. This is selectable in the properties of the connection, as shown in Figure 3.19.

You can launch the Remote Desktop Connection tool with the /admin option, but it doesn't include a check box within the GUI to do so. Instead, you can launch Remote Desktop Connection at the Run line or the command line using the following command: mstsc /admin.

If the /admin option is used, then a connection does not consume a Terminal Services Client Access License (TS CAL).

This is meaningful only if the Terminal Services role is installed on the server. You are still limited to only two administrative sessions, but these sessions do not count against the total number of Terminal Services CALs available on the server.

Admittedly, you can connect to multiple servers using RDC. However, with RDC, you'd have to create a separate instance for each connection. With Remote Desktops, you have the capability of using one instance, instead of several instances.

Some people like RDC. Others like Remote Desktops. Feel free to pick your favorite.

FIGURE 3.19 Remote Desktops connection properties

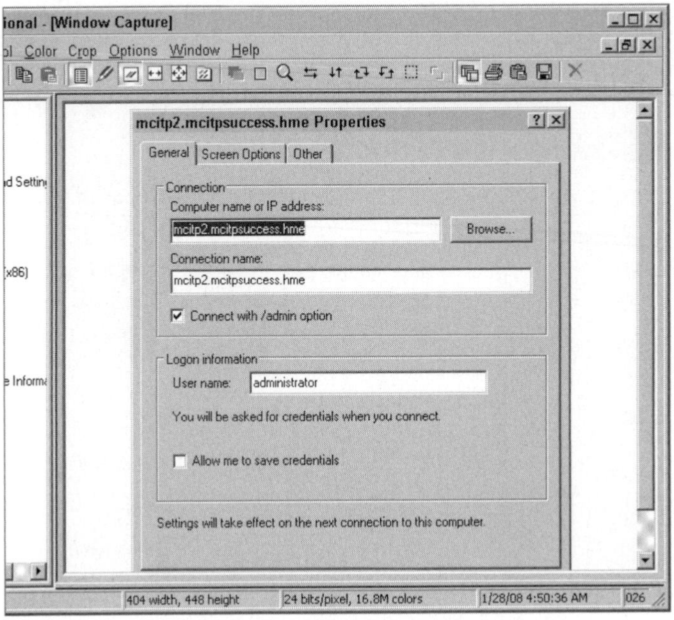

Remote Server Administration Tools

The Remote Server Administration Tool (RSAT) pack includes tools that can be used in addition to the previously discussed tools to remotely administer both Windows Server 2003 and Windows Server 2008 servers. They can only run on Windows Vista with at least SP1 installed.

In past versions of Windows Server, the adminpak.msi file has been used to install administration tools on desktop computers. By installing the adminpak.msi file, any desktop computer could be used to remotely administer servers within a domain. The RSAT pack is the replacement of adminpak.msi.

RSAT includes remote management tools that can be used to remotely manage several different server roles using Microsoft Management Console (MMC) snap-ins. Snap-ins are added for many different uses including:

- Active Directory roles (such as Active Directory Domain Services, Active Directory Certificate Services, Active Directory Lightweight Directory Services, and Active Directory Management Services)
- Network infrastructure roles (including DNS, DHCP, and Network Policy and Access)
- File and Print server roles
- Group Policy Management Console (GMPC)

You can add the RSAT pack using the Server Manager Add Features wizard to a Windows Server 2008 server. You can also download and install it on a Windows Vista system. You can find links for the download in Knowledge Base article 94134 (`http://support.microsoft.com/kb/941314`).

Server Core

In Chapter 2, "Planning Server Deployments," I covered Server Core and the methods of remote management that can be used with Server Core. As a reminder, they are as follows:

Access Server Core with Remote Desktop Connection   Configure the server using the Server Core Registry Editor Windows script file (`scregedit.wsf`) as follows:

```
Cscript c:\windows\system32\scregedit.wsf /AR 0
```

Manage Server Core remotely using a MMC snap-in   Configure using the NetShell (`netsh`) command to manipulate the firewall settings. The following NetShell command will properly configure it:

```
Netsh advfirewall firewall set rule group = "Remote Administration" new
enable = yes
```

Manage Server Core with Windows Remote Shell   Use the `WinRm` command to create a WinRM listener on the server, and the `WinRS` command on the client will remotely connect to the server. The `WinRM` command that you'd run on the Server Core server is as follows:

```
WinRM quickconfig
```

For the client accessing the server, run this command:

```
Winrs -r:computername command
```

Using Terminal Services Gateway Servers

Although I'll explain Terminal Services in greater depth in Chapter 7, for this section I'll tie in how you can use it for remote management.

To access a Remote Desktop connection inside a private network from the Internet, you'd have to open port 3389 at the firewall. That sounds easy enough until you try to get your firewall experts to open a firewall port. Their goal is to keep the network protected, and generally the way to do that is to open as few ports as possible. Every open port represents a potential vulnerability.

However, some ports are already open. For example, HTTP uses port 80, and HTTPS uses port 443. Both ports are already open on almost any firewall allowing Internet traffic (secure on port 443 and nonsecure on port 80). If you could use a port that's already open, you don't need to add a vulnerability to your network.

A Terminal Services Gateway is used to transfer Remote Desktop Protocol traffic over an HTTPS session. In other words, the RDP traffic goes through port 443 instead of port 3389. Figure 3.20 shows the big picture of how TS Gateway works.

FIGURE 3.20 Remote Desktops connection properties

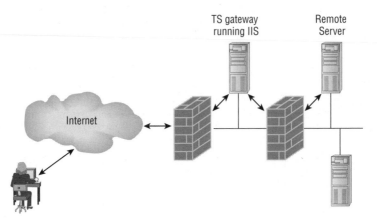

The client would connect to the TS Gateway (running Internet Information Services) via the Internet using the HTTPS protocol. Since the connectivity is with HTTPS, the traffic goes through the firewall using port 443, which is typically already open and secured with Secure Sockets Layer (SSL).

The TS Gateway strips off the HTTPS protocol and uses RDP to connect to the internal server. With the session established, the client can now use the session to remotely administer the server.

Windows Server Update Services

Operating systems and applications are never released in a perfect state. Even after extensive testing, bugs and flaws appear that need to be corrected before the next version. Updates come in the form of *patches*.

Windows Server Update Services (WSUS) provides an automated method for an organization to manage patches. Instead of servers and clients receiving patches from the Microsoft Update site, you can use WSUS to control which patches are deployed to clients.

> **NOTE** Windows *Server* Update Services started as *Software* Update Services (SUS), which provided only operating system updates and patches. With the release of WSUS 2.0, the name was changed from *Software* to *Server* and significantly expanded updates to include updates and patches to a wide range of software from a central server.

Figure 3.21 shows the typical hierarchy of a WSUS server within a network. The WSUS server would be configured to receive all the updates from the Microsoft Update site. Internal servers and clients will be configured to receive all of their updates from the WSUS server.

FIGURE 3.21 WSUS within a network

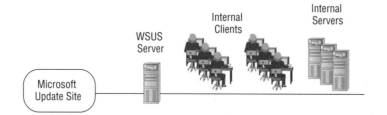

Although the list of products that are updated with WSUS frequently changes, here's a fairly comprehensive list of products that can be kept up-to-date with WSUS.

- Operating systems:
  - Windows Server 2008
  - Windows Server 2003
  - Windows 2000
  - Windows Vista
  - Windows XP
  - Windows Small Business Server
- Server applications:
  - SQL Server
  - Exchange Server
  - Internet Security and Acceleration (ISA) Server
  - Microsoft Data Protection Manager
- Desktop applications:
  - Microsoft Office
  - Visual Studio
  - Windows Live
  - Microsoft Forefront
  - Windows Defender

As you can see, it's not just the operating system that is being updated. Windows Update and WSUS also update server and desktop applications.

WSUS is not installed as a role or a feature of Windows Server 2008 but instead is installed as a separate application. WSUS is free and can be found rather easily with an Internet search for *download WSUS*.

For more detailed information on the deployment of WSUS, check out the WSUS 3.0 Deployment Guide available from Microsoft. You can get the deployment guide from the WSUS home page (http://technet.microsoft.com/en-us/wsus). At 154 pages, it has a whole lot more in-depth information on WSUS than I was able to put into this section.

Real World Scenario

Windows Update History

Years ago, I was one of several administrators who shared responsibility for a Windows 2000 network. None of us were full-time administrators, and no one had specific defined responsibilities, but instead each of us did what needed to be done as our primary job responsibilities allowed.

We had an IIS server hosting an intranet site. About three weeks before we were hit by the Nimda worm, Microsoft released a patch for IIS that would have prevented the damage from Nimda. All we had to do was go to the Microsoft site, check for updates, and download and install the patch. Unfortunately, none of us did so.

Ultimately we were hit, and we all spent a lot of extra hours fighting Nimda.

At the time, I remember thinking there must be a better way to keep servers updated. Apparently people at Microsoft were thinking the same thing. They soon came up with Automatic Updates that could be used for both servers and desktop systems.

Automatic Updates is still in existence. It allows you to set up individual systems (or multiple systems with Group Policy) to automatically check Microsoft's Windows Update site for relevant patches, download them, and automatically install them.

However, there is a drawback with Automatic Updates. Although most updates are benign, occasionally an update can cause problems with the operating system, hardware, or applications running on a server. In a worst-case scenario, an update can break the server.

To prevent this, Microsoft released Software Update Services (SUS, the precursor to WSUS). This allowed administrators to set up an SUS server to download the updates. Administrators could test the updates and approve or disapprove the updates as desired. Clients would be configured to receive updates from the SUS server, instead of Microsoft's Windows Update site.

SUS was improved with WSUS 2.0 and then WSUS 3.0.

The process of updates has gone through several iterations over the years. Each method was designed to improve the previous method. The following are the update methods in recent years:

- Manually connecting to Microsoft site and download required updates

- Automatic Updates

- Software Update Services (SUS)

- Windows Server Update Services (WSUS) 2.0

- Windows Server Update Services (WSUS) 3.0

WSUS Prerequisites

Before you can install WSUS, you need to have the following prerequisites installed:

- Windows Server 2003 SP1 or Windows Server 2008
- Internet Information Services 6.0 or later
- Microsoft Management Console 3.0
- Windows Installer 3.1
- Microsoft .NET Framework v2.0
- Background Intelligent Transfer Service (BITS) 2.0
- Microsoft Report Viewer 2005 Redistributable

With the prerequisites installed, you can then launch the WSUS executable downloaded from Microsoft's site and follow the wizard.

When following the wizard, you'll have to decide whether WSUS will use the default website. If it uses the default website, it will use port 80. If another website will be hosted on this web server as the default site, then WSUS will assign port 8530. Additionally, you'll need to identify the location for the WSUS updates and the WSUS database.

Downloading and Deploying Updates

The steps involved in receiving and deploying updates are as follows:

Step 1: Synchronize   Synchronization is the process or connecting to the public Microsoft Update site or another WSUS server and downloading updates. Synchronization can be scheduled or done manually. When set to manual, an administrator must initiate the synchronization.

When set to synchronize according to a schedule, you have the option of setting the starting time and the number of synchronizations each day. For example, you can choose to start at 1 a.m. and specify four synchronizations a day. Synchronizations will occur at 1 a.m., 7 a.m., 1 p.m., and 7 p.m.

Step 2: Approve   After synchronization, an administrator must approve the updates before they are deployed.

Updates should be tested before being approved. By configuring computer groups, you can approve and deploy updates to your test systems first. Then, after testing, you can approve the updates to other computer groups in your production environment.

After an update is approved, it will be deployed to all the computers in the computer group where it was approved.

WSUS also allows you to set some updates to Auto Approve. This can be done with critical updates and certain classes of updates.

Step 3: Verify Deployment WSUS clients are configured to check in with the WSUS server every 22 hours by default. (You can configure this in Group Policy.) After checking in with the WSUS server, approved updates are deployed to the WSUS client.

You can use the WSUS console to verify the status of updates, the status of computer groups, or the status of individual clients.

WSUS in a Distributed Environment

When deploying WSUS in a distributed environment, you can have your WSUS servers work together to make the best use of available resources. A distributed environment is one where you have more than one physical site connected via a wide area network (WAN) link.

Each WSUS server can be configured in either autonomous or replica mode. The primary difference between the two is in where they get their updates.

Autonomous mode WSUS servers using autonomous mode receive their updates from the public Microsoft Update site. They can still be configured to report summary status information to a parent server. You would use autonomous mode when you have enough IT support at the location to synchronize, analyze, and approve all of the necessary updates. A primary benefit of autonomous mode is that the branch office is able to approve and deploy the updates that are appropriate for the branch office.

In Figure 3.22, both headquarters and the larger branch office are configured in autonomous mode. Both sites receive their updates directly from the Microsoft Update site. All of the internal clients and servers at the larger branch office receive their updates from WSUS2. All of the internal clients and servers at headquarters receive their updates from WSUS1.

Replica mode WSUS servers using replica mode receive their updates from an upstream server (typically over a WAN link). In addition to receiving updates from the upstream server, they also report detailed status information to any server designated as a parent.

In Figure 3.22, the smaller branch office WSUS server (WSUS3) is receiving its updates from WSUS1. In this example, WSUS1 would be considered an upstream server, and WSUS3 would be considered a downstream server.

One of the primary reasons to configure the smaller branch office in replica mode is because of a lack of enough IT support at the smaller branch office. Instead of requiring IT personnel at the branch office to regularly synchronize, analyze, and approve the updates, the replica server inherits the approved update approvals.

Configuring Clients

When configuring clients to use WSUS, two important concepts must be examined: Group Policy objects and targeting.

Group Policy is used to configure clients to receive their updates from the WSUS server. Targeting is used to populate the WSUS server with the names of the clients that will be targeted and managed by the WSUS server.

FIGURE 3.22   Multiple-site enterprise using WSUS in both autonomous and replica modes

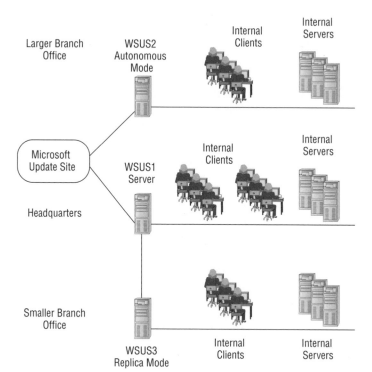

WSUS can also be used to deploy updates to nondomain clients, though it's not as simple as setting a single Group Policy object for all the clients. Instead, you'll need to either set local group policy or modify the registry on each of the clients.

Group Policy Configuration

The magic of Group Policy is that it allows you make one or more settings within a Group Policy object (GPO) and have it apply to many objects (computers and users) within your domain.

In other words, you can cause all your computers in the entire domain to receive their updates from a WSUS server by creating a GPO and applying it at the domain level. This single GPO changes the settings for all the computers in your domain to receive their updates from your WSUS server.

A minor problem with this configuration is that it would also cause your WSUS server to receive updates from itself, which simply wouldn't work.

By creating an organizational unit (OU) for your WSUS server, you can create a separate OU for your WSUS server and either block inheritance of all inherited Group Policy objects (which makes things much more complex) or create a separate OU and configure the GPO to receive the updates from the Windows Update site.

Figure 3.23 shows the latter choice. You'd configure the domain-level GPO (named Updates from WSUS Server) so that all computers within your domain receive their updates from the WSUS server. You'd then configure the GPO (named Updates from the Windows Update site) within the WSUS Servers OU so that any servers in this OU receive their updates from the Windows Update site. Of course, you'd also make sure the WSUS computer object is in the WSUS OU.

FIGURE 3.23 Using two Group Policy objects for WSUS

The order of precedence of Group Policy is as follows:

- Local
- Site
- Domain
- OU

If there are any conflicts, the last one applied wins. In other words, since the OU GPO (named Updates from Windows Update site in the WSUS Servers OU) is applied *after* the Domain GPO (named Updates from WSUS Server in the domain mcitpsuccess.hme), the OU GPO would take precedence for any objects in the WSUS Servers OU.

Admittedly, you can apply the Group Policy in other ways. Instead of applying the updates from WSUS Server at the domain level, you could apply at each of the high-level OUs in your domain (except for the OU holding the WSUS server). A drawback from this method is that GPOs cannot be linked to the computer container since it's not an OU. You'd need to take additional steps to ensure computer objects are not placed into the computer container. Capped Group Policy. This refers to back to the figure. The GPO is named Updates from WSUS server. The OU holding the WSUS servers is "WSUS Servers."

With the GPOs created, you then need to configure them. The GPO settings you want to modify are in Computer Configuration ➢ Administrative Templates ➢ Windows Components ➢ Windows Updates.

When configuring updates through Group Policy, you can select four settings for automatic updating. These are listed as options 2 through 5.

Listing the options as options 2 through 5 looks like a typo, but this is exactly how the options are listed in the Group Policy settings. Of course, this begs the question, where's option 1? Option 1 is implied when the settings are disabled.

2 – Notify for Download and Notify for Install   With this selection, an icon will appear in the status area (at the far right of the taskbar) with a message that indicates updates are ready to be downloaded. This is useful for a computer with a slow network connection (such as dial-up). It prevents the entire bandwidth from being consumed with the update and instead allows the user to choose when to download and install.

3 – Auto Download and Notify for Install   This is the default setting. Updates are automatically downloaded. When the download is complete, the user is notified with a status icon in the status area that updates are ready to be installed.

4 – Auto Download and Schedule the Install   Updates are automatically downloaded and then installed based on the scheduled install time. The default installation time is 3 a.m., but you can modify this.

5 – Allow Local Admin to Choose Setting   With this selection, load administrators can access the Automatic Updates applet in Control Panel to select different configuration options. They cannot disable Automatic Updates but can choose different settings.

Exercise 3.6 leads you through the steps to create and configure a domain-level GPO to receive updates from a WSUS server named WSUS1 in the mcitpsuccess.hme domain. This exercise assumes you have access to a server configured as a domain controller. The name of the domain isn't important.

EXERCISE 3.6

Configuring a WSUS GPO

1. Launch the Group Policy Management console by selecting Start ➤ Administrative Tools ➤ Group Policy Management.

2. In the Group Policy Management onsole, browse to Forest ➤ Domain ➤ mcitpsuccess .hme, and click Group Policy Objects.

3. Select Action ➤ New, and enter the name **Updates from WSUS Server**. Leave Source Starter GPO as the default value. Click OK.

4. In the pane on the right, right-click the new Updates from WSUS Server GPO name, and click Edit.

5. In the Group Policy Management Editor, browse to the Computer Configuration ➤ Policies ➤ Administrative Templates ➤ Windows Components ➤ Windows Update container.

6. Double-click the Configure Automatic Updates setting.

7. With the Setting tab selected, click the Enabled selection.

8. In the Configure Automatic Updating area, select 4 – Auto Download and Schedule the Install. Your display will look similar to the following graphic.

9. Click Next Setting to access the properties of the Specify Microsoft Update Service Location setting.

10. For the Specify Intranet Microsoft Update Service Location selection, select Enabled.

11. In the Set the Intranet Update Service for Detecting Updates text box, **enter http:// wsus1**.

12. In the Set the Intranet Statistics Server text box, **enter http://wsus1**. Your display will look similar to the following graphic. Click OK to close the properties dialog box.

13. Click File ➢ Exit to close the Group Policy Management Editor.

The remaining steps would be to create the updates from Windows Update Site GPO, create the WSUS Servers OU, move WSUS server objects, and link the new GPOs.

Client-Side or Server-Side Targeting

Within WSUS, you have computer groups that are used to organize computers. With computer groups, you are able to approve updates for individual computer groups instead of just approving updates for all computers.

For example, you may choose to create a computer group for sales computers (used by people in the sales department) and another computer group for IT computers (used by people in the IT department). This allows you to target approved updates to specific computers.

Testing may show that an update causes problems with a line-of-business application run by users in the sales department but does not cause problems for users in the IT department. You could approve the update for the IT computer group but not the sales computer group.

You can place computers in the computer groups through two methods:

Client-side targeting   With client-side targeting, clients are able to add themselves to target computer groups on the WSUS server. Client-side targeting is configured via Group Policy and will work only if Automatic Updates has been configured to retrieve updates from a WSUS server.

The Group Policy setting is Computer Configuration ➢ Policies ➢ Administrative Templates ➢ Windows Components ➢ Windows Update ➢ Enable Client-Side Targeting.

Figure 3.42 shows the setting configured for client-side targeting to put this computer in the WSUS Sales group. A group must exist on the WSUS server named Sales.

FIGURE 3.24   Configuring client-side targeting through Group Policy

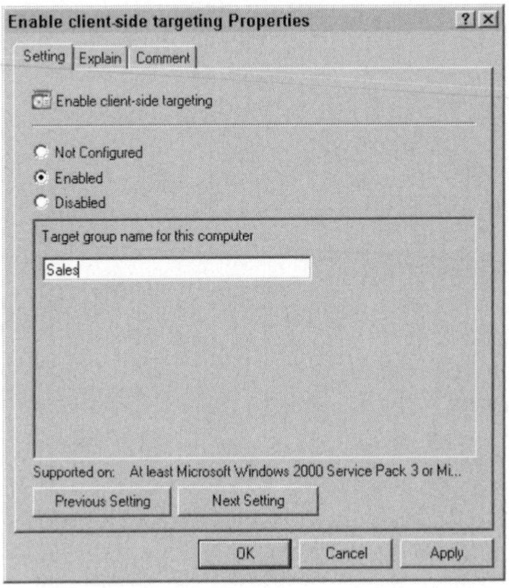

If you use client-side targeting, you will need to configure multiple GPOs. For example, if you want all the computers in the Sales organizational unit to be added to the Sales computer group on WSUS, you would create a GPO and link it to the Sales OU. This affects only computers in the Sales OU. To add computers from the IT OU to a computer group on WSUS named IT, you'd need to create and link another GPO to the IT OU.

Server-side targeting   With server-side targeting, you manually add computers to specific groups using the WSUS console.

Nondomain Clients

Although it's a lot easier to configure clients within a domain to use WSUS (using Group Policy), it's also possible to configure nondomain clients to retrieve updates from a WSUS server. Although this may take a little more time in the short run, once all the clients are configured, you'll be able to sleep a little easier knowing that the clients are getting updated properly.

You can use two methods to configure nondomain clients:

Using the Local Group Policy object   You can use the Group Policy object editor and edit the Local Group Policy object on individual systems. Ensure you have the correct version of the administrative template (wuau.adm), and make the changes on each computer. Edit the same settings that you would edit in Group Policy within a domain.

Depending on how many clients you need to configure, this may or may not be feasible. However, if you use imaging technologies (such as Microsoft's Windows Deployment Services or Symantec's Ghost), you can configure Local Group Policy on your reference computer, and all computers you deploy afterward with this image will be correctly configured.

Editing the registry   You can also use the Registry Editor (regedit) to modify the appropriate registry entries. There are about 20 entries that need to be modified in the registry (see the WSUS 3.0 Deployment Guide for the details). However, one good thing about making modifications to the registry is they can be scripted. Once you create and test your script, you need to execute only once on each nondomain client.

WSUS 3.0 Remote Management

It's possible to remotely manage WSUS using the WSUS 3.0 administration console. This can be installed on Windows Vista or Windows XP Professional using the same WSUS program used to install the full WSUS application on a server.

 Although previous versions of WSUS allowed remote management via a web interface, WSUS 3.0 doesn't include a web interface.

Some requirements to install the WSUS administration console on desktop computers are as follows:

- The computer must be a member of the same domain as the WSUS server or a member of a domain with a trust relationship with the domain of the WSUS server.

- Prerequisites such as .NET Framework 2.0 and Microsoft Management Console 3.0 are required on the remote administration computer. The install program will inform you if any prerequisites are needed. (IIS and SQL Server 2005 are not required on the remote administration computer.)

- Multiple WSUS 3.0 servers can be added to a single remote administration console.

    Of course, it's also possible to use Remote Desktop tools to connect to the WSUS server.

System Center Configuration Manager

The System Center Configuration Manager (SCCM) is the replacement for Systems Management Server. SCCM is designed to allow you to easily assess, deploy, and update your clients, servers, and mobile devices.

    SCCM is not a free product but instead is a server application like Microsoft SQL Server or Microsoft Exchange. Additionally, it's a product you'll expect to find only in large enterprises.

    Many of the basic capabilities of SCCM are available in free products such as Windows Deployment Services, Windows Server Update Services, or Group Policy objects. However, SCCM adds significant features that make it a popular choice for larger organizations that need the extra capabilities.

SCCM is used to provide administrators with assistance in managing the IT infrastructure in several key areas:

Operating system deployment   Deploying operating systems can be a challenging endeavor in large organizations. Not only do you have to deploy the operating system, but you also have to deploy drivers, updates, patches, and security fixes. Using SCCM, you can deploy fully configured systems (both desktops and servers) including applications, if desired.

Although you can use Windows Deployment Services (covered in Chapter 2, "Planning Server Deployments") to deploy images, SCCM provides added capabilities and increased flexibility.

Software distribution   Using SCCM, you can automate the installation and updates of software applications on systems throughout an enterprise. Although you can also use Group Policy (covered in greater depth in Chapter 5, "Monitoring and Maintaining Active Directory") to install, upgrade, and remove applications on computers, SCCM provides a lot more convenience through added capabilities.

A significant capability of software distribution using SCCM over Group Policy is the ability to schedule deployments. For example, you can schedule the deployments to occur after-hours to minimize the impact on end users. Additionally, you can use SCCM to view detailed reports showing which systems have received the deployment and which systems have not received it.

Update management   As covered earlier in this chapter, it's extremely important to keep systems up-to-date. This helps keep the systems running at peak efficiency, but even more important, it protects against constantly emerging security threats. The Update Management portion of SCCM uses WSUS technologies to provide updates to your systems. It can also be integrated with Network Access Protection (NAP) to ensure your systems meet certain "health" requirements.

Asset management   Maintaining accurate inventories of both hardware and software in your enterprise can be streamlined with SCCM. Inventories can be automatically collected and maintained through SCCM, giving administrators information about hardware and software assets, who is using them, and where they are. Detailed information can be used for a wide variety of purposes such as ensuring your organization is in compliance with licensing agreements or simply whether legacy applications are still by used by anyone in the organization.

Configuration management   Configuration management can be one of the most challenging aspects of IT organizations today. Often, a lot of time and effort is expended to evaluate a change to determine the impact on the existing infrastructure. This is referred to as *change management.*

However, other times, a well-intentioned administrator simply makes a change to resolve a problem without taking the time evaluate the impact. Suddenly, a significant portion of your network infrastructure is down, and no one (at least no one who is talking) knows why.

Configuration management is used to ensure that IT systems comply with specific configuration states. You can use SCCM to quickly assess the compliance of computers with established configuration standards and ensure operating system and application installations meet all requirements.

Summary

In this chapter, we covered the details of several tools you have available to monitor and manage systems in your network. These tools can be used on any server roles, such as the specific server roles covered in Chapters 4 through 7.

You can use the Reliability and Performance Monitor to quickly and easily determine how well your system is currently running and, if there are problems, quickly narrow down your focus into what is causing the problem. Data collector sets templates can be run as is or be used to create your own user-defined data collector set including baselines used for trend analysis.

Event management is streamlined in Windows Server 2008 with both event subscriptions and event tasks. Event subscriptions allow you to centrally monitor several servers by forwarding events to a central server. Event tasks can be configured to respond to specific events and execute a task, such as running a program, sending an email, or creating a message box.

Remote Management tools allow you to remotely administer your servers. One of the new components is Remote Desktop Connection 6.0, which adds security features such as Network Level Authentication. It's important to remember that although RDC 6.0 is supported on Windows Vista and Windows Server 2008, it is not supported on all legacy clients. You must have SP2 to use it on Windows XP and SP1 to use it on Windows Server 2003.

Windows Server Update Services is a powerful tool to keep both domain and nondomain systems updated. Clients are configured to receive their updates through Group Policy (nondomain clients use Local Group Policy or registry hacks). Within WSUS, clients are added to computer groups (either through client-side targeting or through server-side targeting). After synchronizing updates with Microsoft's Update site, updates can be approved for specific computer groups.

For larger distributed networks, you can configure multiple WSUS servers, and these servers can be configured to receive their updates from Microsoft's Update site or through another WSUS server. If a WSUS server in a distributed network receives its updates from Microsoft, it is configured in autonomous mode. If the WSUS server receives updates from an upstream server, it is configured in replica mode.

System Center Configuration Manager is the replacement of Systems Management Server and can be used to centrally manage systems within a network. SCCM is a purchased server product and provides significant enhancements to many of the free capabilities of Windows Server 2008. It includes the capabilities of Windows Deployment Services, Windows Server Update Services, Group Policy's ability to deploy software, and much more. For each of these capabilities, SCCM provides significant improvements useful in a large enterprise.

Exam Essentials

Know how to monitor a server using Reliability and Performance Monitor.   You should know how to use Reliability and Performance Monitor. This includes using data collector set templates and creating and running your own data collector sets. Although the templates provide a lot of capabilities to create baselines used for trend analysis, you need to create your own data collector set.

Be able to manage events.   Event management is an important skill on the job and for the exam. By using Event Viewer, you can create event subscriptions to manage events for multiple servers from a single server. By using event tasks, you can attach specific tasks to specific events or to an entire event log. You should be able to configure and create both event subscriptions and event tasks.

Know the different methods of remotely managing a server.   You should know Remote Desktop capabilities, options and requirements. This includes Remote Desktop Connection 6.0 and Network Level Authentication and how Windows XP needs at least SP 2 and Windows Server 2003 needs at least SP1 to install Remote Desktop Connection 6.0. You should also have a basic understanding of how TS Gateway works.

Know about Remote Server Administration Tools (RSAT)   You should know that the Remote Server Administration Tools (RSAT) can be used to remotely administer many different server roles running on Windows Server 2003 and Windows Server 2008. RSAT is the replacement for the adminpak.msi and can be added as a feature on Windows Server 2008 computers, or run from Windows Vista to add to your remote administration capabilities.

Understand the capabilities of WSUS.   You should know the primary purpose of WSUS (automating the deployment of updates) and its different capabilities. For example, you should know the difference between replica mode and autonomous mode, the difference between an upstream and a downstream server, and the difference between client-side targeting and server-side targeting. You should also know how to configure both domain clients and nondomain clients to receive their updates from a WSUS server.

Understand the purpose of WSRM.   The Windows System Resource Manager allows you to control resources allocated to individual applications (process-based) or individual users (user-based). You should know that you can allocate both CPU and memory resources. Further, in a multiple-processor system, you can use processor affinity to link a specific process with a specific processor.

Understand the capabilities of SCCM.   Although you don't have to be an expert on System Center Configuration Manager, you should know that it builds on the strength of several existing technologies and adds capabilities to each of the technologies. For example, Group Policy can be used to deploy software, but SCCM can deploy software based on schedules and provide detailed reports on the results.

Review Questions

1. You are responsible for monitoring and maintaining five Internet Information Services (IIS) servers. You want to centrally monitor them on a single server using the Performance and Reliability Monitor. However, you find that you can't connect to remote computers using the monitor, even though they are fully operational on the network. What's the likely problem?

   A. The Remote Reliability Monitor service is not running.

   B. The Remote Registry service is not running.

   C. The RACAgent service is not running.

   D. The Perfmon service is set to Local mode.

2. You have been assigned management responsibilities of a SQL Server 2008 server. You check the Reliability Monitor to view the overall performance of the server, but you find it does not have any data. Why wouldn't the data for the Reliability Monitor be available?

   A. The RACAgent is not running.

   B. The SACAgent is not running.

   C. The Reliability Monitor is not compatible with SQL Server.

   D. The Remote Registry service is not running.

3. You manage a file server, and you want to identify the overall resource usage of the server. What would be the easiest method?

   A. Run the System Performance data collector set template.

   B. Run the System Diagnostics data collector set template.

   C. Create a data collector set from the System Performance data collector set template, and run it.

   D. Create a data collector set from the System Diagnostics data collector set template, and run it.

4. You have been assigned responsibility to manage a file and print server. You suspect that the performance of the server could be significantly improved, but before you start, you want to document the current performance characteristics of the server. What tool could you use to create a baseline?

   A. Use Reliability and Performance Monitor, and run a data collector set template.

   B. Use Reliability and Performance Monitor, and create a user-defined data collector set.

   C. Use WSRM.

   D. Use WSUS.

5. You manage several Internet Information Services (IIS) servers in a web farm. You want to configure events so that they can be centrally managed on a single server. Further, you want the monitoring server to pull the events from each IIS server on a regular basis. What should you create?

    A.   Collector-initiated subscriptions

    B.   Source computer–initiated subscriptions

    C.   A Minimize Bandwidth delivery method

    D.   A Minimize Latency delivery method

6. You are trying to configure event subscriptions so that events from several servers are forwarded to a monitoring computer. What command must be entered at the source computers to allow events to be forwarded to the monitoring computer?

    A.   `WinRM quickconfig`

    B.   `WinRM /Forward:1`

    C.   `Wecutil qc`

    D.   `Wecutil /Forward:1`

7. You have been having problems with a SQL Server machine. You've found that when a specific critical event is recorded, within 30 minutes the SQL Server machine stops responding to all queries. You want to be notified when this critical event occurs. What could you do?

    A.   Configure an event subscription to forward this event to your system.

    B.   Configure an event subscription to send you an email if the event occurs.

    C.   Create an event task to forward this event to your system.

    D.   Create an event task to send you an email if the event occurs.

8. You have created an event task that will run a program in response to the event's occurrence. You have created an account with administrator privileges named EventTask and have configured the task, as shown here.

However, testing shows that even though the event occurs and the task begins, the task never completes. What's the likely problem?

A. The task is hidden.

B. User Account Control (UAC) is disabled.

C. The task is disabled.

D. The Run with Highest Privileges check box is not selected.

9. You are several different applications on a server, and you want to ensure that each application gets the same amount of resources. What tool could you use?

A. SCCM

B. RDC

C. WSUS

D. WSRM

10. You are a network administrator where you work. You run Windows XP SP1 on your client workstation and Windows Vista on a laptop. You want to use Remote Desktop Connection to connect and manage a Windows Server 2008 server. This works on your Windows Vista computer but not on your Windows XP computer. Why not?

A. Remote Desktop Connection is not supported on Windows XP.

B. Windows XP must be upgraded to SP2.

C. Remote Desktop Connection needs to be upgraded to version 5.0.

D. You must the following command on the Windows Server 2008 server: `WinRM /XP 1`.

11. You want to remotely manage a Windows Server 2008 server using Remote Desktop Connection. Which of the following operating systems will support this? (Choose all that apply.)

A. Windows XP SP1

B. Windows XP SP2

C. Windows Server 2003 SP1

D. Windows Server 2008

12. Your network is used by research analysts who use the Internet for research and reporting. You want to be able to remotely manage one of your servers from home while not sacrificing any security. Security policies state that a VPN can't be used to do this and additional ports cannot be opened in the firewall. What could you use?

A. Configure a Terminal Services server running IIS to act as a gateway.

B. Install RDC 6.0, and configure it to accept port 80 requests.

C. Move the server to the Internet with a public address.

D. Open port 3389 to remotely access the server.

13. You have deployed WSUS in your enterprise. You have a large branch location with an IT staff. They want to approve their own updates, but you also want to ensure summary information is reported to the primary WSUS server at the main location. Which mode should you use for the WSUS server in this location?

   A. Replica

   B. Autonomous

   C. Upstream

   D. Downstream

14. You have configured WSUS to deploy updates in your organization. To have updates sent to your clients, what two steps must be done on the WSUS server?

   A. Synchronize and approve.

   B. Synchronize and deploy.

   C. Download and deploy.

   D. Download and schedule.

15. You are using WSUS to deploy updates in your domain and have configured computer groups to organize computers within WSUS. You want to have computers automatically add themselves to the appropriate computer group. What would you do?

   A. Modify the registry of the computers.

   B. Configure a Local Group Policy to add the computers.

   C. Configure client-side targeting.

   D. Configure server-side targeting.

16. You have deployed a WSUS server that is successfully being used to deploy updates to computers within a domain. You are asked whether the WSUS server can be used to deploy updates to nondomain clients. How do you respond?

   A. No. WSUS can be used to deploy updates only for domain computers.

   B. No. WSUS can be used to deploy updates to domain computers or nondomain computers, but not both.

   C. Yes. The computers can be configured either by using Local Group Policy or by editing the registry.

   D. Yes. You would use server-side targeting.

17. You are an administrator of a domain with several branch locations. Each branch location is configured as an organizational unit (OU) in the domain. You have installed a WSUS server in the Virginia Beach branch locations, which has become quite large. The WSUS server is receiving updates from a WSUS server at the main location. How can you configure the clients at the Virginia Beach location to receive their updates from the WSUS server at the branch location?

   A. Create a script to modify the registry, and run it on each of the computers at the branch location.

   B. Modify the default domain policy to redirect clients to use the new WSUS server.

   C. Create a GPO and link it to the Virginia Beach OU to redirect clients to use the new WSUS server.

   D. Change the clients at the Virginia Beach OU to use client-side targeting.

18. You want to remotely manage several DNS servers from your Windows Vista SP1 desktop computer. Each of the DNS servers is running on Windows Server 2008 Server Core. What should you install on your system to remotely administer the DNS servers via a MMC?

   A. Adminpak.msi

   B. RSAT

   C. GPMC

   D. ADUC

19. You are an administrator in a large enterprise. You need to identify a technology that can be used to deploy applications to desktop computers based on a schedule. What tool should you recommend?

   A. SCCM

   B. WSUS

   C. WSRM

   D. Group Policy

20. You need to implement a solution that will allow you to easily deploy applications to desktop computers. After the deployment, you need to be able to view reports indicating who has received the updates. What tool could you use?

   A. Group Policy

   B. WSUS

   C. SCCM

   D. WSRM

Answers to Review Questions

1. **B.** The Remote Registry service needs to be running to connect to a remote computer. There is no such thing as the Remote Reliability Monitor service. The RACAgent is a scheduled task that collects data for the reliability monitor. Perfmon is the command to launch the Performance and Reliability Monitor, but it does not have a local mode setting.

2. **A.** Data for the Reliability Monitor is provided by the RACAgent scheduled task. There is no such thing as the SACAgent. The Reliability Monitor is part of the operating system and is compatible with any server products. The Remote Registry service is not needed to view data on a local system.

3. **A.** The System Performance data collector set template can be run to quickly identify the overall resource usage. The System Diagnostics data collector set can be used to identify status details of the system but is more useful to troubleshoot and improve performance rather than report overall usage. It would be easier to run the template than create your own data collector set.

4. **B.** By using Reliability and Performance Monitor and creating a user-defined data collector set, you could specify details of the collected data (such as how often to capture the data and how long to run the data collector set). The data collector set template could not be modified for a baseline. Windows System Resource Manager (WSRM) can limit or manage resources to users or applications but can't be used to create a baseline. Windows Server Update Services (WSUS) is used to deploy updates to systems.

5. **A.** In a collector-initiated subscription, the monitoring server will pull the events from the monitored servers. In source computer–initiated subscriptions, the events are pushed to the monitoring server. Collector-initiated subscriptions use the Normal delivery method (events are batched and sent within 15 minutes). Source computer–initiated subscriptions can use either a Minimize Bandwidth or Minimize Latency delivery method.

6. **A.** The Windows Remote Management tool needs to be run to configure the source computer to forward events. `WinRM quickconfig` is the correct command. The collector computer is configured with the Windows Event Collector utility (using `wecutil qc`). There is no `/Forward` switch for either `WinRM` or `Wecutil`.

7. **D.** You can create an event task to respond to specific events. The response can be to send an email, run a program, or display a message box. An event subscription could be configured to forward the event to your system, but you wouldn't know unless you looked at the log or configured an event task. Event subscriptions can't be configured to send emails. Although an event task could be configured to run a script to forward a subscription, you wouldn't know the event was forwarded until you looked at the log.

8. **D.** The Run with Highest Privileges check box needs to be selected. Without this selected, User Account Control (UAC) will prompt the user to run using higher privileges, but the task can't respond to this prompt. A hidden task won't prevent it from running. If UAC were disabled, the task would run. The task begins, so the task is not disabled.

9. D. You can use the Windows Server Resource Manager to ensure that specific applications receive a certain amount of resources. System Center Configuration Manager (SCCM) is used to manage a large enterprise by including and improving many of the free tools available in Windows Server 2008. Remote Desktop Connection (RDC) is used to connect to the desktop of a remote computer. Windows Server Update Services (WSUS) is used to deploy updates and patches to systems within an enterprise.

10. B. To support Remote Desktop Connection on Windows XP and connect to a Windows Server 2008 server, you must install the Remote Desktop 6.0 client. Before this can be done, you must upgrade Windows XP to at least SP2. WinRM does not have a XP switch.

11. B, C, D. To support Remote Desktop Connection, you must have Windows XP SP2, Windows Server 2003 SP1, or a Windows Server 2008 server. The Remote Desktop 6.0 client must be installed on at least Windows XP SP2 or Windows Server 2003 SP1. It is not supported on Windows XP SP1.

12. A. You can use Terminal Services Gateway to accomplish these goals. It can be configured to accept traffic on port 80 (which is already open on any firewall granting Internet traffic) and forward Remote Desktop Protocol (RDP) traffic over an HTTPS session (port 443). RDC 6.0 can't be configured to accept port 80 requests. Moving a server to the Internet will definitely sacrifice security. Although RDP does use port 3389, the security policy states that additional ports can't be opened.

13. B. When in autonomous mode, WSUS servers will receive their updates from the Microsoft Update site. Updates must be synchronized and approved on the WSUS if in autonomous mode. If in replica mode, updates are received from the upstream server, and the WSUS server is referred to as the *downstream server*.

14. A. Synchronization is the process of connecting with the public Microsoft Update site or another WSUS server and downloading the updates to the WSUS server. After updates have been tested, they can be approved. Approved updates are deployed to the clients.

15. C. Client-side targeting is configured via Group Policy. When configured, clients will automatically add themselves to the appropriate computer group on the WSUS server. There is no way to modify the registry to configure client-side targeting. A Local Group Policy within a domain will require you to configure every computer individually. Server-side targeting requires you to add the computers to the appropriate group manually.

16. C. It is possible to have WSUS deploy updates to nondomain clients. The clients would be configured either by using local group policy or by modifying the registry. Server-side targeting adds the computers to a computer group at the server, but it does not configure the clients to receive their updates from the WSUS server.

17. C. By creating a GPO and linking to the Virginia Beach OU, you can change the settings for the computers in that OU. Modifying the registry can be done for nondomain clients but is not the best method for domain clients; we know the clients at the Virginia Beach location are domain clients since the branch locations are part of an OU. Modifying the default domain policy will cause all clients in the domain (the main location and all branches) to receive their updates from the Virginia Beach location. Client-side targeting identifies how computers are added to computer groups in the WSUS server but doesn't identify where clients receive their updates from.

18. B. The Remote Server Administration Tools (RSAT) can be installed on Windows Vista SP1 to add Microsoft Management Console (MMC) snap-ins for the management of several different server roles including DNS. The adminpak.msi file was used to install similar snap-ins for managing a Windows Server 2003 domain but is replaced by RSAT in Windows Server 2008. The Group Policy Management Console (GPMC) is used to manage Group Policy, not DNS. The Active Directory Users and Computers (ADUC) is used to manage Active Directory Domain Services.

19. A. System Center Configuration Manager (SCCM) is the replacement of Systems Management Server (SMS) and can be used to automate the deployment of software including scheduling the deployment. WSUS is used to deploy updates, not applications. Windows System Resource Manager (WSRM) is used to allocate resources. Although Group Policy can be used to deploy software, it can't schedule the deployment.

20. C. System Center Configuration Manager (SCCM) is the replacement of Systems Management Server (SMS) and can be used to automate the deployment of software. SCCM provides detailed reports on the results of the deployment. Although Group Policy can be used to deploy software, it doesn't have any reporting capabilities. WSUS is used to deploy updates, not full versions of applications. Windows System Resource Manager (WSRM) is used to allocate resources.

Chapter

4

Monitoring and Maintaining Network Infrastructure Servers

MICROSOFT EXAM OBJECTIVES COVERED IN THIS CHAPTER:

✓ **Planning for Server Deployment**

- Plan Infrastructure Services Server Roles. May include but is not limited to: address assignment, name resolution, network access control, directory services, application services, certificate services.

✓ **Monitoring and Maintaining Servers**

- Monitor and Maintain Security and Policies. May include but is not limited to: remote access, monitor and maintain NPAS, network access, server security, firewall rules and policies, authentication and authorization, data security, auditing.

Computers within networks need to be able to easily communicate with each other. Network infrastructure servers help automate the process of configuring the computers and the network so that communication is easy and secure. In this chapter, you'll learn some of the key aspects of Dynamic Host Configuration Protocol (DHCP), Domain Name System (DNS), Windows Internet Naming Service (WINS), and Network Access Protection (NAP) within the network.

DHCP servers are used to automatically configure DHCP clients with TCP/IP configuration information such as IP addresses, default gateways, addresses of DNS servers, and more.

DNS servers are primarily used to provide name resolution of hostnames within a network. It's important to understand the various types of zones, zone files, and zone records to adequately monitor and maintain DNS. Clients, DHCP, and DNS work together in a Windows Server 2008 network to automatically update records within DNS in the dynamic update process.

WINS also provides name resolution but for NetBIOS names instead of hostnames. Before Windows 2000 (NT 4.0), WINS was the primary method of name resolution within a network. Since Windows 2000, WINS has been increasingly less important, but you'll still find it in many networks today.

NAP provides some significant new abilities to implement security within a network in Windows Server 2008. NAP is used to monitor the health of clients. An administrator creates a health policy, and NAP components check clients to ensure they are compliant. If not, clients can be removed from the network and given only limited access to remediation servers.

You'll notice in the list of objectives that directory services, application services, certificate services, network access, server security, firewall rules and policies, authentication and authorization, data security, and auditing are listed. Chapter 5, "Monitoring and Maintaining Active Directory," covers directory services and certificate services. Chapter 7, "Planning Terminal Services Servers," covers application services. Network access, server security, firewall rules and policies, authentication and authorization, data security and auditing are covered in Chapter 8, "Planning Windows Server 2008 Security."

Dynamic Host Configuration Protocol

The purpose of Dynamic Host Configuration Protocol (DHCP) is to provide TCP/IP configuration information to clients. Notice I didn't say the purpose of DHCP is to provide IP addresses. DHCP certainly does provide IP addresses, but it provides much more.

A DHCP server within a Windows Server 2008 domain will typically provide the following information to clients:

- IP address
- Subnet mask
- Default gateway
- DNS domain name
- Address of DNS server
- Address of WINS server
- And possibly more

The DHCP server can provide 70 different TCP/IP options to clients. I won't cover them all in this chapter but will instead focus on what is most important within a Windows Server 2008 domain.

Overview

Before getting too far into some of the specifics of DHCP that you'll need for the exam, I'll start with a basic review of DHCP and the process a client goes through to get TCP/IP configuration.

Figure 4.1 shows both the DHCP client and the DCHP server right after the client turns on. When a client is turned on, it has a name but doesn't have an IP address. Also, it doesn't know the IP address of the DHCP server, so it must broadcast its request, and the DHCP server must broadcast the answer. A total of four packets are exchanged between the client and server.

FIGURE 4.1   DHCP client and server in the DORA process

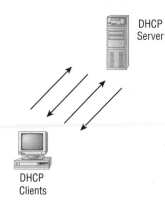

DHCP
Server

DHCP
Clients

Many people remember the four packets by using the acronym DORA. The four packets exchanged between a DHCP client and a DHCP server are as follows:

DHCP discover (the *D* in DORA)   The DHCP discover packet broadcasts out looking for any server running the DHCP service.

DHCP offer (the *O* in DORA)   When a DHCP server receives a DHCP discover, it responds by broadcasting an offer, which includes a lease length and specific TCP/IP options. Options would include an IP address, subnet mask, and any other TCP/IP options that have been configured on the DHCP server. It's possible for more than one DHCP server to receive the request and respond with an offer.

DHCP request (the *R* in DORA)   The DHCP client will respond to the first DHCP offer with a DHCP request. In essence, the DHCP client is requesting to confirm the lease. If a DHCP server doesn't receive a DHCP request (for example, the second DHCP server that sent an offer), the DHCP offer will time out, and the IP address will be available to give to another client.

DHCP acknowledge (the *A* in DORA)   After receiving the DHCP request, the DHCP server will respond with a DHCP acknowledge. At this point, the DHCP server confirms the IP address is allocated and not available to give to other clients, and the client begins to use the IP address.

Without DHCP, you'd have to manually configure DHCP on your clients. In most enterprise environments, this is just too time-consuming and expensive.

🌐 Real World Scenario

Manually Assigning IP Addresses

The only large network I've worked in that didn't use DHCP was a secure network since DHCP is inherently insecure. If a computer plugs into the network and requests the address, it gets one.

In this secure network, every computer was manually assigned a specific IP address and manually configured in DNS. Although this was quite a bit of work, it prevented clients from accessing network resources and even from gaining access to the subnet (unless they previously knew information about the subnet).

If a client plugs into the network, instead of receiving an IP address from DHCP, the client will instead assign itself an automatic private IP address (APIPA) in the range of 169.254.0.0 with a subnet mask of 255.255.0.0. An APIPA address is assigned by the client and includes only the IP address and subnet mask. It doesn't include a gateway or any other domain information since the client doesn't know anything about the network.

With an APIPA address, unknown clients cannot obtain information about the network.

If you don't have DHCP installed on a system, you can follow the steps in Exercise 4.1 to install it.

EXERCISE 4.1

Installing DHCP

1. Before you can begin the installation of DHCP, you need to have statically assigned IP addresses. If you already have statically assigned IP addresses, you can skip these steps and start with step 2.

    a. Click Start, right-click Network, and select Properties.

    b. In the Network and Sharing Center window, select the Manage Network Connections task in the Tasks pane on the left.

    c. Right-click your NIC (typically labeled Local Area Connection), and select Properties.

    d. Select Internet Protocol Version 4 (TCP/IP v4), and click Properties.

    e. Type an IP address of **192.168.1.2**, a subnet mask of **255.255.255.0**, and a preferred DNS server with the IP address of your preferred DNS server. On my system, the DHCP server is also the DNS server, so I've entered **192.168.1.2**. Click OK.

    f. Select Internet Protocol Version 6 (TCP/IP v6), and click Properties.

    g. Type an IP address using mixed notation in the following format: **E3D7::5154:9BC8:192.168.1.2**. Enter a subnet prefix length of **64**. Enter the IP address of your DNS server. DNS is installed on my system, so I entered the shortcut to indicate this system as **::1**. Your display will look similar to the following image. Note that you can enter IPv6 addresses in mixed notation. This allows you to add the IPv4 address in place of the rightmost 4 bytes in the IPv6 address. Once entered, it will be displayed (such as when entering IPCONFIG at the command line) with the IPv6 address. Click OK.

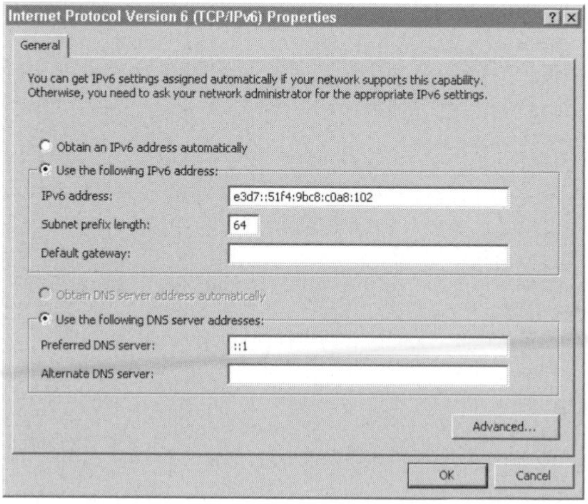

2. If not displayed, launch Server Manager by clicking Start, right-clicking Computer, and selecting Manage.

3. In Server Manager, select Roles.

4. In the Roles Summary area, click Add Roles.

5. On the Before You Begin page, click Next.

6. On the Select Server Roles page, click the DHCP Server check box, and click Next.

7. On the DHCP Server page, review the notes, and click Next.

8. On the Select Network Connection Bindings page, ensure the IP address for your NIC is checked, and click Next.

9. On the Specify IPv4 DNS Server Settings page, review the material. You can test the DNS server addresses by clicking Validate. Click Next.

10. On the Specify IPv4 WINS Server Settings page, accept the default of WINS Is Not Required for Applications on this Network, and click Next.

11. On the DHCP Scopes page, click Next. We'll create the scope in the next exercise.

12. On the Configure DHCPv6 Stateless Mode page, accept the default of Enable DHCPv6 Stateless Mode for This Server. Click Next.

13. On the Specify IPv6 DNS Server Settings page, review the material, and click Next. If the Preferred DNS Server IPv6 Address field is blank with the error "Enter an IP Address," enter **::1**, and then click Next.

14. On the Authorize DHCP Server page, identify the credentials of the account you used to log onto the system.

    a. If you are logged onto the server with an account that has authority to authorize the DHCP server, accept the default to use your current credentials, and click Next.

    b. If your account does not have the authority to authorize the DHCP server, click Use Alternate Credentials, click Specify, and enter the credentials of an account with the appropriate permissions. Click OK and then click Next.

15. On the Confirm Installation Selections page, review your choices, and click Install.

If the DHCP server is not authorized, it will not issue IP addresses to DHCP clients. The goal is to prevent someone from standing up a rogue server. To authorize a DHCP server in a domain, you must be in the Enterprise Admins group.

In Exercise 4.1, you chose DHCPv6 Stateless mode. You can choose either DHCPv6 Stateless mode or DHCPv6 Stateful mode:

DHCPv6 Stateless mode   DHCPv6 Stateless mode indicates that the DHCP server is not issuing IPv6 addresses to clients. DHCP will still issue other DHCP options such as the address of the DNS server or the default gateway.

In this mode, clients normally will use the IPv6 prefix from a router advertisement and autoconfigure an IPv6 address. This address will be assigned to the NIC.

DHCPv6 Stateful mode   DHCPv6 Stateful mode indicates the DHCP server is being used to issue IPv6 addresses to clients.

The mode used by clients within a Server 2008 environment is controlled by router advertisements within the network. Clients send a router solicitation to the router, and depending on the flags that are sent in the response, the client will use either the Stateless mode or the Stateful mode.

Scopes

DHCP is configured with scopes to identify the range of available IP addresses to give to computers on that scope. A scope usually relates directly to a subnet, though subnets can contain more than one scope.

Creating Scopes Using All of the Possible Addresses

Take a look at Figure 4.2. This network has two subnets—subnet 1 to the left of the router and subnet 2 to the right of the router. It would be logical to configure the two subnets with two separate scopes.

FIGURE 4.2   DHCP client and server in the DORA process

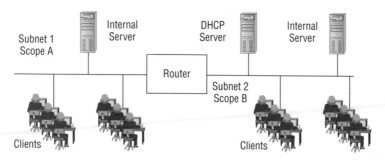

For example, you could configure the two scopes related to the two subnets, as shown in Table 4.1. In this table, we've assigned a network ID to each subnet and created scopes matching the network ID.

TABLE 4.1   Using All Available Subnet IP Addresses in the Scopes

Subnet	Network ID	Scope
Subnet 1	192.168.1.0/24	192.168.1.1/24 to 192.168.1.254/24
Subnet 2	192.168.22.0/24	192.168.22.1/24 to 192.168.22.254/24

The /24 in the scope range is referred to as *CIDR notation*. Instead of indicating the subnet mask as 255.255.255.0, the /24 indicates how many bits are a binary 1 in the subnet mask. A subnet mask (and an IP address) has four octets of 8 bits each. The /24 indicates that the first three octets ($3 \times 8 = 24$) are all a binary 1, or said another way, the subnet mask is 255.255.255.0.

Creating Scopes Using Only Some of the Addresses

Creating scopes using all the available TCP/IP addresses within a subnet is certainly possible, but it's not always done.

For example, you may want to manually assign IP addresses to several hosts such as routers and some servers. If you included these addresses in the scope, you'd have to configure exceptions within DHCP to ensure duplicate IP addresses aren't assigned.

You can fine-tune your scopes by not including the first 10 available IP addresses in your scope. Table 4.2 shows a different plan.

TABLE 4.2   Using Only Some of the IP Subnet Addresses in the Scopes

Subnet	Network ID	Scope
Subnet 1	192.168.1.0/24	192.168.1.11/24 to 192.168.1.254/24
Subnet 2	192.168.22.0/24	192.168.22.11/24 to 192.168.22.254/24

Notice that in subnet 1, the IP addresses of 192.168.1.1 through 192.168.1.10 are not included. Similarly, the IP addresses of 192.168.22.1 through 192.168.22.10 are not included in subnet 2. This gives you 10 addresses in each scope that can be manually assigned to servers, routers, or any other hosts that need a manually assigned address.

Exercise 4.2 includes the steps needed to add a scope to a DHCP server. It will lead you through the steps to create a second scope for subnet 1. This exercise assumes you have completed Exercise 4.1 or have at least installed DHCP through some other method.

EXERCISE 4.2

Creating a DHCP Scope

1. Launch the DHCP console by clicking Start ➤ Administrative Tools ➤ DHCP.

2. In the left pane of the DHCP console, click the plus sign to open the domain and then select IPv4.

3. Right-click IPv4, and select New Scope.

4. On the New Scope Welcome page, click Next.

5. On the Scope Name page, enter **TestScope** as the name and **Exercise 4.2** as the description. Click Next.

6. On the IP Address Range page, enter **192.168.1.11** as the start IP address, **192.168.1.200** as the end IP address, and **24** as the length. The subnet mask will automatically fill in based on the Length setting. Your display will look similar to the following image. Click Next.

7. No exclusions are necessary, so on the Exclusions page, click Next. Exclusions are needed if you have a client that needs an IP address within the scope range. For example, if an IIS server had to have the IP address of 192.168.1.200 manually assigned, you could exclude this IP address from the range. The DHCP server would exclude this address from the list of addresses that can be assigned.

8. On the Lease Duration page, accept the default of 8 days, and click Next.

9. On the Configure DHCP Options page, change the setting to No, I Will Configure These Options Later, and click Next.

10. On the Completing the New Scope Wizard page, click Finish.

Notice in Figure 4.3 that the scope has a red down arrow. The red down arrow indicates the scope hasn't been authorized yet, and it won't issue IP addresses to any clients.

FIGURE 4.3   DHCP with an inactive scope named TestScope

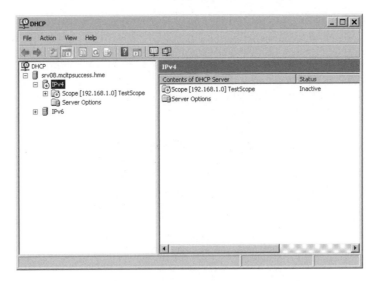

Modifying an Existing Scope to Use More Addresses

It's also possible that someone could have created a scope without using the full subnet. For example, a business may have anticipated only 100 clients on a subnet, so the scope was created using the address range of 192.168.1.11 to 192.168.1.200.

This address range may have worked fine for a while, but at some point it's recognized that the full IP range is needed. What do you do?

You cannot create a second scope using the same network ID. In other words, with a subnet mask of 255.255.255.0, the network ID of your scope is 192.168.1.0. If you tried to create a second scope using a range of 192.168.1.201 to 192.168.1.254 with a subnet mask of 255.255.255.0, you would get an error message indicating a scope has already been created in that range. Instead, you would need to modify the existing scope.

Use Exercise 4.3 to modify the existing scope that you created in Exercise 4.2.

EXERCISE 4.3

Modifying a DHCP Scope

1. If it's not open, launch the DHCP console by clicking Start ➢ Administrative Tools ➢ DHCP.

2. In the left pane of the DHCP console, click the plus sign to open the domain and then select IPv4.

3. Right-click IPv4, and select New Scope.

4. On the New Scope Welcome page, click Next.

5. On the Scope Name page, enter **Test2e** as the name and **This will fail** as the description. Click Next.

6. On the IP Address Range page, enter **192.168.1.201** as the start IP address, **192.168.1.254** as the end IP address, and **24** as the length. The subnet mask will automatically fill in based on the Length setting. Click Next. Your will see a dialog box similar to the following image indicating this can't be done.

7. Click OK to dismiss the warning. Click Cancel.

8. Back in the DHCP console, right-click the TestScope created in the previous exercise, and click Properties. The only property that can't be modified is the subnet mask. All other properties (including Starting IP Address, Ending IP Address, and Lease Duration) can be modified after the scope has been created.

EXERCISE 4.3 *(continued)*

9. On the Scope properties page, modify the End IP Address setting to 192.168.1.1.254. Your display will look like the following image. Click OK.

Ports Used by DHCP

If you know a little about networking, you may have noticed an inconsistency with how DHCP works. In the earlier explanation, I stressed that the four packets passed back and forth between the DHCP client and the DHCP server are broadcast packets.

Take a look at Figure 4.4, which shows a typical network. The clients on the right side of the router broadcast, and the DHCP server hears the broadcasts with no problem. However, consider the clients on the left side of the router. By default, a router does not pass broadcasts, so how do these packets get through?

You should understand the following two subtleties:

- DHCP broadcasts aren't normal broadcasts but instead are referred to as *BOOTP broadcasts*. A BOOTP broadcast uses UDP ports 67 and 68.

- Most routers today are RFC 1542 compliant, which means they can be configured to pass BOOTP broadcasts. In other words, if a broadcast message is using ports 67 and 68, the router will pass the broadcasts.

With this knowledge, you can see how DHCP clients on the other side of the router can pass DHCP broadcast messages back and forth to the DHCP server. The router should be configured to pass BOOTP broadcasts on NICs labeled 1 and 2 in the figure.

FIGURE 4.4 DHCP within a network

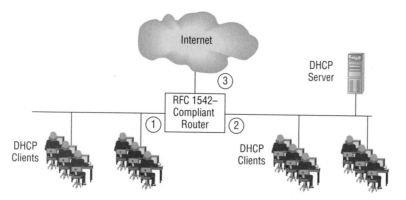

Another consideration is security. If you look back at Figure 4.4, the NIC labeled 3 would be your firewall. It should have ports 67 and 68 closed.

If ports 67 and 68 are open, someone outside your network would be able to issue DHCP requests and receive leases. The leases provide valuable information on your network such as IP addresses and subnet masks, routers, DNS servers, and more. This is known as *footprinting*.

Options

You can add options to any DHCP lease. These provide the DHCP client with additional TCP/IP configuration settings. Common DHCP options and their option numbers are as follows:

- 003 Router (also referred to as *default gateway*)
- 006 DNS Servers
- 015 DNS Domain Name
- 032 Router Solicitation Address
- 044 WINS/NBNS Servers
- 046 WINS/NBT Node Type
- 060 PXE Client

You can add options at the server level or at the scope level. Options added to the server level will apply to all clients unless the option is also assigned at the scope level.

In other words, if you created a server option to assign the IP address of 192.168.1.2 for the 006 DNS Servers option, it would assign this option to all clients served by the server.

If you then assigned the IP address 192.168.1.3 as the 006 DNS Servers option for a scope, the scope option would take precedence. All clients in this scope would receive the IP address of 192.168.1.3 for the DNS server.

Windows Deployment Services Interaction

Windows Deployment Services (WDS) was covered in depth in Chapter 2, "Planning Server Deployments." One of the possible issues with WDS is when DHCP and WDS are installed on the same system.

Both WDS and DHCP listen on port UDP 67. If WDS and DHCP are both installed on the same server, you have to modify the default settings. Since a client machine must have an IP address before it can connect to DHCP, disabling DHCP wouldn't be an option.

Instead, you configure WDS so that it does not listen on port 67 and configure DHCP option 060 on the DHCP server. Figure 4.5 shows the option configured as a server option.

FIGURE 4.5   Configuring option 060 when DHCP and WDS are on the same server

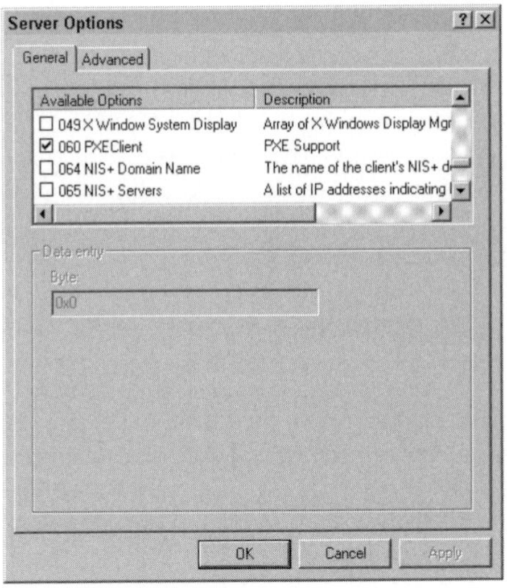

![Server Options dialog box showing the General tab with Available Options list. Checkboxes show 049 X Window System Display, a checked 060 PXE Client, 064 NIS+ Domain Name, and 065 NIS+ Servers, with corresponding descriptions. A Data entry section shows a Byte field with value 0x0. OK, Cancel, and Apply buttons are at the bottom.]

The DHCP option 060 PXE Client does not appear unless your server has the WDS role installed.

The same as any other options (such as default gateway or DNS addresses), option 060 is included in the DHCP response to the client. Option 060 informs the client that the DHCP server is also the WDS server.

If you have DHCP installed when you install a WDS server, the WDS Configuration Wizard will recognize the configuration and prompt you to configure this automatically.

On the other hand, if you add DHCP to a WDS server, you'll have to configure these options yourself.

DHCP Management

When planning for the management of DHCP, you need to consider two built-in groups. Both groups are in the Users container within Active Directory Users and Computers. They are as follows:

DHCP Administrators   Users in the DHCP Administrators group can fully administer DHCP with one exception. DHCP Administrators cannot authorize a DHCP server.

DHCP administrators can create and modify scopes, add and modify options, add scope options, and add and modify reservations. If an administrator is assigned responsibility for a DHCP, she should be added to the DHCP Administrators group.

DHCP Users   The DHCP Users group can view but not modify settings and information within the DHCP console.

As an example, you may have a midnight shift that monitors a group of servers. To give them permissions to view the DHCP console for troubleshooting purposes, you'd add them to the DHCP Users group. They could view the information but would not be able to make any changes (either on purpose or accidentally).

Of course, users in the Domain Admins group (who can do anything in the entire domain) and the Enterprise Admins group (who can do anything in the entire forest) can also fully administer DHCP. However, with the principle of least privilege in mind, you wouldn't want to add a user to one of these groups just to administer DHCP.

Domain Name System

Domain Name System (DNS) servers are primarily used to provide name resolution of hostnames. Every host that has an IP address can also have a hostname. Instead of remembering the IP address, we remember the name, and then DNS resolves the name to an IP address.

Within a Windows network using Active Directory Domain Services, DNS is also used to find specific servers through the use of SRV records. For example, a service may need to find a global catalog server or a PDC emulator. SRV records are used to find servers with these capabilities, and more.

When learning DNS (and preparing for the 70-646 exam), it's important to have a solid understanding of DNS zone types, zone files, and zone records. This chapter will cover each of these to help you reinforce the important pieces of DNS.

DNS has been in use on the Internet since the early days of the ARPANET. However, DNS has not always been the primary name resolution within networks. In the NT 4.0 days, DNS was rarely used on internal networks simply because it was too difficult to register the names.

On the Internet, each record added to a DNS must be added manually. This works fine since hosts on the Internet rarely change. For example, if you host a website, it would be hosted on a specific server. The address of that server would rarely, if ever, change.

That's not the same on internal networks. Typically DHCP is used to dynamically assign IP addresses, so it's very possible for a client to get a new address if turned off one day and turned back on the next.

Since clients can receive different IP addresses, a method is needed to update DNS with the new IP for the client. This process is called *dynamic update*.

Names

When discussing name resolution, it's important to understand that we traditionally have two types of names: hostnames and NetBIOS names. With the introduction of GlobalNames Zone in Windows Server 2008, we also have the addition of a third name: global names.

Hostnames   Hostnames are used on the Internet and within Windows domains to identify systems within the network. A hostname can have as many as 256 characters, though within a network, the name is generally kept to fewer than 16 characters. A name that is fewer than 16 characters is compatible with NetBIOS names.

Hostnames are used within the hierarchy of DNS and are supported in both IPv4 and IPv6. Hostnames must be unique within the namespace but can be duplicated in different namespaces.

For example, the hostname MCITP1 cannot be repeated within the domain of `mcitpsuccess` `.hme`. It would have a fully qualified name of `MCITP1.mcitpsuccess.hme`, and there can be only one such fully qualified domain name.

If you expand the DNS hierarchy, you could have additional domains such as `north` `.mcitpuccess.hme`, `south.mcitpsuccess.hme`, and so on. Within each namespace you could have another server named MCITP1, giving it a fully qualified name of `MCITP1.north` `.mcitpuccess.hme` and `MCITP1.south.mcitpsuccess.hme`, respectively.

Notice that the hostname can be repeated, but only within different namespaces.

Hostnames and NetBIOS names are not case sensitive. In other words, MCITP1 is the same as mcitp1. Additionally, the fully qualified domain name is not case sensitive. `MCITP1.MCITPSUCCESS.HME` is the same as `mcitp1` `.mcitpsuccess.hme`. It's not uncommon to mix cases for readability.

NetBIOS names   NetBIOS names are used only within internal networks and are used to identify systems within the network. A NetBIOS name is composed of 16 characters, but only the first 15 characters are readable. The last character identifies the service running on the computer.

A NetBIOS name is a single name; said another way, it exists within a flat namespace and does not use any type of hierarchy giving it a fully qualified domain name. A server named MCITP1 is simply MCITP1. It doesn't matter in which domain the server exists.

NetBIOS names are not supported in IPv6.

Global names   A global name is new to Windows Server 2008 and is a name that can be resolved using the new GlobalNames Zone feature. The addition of GlobalNames Zone and global names is intended to assist enterprises in eliminating the use of WINS in the network.

Remember, a hostname can be 256 characters, but a NetBIOS is limited to only 15 readable characters. If a longer hostname is used for a computer, the name will be truncated to only the first 15 characters for the NetBIOS name.

For example, if a longer hostname were used for a computer such as microsoftcertifieditpro1 (instead of MCITP1), it would be truncated to microsoftcertif. This is not so bad in itself, but if you created another server and named it microsoftcertifieditpro2, it would also be truncated to microsoftcertif. With two computers holding the same NetBIOS name, you'd have problems. This is why administrators generally limit hostnames to 15 characters.

If you examine how a simple command such as `PING` works using these two names, you'll see how the name can be interpreted either as a hostname or as a NetBIOS name. Consider a computer named MCITP1 within the domain named `north.mcitpsuccess.hme`.

If you enter `PING MCITP1` at the command line, here's what typically happens:

1. First, the domain name is appended to the hostname as `MCITP1.north.mcitpsuccess.hme`. `PING` tries to resolve this hostname using the methods available (DNS, hosts file, and host cache).

2. Next, the address is devolved. This is a fancy way of saying that the child domain name (north in this example) is removed from the fully qualified domain name. `PING` then tries to resolve the hostname `MCITP1.mcitpsuccess.hme` to an IP address.

3. If `PING` doesn't have an IP address at this point, it uses the flat NetBIOS name MCITP1 and tries to resolve it using the methods available (WINS, LMHosts file, NetBIOS cache, and broadcast).

In other words, a name of MCITP1 could be either a hostname or a NetBIOS name. The application assumes it's one or the other and attempts to resolve it based on the assumption. If unsuccessful, most applications will attempt to resolve it using the remaining name resolution methods.

In a forest with multiple namespaces, it's common to use Group Policy to populate the DNS suffix list on clients. For example, a forest with multiple namespaces such as `mctipsuccess.hme`, `contoso.msft`, and `nwtraders.msft` could all be within a client's suffix list. The hostname would be added to these suffixes, and each fully qualified name would be attempted until the name was resolved.

Name Resolution Methods

It's easy to get caught up in the idea that DNS does all name resolution within a network, but actually several types of name resolution are still in use in Microsoft networks today. They are aligned with the three types of names in use: hostnames, global names, and NetBIOS names.

Table 4.3 shows the three name types with their primary methods of name resolution. However, it's important to realize that applications rarely stop with just one method. They instead keep trying name resolution methods until they get an answer or have used all methods.

TABLE 4.3 Name Resolution Methods

Type of Name	Static Method	Dynamic Method	Cache	Vista and Server 2008 only
NetBIOS name	LMHosts file	WINS	NetBIOS cache	
Hostname	Hosts file	DNS	Host cache	LLMNR
GlobalNames*		DNS GNZ		
All	Broadcast			

* Globalames are new to Windows Server 2008 and won't be found elsewhere. They are used for single-label names.

NetBIOS names are considered legacy today, and whenever possible, it's recommended to disable the NetBIOS service within a network today because of security issues. However, many applications still expect a name to be a NetBIOS name and try to use the NetBIOS methods of name resolution.

The three primary types of name resolution for NetBIOS names are as follows:

LMHosts. This is a straight text file that you can use to enter NetBIOS names and IP addresses. When used, it is located in the `C:\Windows\System32\Drivers\etc` folder by default. The `LMHosts.sam` file is a sample file and can be renamed to LMHosts with no extension.

WINS. The WINS server can be used to dynamically resolve NetBIOS names. When used, clients dynamically register their names and IP addresses when they first boot. WINS then responds to queries that include the NetBIOS name with an IP address. In Windows Server 2008, WINS is a feature rather than a full server role.

NetBIOS cache. Once a NetBIOS name is resolved, it is placed into cache. Before querying a WINS server again, the NetBIOS cache is checked. You can view the NetBIOS cache entries with the NetBIOS over TCP/IP Statistics (NBTStat) command: `nbtstat -c`.

The following types of name resolution methods are used to resolve hostnames:

Hosts. This is a straight text file that you can use to enter hostnames and IP addresses. When used, it is located in the C:\Windows\System32\Drivers\etc folder by default. Once a name mapping is placed in the hosts file, it is immediately placed in the host cache.

DNS. The DNS server is used to dynamically resolve hostnames. Within a Windows Server 2000, 2003, or 2008 network, dynamic DNS is used, and clients automatically register their names with the DNS server when booted. Records for DNS servers on the Internet must be manually updated.

DNS GNZ. DNS servers in Windows Server 2008 can host a GlobalNames zone that is used for single-label name (GlobalNames) resolution. This works similarly to how NetBIOS names are resolved by a WINS name server.

Host cache. When a name is resolved from DNS, it is automatically placed in the host cache. Additionally, when names and IP addresses are entered into the hosts file, they are automatically added to cache. You can view the host cache using the IPConfigure/DisplayDNS command. You can purge records from the host cache with the IPConfigure /FlushDNS command.

Link-Local Multicast Name Resolution (LLMNR). LLMNR is new and is supported on Windows Vista and Windows Server 2008 clients. LLMNR is sometimes referred to as *multicast DNS* (mDNS) and is used to resolve names on a local network segment when a DNS server is not available. For example, if a failed router cuts a subnet off from all DNS servers on the network, LLMNR can still be used to resolve some hostnames.

The last method can be used with either NetBIOS or host names.

Broadcast. The last method reminds me of my wife (though I dearly love her). She may be downstairs, but when she wants something, she broadcasts, and everyone knows she wants something. Similarly, the broadcast method sends out a name request to all computers within earshot, and if any host has that name, it will answer with an IP address. It's worth mentioning that routers do *not* pass broadcasts, so "within earshot" means only on the same subnet.

Zones

When discussing DNS, we use the term *zones*. A DNS zone is group of resource records associated with a specific namespace. It includes mappings of names to IP addresses, IP addresses to names, names to services, and more.

If you know DNS from Windows Server 2003, you'll be happy to know that there aren't many significant differences between DNS zones in Server 2003 and Server 2008. The primary differences are related to read-only domain controllers and WINS.

If a DNS server is responsible for maintaining records for a given namespace, it is considered authoritative for that zone.

For example, you could have a domain named mcitpsuccess.hme with a DNS Server named DNS1 that is authoritative for the namespace mcitpsuccess.hme. Imagine querying DNS1 asking for the IP of a server named MCITP7 and DNS1 replies negatively implying there is no host named MCITP7. You've received a definitive answer since DNS1 is the authority for the namespace mcitpsuccess.hme.

Zones are divided into zone types, zone files, and zone records. Any of the zone types can have one or two zone files, and zone files contain zone records.

The primary tool used to manage DNS is the DNS Manager console. Figure 4.6 shows the DNS Manager console as viewed on server MCITP1. This server is hosting an Active Directory–integrated (ADI) primary zone for the mcitpsuccess.hme namespace. It shows several records in the display pane.

FIGURE 4.6   Viewing the DNS Manager console

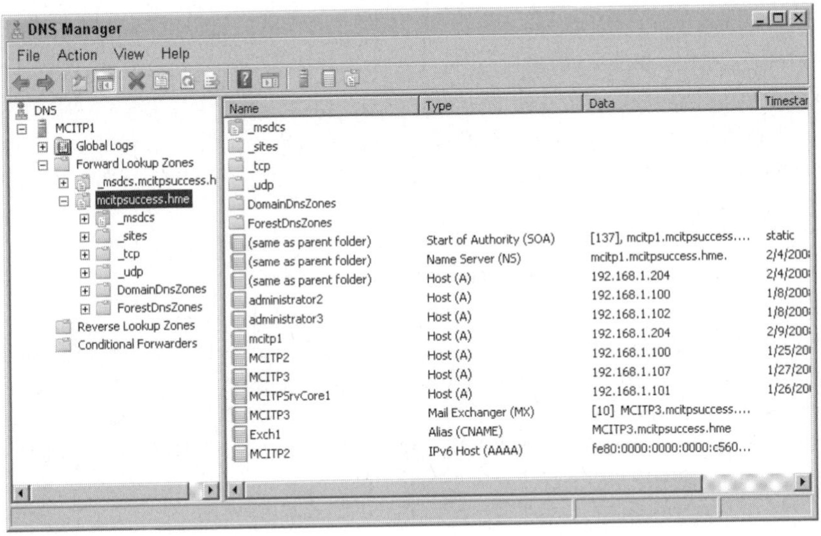

Several of the folders start with an underscore (_). The underscore indicates the folders that are holding SRV records. SRV records are required within a domain. In other words, by looking at Figure 4.6, you can easily tell that this DNS server is hosting records for a domain.

In the following sections, we'll explore zone types, zone files, and zone records, but it's good to have an understanding of the big picture. Zones (primary, secondary, GlobalNames or stub) hold one or two zone files, and zone files hold zone resource records.

Zone types   The following are the zone types:

- Primary
- Secondary
- Stub
- Active Directory–integrated
- GlobalNames

Zone files   The following are the zone files:

- Forward lookup zone file (holds A records, and more). This primarily provides hostname to IP address resolution.
- Reverse lookup zone file (holds PTR records). This provides IP address to hostname resolution.

Zone resource records   The following are the zone resource records:

- A (host) IPv4
- AAAA (host) IPv6
- PTR
- SOA
- SRV
- NS
- MX
- CNAME (alias)

Zone Types

Windows Server 2008 DNS includes three zone types:

Primary zone   A primary zone is a zone hosted by a DNS server where the server is the primary source of information about the zone. In other words, the DNS server for a primary zone is authoritative for that zone.

If the zone is not an Active Directory–integrated zone, the primary DNS server holds the only read/write copy of the database. In this situation, you would have only one primary DNS server.

When using Active Directory–integrated zones (and this is recommended), you can have multiple primary DNS zones. However, each DNS server hosting a primary zone would have to be Active Directory–integrated.

Secondary zone   A secondary zone is created on a different DNS server to provide load balancing for the DNS server holding the primary zone. The secondary zone is a read-only copy of the zone data. It cannot be modified except through zone transfers.

Periodically, the DNS server hosting the secondary zone is updated through a process known as a *zone transfer*. Either the secondary DNS server queries the primary DNS server to determine whether it is out-of-date or the primary DNS server can notify the secondary server that a change has occurred.

Zone transfers transfer only the records that have been added, deleted, or modified, not the entire zone file.

Stub zone A stub zone is a copy of key records in another zone. The purpose is to identify the DNS server that is authoritative for the zone. A stub zone does not contain all of the records in the zone but instead only enough records needed to communicate with the authoritative DNS server.

Records contained in the stub zone are the name server (NS) record, the start of authority (SOA) record, and possibly the host (A) records.

Active Directory–integrated zones Both primary zones and stub zones can also be Active Directory–integrated zones. An ADI zone is one that is included in the Active Directory database.

A significant benefit of using ADI zones is that DNS zone transfers are now part of Active Directory replication. Whenever a change occurs to objects (such as users, computers, and in this case DNS zone records) within Active Directory, the replication process recognizes the change and sends the changes to other domain controllers in the domain.

Since the zone transfer is part of Active Directory replication, it is automatically encrypted. Additionally, since all DNS servers that are ADI zones are also primary zones, an ADI zone provides built-in fault tolerance. If a single DNS server fails, other DNS servers will automatically take on the load.

The three options you have when selecting Active Directory replication are as follows:

> **To all DNS servers in the forest.** When this option is selected, DNS zone data will be replaced to all Windows Server 2003 and Server 2008 domain controllers in the forest that are also DNS servers.

> The DNS zone data is replicated as part of the ForestDNSZones partition.

> **To all DNS servers in the domain.** This option will replicate the DNS zone data information to all Windows Server 2003 and Windows Server 2008 domain controllers in the domain that are also DNS servers.

> The DNS zone data is replicated as part of the DomainDNSZone partition.

> **To all domain controllers in the domain.** If you have DNS servers running Windows Server 2000 and you want them to be ADI, you have to select this option.

> Windows 2000 doesn't have the capability to use Active Directory application partitions, so zone data must be replicated to all domain controllers in the forest.

If you don't have any Active Directory–integrated zones running on Windows Server 2000 servers, don't use this option. Application partitions provide better performance.

Microsoft recommends you use Active Directory–integrated zones whenever possible. It is easier to manage DNS with ADI zones, and if you want to secure DNS, an ADI zone provides extra security capabilities such as the ability to enable secure dynamic updates.

As a reminder, to enable secure dynamic updates, the following requirements must be in place:

- The DNS server is running on a domain controller.
- The Active Directory–integrated zone has been enabled.
- Dynamic updates are set for Secure Only in the properties of the zone.

To fully administer DNS, you need to be a member of the DNS Administrators group. This also allows you to configure individual permissions for Active Directory–integrated zones.

GlobalNames Zone   GlobalNames zone (GNZ) is a new feature in Windows Server 2008, and it provides single name resolution in networks that do not use WINS. It's somewhat of a misnomer to refer to it as a different type of zone. To be more technically accurate, it is a special type of primary zone.

To put GNZ into context, remember that hostnames are traditionally resolved using the fully qualified name (such as MCITP1.mcitpsuccess.hme) by DNS and that NetBIOS names are typically resolved using a single label or flat namespace (such as only MCITP1) by WINS. When using a GNZ, DNS is able resolve names using the single label name.

GNZ is not intended to replace WINS. It can aid in the retirement of WINS in networks where WINS is rarely used. WINS uses name registration to dynamically add records to the WINS database. DNS uses dynamic update to dynamically add records to DNS zones. However, GNZ does not support dynamic updates, so records must be added manually.

A GNZ can be hosted only on a DNS server that is authoritative for the zone and running on a Windows Server 2008 domain controller. It's recommended the zone be Active Directory–integrated and replicated to all DNS servers in the forest, but remember that all DNS servers must be running Windows Server 2008 to support the GNZ.

Before a GlobalNames zone can be created, you must enable it. The following command can be run from the command line to enable the creation of a GlobalNames zone:
Dnscmd ServerName /config /EnableGlobalNamesSupport 1.

The command is not case sensitive.

The GNZ would then be created as a primary zone. Figure 4.7 shows a GlobalNames zone added to a DNS server.

The record types added to the GNZ are CNAME records. Each CNAME record must be manually added and points to a host record within another DNS zone.

Zone Files

Zones can contain one or two zone files:

Forward lookup zone file   The forward lookup zone file is primarily used to provide hostname to IP address resolution using host (A) records. In other words, a client queries the DNS server with a hostname, and the DNS server answers with the IP address based on the record within the forward lookup zone.

You must have a forward lookup zone file within a DNS zone of any type.

Although forward lookup zones primarily hold host (A) records, they typically hold other records. Forward lookup zones can hold any zone records except PTR records, which are used for reverse lookups.

Reverse lookup zone file   The reverse lookup zone file is used to hold PTR (commonly called *pointer*) records. PTR records are found only in reverse lookup zones and provide an IP address to name resolution method. In other words, the client passes an IP address to the DNS server, and the DNS server replies with the hostname. PTR records are commonly used for security purposes.

For example, imagine that Microsoft enters into an agreement with Sybex. Sybex is allowed access to Microsoft's internal network through the Internet but only when accessed from Sybex's network (not through someone's home computer).

When a request is received at Microsoft, the IP address is included in the packet. Microsoft can then query a DNS server with a reverse lookup using the IP address. The reverse lookup will verify the connection is from a computer from sybex.com.

If instead a reverse lookup reports the name associated with the IP address is hackersRus.com, the traffic would be stopped.

Reverse lookup zones are optional. A DNS server can function without a reverse lookup zone but cannot operate without a forward lookup zone.

Zone Resource Records

Zone resource records are contained with zone files. The PTR record is contained with the optional reverse lookup zone file, but all other resource records are found in the forward lookup zone file. The following are the common zone records you'll see within a Windows Server 2008 DNS server:

A (host) IPv4   The A, or host record, maps a hostname to an IPv4 address. This is the most common type of record within DNS. When using dynamic update, the A record is automatically created by DNS. It can also be created manually.

AAAA (host) IPv6   Within IPv6, the A record is replaced with the AAAA record. It maps a hostname to an IPv6 address. Just like an A record, if you're using dynamic update, the AAAA record is automatically created by DNS, and it can also be created manually in the DNS Manager console.

PTR   The PTR record is contained within the reverse lookup zone file. It provides mapping from the IP address to a name. PTR records can be automatically created when the A or AAAA is created with dynamic update. Additionally, when creating an A or AAAA record manually, you can check a box to also create the associated PTR record.

SOA   The start of authority (SOA) record provides a lot of key information on the DNS server and is created when DNS is installed.

Figure 4.8 shows the values contained within the SOA record. You can view this either by double-clicking the SOA record within the DNS Manager console or by right-clicking the zone, selecting Properties, and then selecting the Start of Authority tab.

Within the SOA record, you have the following properties:

Serial number. When a record is added, deleted, or modified, the serial number is incremented on the SOA record of the primary DNS server. When a secondary DNS server queries the primary DNS server, a copy of the SOA record is sent. If the serial number is different, the secondary DNS server requests a zone transfer.

Primary server. This shows the fully qualified name of the DNS server that is authoritative for the zone.

Responsible person. This indicates an email address that administrators can use to contact someone in case a problem with DNS is discovered. The email address is entered as username.mcitpsuccess.hme but is interpreted as username@mcitpsuccess.hme.

Refresh interval. The refresh interval determines how often secondary DNS servers request a copy of the SOA from the primary DNS server. When the SOA is received, the secondary DNS server compares the value of the serial number to see whether a zone transfer should be requested.

FIGURE 4.8   The SOA record

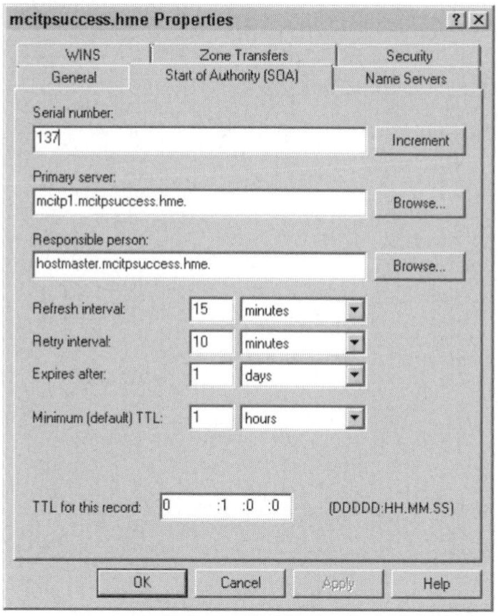

Retry interval. If the secondary DNS server can't reach the primary DNS server after the refresh interval has been reached, the retry interval identifies how often it should retry.

Expires after. If the secondary DNS server consistently cannot reach the primary DNS server, the Expires After value will be used. After this period of time, the secondary DNS server will consider its records stale and no longer answer queries for this zone.

Minimum (default) TTL. The default Time to Live (TTL) indicates the TTL value of manually created records. Minimum is really a misnomer. Records created from dynamic updates have a default TTL value of 20 minutes, which is set in the registry.

The TTL indicates how long records should be cached. You can view remaining TTL values for any records in the cache by using IPConfig /DisplayDNS.

TTL for this record. The TTL for the SOA record is listed in this box.

SRV   SRV records are used to identify servers running specific services within the domain. DNS is required within an Active Directory Domain Services domain, and the existence of SRV records is a core reason why DNS is required.

Figure 4.9 shows some of the SRV records within the mcitpsuccess.hme namespace. The _gc record identifies a server holding the role of the global catalog server. The _kerberos record identifies the domain controller that can be used for authentication. The _ldap record identifies the server that can be used for generic LDAP queries.

FIGURE 4.9   Viewing SRV records in the DNS Manager console

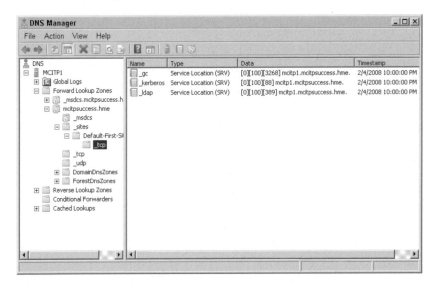

Since my domain has only one domain controller, all three records point to the server named MCITP1. Notice the SRV record doesn't have the IP address, but instead only the name. The name is then used to query the A record for the IP address.

The SRV records are created by the NetLogon service. Occasionally, the SRV records do not appear as they should. You can stop and restart the NetLogon service to force the SRV records to be regenerated. You can use the Services applet, or you can restart the service from the command line with the following commands:

```
Net Stop Netlogon
Net Start Netlogon
```

NS The NS record is used to identify DNS name servers. A NS record can be created within a zone by viewing the properties of the zone and selecting the Name Services tab. Figure 4.10 shows the Name Servers tab. By clicking Add, you can create an NS record.

MX Mail exchanger (MX) records are used to identify mail servers. An MX record is sometimes referred to as a *mail exchange record*.

CNAME (alias) A CNAME record is used to allow a single server to respond to multiple names. DNS queries with any of the names (from the A record or any of the CNAME records) will respond with the same IP address.

For example, a server could be named MCITP1, but since it's running Microsoft Exchange, you decide you also want it to be known as EXCH1. By adding a CNAME record that points to the MCITP1 A record, queries for either MCITP or EXCH1 will be answered with the same IP address.

CNAME records are used within the GlobalNames zone for single-label name resolution.

FIGURE 4.10   Viewing the Name Servers tab to create a new NS record in the DNS Manager console

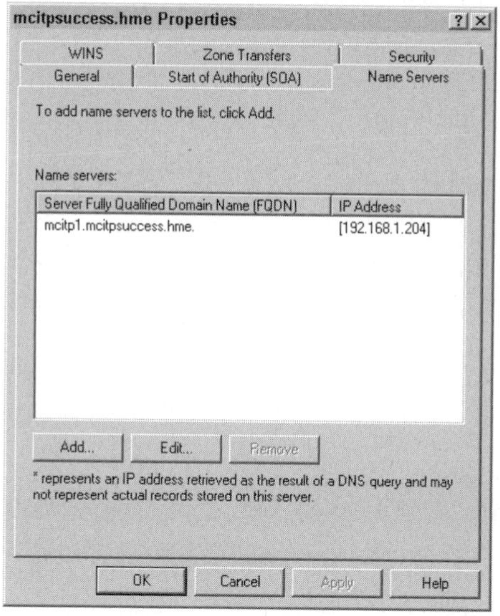

Exercise 4.4 shows you how to create a DNS forward lookup zone file. This exercise assumes you have DNS installed on your system. If you don't have a system with DNS installed, you can do Exercises 1.3 and 1.4 in Chapter 1, "Introducing Windows Server 2008." These exercises install Active Directory Domain Services and DNS on your Windows Server 2008 system.

EXERCISE 4.4

Creating a Forward Lookup Zone

1. Launch the DNS Manager console by clicking Start ➤ Administrative Tools ➤ DNS.

2. Click the plus sign next to the server to open the DNS tree.

3. Right-click the server name, and select New Zone.

4. On the Welcome page, click Next.

5. On the Zone Type page, ensure Primary Zone is selected. Additionally, ensure the check box next to Store the Zone in Active Directory is selected. Click Next.

6. On the Active Directory Zone Replication Scope page, select the option To All DNS Servers in This Domain. Click Next.

7. On the Forward or Reverse Lookup Zone page, accept the default of Forward Lookup Zone, and click Next.

8. On the Zone Name page, enter the name **sybex.mcitpsuccess.bk**. Notice this name does not need to match the namespace of other zones hosted on this DNS server. Since we are creating it just to create dummy records, it doesn't even need to match the name of an existing domain.

9. On the Dynamic Update page, accept the default of Allow Only Secure Dynamic Updates, and click Next.

10. On the Completing the New Zone Wizard page, click Finish.

Exercise 4.5 shows how to create DNS records within your forward lookup zone file. This exercise assumes you have completed Exercise 4.4

EXERCISE 4.5

Creating Records within a Forward Lookup Zone

1. If not already launched, launch the DNS Manager console by clicking Start ➤ Administrative Tools ➤ DNS.

2. Click the plus sign next to the server to open the DNS tree.

3. Select the sybex.mcitpsuccess.bk zone.

4. Right-click the zone, and select New Host (A or AAAA).

5. In the New Host dialog box, enter **MCITP_IPv4** in the Name box. Notice that the fully qualified domain name fills in as you type. For the IP address, enter **192.168.7.4**. The New Host dialog box creates an A record if you enter an IPv4 address and creates an AAAA record if you enter an IPv6 address. Your display will look similar to the following image. Click the Add Host button.

6. In the DNS dialog box that indicates success, click OK. The New Host dialog box will clear, allowing you to create another record.

7. In the New Host dialog box, enter **MCITP_IPv6** in the Name box. Enter **E3D7::5154:9BC8:C0A8:74** as the IP address. Click the Add Host button.

8. In the success dialog box, click OK. In the New Host dialog box, click Done. Your display will look similar to the following image. Notice that the SOA and NS records were created from creating the zone file. The A and AAAA records were created in the steps in this exercise.

EXERCISE 4.5 *(continued)*

9. Right-click the sybex.mcitpsuccess.bk zone, and select New Mail Exchange.

10. In the New Resource Record dialog box, click the Browse button.

11. In the Records section, double-click your server name. Double-click the Forward Lookup Zones folder. Double-click the sybex.mcitpsuccess.bk name. Select the MCITP_IPv4 record, and click OK.

12. Right-click the sybex.mcitpsuccess.bk zone, and select New Alias (CNAME).

13. In the New Resource Record dialog box, enter **EXCH1** as the alias name.

14. Click the Browse button. In the Records section, double-click the name of your server. Double-click the name of the Forward Lookup Zones folder. Double-click the sybex .mcitpsuccess.bk zone. Select the MCITP_IPv4 record. Click OK.

15. The fully qualified name of the server you selected will be added to the Fully Qualified Domain Name box. Click OK. The following image shows a partial view of the DNS Manager console with the records you just created.

Name	Type	Data
(same as parent folder)	Start of Authority (SOA)	[1], mcitp1.mcitpsuccess.hme., hostmaster.mcitpsuccess.hme.
(same as parent folder)	Name Server (NS)	mcitp1.mcitpsuccess.hme.
MCITP_IPv4	Host (A)	192.168.7.4
MCITP_IPv6	IPv6 Host (AAAA)	e3d7:0000:0000:0000:5154:9bc8:c0a8:0074
(same as parent folder)	Mail Exchanger (MX)	[10] MCITP_IPv4.sybex.mcitpsuccess.bk
EXCH1	Alias (CNAME)	MCITP_IPv4.sybex.mcitpsuccess.bk

You can use the DNS Manager console to create as many manually created records as you need.

Another record you may create manually is the MX record. If you have multiple mail servers, you can create multiple MX records within the same zone.

By modifying the mail server priority value in the different records, you can affect which mail server will be contacted. The response to the MX query will include all MX records, but the record with the lowest priority value will be attempted first. If that attempt fails, the next priority server is tried. If the priority values are the same for all MX records, the servers are chosen at random.

Although you should know how to create the records, most records are not created manually within a domain. Instead, most records within a domain are created through the dynamic update process. Of course, that begs the question, "What is dynamic update?"

I'm so glad you asked …

Dynamic Update

Since Windows 2000, Microsoft networks have supported dynamic DNS, or dynamic updates. The dynamic update feature allows the A and PTR records within DNS to be created automatically without any manual intervention. Figure 4.11 shows the process of dynamic updates.

FIGURE 4.11   Dynamically updating DNS records

When the client boots, it receives the TCP/IP configuration information from DHCP, including the IP address and the address of DNS. The client will then update the A record in DNS. Additionally, DHCP will update the PTR record if a reverse lookup zone exists.

Dynamic update is configured in three locations:

DNS settings for dynamic update   In the General properties tab of a DNS zone, you can configure dynamic updates. Figure 4.12 shows the three possible selections.

FIGURE 4.12   Configuring DNS for dynamic updates

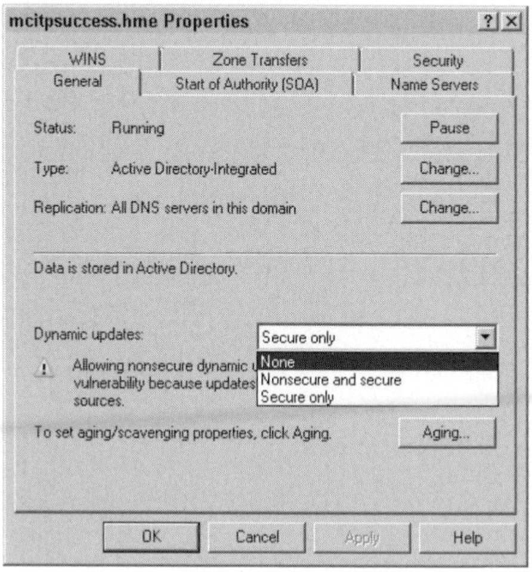

None   Dynamic updates are not allowed. This is rare.

Secure Only   Only computers with an account in the domain can update the records after receiving a DHCP address. Additionally, security zones can be secured with permissions.

> Microsoft consistently repeats the recommendation to use Secure Only. A requirement to enable this feature is that the zone must be in Active Directory–integrated mode, meaning it must be a domain controller. It makes a lot of sense for ease of administration to run DNS on a domain controller and use Active Directory–integrated mode. As long as you've gone that far, follow the recommendation and use Secure Only.

Nonsecure and Secure   Both nonsecure and secure updates are allowed.

DHCP settings for dynamic update   The DHCP server is configured by default to use dynamic updates. Figure 4.13 shows the default settings.

FIGURE 4.13   Configuring DHCP for dynamic updates

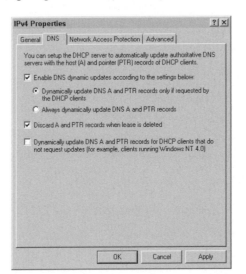

As long as all your clients are running Windows 2000 or later, these settings will work. If you have down-level clients (Windows NT 4.0 or earlier), you should select one of the following two settings:

- Always Dynamically Update DNS A and PTR Records
- Dynamically Update DNS A and PTR Records for DHCP Clients That Do Not Request Updates

Windows XP and Vista clients are aware of dynamic update so can be configured to update the records themselves. If you don't have any down-level clients, there is no need to modify the default settings for DHCP.

Client settings for dynamic update   The client settings for dynamic update can be configured in the NIC's properties. Figure 4.14 shows the DNS tab of the Advanced TCP/IP Settings dialog box, which you can access via the Transmission Control Protocol/Internet Protocol v4 (TCP/IPv4) properties of the NIC.

FIGURE 4.14   Configuring the client for dynamic updates

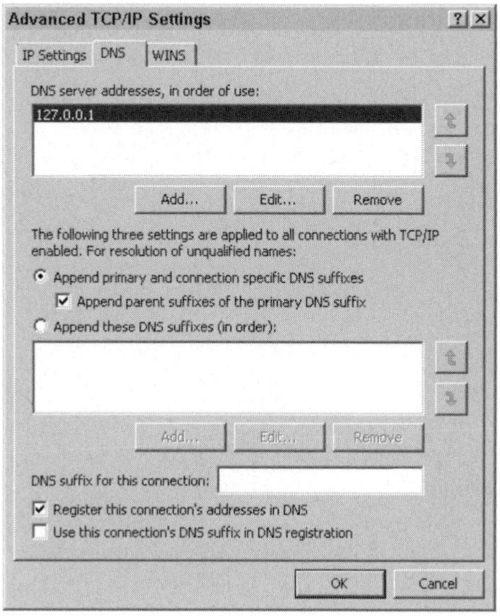

DNS and RODCs

A new feature in Windows Server 2008 is the introduction of read-only domain controllers (RODCs). When placing an RODC at a remote site, you should also configure DNS appropriately.

As a reminder, an RODC is placed in a branch office that needs a local domain controller but doesn't have adequate physical security to support placing a regular domain controller at the site. Inadequate physical security means someone could easily come in and steal the domain controller. With unrestricted access to the domain controller, the entire domain could be compromised as the thief slowly learns the passwords of key accounts like Enterprise Admins or Domain Admins.

With an RODC, only the credentials needed to support the remote branch office are maintained on the RODC. RODCs are typically configured so that administrative account credentials are not stored locally.

Now consider DNS.

If you place a domain controller at a remote site, you should also place a DNS server there. When a user logs on, SRV and host records need to be queried to locate a domain controller. If the DNS server is not located locally, multiple queries would have to traverse the WAN link.

Further, if you place a DNS server locally, it makes a lot of sense to place it on the domain controller and make it Active Directory–integrated. Last, clients at the remote site should be configured to use the local DNS server.

You might notice a conflict with dynamic update. The domain controller is read-only, and the DNS zone is Active Directory–integrated, so this indicates that dynamic update can't work. Rest assured, it still does.

Figure 4.15 shows the process of dynamic update when using an RODC. The four overall steps are labeled as 1 through 4.

FIGURE 4.15 Configuring the client for dynamic updates

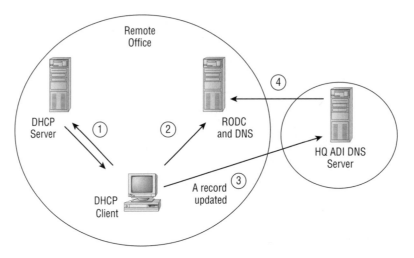

The DHCP server provides the IP address and other TCP/IP configuration information as normal in step 1. In step 2, the local DNS server receives a dynamic update request. The local DNS server redirects the client to a writable DNS server. In step 3, the client completes the dynamic update with the writable DNS server. In step 4, the writable DNS server replicates this record to the local DNS server via Active Directory replication.

Although not shown in the figure, DHCP updates the PTR record using the same referral process. The local DNS server redirects DHCP to a writable DNS server.

In summary, when using RODCs, configure DNS as follows:

- Add DNS to the RODC as an Active Directory–integrated zone.
- Configure DNS to accept dynamic updates.
- Configure clients with address of local DNS server.

Windows Internet Naming Service

Windows Internet Naming Service (WINS) is used to map NetBIOS names to IP addresses. Don't be fooled by the name, though. WINS has nothing to do with the Internet. The Internet uses hostnames, not NetBIOS names. You will find WINS servers only on internal networks.

However, the use of NetBIOS names has been significantly reduced over the years since dynamic update with DNS was introduced. When dynamic update was first introduced with Windows 2000, a wave of administrators predicted we could get rid of WINS. Unfortunately, since so many applications were still expecting a WINS server out there, WINS was still needed.

In Windows Server 2003, the predictions were repeated by many administrators—WINS won't be needed anymore. Yet it remained in many environments (including mine).

With Windows Server 2008, the predictions are more cautious. You may be able to get rid of WINS. It depends on the applications you use in your environment. However, Windows Server 2008 DNS introduced the GlobalNames Zone feature, which does get us another step closer. The GNZ resolves single-label names that look like NetBIOS names but are resolved within DNS.

Figure 4.16 shows the name registration process for WINS. When a client turns on, it receives an IP address and other TCP/IP configuration information, such as the address of the WINS server. The client then registers its NetBIOS name and IP address in WINS. Other clients can then query WINS to resolve NetBIOS names to IP addresses.

FIGURE 4.16   Name registration in WINS

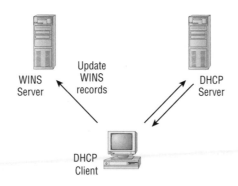

You may notice some similarities between WINS and dynamic DNS. As a matter of fact, when I teach name resolution in the classroom, I use the same diagram on the white board for both DNS and WINS. I just change the name of the server.

Both DNS and WINS can have the majority of their records updated automatically without an administrator having to add each of the records. WINS uses a registration process, and DNS uses dynamic update.

WINS Is a Feature

A significant difference with WINS in Server 2008 and previous Windows Server products (such as Windows Server 2003) is that WINS is not considered a full server role. Instead, WINS is a feature. All this really means is that when you add WINS, you use Server Manger and add it as a feature. It is not available as a server role. Since NetBIOS names are used less and less and the need for WINS is significantly reduced from the NT 4.0 days, it's less likely you'll need to dedicate a server to be only a WINS server.

Although in the past a WINS server could have a primary role as a WINS server and be highly utilized as a WINS server in a large environment, that's just not likely today. Instead, you would have a server with another primary role, and you add on the WINS feature to the server to resolve NetBIOS names. You can compare this to adding the Windows Backup feature to enable the use of backups.

DNS and WINS

If you don't have many applications that need WINS but still need to occasionally resolve some key servers with a single-label name, you can consider retiring WINS and using GlobalName zone within DNS.

It's worth noting that GNZ records cannot be created dynamically. Instead, CNAME records are added manually to the GNZ for each server that you need to resolve with a single-label name. However, since the CNAME record maps to an A record to resolve the name to an IP address, you need to add the CNAME only once to a GNZ, even if the IP address may change.

Network Access Protection

Network Access Protection (NAP) is used to ensure that any clients that connect to a network are healthy. Health is determined by the administrator and is enforced with health policies.

Network access is used to provide access to the network from outside the network. Clients can connect using dial-up, a virtual private network (VPN), or wireless. One of the significant security challenges with network access is ensuring that clients are compliant with specific security policies.

Within a network, clients can be controlled. Hotfixes and patches are easily deployed. Antivirus software can be kept up-to-date. Security settings can be maintained via Group Policy.

In contrast, a client connecting via a network access method often cannot be controlled, at least until they're granted access to the network. By that time it may be too late. When a client connects, you need to know whether it is healthy and not a risk or whether it is significantly unhealthy (such as being infected with viruses or worms), posing significant risks to the network.

Figure 4.17 shows a typical network that is using Network Access Protection. Consider a VPN client that accesses the network via the Internet through the VPN server. The NAP health policy server holds the policy configured by the administrator. The health registration authority (HRA) verifies the health of the clients and issues health certificates to healthy clients.

FIGURE 4.16   Network with NAP deployed

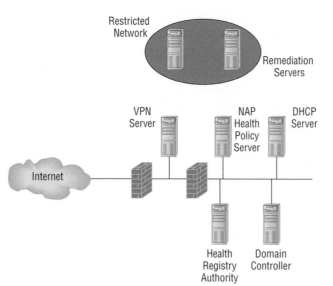

If a client is determined to be healthy, it is granted regular access to the network. If a client is not issued a health certificate from the HRA, then it is granted access only to the restricted network. The restricted network is also referred to as the *limited-access network* and will contain remediation servers that can be used to help the client become healthy.

For example, if the health policy specifies the clients must be up-to-date with current hotfixes and patches, a WSUS server could be placed in the restricted-access environment. Similarly, an antivirus software server could be in the restricted-access network to allow the client to download up-to-date antivirus signatures.

Network Access Protection has four primary enforcement methods that you can use to help ensure that security policies are being enforced on your network:

- VPN enforcement
- IPSec enforcement
- 802.1x enforcement
- DHCP enforcement

Each of the methods is described more fully in the following pages. Additionally, each of the four methods can be used in a monitoring-only environment or a limited-access environment.

Monitoring-only environment   Clients are checked to ensure they are healthy in compliance with the health policy. The compliance state of each computer is logged. However, unhealthy clients are still allowed access to the network the same as healthy clients.

Before deploying a full-scale NAP solution, administrators can use the logs to help determine the issues that need to be addressed.

Limited-access environment   In a limited-access environment, unhealthy clients are not granted access to the network but instead granted only limited access to the restricted network. The limited-access environment includes remediation servers that can help the client become compliant with the health policy.

Three important aspects of Network Access Protection are shared with each of the enforcement methods. They are as follows:

Health state validation   Health requirement policies are defined by an administrator and held on the NAP health policy server. When a computer connects, the policy is used to check the computer's health by the health registration authority. If healthy, the client is issued a health certificate from the health registration authority.

It's important to realize that just because the client isn't issued a health certificate, it doesn't necessarily mean that it's infected with a virus or worm or has any other significant problems. Instead, the health certificate indicates only that the client is in compliance with the health policy.

Health policy compliance   When a computer is determined to be unhealthy, an administrator has many choices on what action to take. Normally, a client will be granted access to the restricted network only until compliant.

If you have the resources on your network, you could set the policy to automatically update unhealthy computers in some situations. For example, a computer may need to have a patch installed to be determined healthy. The patch could be deployed via Systems Management Server (SMS) or via System Center Configuration Manager (SCCM) to bring the computer into compliance.

Additionally, you can configure exceptions so that some noncompliant computers are still granted network access.

Limited access   Limited access refers to granting a client access only to a restricted network. The restricted network contains remediation servers that can be used to help the client become healthy. Once a client utilizes the remediation servers to become healthy, the health registration authority again tries to validate the client. If healthy, the health registration authority issues a health certificate, and the client has regular access to the network.

VPN Enforcement

Many networks allow network access via a VPN. Figure 4.18 shows a typical VPN configuration. The client connects to a local ISP and then tunnels through Internet to create a VPN connection with the VPN server.

FIGURE 4.18   Typical VPN configuration

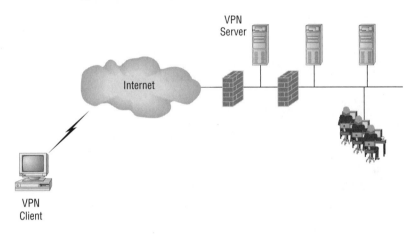

VPN servers use some form of authentication to ensure only authorized users can gain access to the back-end network. Additionally, VPN protocols include encryption mechanisms to ensure the data isn't intercepted. A common VPN combination is the Layer 2 Tunneling Protocol used over IPSec (commonly referred to as L2TP/IPSec).

NAP can be configured to work with VPNs using VPN enforcement. Instead of just allowing clients through that can authenticate themselves, VPN enforcement adds the capability of ensuring clients are healthy before being granted access to the back-end network.

Health policies are created on the NAP health policy server. When the client connects, the health registration authority is used to compare the client against the policies. If the client is determined to be in compliance with the health policies, a health certificate is issued. If noncompliant, the computer would be granted only limited access.

Once the computer uses the remediation servers to become compliant, the health registration authority once again checks the client. If healthy at this time, a health certificate is issued, and the client gains access to the network.

IPSec Enforcement

IPSec enforcement is the strongest form of limited network access protection you can deploy in the network. It is used to ensure traffic is protected based on a policy created by the administrator.

IPSec can be used with both IPv4 and IPv6 and is used to protect communications between computers. It can be used to encrypt the traffic to prevent it from being intercepted and read by a third party. IPSec can also be used to verify authentication of each of computers.

Encryption is done with IPSec's Encapsulating Security Payload (ESP). Authentication is accomplished with an authentication header (AH) embedded in the IP packet.

Although IPSec is commonly used with VPNs (such as with L2TP/IPSec), it can also be used to encrypt traffic beyond VPNs. For example, a file server holding key financial data can be configured to ensure that all connections use IPSec. When properly configured, data would be transferred only from the financial servers using IPSec technologies.

For computers to be able to communicate with IPSec with other computers, they must have an IPSec policy configured. IPSec policies can be configured through Group Policy in an Active Directory Domain Services environment or through a local policy.

With IPSec enforcement, you have the ability to ensure that clients can communicate with IPSec. Using IPSec enforcement, you can define requirements for secure communications between compliant computers. As long as a client's IPSec policy is compliant with the IPSec enforcement policy, it will be issued a health certificate.

If a client is not compliant with the IPSec enforcement policy, network access will be limited.

802.1x Enforcement

802.1x enforcement can be used in networks using 802.1x authentication. In addition to the authentication mechanisms with 802.1x, you can add NAP to ensure the clients are healthy before they are granted full access to the network.

Although 802.1x can be used for both wired and wireless networks, it is more commonly associated with wireless networks. To get a better understanding of 802.1x, compare a home or small-office network to a large enterprise.

You may be running a wireless network at home or know someone who is. They are fairly easy to set up and are very popular in areas that have broadband access such as through a cable TV company.

The broadband modem connects to the Internet service provider (ISP). Most computer stores sell wireless routers that can be connected to the modem and then be used to connect wireless (and wired) connections to the Internet with just the single line to the Internet through the cable company.

Thinking about a wireless network at a home or even a small business, what's needed to connect to the router? Typically you'd use some type of encryption such as WEP (which is old and easy to decrypt; I hope you're not using this anymore), WPA, or WPA2. Now, any client that knows the encryption key can connect. Although this works effectively at homes and small offices, it isn't an effective solution in larger networks.

In a large enterprise, you may want each user to log on before being granted access to the network. A Remote Authentication Dial-In User Service (RADIUS) is used within an 802.1x configuration to authenticate users before they are granted access to the network.

If you have an 802.1x configuration, you can also add NAP to the setup. 802.1x enforcement can be used to determine the health of a client before the client is granted full access to the network. If a client is not healthy, it will be granted only limited access. It can then access the remediation servers, get healthy, and try again.

DHCP Enforcement

One of the security issues with DHCP is that if a client plugs in and broadcasts a discover packet, DHCP answers. It doesn't matter who the client is; DHCP sends it a lease including an IP address and other options.

From a workability perspective, this is great. It doesn't require any intervention from the administrator. From a security perspective, this is not good.

An unpatched computer infected with a new virus or worm could connect, and in no time, your day is ruined.

If the computer was completely under your control, you could ensure that it was fully patched and had the correct virus signatures installed. However, a mobile computer is, well ... mobile. It's here one day and gone the next.

You can use NAP enforcement with DHCP (also called *DHCP enforcement*) to check a client's health before issuing a normal lease.

DHCP Enforcement Process

Remember earlier in this chapter when I explained the DHCP process? The client sends a discover packet, the DHCP responds with a lease offer (including the IP address and all the option information), the client sends a request packet to request the lease, and last, the DHCP server sends an acknowledgment.

The difference when DHCP enforcement is used starts right away. Instead of issuing a lease, DHCP works with NAP to determine the health of the client:

- If the client is found to be healthy, a regular lease is offered, requested, and acknowledged.

- If the client is not healthy, a different lease is offered. This lease includes an IP address, subnet mask, and set of host routes to remediation servers.

The client can then connect with the remediation servers to do whatever is necessary to make it healthy. For example, remediation servers can be used to help the client receive the currently approved patches or update antivirus signatures.

Once the client is updated, it repeats the process with DHCP. The statement of health is presented to the NPS server, and if it passes, the client is issued a normal lease.

Requirements

The requirements to use DHCP enforcement are as follows:

- The DHCP server must be running on Windows Server 2008.

- The DHCP server must have the Network Policy Server (NPS) role installed as a RADIUS server or as a RADIUS proxy to forward requests to an NPS server.

- The Network Access Protection (NAP) service must be running on the DHCP clients.

The last requirement may look like a security hole, but it isn't. It is a hole for operability, but not for security. The NAP service doesn't run on non-Microsoft clients, so it can't be used in heterogeneous environments.

Only Windows XP (with SP3), Windows Vista, and Windows Server 2008 can run the service. Microsoft doesn't have any current plans to expand the NAP service to other clients such as Mac, Linux, Unix, or any Microsoft down-level clients before Windows XP with SP3.

Summary

A solid network infrastructure design is key to a consistently working network. DNS, DHCP, WINS (when used), and NAP can all come together to ensure your network components work together and clients can access exactly what they need to access, when they need to access it.

If you took the 70-642 MCTS exam (Configuring Windows Server 2008 Network Infrastructure), you probably noticed a lot of familiar material. In this chapter, you didn't learn all the details about each of these network components but instead reviewed and refreshed some of the important details you'll need as an MCITP: Server Administrator.

You learned basics of DHCP, how to add it as a role, and how to configure scopes and options. On the job, it's not unreasonable for you to need to modify DHCP properties. As long as you're in the DHCP Administrators group, you can modify anything within DHCP (except authorize the server itself).

Within DNS, you learned the basics of zone types, zone files, and zone records. You should have a solid understanding of the different zone types (primary, secondary, stub) and the specialized zone types (Active Directory–integrated and GlobalNames zone) in a Windows Server 2008 environment.

The two zone files are forward lookup and reverse lookup zone files. The reverse lookup zone file uses PTR (pointer) records to resolve IP addresses to names (the reverse of a host record, which resolves names to IP addresses). The forward lookup zone holds the A (IPv4) and AAAA (IPv6) records but can also have other record types such as SRV, NS, MX, and CNAME records. All zone files have the Start of Authority record that holds key information about the zone.

WINS is used to resolve NetBIOS names in a network. If you are close to being able to get rid of WINS, you may be able to implement a GlobalNames zone to speed the process.

Last, the chapter presented Network Access Protection. You learned that network access policies can be created to identify what a healthy client looks like. The health registration authority is then used to check clients. Healthy clients are issued a health certificate and granted access to the network. Unhealthy clients are given only limited access to a restricted network where they can use remediation servers to get healthy.

NAP has four enforcement methods used to ensure security policies are being enforced on your network: VPN enforcement, IPSec enforcement, 802.1x enforcement, and DHCP enforcement.

Exam Essentials

Know how to create and modify scopes within DHCP.   You should know the purpose of scopes and how to manipulate them. For example, you should know how to add options and modify the scope size if it was created incorrectly originally.

Know how to configure DHCP to work with WDS.   Understanding that both DHCP and WDS use port 67 to listen, you should know how to configure both when installed on the same server. WDS needs to be configured to not use port 67, and DHCP should be configured with option 060.

Know the different groups that can be used to grant permissions to administer DHCP and DNS.   You should know the permission capabilities of the DHCP Users group (read-only), the DHCP Administrators group (full control in DHCP), and the DNS Administrators group (full control in secure zones).

Understand the capabilities the different types of zones in DNS.   You should know the primary purpose of each type of zone. This includes primary, secondary, stub, Active Directory–integrated (ADI), and GlobalNames. You should be aware that GlobalNames Zones can be used to aid in the retirement of WINS, and ADI zones are replicated security and provide built-in fault tolerance.

Understand the purpose of zone files and the types of records typically used.   You should know the purpose of the forward lookup and reverse lookup zones and the different types of records typically found in a Windows Server 2008 DNS server. These records include A, AAAA, PTR, SOA, SRV, NS, MX, and CNAME.

Understand the purpose of Network Access Protection (NAP).   You should understand the big picture of how NAP uses health policies to define health, to define a health registration authority, to check health, and to define health certificates to verify health. For unhealthy clients, you should understand how remediation servers are placed in restricted networks to help them become healthy.

Understand the capabilities of NAP   This includes the four primary methods of NAP enforcement including VPN enforcement, IPSec enforcement, 802.1x enforcement, and DHCP enforcement.

Review Questions

1. You manage a network consisting of two subnets. On one of the subnets, the network ID is 172.16.0.0/20. The scope for this subnet is 172.16.0.1/20 through 172.16.7.254/20. There are no contention problems, but DHCP has run out of addresses to assign. What could you do that would have the least impact on the network?

   A. Move clients from one subnet to another.

   B. Create a superscope using the two subnets.

   C. Modify the scope to include the full range of IP addresses.

   D. Create a second scope from 172.16.8.1/20 through 172.16.15.254/20.

2. You administer a network that is slowly integrating IPv6 with existing IPv4. You now want DHCP to issue IPv6 addresses. What mode should DHCP be using?

   A. DHCPv6 Stateless mode

   B. DHCPv6 Stateful mode

   C. IPv4 Compatibility mode

   D. IPv6 Compatibility mode

3. You need to manually create a record within DNS to allow clients using IPv6 to resolve the MCITP1 server name only to an IP address. What would you create?

   A. A record

   B. AAAA record

   C. PTR record

   D. CNAME record

4. You have added DHCP to a server running Windows Deployment Services (WDS). What do you need to configure so that both services can work together on the same server? (Choose two.)

   A. On the DHCP server, configure option 060.

   B. On the DHCP server, set it so that DHCP does not listen on port 67.

   C. On the WDS server, configure option 060.

   D. On the WDS server, set it so that WDS does not listen on port 67.

5. A new administrator is tasked with managing a DHCP server, including creating and modifying scopes. However, she finds that she can't add an option to a scope. Which group should you add her to so that she can accomplish the task?

   A. DCHP Administrators

   B. DHCP Users

   C. Domain Admins

   D. Enterprise Admins

6. You manage a DHCP server on the network that has been working fine for several months. A router on the network fails and is replaced with a legacy router. After a few days, several clients begin receiving APIPA addresses in the 169.254.0.0/16 range. Other clients are receiving DHCP leases as expected. What is the likely problem?

    A. The router is passing broadcasts over ports 67 and 68.

    B. The DHCP server is not authorized.

    C. The router is not RFC 1542 compliant.

    D. There is no problem. APIPA addresses are expected in a routed network.

7. After rebooting your DNS server that is also a domain controller, you having a wide variety of problems. A significant problem is that users aren't able to access any network resources, but you verify that they received the correct DHCP lease. You suspect that SRV records haven't been created. What can you do to create them?

    A. Use the DNS Manager console to manually create the SRV records.

    B. Stop and restart the NetSRV service.

    C. Stop and restart the NetLogon service.

    D. Stop and restart the SRV service.

8. You administer an Active Directory Domain Services domain running Windows Server 2008 servers. You want to configure your network so that a few key servers can be resolved using a single label name. WINS is not deployed on your network. What should you do?

    A. Deploy WINS.

    B. Add CNAME records to your forward lookup zone.

    C. Create a reverse lookup zone.

    D. Create a GlobalNames zone.

9. You administer the DNS server in your network. The administrator who manages two Microsoft Exchange servers (EXCH1 and EXCH2) asks you to modify DNS so that the EXCH1 server is the primary server used.

    A. Delete the existing MX records, and add them in the following order: EXCH1 and then EXCH2.

    B. Delete the existing MX records, and add them in the following order: EXCH21 and then EXCH21.

    C. Modify the priority of the EXCH1 server so that it has a higher value than EXCH2.

    D. Modify the priority of the EXCH1 server so that it is a lower-priority value than EXCH2.

10. DNS clients within your network need to be able to determine the name of computers based on their IP address. What can you create to allow this functionality?

    A. A forward lookup zone

    B. A reverse lookup zone

    C. A records

    D. AAAA records

11. You are an administrator for a Windows Server 2008 domain that includes DNS but not WINS. Clients within your network need to be able to connect to an intranet web server named MCTIP1 using the address of `http://mcitp1`. Of the following, what should you do to ensure this works correctly?

    A. Add WINS.

    B. Create a reverse lookup zone.

    C. Add an Active Directory–integrated zone.

    D. Create a GlobalNames zone.

12. What kind of record would be created within a GlobalNames zone in DNS?

    A. Global

    B. MX

    C. CNAME

    D. PTR

13. An administrator needs to fully administer a DNS server used within a Windows Server 2008 domain. Zones within DNS are Active Directory–integrated. What group should you add the administrator to so that she can do her job?

    A. Enterprise Admins

    B. Domain Admins

    C. DNSAdmins

    D. DHCP Admins

14. You want to enable secure dynamic updates on your network. What are the prerequisites? (Choose all that apply.)

    A. The DNS server must be on the DHCP server.

    B. The DNS server must be on a domain controller.

    C. The zone must be ADI.

    D. You must have a GlobalNames zone on the DNS server.

15. You administer a domain using only Windows Server 2008 servers as domain controllers. You are planning a strategy for network access. You need to ensure that clients have up-to-date service packs and up-to-date anti-virus software definitions installed before they are granted access to the network. What should you include in the plan?

    A. NAP using 802.1x enforcement

    B. NAP using DHCP enforcement

    C. NPS using GNZ

    D. NPS using DHCP enforcement

16. You administer a Windows Server 2008 domain that uses DHCP and DNS. You are tasked with ensuring that clients have certain patches and hotfixes installed. If they don't, you must ensure that DHCP does not give them a lease to the full network. What could you configure?

A. NAP with DHCP enforcement

B. NAP with 802.1x enforcement

C. Dynamic updates

D. Secure Active Directory–integrated zones

17. A Network Access Protection (NAP) is deployed within your network. What is issued to clients to show that they comply with NAP policies?

A. An IPSec authentication certificate

B. A health token

C. A NAP ticket-granting ticket

D. A health certificate

18. An administrator has configured a Network Access Policy so that clients are checked to ensure they are up-to-date with antivirus signature files. If the clients are not up-to-date, he wants to ensure they are not granted access to the network. What should be done? (Choose two.)

A. Add remediation servers to the restricted network.

B. Deploy WSUS.

C. Grant the clients limited access to a restricted network.

D. Grant the clients limited access to the antivirus server used to deploy updates to clients.

19. You administer a Windows Server 2008 domain used to connect several research and development computers in a private network. You need to ensure that all computers are using encryption for all communications, and if they lose the ability to communicate with encryption, they will lose connectivity with all computers within the network. What should you implement?

A. NAP with IPSec enforcement

B. L2TP/IPSec

C. NAP with 802.1x enforcement

D. Group Policy

20. Clients connect to your network using remote access technologies. The company policy states that clients must be up-to-date with current hotfixes and patches before they are allowed access to the internal network. What should be implemented?

A. NAP with 802.11x enforcement

B. NAP with VPN enforcement

C. WSUS

D. SCCM

Answers to Review Questions

1. **C.** The full range of addresses with a network ID of 172.16.0.1/20 is 172.16.0.1 through 172.16.15.254. You can modify the existing scope to include the full range of IP addresses. Moving clients may work and would be a good solution if there were contention problems, but the real problem is that DHCP has run out of IP addresses. Creating a superscope with the two scopes wouldn't give more addresses to the first range. It is not possible to create a second scope with the network ID as an existing scope.

2. **A.** In DHCPv6 Stateless mode, it does not issue IPv6 addresses. It will issue IPv6 addresses in DHCPv6 Stateful mode. There is no such thing as a Compatibility mode in DHCP.

3. **B.** Within DNS, an AAAA record is used to map a hostname to an IPv6 record. An A record is used to map a hostname to an IPv4 address. PTR records are used for reverse lookup (identifying the name from an IP address). CNAME is used to give the host an alias so that multiple names can be mapped to the same IP address.

4. **A, D.** You must configure WDS so that it does not listen on port 67 and configure option 060 to inform the PXE client that the WDS server is on the network. If you configure DHCP so that it does not listen on port 67, DHCP clients will not receive responses from DHCP. There is no option 060 on WDS servers.

5. **A.** When added to the DHCP Administrators group, she will be able to fully administer DHCP, including adding options to scopes. The DHCP Users group allows read-only access to DHCP. Both the Domain Admins and Enterprise Admins groups would allow her to accomplish the task but much, much more. A standard security principle is the principle of least privilege; give users only what they require and no more.

6. **C.** A router that is RFC 1542 compliant will pass BOOTP broadcasts on UDP ports 67 and 68. If a router is not RFC 1542 compliant, then DHCP clients on the other side of the router will not receive DHCP leases. Since some clients are receiving DHCP leases, the DHCP server must be authorized. APIPA addresses do not include default gateways, so they would not work in a routed network.

7. **C.** The NetLogon service is responsible for creating the SRV records. If they haven't been created in DNS, you can stop and restart the NetLogon service to cause them to be recreated. It is much too time-intensive, and not necessary, to create the SRV records manually. There is no such thing as a NetSRV or an SRV service.

   Though not stated in the question, you can verify the SRV records are created (or not created) by looking for the folders that start with an underscore (_). These folders hold the SRV records.

8. **D.** A GlobalNames zone (GNZ) can be added to DNS with CNAME records to resolve single-label names. It is not intended to replace WINS since dynamic updates are not supported in a GNZ. There is no need to deploy WINS for only a few key servers. Adding CNAME records to the regular forward lookup zone won't cause the names to be interpreted as single-label names. A reverse lookup zone is used to resolve IP addresses to names but won't resolve single-label names.

9. D. By modifying the priority value within the MX record, you can affect which mail server will be contacted first. The server with the lower-priority value in the MX record would be contacted first. The order of creation of MX records does not affect the priority.

10. B. A reverse lookup zone is used within DNS to resolve IP addresses to names. A forward lookup zone resolves names to IP addresses. A records are host records for IPv4, and AAAA records are host records for IPv6. Both A and AAAA records are used within forward lookup zones.

11. D. A GlobalNames zone is used to provide single-label name resolution. In this example, a web server needs to be identified with the single-label name of MCITP1 (not with a fully qualified domain name). By creating a CNAME record within a GlobalNames zone, DNS will resolve the single-label name. Adding WINS would be much more work than necessary for this single server. Reverse lookup zones are used to resolve IP addresses to names. An Active Directory–integrated zone does not use single-label names.

12. C. CNAME records are created within a GlobalNames zone to allow DNS to resolve single-label names to IP addresses. While other types of records could be created within the GlobalNames zone, the CNAME record is used to provide single-label name resolution. The CNAME record is mapped to a host record. There is no such thing as a Global record. MX records are used to locate mail servers. PTR records are used to resolve IP addresses to names.

13. C. The DNSAdmins group grants enough permission to members to fully administer DNS. Both the Enterprise Admins and Domain Admins would grant significantly more permission than needed so aren't appropriate. The DHCP Administrators group (not the DHCP Admins group) grants full permissions over DHCP, not DNS.

14. B, C. To configure secure dynamic updates for a zone, the zone must be Active Directory–Integrated (ADI). To configure a zone as ADI, the DNS server must be running on a domain controller. There is no need for the DNS and DHCP server roles to be on the same server. A GlobalNames zone can be used to allow DNS to resolve single-label names to IP addresses, but it is not needed for secure dynamic updates.

15. A. Network Access Protection (NAP) is a group of technologies that can be used to verify the health of a client before granting access. Used with 802.1x enforcement, it can be used to verify the health of clients accessing the network using network access methods (such as dial-up). NAP using DHCP enforcement is used within a network (not for clients using network access). A Network Policy Server (NPS) is part of NAP; however, using NPS with a GlobalNames Zone (GNZ) doesn't make sense and using NPS with DHCP wouldn't affect network access clients.

16. A. NAP with DHCP enforcement can be used to ensure clients meet a specified health policy. Healthy clients receive one lease, and unhealthy clients receive a separate lease. NAP with 802.1x enforcement is typically used with wireless clients and does not use DHCP. Dynamic update is a process that updates DNS records after a client receives a lease. Secure ADI zones can't enforce a health policy.

17. D. If a client complies with a NAP policy, the health registration authority issues the client a health certificate. Certificates are used with IPSec as one of the authentication mechanisms, but the authentication certificate does not validate health. There is no such thing as a health token or a NAP ticket-granting ticket.

18. A, C.   Network Access Protection (NAP) can be used to check the clients for health based on a health policy. Unhealthy clients can be granted access only to a restricted network that includes remediation servers (such as a server that includes up-to-date antivirus signature files). WSUS is used to deploy patches and fixes, but not antivirus signature files. NAP can't be used to grant limited access to a server, only limited access to a network (such as a specific subnet).

19. A.   Network Access Protection (NAP) with IPSec enforcement can ensure that clients have specific IPSec policies configured. If these policies are changed, the health certificate will be revoked, and connectivity can be limited. L2TP/IPSec is used with VPNs, not private networks. NAP with 802.1x enforcement is typically used with wireless networks. Group Policy can be used to configure clients, but if they are manually changed or overridden by other policies, they would not lose connectivity.

20. B.   Network Access Protection (NAP) with VPN enforcement can be used to ensure clients are up-to-date. 802.1x enforcement (not 802.11x enforcement) can also be used and is commonly implemented with wireless networks. Neither WSUS nor SCCM could be used to patch clients until they were on the network. However, with NAP, WSUS and SCCM could be used to patch the clients after they were checked.

Chapter 5

Monitoring and Maintaining Active Directory

✓ **Planning for Server Deployment**

- Plan Infrastructure Services Server Roles. May include but is not limited to: address assignment, name resolution, network access control, directory services, application services, certificate services.

✓ **Planning for Server Management**

- Plan Server Management Strategies. May include but is not limited to: remote administration, remote desktop, server management technologies, Server Manager and ServerManagerCMD, delegation policies and procedures.

- Plan for Delegated Administration. May include but is not limited to: delegate authority, delegate Active Directory objects, application management.

- Plan and Implement Group Policy Strategy. May include but is not limited to: GPO management, GPO backup and recovery, group policy troubleshooting, group policy planning.

✓ **Planning Application and Data Provisioning**

- Provision Applications. May include but is not limited to: presentation virtualization, terminal server infrastructure, resource allocation, application virtualization alternatives, application deployment, System Center Configuration Manager.

✓ **Plan for Business Continuity and High Availability**

- Plan for Backup and Recovery. May include but is not limited to: data recovery strategy, server recovery strategy, directory service recovery strategy, object level recovery.

Any server administrator within a Microsoft Server 2008–based enterprise needs to understand Active Directory. Although the high-level design of a full Active Directory forest will fall to the enterprise administrator, day-to-day tasks will fall to the server administrator.

You need to understand the basic Active Directory roles — especially the Active Directory Domain Services (AD DS) and Active Directory Certificate Services (AD CS) roles. You should also understand the purpose of a read-only domain controller (RODC). Active Directory includes many built-in groups that can be used to ease administration, and you'll need to know what they are and how to use them.

No one wants to see a domain controller crash, but if it happens, you need to be prepared. You'll learn some basics of Active Directory backup and recovery in this chapter.

Last but certainly not least, you'll learn about Group Policy, including how Group Policy is applied and some key settings you can use to manage an enterprise.

You'll notice in the list of objectives that address assignment, name resolution, network access control, application services, application management, presentation virtualization, terminal server infrastructure, resource allocation, application virtualization alternatives, System Center Configuration Manager, data recovery strategy, and server recovery strategy, are listed. Presentation virtualization and application virtualization alternatives was covered in Chapter 2, "Planning Server Deployments." Chapter 3, "Using Windows Server 2008 Server Management Tools," covered resource allocation and System Center Configuration Manager. Chapter 4, "Monitoring and Maintaining Infrastructure Servers," covered address assignment, name resolution, and network access control. Chapter 7, "Planninng Terminal Services Servers," covers application services and application management. Data recovery and server recovery strategies are covered in Chapter 9, "Planning Business Continuity and High Availability."

Active Directory Roles

Active Directory is the core of Microsoft's network operating system. It contains data on all of the objects within the forest, and it allows administrators to centrally manage the network.

In Windows Server 2008, Active Directory has been expanded to include additional Active Directory roles that weren't previously available. Although the basic domain controller capabilities still exist, the additional roles provide a separation and expansion of Active Directory's role within a forest.

The Active Directory roles supported in Windows Server 2008 are as follows:

- Active Directory Domain Services (AD DS)
- Active Directory Certificate Services (AD CS)
- Active Directory Lightweight Directory Services (AD LDS)
- Active Directory Rights Management Services (AD RMS)
- Active Directory Federation Services (AD FS)

When preparing for the 70-646 exam, you should focus on on the AD DS and AD CS roles. These roles, and the read-only domain controller (RODC), are explained in-depth in the following sections.

Active Directory Domain Services

The AD DS role is the primary role of Active Directory. It holds information about objects on the network and allows administrators to centrally manage the network. The server hosting this role is commonly referred to as a *domain controller.*

Active Directory refers to the directory services (the database) that contains all the objects (such as users, computers, and groups) within the environment. This database is contained on server hosting the role of Active Directory Domain Services (AD DS). A server hosting AD DS is called a domain controller. Other Active Directory roles exist, but the primary server that you'll do most of the day-to-day domain administration with is the domain controller that hosts the role of the Active Directory Domain Services server.

Objects contained within the AD DS role are users, computers, groups, and more. When a user needs to access the domain, you create a user account for the user. This user account is referred to as an *object* within Active Directory.

In the classroom, I've noticed that the word *object* sometimes trips people up because it isn't a common term. Let me state something obvious that often helps people put this into perspective: When you create a user account in Active Directory, you don't create a person. Instead, you create an object that directly relates to a person.

You can think of most objects in Active Directory in this way. You are using the objects in Active Directory to teach Active Directory Domain Services about the real world. You can create computer objects that relate to computers. You can create group objects that relate to how people are grouped together.

The primary tool you'll use to interact with AD DS is Active Directory Users and Computers, often called ADUC (pronounced "a duck"). Figure 5.1 shows Active Directory Users and Computers.

FIGURE 5.1 Active Directory Users and Computers

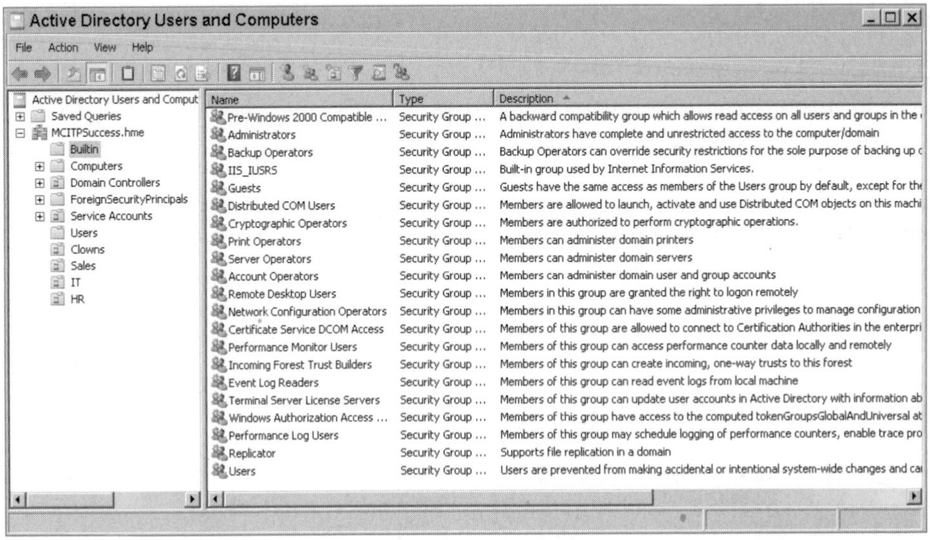

A domain is typically organized with organizational units (OUs). There are two reasons to create OUs within your domain:

Delegate control to an individual or group If you have a domain of 50 users, you may do all the administration for the domain. However, if you manage a domain of 5,000 users, you need some help. Individual departments could have their own IT support, and you may want these IT support personnel to manage the accounts for the users and computers in their department.

For example, you could create a Sales OU to support the sales department. You'd place all the sales department users and computers into the Sales OU. Additionally, you'd create a group (such as SalesITAdmins) for all the users who should have administrative privileges for the Sales OU.

Then, you'd delegate control of the Sales OU to the SalesITAdmins group. Now, you can still oversee the domain, but IT personnel in the sales department can take care of the needs for the users in the Sales OU.

When delegating control to users or groups, it's best to use the Delegation of Control Wizard available within Active Directory Users and Computers. Exercise 5.1 will show how to use the Delegation of Control Wizard.

Manage with Group Policy Group Policy allows you to manage many users and computers by making a single setting. If you have a group of users or computers that need common settings, it makes sense to create an OU to organize these objects.

For example, all the personnel in the HR department may have a need for a specific application. You could use Group Policy to deploy the application. To support this, you'd first need to create an OU for the HR department, place all the HR users into this OU, and then create and link a GPO to the OU.

Group Policy is covered in greater depth later in this chapter.

Exercise 5.1 shows the steps used to delegate control of an OU to a group. You'll also create a user account, a group, and an OU. This exercise assumes you are running a Windows Server 2008 server that has been promoted to a domain controller.

EXERCISE 5.1

Delegating Control to an OU

1. Launch Active Directory Users and Computers by clicking Start ➢ Administrative Tools ➢ Active Directory Users and Computers.

2. Right-click the domain, and select New ➢ Organizational Unit, as shown here.

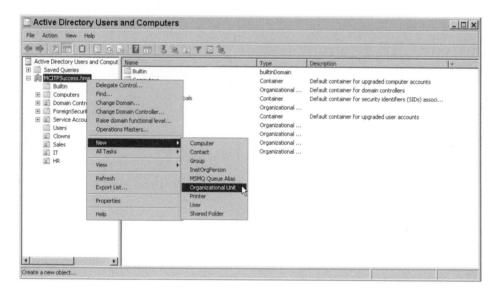

3. In the New Object – Organizational Unit dialog box, enter **Sales**, and click OK. This creates your Sales OU.

4. Right-click the Sales OU, and select New ➢ User.

5. In the New Object – User dialog box, enter your first and last names in the First Name and Last Name boxes. For User Logon Name, enter your first and last names separated by a period. Click Next.

6. In the New Object – User Password dialog box, enter **P@ssw0rd** in the Password and Confirm Password text boxes. Deselect the User Must Change the Password at Next Logon box. Click Next. Click Finish to create the user account.

EXERCISE 5.1 *(continued)*

7. Right-click Sales OU, and select New ≻ Group.

8. In the New Object – Group dialog box, enter **SalesITAdmins** as the group name. Ensure that Global is selected as the group scope and Security is selected as the group type, as shown here. Click OK.

New Object - Group		$\times$
	Create in: MCITPSuccess.hme/Sales	

Group name:

SalesITAdmins

Group name (pre-Windows 2000):

SalesITAdmins

Group scope
- ◯ Domain local
- ⦿ Global
- ◯ Universal

Group type
- ⦿ Security
- ◯ Distribution

[OK] [Cancel]

9. Double-click your user account to access the properties page. You can also right-click the account and select Properties.

10. Select the Member Of tab, and click Add.

11. In the Select Groups dialog box, enter **SalesITAdmins**, and click OK. On the properties page of you user account, click OK.

    At this point, you have an OU, a user account, and a group. Further, you have added the user account to the group. In the following steps, you'll delegate control of the Sales OU to the SalesITAdmins group. This will give your user account the same permissions granted to the group.

12. Right-click the Sales OU, and select Delegate Control.

13. On the Delegation of Control Wizard Welcome page, click Next.

14. On the Users or Groups page, click Add.

15. On the Select Users, Computers, or Groups page, enter **SalesITAdmins** as the group. Click OK.

As a best practice, whenever possible you should assign permissions to groups instead of users. To grant another user the same permissions, you only need to add them to the group. This practice is easier to manage in the long run.

16. Back on the Users or Groups page, click Next.

17. On the Tasks to Delegate page, select the Create, Delete and Manage User Accounts box. You display will look similar to this.

> **Delegation of Control Wizard**   ☒
>
> **Tasks to Delegate**
> You can select common tasks or customize your own.
>
> ⦿ Delegate the following common tasks:
>
> ☑ Create, delete, and manage user accounts
> ☐ Reset user passwords and force password change at next logon
> ☐ Read all user information
> ☐ Create, delete and manage groups
> ☐ Modify the membership of a group
> ☐ Manage Group Policy links
>
> ○ Create a custom task to delegate
>
> [< Back] [Next >] [Cancel] [Help]

Although we are delegating control only over user accounts in this exercise, it's possible to delegate control over any type of objects available in an OU. If desired, you can select Create a Custom Task to Delegate and then select Full Control to grant a group permission to do anything and everything in the OU.

18. On the Tasks to Delegate page, click Next. On the Completing the Delegation of Control Wizard page, click Finish.

Read-Only Domain Controller

The read-only domain controller was presented in Chapter 1, "Introducing Windows Server 2008," as a new feature.

To create an RODC, you would run DCPromo on the server after joining it to a domain. When selecting roles, you have the option of selecting the check box for a read-only domain controller. Once you select this option, you identify a user or group that will be designated to manage the server.

As a reminder, the primary purpose of the RODC is to support remote offices that need the benefits of a domain controller (DC) but don't have either the technical support or the physical security required to support the DC.

Remember, the DC holds a copy of all objects (such as users and computers) within the domain. If the DC was stolen because of inadequate physical security, the thief would have unrestricted access to the Active Directory database, and it would be only a matter of time before passwords were discovered and the entire domain would be compromised. Your only security solution is to flatten the entire domain and start from scratch.

However, the entire Active Directory database is not contained on the RODC. If the RODC is stolen, the entire domain is not compromised.

The RODC could contain some credentials depending on how the Password Replication Policy is configured for the RODC. It is common to configure the policy to cache local users' credentials but not cache any administrator credentials.

Take a look at Figure 5.2 for an overview of how the RODC works. Imagine that a user named Bob logs in from the remote office. When he sends his credentials to the RODC the first time, the RODC passes the credentials to a DC at headquarters. The HQ DC then responds, directing the RODC to cache the credentials. The next time Bob logs on to the RODC, his credentials can be checked locally.

FIGURE 5.2   An RODC in a remote office

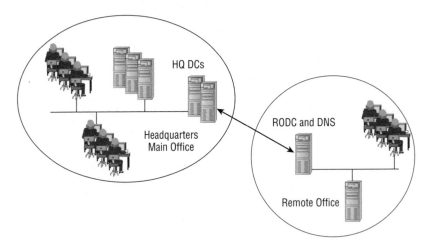

One of the benefits of the RODC is that even if the WAN link between the main office and the remote office is lost, users at the remote office can still log in and have access to resources at the remote site.

If an RODC was not used at the remote site, users would have to access a DC over the WAN link. If the WAN link were lost, then users would use locally cached credentials to access their local computers. However, with locally cached credentials, users would not be able to access any LAN resources at the remote office.

Password Replication Policy

The Password Replication Policy is used to define which users, groups, and computers will have passwords cached on the RODC and which ones will not have passwords cached.

Users, groups, and computers can be added to the policy with either the Allow setting or the Deny setting selected. If Deny is selected, passwords will not be cached on the RODC. If Allow is selected, then the password can be cached on the RODC. For the password to be cached, it must *not* be in the Deny list and must be the Allow list.

With this in mind, what exactly does it mean to cache the password? Frequently, *cache* refers to memory and implies it will be lost once the system loses power. This is not the case here.

Instead, stating that the password will be cached means that a writable DC will replicate the password back to the RODC, allowing it to be stored semipermanently. It will survive reboots. Once a user changes their password, the cached value will be changed.

You can set the Password Replication Policy in the properties page of the RODC server from within Active Directory Users and Computers. Figure 5.3 shows the Password Replication Policy tab selected from the properties of the RODC server.

FIGURE 5.3   An RODC in a remote office

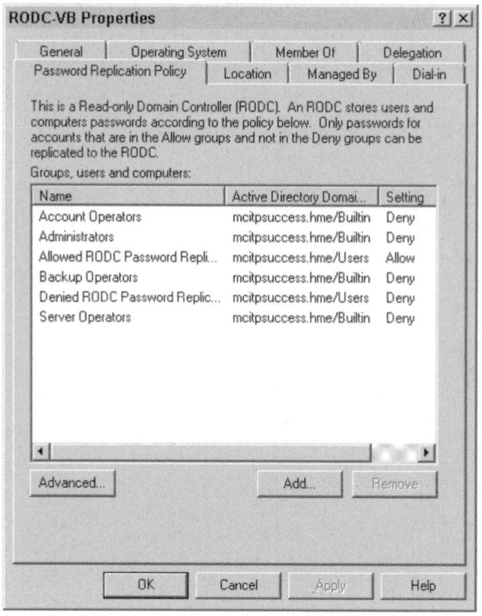

Figure 5.3 also shows the accounts added by default. Notice that the groups with high levels of rights and permissions (Account Operators, Administrators, Backup Operators, and Server Operators) are set to Deny. This prevents the credentials for members of these groups from being cached on the RODC.

It's common and recommended to have Administrator accounts in the Deny list of the Password Replication Policy on the RODC. This specifically prevents any Administrator accounts from being cached on the RODC. This way, if an RODC is stolen, Administrator accounts will not be compromised.

Two groups are worth exploring further: the Denied RODC Password Replication Group and the Allowed RODC Password Replication Group. Both groups are added to the RODC Password Replication Policy when the RODC is created.

Using these groups, you have the ability to globally affect which accounts are cached on RODCs. In contrast, you can use the Password Replication Policy of individual RODCs to allow or deny caching of specific users in individual remote offices.

Both of these groups can be accessed in the Users container of Active Directory Users and Computers. They are as follows:

Denied RODC Password Replication Group Accounts and groups added to this domain local group are automatically denied the ability to cache their passwords on any RODC. Figure 5.4 shows the default membership of this group. Notice that the high-level administrators (Domain Admins, Enterprise Admins, and Schema Admins) are added to this group by default.

Allowed RODC Password Replication Group By default, this group does not have any members. However, if you want to ensure a specific group of users have their passwords cached on each RODC in your enterprise, you can add them to this group.

FIGURE 5.4 Members of the Denied RODC Password Replication Group

Denied RODC Password Replication Group Properties

Object	Security	Attribute Editor
General	Members	Member Of	Managed By

Members:

Name	Active Directory Domain Services Fo
Cert Publishers	MCITPSuccess.hme/Users
Domain Admins	MCITPSuccess.hme/Users
Domain Controllers	MCITPSuccess.hme/Users
Enterprise Admins	MCITPSuccess.hme/Users
Group Policy Creator Owners	MCITPSuccess.hme/Users
krbtgt	MCITPSuccess.hme/Users
Read-only Domain Controllers	MCITPSuccess.hme/Users
Schema Admins	MCITPSuccess.hme/Users

Add... Remove

OK   Cancel   Apply   Help

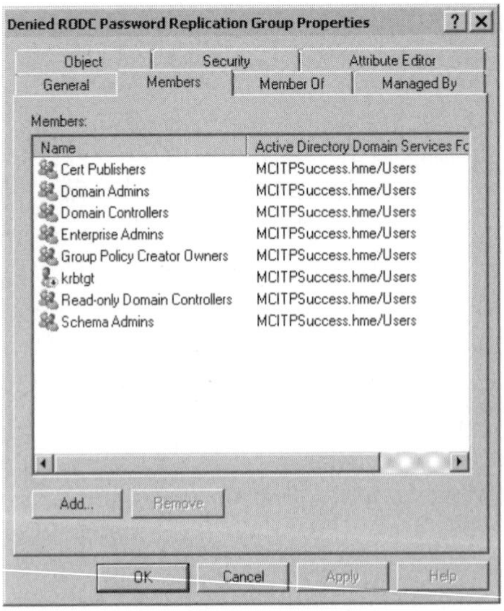

Prerequisites for RODCs

To support RODCs, the following prerequisites must be met:

- The domain functional level must be Windows Server 2003 or higher.

- The forest functional level must be Windows Server 2003 or higher.

- Run `adprep /rodcprep`. This must be run once in the forest. It will modify the permissions on DNS application directory partitions and allow RODCs that are also DNS servers to replicate their permissions correctly.

- The Password Replication Policy must be set on a writable domain controller running Windows Server 2008. The RODC forwards authentication requests to this DC and the Password Replication Policy determines whether credentials are replicated back to the RODC.

- The domain controller holding the Flexible Single Master Operations (FSMO) PDC Emulator role in the domain must be running Windows Server 2008.

Active Directory Certificate Services

The AD CS role is used to create certification authorities and issue certificates. Certificates and certification authorities are part of a public key infrastructure (PKI).

Only the Enterprise and Datacenter editions of Windows Server 2008 fully support all the features of AD CS. You can install AD CS on a Standard edition of Windows Server 2008, but it won't support many of the components and features such as the Online Responder service.

When discussing AD CS, it's important to understand some basic terminology related to certificates and certificate services:

Public key infrastructure   PKI is a group of technologies that work together to allow certificates and keys to be used for authentication and encryption. Just as the IP protocol and IP addresses are part of the TCP/IP suite of protocols used on the Internet, certificates and keys are only part of the public key infrastructure. PKI includes all the pieces such as software, hardware, certificate authorities, the Online Certificate Status Protocol, online responders, and more.

Certificates   A certificate is an electronic file that holds information about the holder of the certificate, the issuer of the certificate (the CA), when it expires, and a key that can be used for encryption. Certificates are used for a wide variety of purposes, but the two primary purposes of a certificate are encryption and authentication.

The key in the certificate is referred to as a *public key* and is available to anyone who has access to the certificate. A matching private key is kept private. The public and private key pair can be used to encrypt and decrypt data between two entities such as a client and a server. Data encrypted with the public key can be decrypted only with the private key. Similarly, data encrypted with the private key can be decrypted only with the public key.

When the certificate is used to encrypt data, the certificate is passed to a client with the public key embedded within it. The client uses the public key to encrypt the data. The server receives the data and uses the private key to decrypt it. If a third party intercepts the encrypted data, they can't read it since the private key is kept private.

Authentication works a little differently, but still one key encrypts and one key decrypts. The difference is that the private key encrypts the data and the public key decrypts it. Imagine a vice president of a company sending an email to the CEO where company policy states that all executive emails must be digitally signed. A digital signature is created from the VP's certificate and encrypted with the private key. The CEO receives the encrypted digital signature with the email. The CEO already has the VP's certificate (or it could be retrieved from Active Directory), which includes the VP's public key. If the public key can decrypt the digital signature, then it must have been encrypted with the VP's private key. Or in other words, the VP must have sent it.

A certificate can be used to prove identify (authentication) or cipher the data (encryption) so that third parties can't intercept and read the data. Although certificates are most often discussed with Internet technologies, they are used for many other purposes such as EFS encryption, smart cards (certificate embedded for authentication), email encryption, email digital signing, code signing (such as ActiveX controls), IPSec authentication, and more.

Certification authority (CA)   A certification authority (CA, commonly pronounced as "cah") issues, manages, and verifies certificates. A CA can be either public or private. Before a CA will issue certificates, the CA goes through a verification and authentication process to identify the requestor. Once it verifies the requestor, the certificate is issued. If the certificate is issued from a trusted CA, then the certificate is automatically trusted.

Think about a person cashing a check. He is asked for identification and provides his driver's license to prove who he is. The driver's license is accepted as valid proof because it is issued from the Department of Motor Vehicles (DMV). Before issuing a driver's license, the DMV verifies someone's identify. We trust the DMV. Since the driver's license is issued from the DMV, we trust the validity of the driver's license.

Similarly, there are several trusted root certification authorities. We trust them just as we trust the DMV. Figure 5.5 shows a partial list of trusted root authorities in Internet Explorer. You can view this page by selecting Tools ≻ Internet Options, selecting the Content tab, clicking the Certificates button, and then selecting Trusted Root Certification Authorities.

VeriSign and Thawte are two well-known certification authorities, but there are many more. If a business purchases a certificate from Thawte and then presents the certificate to your computer as proof of identity, the certificate is trusted. Your computer trusts Thawte, so it also trusts the businesses certificate sold by Thawte.

A CA also maintains the certificate revocation list (explained in the following text) and can also run the Online Certificate Status Protocol (OCSP) to respond to status requests for certificates.

Types of certification authorities include stand-alone root CAs, enterprise root CAs, and subordinate CAs. All of these will be explored in the next section.

FIGURE 5.5   List of trusted root authorities

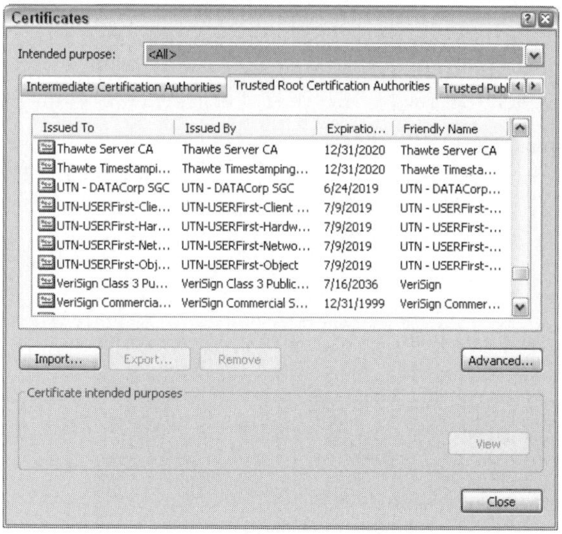

Certificate revocation list (CRL)   Certificates can be revoked if compromised. For example, if it's discovered that a certificate has been improperly issued or the private key has been discovered, then the certificate should no longer be used.

A revoked certificate is published in a certificate revocation list (CRL, often pronounced as "crill"). When a certificate is presented to a client from a server, the client can consult the CRL to verify the certificate has not been revoked. If the certificate is on the CRL, then an error is presented to the user.

CRLs are digitally signed to prevent invalid CRLs from being used. Additionally, CRLs expire after a period of time set by the CA to prevent CRLs from being cached indefinitely.

Online Certificate Status Protocol (OCSP)   The Online Certificate Status Protocol (OCSP) is used to check the status of a certificate. This is often used as an alternative to checking the CRL. Instead of checking the CRL, the client sends a status request to the server, and the server responds with the current status of the certificate.

OCSP requests and responses are generally quicker than sending the entire CRL and forcing the client to check all the entries. For example, the CRL may have 100 entries. The list of 100 entries is retrieved and sent over the network, and then the client needs to check each of the 100 entries. In contrast, with OCSP, one request is sent, the server checks the CRL, and a simple status response is sent back to the client. Servers running the OCSP protocol are referred to as *online responders*.

Online responders   An online responder is a server running the Online Responder service. It receives OCSP status requests from clients and sends back a response. The response is "good," "revoked," or "unknown."

Clients that receive a "good" response trust the certificate and continue with the session. Anything other than a "good" response results in an error message.

An online responder can be the same server that is running the certification authority or a different server. With Internet applications, the online responder will likely be a different server, but within an enterprise PKI, it's possible that the CA is also acting as the online responder.

With an understanding of the different terms related to certificates, take a look at Figure 5.6 to put the entire process together. In step 1, the client makes an HTTPS request to the web server. The web server sends its certificate with the public key embedded in step 2. The client needs to verify the validity of the certificate so uses OCSP to query the online responder in step 3. The online responder may have access to the CRL or may need to query the CA for the CRL. Once the online responder verifies the status of the certificate, it sends the OCSP response to the client shown in step 4.

Using a Certificate in an SSL Session

You use certificates whenever you create a Secure Sockets Layer (SSL) session on the Internet. You can tell it's secure because the URL shows it as https instead of http, and most browsers also show a lock icon somewhere on the browser. A secure session is created quickly, but there are a lot of events that occur under the hood.

For example, consider what happens when you purchase something from Amazon online. Once you start to check out, the server initiates an HTTPS session by sending you a certificate. Embedded in the certificate is Amazon's public key.

Before trusting the certificate, the certificate is checked to see whether it was issued from a company with a certificate in the trusted root authority. If so, then OCSP is used to check the status of the certificate, ensuring it is valid and hasn't been revoked. If these checks pass, the process continues.

Your system creates an encryption key that will be used for the entire session. However, it needs to let Amazon know what that key is without letting Hacker Joe know. The session key is encrypted with the public key received from Amazon's certificate. The only thing that can decrypt this encrypted session key is Amazon's private key, which is paired with the public key you received in their certificate.

Amazon receives the encrypted session key and uses its private key to decrypt the session key. At this point, both your computer and Amazon's server know what the session key is, and the entire session is encrypted with the session key. Using symmetric encryption (one session key) instead of asymmetric encryption (two keys, public and private) is much cheaper in terms of processing cost.

What I find exceptionally amazing about all of this is that it happens in seconds.

FIGURE 5.6   Certificate verification process

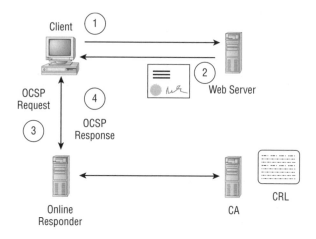

Types of Certification Authorities

Certification authorities receive requests for certificates and issue certificates. But who a CA issues certificates to and how the CA is configured can be different in different situations.

All CAs have a root CA, and it's also possible to have subordinate CAs. Additionally, a CA can be either a stand-alone CA or an enterprise CA. The following sections describe the differences between these different types of CAs.

Root and Subordinate Certification Authorities

A *root CA* is the very first server stood up as a certification authority in the namespace. In a small organization, you may have only a root CA. It is used to issue certificates for all purposes in the organization.

In larger organizations, the root CA can be used to issue certificates to subordinate CAs. Both stand-alone and enterprise CAs (which I'll detail shortly) can have either a single root CA or a root and subordinate CAs.

Consider Figure 5.7. It shows a root CA and several subordinate CAs. The root CA issues certificates to subordinate CAs, and the subordinate CAs can then issue certificates to other subordinate CAs. The lowest-level CAs issue certificates to end users.

When a company has a hierarchy such as Figure 5.7, it's not uncommon to remove the root CA from the network and provide it with the most protection possible.

Imagine that one of the certificates issued from the lowest-level subordinate CA is issued to a web browser. This web browser could then use the certificate to initiate SSL sessions. To ensure that clients trust this certificate, a copy of the certificate from the root CA would need to be in the trusted root authority.

FIGURE 5.7 Root and subordinate CAs

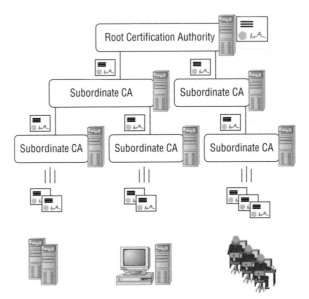

As long as the web browser purchased the certificate from a public CA that was in the trusted root authority, this will work fine. If the certificate were purchased from Gibson's Cheap Certificates (or some other unknown entity), it would be a problem. SSL sessions would start with an error stating that the certificate wasn't trusted.

From an e-commerce perspective, an error stating the certificate isn't trusted is unacceptable. Imagine yourself getting ready to buy a case of widgets online. You have your credit card in hand; then suddenly an error message pops us saying the certificate isn't trusted, bad things will happen, and it's not recommended that you continue. Most reasonable people put their credit card away.

Stand-Alone Certification Authority

A stand-alone CA does not need Active Directory Domain Services. Instead, it's a server that is completely separate from a domain. Public certification authorities (such as VeriSign or Thawte) are known as stand-alone CAs.

Certificate requests to stand-alone CAs are submitted via web enrollment tools or sometimes through other electronic means such as an email attachment. Once a certificate request is received, the request is marked as pending. The certification authority will follow its own internal rules to determine the identity of the requestor. This can sometimes be quite involved. Once the identity of the requestor is verified, the request is approved, and the certificate is issued.

Enterprise Certification Authority

An enterprise certification authority exists within an Active Directory Domain Services domain and requires access to Active Directory Domain Services. It is used to issue certificates to entities within a business or organization. Since it's intertwined with Active Directory Domain Services, you can take advantage of many of the benefits within a domain, such as Group Policy.

For example, you can use Group Policy to set the Trusted Root Certification Authorities certificate store for all users and computers in the domain. You can also use Group Policy to configure autoenrollment settings within a domain.

> Autoenrollment sounds like the user is being enrolled in some type of club ("Thanks for subscribing to our magazine. We have automatically enrolled you in the Fruit of the Month Club. Next month: apricots!"). However, what autoenrollment means in this context is that the user is automatically being issued a certificate without having to request the certificate.

Autoenrollment can be used to automatically issue and renew certificates to users and computers within a domain. This can be done without any user intervention after being configured by an administrator.

Before issuing certificates, any CA needs to verify the identity of the requestor. Within a domain, Kerberos is used as the primary authentication mechanism, so users and computer have already been reliably identified. With autoenrollment, there's no need for manual intervention.

In addition to issuing certificates to users and computers, AD CS in Windows Server 2008 also includes the integrated Simple Certificate Enrollment Protocol (SCEP) enrollment services that can be used to issue certificates for network devices such as routers.

A logical question is, when should I use an enterprise certification authority, and when should I use a stand-alone certification authority? Generally, if you need a certificate for your users and computers only, you'd use an enterprise CA. If users external to your company need to use the certificates, you should consider purchasing a certificate from a stand-alone CA from a trusted root authority.

Remember the example of purchasing something online. You have your credit card in hand and an error pops up. This could easily result in a lost sale. If you envision a lost sale or lost revenue, then the cost of certificate from a public CA is justified.

However, consider something like Outlook Web Access (OWA). Using Exchange Server 2007, you have the capability of allowing employees to connect to an Internet-facing server with a web browser and connect to their email accounts. This session needs to be encrypted, so an HTTPS session is initiated, and a certificate is required. You could purchase the certificate, but what's the impact if you didn't? The worst case is that employees will receive an error message saying the certificate is not trusted and asking them whether they want to continue.

Since the website is from their employer and they're accessing the site from directions issued from the employer, users will continue. There is no lost revenue. It makes sense to stand up an internal enterprise CA in this example.

Further, you have the capability of using Group Policy to push a list of trusted root authorities, adding your enterprise root CA to the list. All of this occurs at no additional monetary cost.

Active Directory Lightweight Directory Services

The AD LDS role is used to store application-specific data for directory-enabled applications. The AD LDS database stores only the data needed for a Lightweight Directory Access Protocol (LDAP) application. It does not store typical domain objects (such as users and computers). LDAP applications are also referred to as *directory-enabled* applications.

The primary benefit of AD LDS is that you can take advantage of the features of Active Directory Domain Services (such as replication, LDAP searches, and LDAP over SSL access) without modifying your domain structure.

If you stored the same information in your domain structure, you'd have to modify the schema. Modifying the schema is dangerous. Remember, the entire forest has only one schema. If things go wrong when you modify the schema, you may have to rebuild your entire forest from scratch.

On the other hand, by creating a separate AD LDS server, you don't need to modify the schema but can still enjoy the benefits of LDAP. You can have one or more AD LDS instances working with your Active Directory Domain Services instance. An AD LDS role can be running on the same server as a domain controller running Active Directory Domain Services.

Active Directory Rights Management Services

The AD RMS role allows owners of documents to define what can be done with their documents. AD RMS is especially useful in preventing sensitive information from being misused. You can define who can open, forward, print, or take other actions on documents and other content.

For example, Sally may send Joe an email attachment and stress that the data is highly sensitive and shouldn't be printed. However, Sally is trusting Joe not to print it. With AD RMS, Sally can assign specific rights to the document to prevent the document from being printed.

The usage rights of the document are contained within the document. This is different from NTFS and Share permissions. With an NTFS file, the NTFS permissions are part of the NTFS drive or partition. Once you email or copy a document, it's no longer part of the drive, so the drive permissions no longer apply.

Rights account certificates are issued from the AD RMS server. Both users that protect their documents and users that open protected documents must have a rights account certificate. A user with a rights account certificate could assign specific rights or conditions to a document. These rights or conditions are then bound to the document in the form of a publishing license.

When a user attempts to open an AD RMS–protected document, a request is sent to the AD RMS server. It ensures the user has a rights account certificate and applies the specific usage rights and conditions specified in the publishing license. If the AD RMS server can't be reached, the document will not open.

Microsoft Office 2007 Enterprise, Professional Plus, and Ultimate editions support the creation of rights-protected content with AD RMS. Third-party applications can also be AD-RMS enabled.

Active Directory Federation Services

AD FS is used to extend single sign-on features to web applications. In other words, it allows select external users to access a company's website without providing additional authentication. Once a user authenticates within their own domain, that authentication can be used to authenticate into an external company's website.

To get a better perspective of how this works, compare how website access works for internal users on internal websites with how it works for external users.

Within a domain, most users have one user account to access everything they need. (Administrators typically have two accounts—one for regular use and a second for administrative purposes.) For example, Sally would log on, provide credentials to Active Directory Domain Services, and be authenticated. She is then issued a token (which includes her group membership information) that is used throughout the day to identify her. When she accesses a file or other resource, the permissions of the resource are compared to the identities in the token to determine whether she should have access.

Similarly, if Sally accesses a website within the enterprise that is using Windows Integrated Authentication, her original token is also used to authenticate her. Sally wouldn't need to authenticate again to access a website that needs authentication.

Compare this to Joe, who is not part of the enterprise but instead is an employee of a partner or supplier, or even a customer. When Joe accesses our website over the Internet, he must provide credentials such as a username or password. From Joe's perspective, he has logged on once to his domain, and each time he accesses our website he needs to log on again.

By adding AD FS, you have the capability of supporting single sign-on for users in a different enterprise. This is done by creating a trust relationship between the two domains for the express purpose of sharing a client's identity in one network with another network. AD FS does not create full trust relationships between the domains but instead just shares enough information between the two domains to allow web single sign-on. AD FS can be very useful in business-to-business (B2B) partnerships where employees in one company will often access a website in another company.

Microsoft's Office SharePoint Services (MOSS) is gaining a lot of popularity both internally to companies and for Internet-facing applications. AD FS has been tightly integrated with Office SharePoint Services 2007 and is likely where you'll see it used most often.

Active Directory Rights and Permissions

Windows Server 2008 includes many built-in groups. By adding a user to the group, you grant the user all the rights and responsibilities of that group. Understanding the groups available can go a long way to easing your job as an administrator. If you know which groups are available, you can quickly and easily grant someone the appropriate rights and permissions to do a job.

Further, by knowing the available groups, you know when a group is available to do a job and when you need to add groups to fulfill specific requirements.

Real World Scenario

Principle of Least Privilege

Most organizations follow the basic security principle of "least privilege." In other words, you grant users only what is necessary to accomplish a job, and no more.

As an extreme example on the other side of the coin, I remember a short consulting gig I had where this wasn't followed. A lone IT administrator was tasked with maintaining a rather large network that had experienced some quick growth. He had requested help in the form of additional employees but was refused. Instead, the company occasionally brought in a consultant to solve an immediate problem.

Looking around I noticed that the Domain Admins group had the Authenticated Users group in it. In essence what this meant was that anyone who logged on was a member of the Domain Admins group and could do anything in the domain. Bluntly, this is pretty scary. Someone could accidentally cause problems, or worse, the legendary disgruntled employee could easily take down the entire domain.

When I asked him about it, he said that he was constantly fighting permission issues. Someone wanted to print. Someone else wanted to access a file or folder or share. He knew the correct way to resolve the problem was to create an administrative model, but he simply didn't have the time or resources with his workload. He finally gave up and added everyone to the Domain Admins group. The immediate problem was solved.

Ultimately he left the job. About six months later, I saw a consultant request to help the company redesign and rebuild the domain. I learned that the company ended up with some significant security issues where a lot of its financial data was compromised.

This is close to the worst-case scenario, but it does help illustrate the importance of following the principle of least privilege. If someone needs to print, give them permission to print. If they need to manage a domain controller, add them to the Server Operators group.

Give them only what they need, and nothing more.

When adding users to a group, you always want to follow the principle of least privilege. In other words, add users to the group that grants them permissions they need and only the permissions they need.

Figure 5.8 shows the default groups in the Users container. You also have many default groups in the Builtin container. Notice how users have an icon of a single person and groups have an icon of two people.

The following are many of the groups you have available to use, including their purposes:

Enterprise Admins   The Enterprise Admins group grants members full administrative access to all computers within the forest. The root domain Administrator account is added to the Enterprise Admins group by default.

FIGURE 5.8   Default groups in the Users container

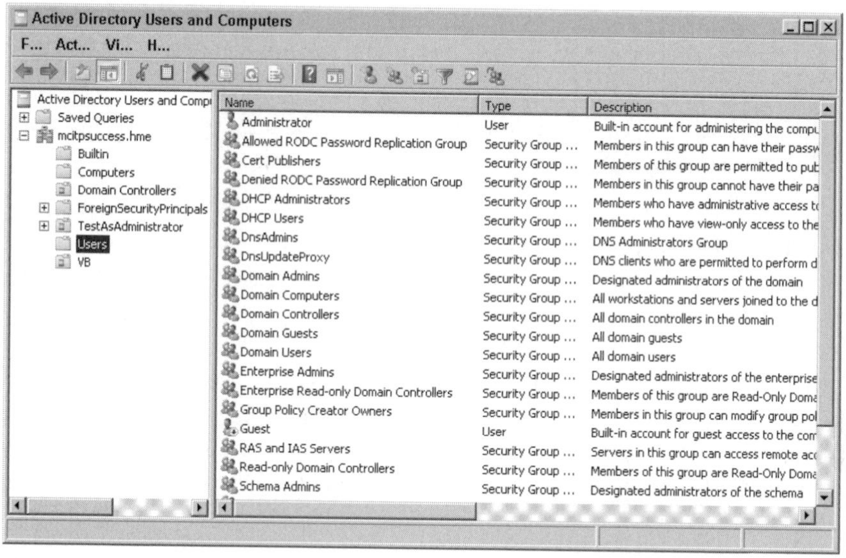

The Enterprise Admins group is a member of the local Administrators group on each computer within the domain and a member of the Denied RODC Password Replication group. Only the root domain of a forest has the Enterprise Admins group.

Domain Admins   Members of the Domain Admins group have full administrative access to all computers within the domain. The domain Administrator account is added to the Domain Admins group by default.

The Domain Admins group is a member of the local Administrators group on each computer within the domain and a member of the Denied RODC Password Replication group. Each domain will have a Domain Admins group.

Schema Admins   Members of the Schema Admins group can modify the schema of the forest. The root domain Administrator account is added to the Schema Admins group by default. This group exists only within the root domain of the forest.

Administrators (local machine)   Members of the local Administrators group have permissions to do anything and everything on the local system. The Domain Admins group is automatically added to the local Administrators group on all computers within the domain.

Administrators (domain controller)   The Administrators group is located in the Built-in (as in Figure 5.8) container of Active Directory Users and Computers. Members of this group have full control on domain controller servers.

The Administrators group in Active Directory is generally misunderstood and often glossed over in documentation. However, be aware (and beware) that when you add users to this group, you are granting almost unlimited permissions to the domain. A member of the built-in Administrators group can log in to a domain controller and add themselves to the Domain Admins and Enterprise Admins groups. This is significantly different from the permissions granted to a member of the local Administrators group.

Server Operators   The Server Operators group is used to grant someone administrative access to a domain controller without granting access to the domain. Server Operators can log onto domain controllers, create and delete shares, start and stop many services, back up and restore files, and shut down the computer.

Remember that a domain controller does not have a local Security Accounts Manager database, or in other words, there are no local accounts. With this understood, you don't have the local Administrators group on a domain controller, and the Administrators group on the domain controller provides significant permissions throughout the domain, so it should be used with caution.

Power Users   The Power Users group is found only on local computers (not on a domain controller). Members of the Power Users group have rights and permissions a step below the local Administrators group.

However, using the Power Users group is no longer recommended. Instead, it is recommended to use a standard user account and an administrative account. Regular users would use a standard user account, and administrators would use the administrative account with the secondary logon feature.

Although some documentation indicates that the Power Users group is gone, you can still find the group in default installations of both Windows Vista and Windows Server 2008.

Account Operators   Members of the Account Operators group can create, delete, and modify most accounts within the domain. This includes users, computers, and groups. Account Operators cannot modify the Administrators or Domain Admins groups.

Users in this group can log onto domain controllers and shut them down. (By default regular users can log onto any computer within the domain *except* domain controllers.)

Backup Operators   The Backup Operators group grants members the ability to both back up and restore data. This group exists within the domain and on individual systems.

Members of the group on a local machine can perform backups and restores on the local system only. Members of the domain group can perform backups and restores on any system in the domain.

Print Operators   Members of the Print Operators group have permission to manage any printers or print queues. Members of this group are granted the equivalent of full control for all printers within the domain.

This group exists only within the domain.

DHCP Users   Members of the DHCP Users group can launch and view the DHCP console. Only read access is granted to DHCP settings.

This group appears only when DHCP has been installed on the server.

DHCP Administrators   The DHCP Administrators group is used to grant members the ability to fully administer the DHCP service. Members can start and stop the service and make changes to DHCP properties, scopes, and options.

Membership in the group allows members to administer DHCP using either the DHCP console or the netsh command-line tool. This group does not grant permissions to administer other server settings.

This group appears only when DHCP has been installed on the server.

DNSAdmins   Members of the DNSAdmins group can fully administer DNS. This includes starting and stopping the service and manipulating zones and zone data. This group appears only when DNS has been installed on the server.

Performance Monitor Users   Members of the Performance Monitor Users group can access performance counter data on local and remote servers. Performance Monitor is part of the Performance and Reliability Monitor.

Performance Log Users   Members of the Performance Log Users group can create performance counter logs and traces on local and remote servers.

The difference between the Performance Monitor Users group and the Performance Log Users group is that the Performance Monitor Users group can only view the data, while the Log group can create and schedule the logs.

Remote Desktop Users   The Remote Desktop Users group is used to grant members permission to log in to systems remotely. When Remote Desktop or Remote Assistance is used by nonadministrators, it's common to add members to this group to allow them to log on remotely.

Network Configuration Operators   This group grants members permission to make changes to network configuration settings. This includes making changes to the network interface card and settings within the Network and Sharing Center.

Allowed RODC Password Replication Group   Users in this group can log onto any read-only domain controller, and their credentials will be replicated back to the RODC. In other words, their password will be stored on the RODC, and the users will be able to log onto the RODC even if the WAN link to a writable DC is broken. By default this group is empty.

This group is global to Active Directory, meaning it applies to all RODCs in the domain. However, the Password Replication Policy of each individual RODC can be modified to specifically allow passwords to be replicated back to the RODC and stored locally.

Denied RODC Password Replication Group Users in this group can log onto any read-only domain controller, and their credentials will *not* be replicated back to the RODC. In other words, their password will *not* be stored on the RODC. If the RODC is stolen, the password of these accounts will not be susceptible to compromise.

By default this group includes the following groups: Cert Publishers, Domain Admins, domain controllers, Enterprise Admins, Group Policy Creator Owners, read-only domain controllers, and Schema Admins.

This group is global to Active Directory, meaning it applies to all RODCs in the domain.

Active Directory Backup and Recovery

Although I'll cover backups more fully in Chapter 9, "Planning Business Continuity and High Availability," for this chapter it's important to understand how to back up and restore Active Directory.

You can backup Active Directory by backing up all the critical volumes on a domain controller or by backing up system state data on a domain controller.

 You can think of a volume in this context either as a partition when using basic disks or as a volume when using dynamic disks. Any physical disk can be a single partition or volume or can be divided into multiple partitions or volumes (such as C:\, D:\, and so on). For a physical disk that has been divided into partitions or volumes, you don't necessarily have to back up the entire physical disk, but instead only the critical partitions or critical volumes.

Critical volumes in Windows Server 2008 are any volumes that include the following data or files:

- The system volume (also referred to as SYSVOL). This volume holds the boot files (bootmgr file and boot configuration data store). This is typically C:\.

- The boot volume. The boot volume is the volume that holds the Windows operating system and the registry. The Windows operating system is typically in the C:\Windows folder, which would make the boot volume C:\. If the Windows were installed in D:\Windows, D:\ would be the boot volume.

- The volume that holds the SYSVOL tree. This folder is typically in C:\Windows\System\Sysvol\sysvol.

- The volume that holds the Active Directory database (ntds.dit). The Active Directory database is held in C:\Windows\NTDS by default, but it can be moved to a drive different from the operating system for optimization.

- The volume that holds the Active Directory database log files. The Active Directory database log files are held in C:\Windows\NTDS by default but can be moved to a different drive from the NTDS.dit database for optimization.

   System state includes key data such as:

- The registry

- Boot files (including system files)

- Files that are protected by Windows File Protection (WFP)

   On a domain controller hosting Active Directory Domain Services, system state also holds the Active Directory database and the Sysvol folder.

   Restoring Active Directory is similar to previous versions of Windows Server 2008. You must first boot into Directory Services Restore Mode (DSRM), and then you can restore Active Directory. The program used to do backups in Windows Server 2008 is the Windows Backup program. The command-line equivalent is the Wbadmin.exe tool. Neither tool is available until the Windows Backup feature is installed on the server.

Windows Server 2008 Backup

The Windows Server 2008 Backup program is not available by default. Instead, you must add it by using Server Manager.

   Exercise 5.2 shows the steps to install the Windows Backup feature on a Windows Server 2008 server.

EXERCISE 5.2

Adding the Backup Feature

1. Launch Server Manager by clicking Start ➤ Administrative Tools ➤ Server Manager.

2. In the Server Manager tree, select Features. Click the Add Features link in the main window.

3. On the Select Features page, scroll down to the Windows Server Backup Features selection, and click the plus sign. Select the Windows Server Backup box. Your display will look similar to this.

EXERCISE 5.2 *(continued)*

4. On the Select Features page, click Next.

5. On the Confirm Installation Selections page, click Install. The Windows Backup Feature will be installed. After a moment, the Installation Results page will appear indicating the installation succeeded.

6. Click Close to complete the installation.

Backing Up Active Directory

In Windows Server Backup for Server 2008, there are two types of backup:

Full server backup   This includes a backup of every volume on the server.

Critical volumes backup   A critical volumes backup backs up only critical volumes. Critical volumes are those that are required to recover Active Directory Domain Services as described earlier in this chapter.

If you have only one volume on your server, there is no difference between the full server backup and the critical volumes backup. They will both back up the same volumes.

You must be a member of the administrators group or the Backup Operators group to start a backup using either the Windows Server Backup GUI or the Wbadmin command-line backup tools.

Using the backup tools, you can back up critical volumes to the following:

- A noncritical volume

- A network share

- A CD or DVD

You *cannot* back up to the following:

- Magnetic tape

- A volume that has been configured as a dynamic volume

Exercise 5.3 shows how to back up critical volumes, giving you a copy of Active Directory. This exercise should be performed on a domain controller.

EXERCISE 5.3

Backing Up Critical Volumes

1. Launch Windows Server Backup by clicking Start ➢ Administrative Tools ➢ Windows Server Backup.

2. In the Actions pane (at the right of window), click the Backup Once link. (In a production environment, you would likely schedule the backup to occur regularly. However, for this exercise you will back up the data once.)

3. On the Backup Options page, ensure Different Options is selected, and click Next.

4. On the Select Backup Configuration page, select Custom, and click Next. Note that if your server includes only one volume, there really is no difference between a full server backup and a custom backup.

5. On the Select Backup Items page, ensure Enable System Recovery is selected. Your display will look similar to the following.

EXERCISE 5.3 *(continued)*

Backup Once Wizard

Select backup items

- Backup options
- Select backup configur...
- **Select backup items**
- Specify destination type
- Specify advanced option
- Confirmation
- Backup progress

What volumes do you want to back up?

Volumes ▲	Status	Size
☑ Local disk (C:)	Included (for system reco...	27.94 GB

☑ Enable system recovery.
This option automatically includes all volumes that contain operating system components for system recovery.

< Previous   Next >   Backup   Cancel

6. Click Next on the Select Backup Items page.

7. On the Specify Destination Type page, click Remote Shared Folder, and click Next. (You could also select another drive or a DVD drive here if desired.)

8. On the Specify Remote Folder page, enter the UNC path of a share available on your network. For example, you could create a share named Backups on the MCITP2 computer, and the Universal Naming Convention (UNC) path would be \\MCITP2\Backups.

A universal naming convention (UNC) path takes the format of \\ *ServerName\ShareName*. As an example, if you had a server named MCITP2, you could create a share named Backups and enter **MCITP2\ Backups**.

9. For Access Control, select Inherit. This allows the backup file to inherit the permissions of the remote shared folder. Click Next.

10. On the Specify Advanced Option page, ensure VSS Copy Backup (Recommended) is selected. This will ensure that your backup will not interfere with any other scheduled backups on your system using the Volume Shadow Copy Service. Click Next.

11. On the Confirmation Page, click Backup. The backup will begin.

12. On the Backup Progress page, observe the status. Depending on the size of the volumes, this backup can take quite a long time. Once it is complete, click Close.

As mentioned previously, it's also possible to backup just the system state data using the Wbadmin command-line tool. Launch a command line and enter the following command:

Wbadmin start systemstatebackup

To restore system state, you can use the following command from with the Directory Services Restore Mode (DSRM).

Wbadmin start systemstaterecovery

Old system state backups can be deleted with the following command:

Wbadmin delete systemstatebackup

Backing Up Critical Volumes on a Server Core Installation

If you're running your domain controller on Server Core, you won't have access to the GUI. Instead, you can use these commands:

First install the Windows Backup feature with this command:

start /w ocsetup WindowsServerBackup

Next, run the Wbadmin command to start the system state backup:

Wbadmin.exe start systemstatebackup -backuptarget:D:

The previous command assumes you have a D:\ drive where you can store the backup. It's also possible modify the registry to allow you to set the backup target to a network share using a UNC path (\\servername\share).

Restoring Active Directory

You can restore Active Directory by restoring system state data. You do this by restoring critical volumes using the Windows Server Backup tool or by using the Wbadmin command-line tool.

If all your system state data is on the same volume where the operating system is located (such as the C:\ drive), you need to use the Wbadmin command-line tool to restore only the system state data.

Tombstone Lifetime

When an object is deleted, it isn't truly deleted. Instead, it is marked for deletion by setting it as tombstoned. This allows the object to be replicated to all other domain controllers in a tombstoned state. When the tombstone lifetime expires, the object is deleted. By default, the tombstone lifetime is 60 days.

The tombstone lifetime restricts how old your backups can be within the forest. Any backups older than the tombstone lifetime cannot be restored.

Normally, this isn't a problem. However, if you want to have the capability to restore backups older than 60 days, you need to change the tombstone lifetime.

The actual method of changing the tombstone lifetime is beyond the scope of this book. However, the tools you can use are: ADSI Edit, the LDIFDE command line tool, or a VBScript.

Nonauthoritative Restore vs. Authoritative Restore

Two types of Active Directory restores are possible: authoritative restores and nonauthoritative restores. It's important to know what each of them are, the differences between the two, and the process of each.

Nonauthoritative restore   In a nonauthoritative restore, you restore Active Directory by restoring system state data. A nonauthoritative restore is done most often when a domain controller suffers a failure and needs to be rebuilt.

While the domain controller is out of service, other domain controllers are up and operational. They are accepting regular changes to domain objects (such as adding users and computers, users changing passwords, users being deleted, and so on).

When the domain controller is brought back online after a nonauthoritative restore, it will replicate with other domain controllers to get any changes that may have occurred since it was taken out of service.

Authoritative restore   An authoritative restore is used to recover objects and containers that have been deleted from Active Directory. An authoritative restore isn't done in response to a failure on the DC but instead to restore deleted objects.

For example, if a user or OU was deleted, you can use an authoritative restore to bring these objects back. When the domain controller is brought back online, it authoritatively replicates these restored objects to other domain controllers.

Remember, in a nonauthoritative restore, the other domain controllers replicate the objects to the domain controller brought back online. In an authoritative restore, the objects are marked to tell the other domain controllers that its version of the object is the real, authoritative version.

To understand how these two restores work, consider the following two scenarios:

Nonauthoritative restore scenario

- **Sunday**—Back up system state by backing up critical volumes.
- **Monday**—DC1 experiences a hard drive failure on the drive holding the `ntds.dit` file (Active Directory).
- **Tuesday**—An account named Maria is created in Active Directory on another domain controller (DC2).
- **Wednesday**—DC1's hard drive is repaired. System state data is restored, and DC1 is brought back online. DC2 will replicate all of the Active Directory changes (since Sunday's backup) to DC1, including the new Maria account.

Authoritative restore scenario

- **Sunday**—Back up system state by backing up critical volumes.
- **Monday**—An account named BigBossCEO is deleted in Active Directory.
- **Tuesday**—Active Directory is restored on DC1 nonauthoritatively from the Sunday backup. (The BigBossCEO account is present in this backup.)

If you rebooted at this point, DC1 would replicate with other domain controllers, and the BigBossCEO account would again be deleted on DC1.

Instead, you need to authoritatively restore the BigBossCEO account before rebooting DC1. When DC1 is rebooted after the authoritative restore, the BigBossCEO account is replicated to other domain controllers as the authoritative version of this account.

An important point of the authoritative restore is that it starts with a nonauthoritative restore. This is done to retrieve a complete copy of the deleted object. If the BigBossCEO account has been deleted, you first have to restore the object and then authoritatively mark it.

Directory Services Restore Mode

To restore Active Directory, you need to boot into Directory Services Restore Mode. You can access Directory Services Restore Mode by restarting the domain controller and pressing F8 upon rebooting. F8 will launch the Advanced Options page.

Advanced Options includes many other troubleshooting options:

- Safe Mode (including With Networking and With Command Prompt)
- Enable Boot Logging
- Enable Low-Resolution Video (640×480)
- Last Known Good Configuration (Advanced)
- Debugging Mode
- Disable Automatic Restart on System Failure
- Disable Driver Signature Enforcement

You select Directory Services Restore Mode from the Advanced Options menu.

It's also possible to use the bcdedit command to restart the domain controller in directory services restore mode. At the command prompt, enter **bcdedit /set safeboot dsrepair**. This will modify the boot configuration data store to boot into directory services restore mode on the next reboot. To restart the server normally after doing the restore, enter **bcdedit / deletevalue safeboot**. If you entered the first bcdedit command but don't run the bcdedit command again, you will constantly be booting into directory services safe mode.

Exercise 5.4 shows how to restore Active Directory. You must have a backup of critical volumes (such as what you created in Exercise 5.3) in order to perform this procedure.

Real World Scenario

Why Should You Do Authoritative Restores?

You may be wondering why an authoritative restore is necessary. If an account is deleted, isn't it easy to just create a new one with the same name?

Although it is easy to create a new account with the same name, the operating system doesn't identify accounts with their names. Instead, any account is identified with a security identifier (commonly called a SID). SIDs are unique within a forest, meaning you would never have the same SID for any two accounts.

Additionally, SIDs are used in access control lists of each and every object that uses permissions to control access.

For example, consider the folder named Projects of an NTFS drive. The Security tab is showing in the following image, which shows the NTFS access control list. Two entities are granted access: the Administrators group and the BigBossCEO account.

What's not apparent is that each of these accounts is actually identified by a SID. The system does a lookup to identify the actual name from the SID, and the account name is displayed.

If you created another account with the same name of BigBossCEO, that account would not have access to this folder or any other resources associated with his original account, since the new account would have a different SID.

By restoring the original account, the user will retain access to all the same resources.

EXERCISE 5.4

Nonauthoritatively Restoring Active Directory

1. Reboot your domain controller.

2. As the system is restarting, press F8 to access the Advanced Options page.

3. On the Advanced Boot Options selection page, use the arrow keys to select Directory Services Restore Mode (DSRM), and press the Enter key. The system will boot into a safe mode used for directory services repair.

4. Once the system completes the reboot process, press Ctrl+Alt+Del to log on.

5. Click Other User, and enter **.\Administrator** for the DSRM administrator name. Notice the dot before the backslash. This indicates the DSRM account. The Active Directory Administrator account won't be available since Active Directory Domain Services and the Active Directory database is not running.

6. Enter the password of the DSRM account created when you first installed Active Directory Domain Services. If you did the previous exercises in this book, the password is P@ssw0rd. Press Enter, and you will be logged into the system in safe mode.

7. Click ➢ Command Prompt.

8. At the command prompt, enter the following command:

    `Wbadmin get versions -backuptarget:UNC path`

    The UNC path is the path where you stored the backup in the previous exercise. For example, if you created a share named Backups on the MCITP2 computer, the UNC path would be \\MCITP2\Backups, and the full command would be as follows:

    `Wbadmin get versions -backuptarget:\\MCITP2\Backups`

    The entire command should be entered on one command line. The Wbadmin command connects to the share and will report key information about the backup. It looks similar to the following:

    `Backup time: 5/1/2008 1:31PM`

    `Backup target: Network share labeled \\MCITP2\Backup`

    `Version identifier: 05/01/2008-18:31`

    `Can Recover: Volume(s), File(s), Application(s), Bare Metal Recovery, and System State.`

    I have bolded the version identifier. It is important and must be entered exactly as it is shown. Notice it looks like a date time stamp, but the time differs from the actual backup time. Identify your version identifier and write it down here: _____.

EXERCISE 5.4 *(continued)*

9. Start the recovery of system state data with the following command:

Wbadmin start systemstaterecovery -version:03/01/2008-18:31

Substitute your version identifier for what is shown in the previous command.

10. When prompted to start the system state recovery operation, press the Y key, and press Enter.

The restore occurs in three phases: processing files, preparing for restore, and restoring files. It will take quite a bit of time to complete.

11. Once the restore completes, reboot your system. Depending on the configuration of your system, it's possible it will automatically reboot.

If you wanted to do an authoritative restore, you would not reboot. Instead, use the following steps to complete an authoritative restore:

1. Launch NTDSUtil from the command line.

2. Set the active instance to NTDS by entering **Activate Instance NTDS**.

3. Access the authoritative restore shell commands by entering authoritative restore.

4. Restore the object or container (such as an OU). Objects are restored using the command Restore object %s. Containers are restored using the command Restore subtree %s.

In both commands, the %s indicates the distinguished name of the object. For example, to restore the entire Sales OU in the MCITPSuccess.hme domain, the distinguished name would be OU=Sales,domain=mcitpsuccess,domain=hme. Similarly, the user named SallySmith in the Sales OU would have a distinguished name of CN=SallySmith,OU=Sale, dc=mcitpsuccess,dc=hme.

Group Policy

The power of Group Policy lies in how it allows you to create a single setting but have it apply to many users and computers. If you're working in a domain environment, you can have hundreds or thousands of users and computers. By creating and linking Group Policy objects (GPOs), you can easily manage all of the users and computers.

If you want everyone in your domain to set their home page to your company's intranet home page, you can go to each individual computer and set it (and hope users don't change it), or you can set it once using Group Policy. By creating a single GPO and linking it to the domain, you cause this setting to be applied to all users in the domain.

By default, two group policies exist in a domain:

The default domain policy   When DCPromo is run to promote the first server in the domain to a domain controller, this GPO is created and a linked to the domain. It includes many default settings and affects all users and computers in the domain.

The default domain controllers policy   This GPO is linked to the Domain Controllers OU and applies to all computers in the Domain Controllers OU. All the domain controllers and only the domain controllers should be in the Domain Controllers OU. In effect, the GPO applies to the domain controllers, but you can't link a GPO to a computer.

Figure 5.9 shows the Group Policy Management Editor with the Default Domain Policy open. Each GPO has two nodes—Computer Configuration and User Configuration.

FIGURE 5.9   Group Policy Management Editor

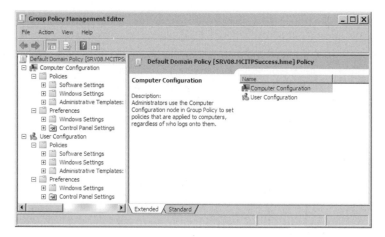

Computer Configuration   Settings in this node apply to computers, regardless of who logs into the computer. You can use it to assign software to users, set a myriad of Windows settings (including setting security and running scripts), and configure the environment with settings for Control Panel, the network, printers, Windows components, and other system settings.

User Configuration   Settings in this node apply to users, regardless of to which computer the user logs on. You can use it to publish or assign software to users, set Windows settings (including implement security, run scripts, redirect folders, and configure Internet Explorer). Administrative templates allow you to set the environment for the user including settings for Control Panel, the desktop, the network, shared folders, the Start menu and taskbar, and more.

Within each node, you have both policies and preferences. Preferences are new to Windows Server 2008.

Policies   Settings configured as policies will be forced on users and computers affected by Group Policy. If a user tries to make a change to the setting, it will be dimmed, and the user cannot make the change on the local machine. Policies are set when Group Policy is first applied and then at refresh intervals (described later in this section).

Preferences Preferences are set as administrator preferences. In other words, the administrator prefers the user accept these settings. However, the user can still make local changes to these settings. Preferences are applied when the Group Policy is first applied. You can choose whether to have preferences reapply at refresh intervals.

Understanding How Group Policy Is Applied

Group Policy is a big animal. No doubt about it. However, when you're trying to understand how Group Policy works, you don't have to know and understand all the possible settings. Indeed, if you try to learn and understand them all right away, you'll get lost in the details.

When trying to understand how Group Policy is applied, it's best to concentrate on a single setting. Although you have literally hundreds of settings, you don't have to understand or know them all to understand how Group Policy works. Once you understand how Group Policy applies to this single setting, it's easy to apply that knowledge to other Group Policy settings.

For example, consider the Prohibit Access to the Control Panel setting, as shown in Figure 5.10. When enabled, users affected by this setting won't be able to access the Control Panel.

FIGURE 5.10 Prohibiting access to the Control Panel

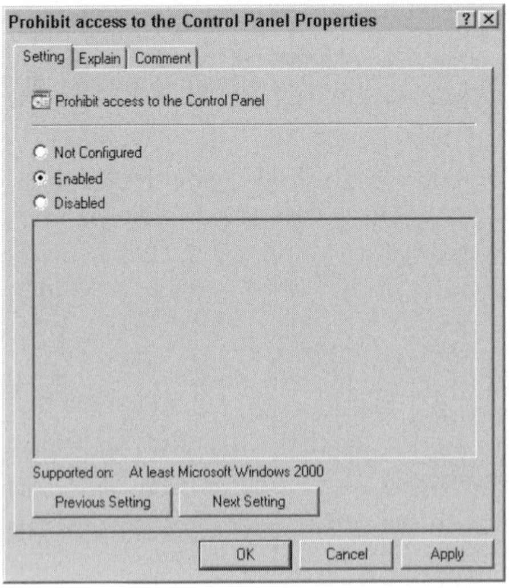

On the other hand, if it is set to Disabled, then it reverses any previous setting that prohibited access to Control Panel. Think of it as two negatives making a positive—if you *disable* a *prohibition*, you are effectively allowing it.

Group Policy objects can be linked to sites, domains, and organizational units (OUs). Say that to yourself about a hundred times. It's that important. GPOs can be linked to sites, domains, and OUs.

Before we go too far, these three terms deserve definitions:

Site A site is a group of well-connected hosts or well-connected subnets.

You can work at a company that has a location in Virginia Beach, Virginia, and another location in Suffolk, Virginia. Each location could be running a 100Mbps network, but they are connected via a T1 line at 1.544Mbps. Each site is well connected within itself, but between the sites, they are connected with a significantly slower connection.

Within Active Directory, you can create a site identifying each location (Virginia Beach and Suffolk). By linking a GPO to the Virginia Beach site, you could affect only the users and computers in Virginia Beach.

There isn't any direct correlation between sites and domains. It's possible to have more than one site within a single domain or to have more than one domain within a single site. Several possibilities exist.

- One domain could contain both the Virginia Beach and Suffolk sites. GPOs applied at the domain level would apply to all users and computers in both sites. However, GPOs applied to only one site apply only to users and computers in that site. You can see this in Figure 5.11.

FIGURE 5.11 One domain holding two sites

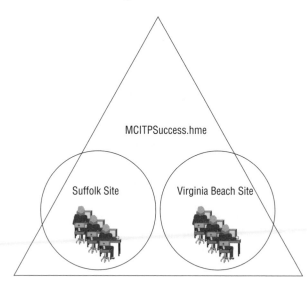

MCITPSuccess.hme

Suffolk Site   Virginia Beach Site

- Each site could have a single domain. There would be no difference between applying GPOs at the site or domain level. GPOs applied at the domain level apply to all users and computers in the site, and GPOs applied at the site level apply to all users and computers in the domain. You can see this in Figure 5.12.

FIGURE 5.12 One domain for each site

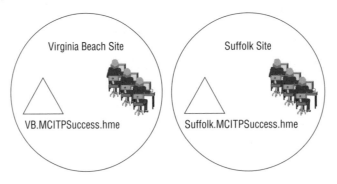

- A single site could hold multiple domains. For example, the Virginia Beach site could hold both the root domain and a child domain. GPOs applied at the site level affect both domains. GPOs applied at either domain level apply only to the individual domain. You can see this in Figure 5.13.

FIGURE 5.13 One site holding two domains

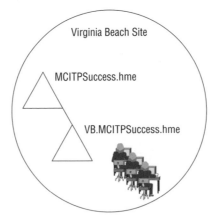

Domain A domain is the collection of users and computers on the network that share a common database (Active Directory) and security policy. The database holds all the objects in the domain such as users, computers, groups, and more.

Any GPO applied to the domain would affect all users and computers in the domain. This includes users in the Users container and computers in the Computers container.

Remember, you can apply GPOs only to sites, domains, or OUs. Neither the Users container nor the Computers container is an OU. If you want to affect the Users and Computers containers, you need to link a GPO at the domain level.

Organizational unit   An OU is an object within Active Directory used to organize objects such as users and computers.

For example, you could have an accounting department within your business. If all users within the accounting department needed access to a specific line-of-business application, you could create an Accounting OU and place all accounting personnel in the OU. You could then create a GPO to deploy the line-of-business application and link the GPO to the Accounting OU. All users would now automatically have access to the application.

Order of Precedence

When Group Policy is applied, it is applied in the following order:

- Local policy
- Site GPOs
- Domain GPOs
- OU GPOs
- Child OU GPOs (if child OUs exist)

> When a local policy is enabled on a local system, these settings will remain applied unless they are overwritten by any site, domain, or OU GPOs. However, in Windows Server 2008, a setting called Turn Off Local Group Policy Objects Processing exists. When this setting is disabled, the local policy will not apply.

The Winning GPO

If there is a conflict between any GPOs, the last GPO applied wins. For example, imagine if you had two GPOs named EnableRemoveControlPanel and DisableRemoveControlPanel. The EnableRemoveControlPanel GPO is linked at the domain level. Its purpose is to remove access to the Control Panel for all users affected by this GPO. On the other hand, the DisableRemoveControlPanel GPO is linked to the ITAdmins OU. Its purpose is to reverse the Remove Control Panel setting.

Figure 5.14 shows these two GPOs and how they are linked to the domain and the ITAdmins OU.

FIGURE 5.14   Prohibiting access to Control Panel

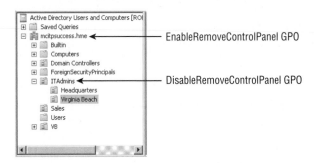

Can you determine what the impact from these two GPOs is on users in the following locations? Is Contol Panel enabled or disabled?

- Users in the Users container in the domain

- Users in the Sales OU

- Users in the ITAdmins OU

- Users in the Headquarters OU

Any GPO linked to the domain affects all users and computers in the domain. Whatever is applied to the domain is inherited by OUs and containers within the domain. This includes users in the Users container, computers in the Computers container, and users and computers in the Sales OU. If no other GPOs are applied, Control Panel will be removed for all users in the domain.

However, another GPO is being applied to the ITAdmins OU. Any GPO linked to an OU will affect all users and computers in the OU and in any child OUs.

The effect of both GPOs on the following locations is as follows:

Users in the users container   Control Panel *disabled*; only the EnableRemoveControlPanel GPO is applied.

Users in the Sales OU   Control Panel *disabled*; only the EnableRemoveControlPanel GPO is applied.

Users in the ITAdmins OU   Control Panel *enabled*; the DisableRemoveControlPanel is the last GPO applied.

Users in the Headquarters OU   Control Panel *enabled*; the DisableRemoveControlPanel is the last GPO applied.

Advanced Settings

Group Policy includes two advanced settings that can affect how Group Policy is applied to OUs: Block Policy Inheritance and Enforced.

Block Policy Inheritance   You can set Block Policy Inheritance on any OU. When set, almost all higher level GPOs set at the site, domain or parent OU levels will be blocked and will not apply. The exception is when an inherited GPO has the Enforced setting enabled.

When higher level GPOs are blocked, they simply don't apply. As an example, you may have an OU named ITAdmins used to hold IT administrator accounts. To prevent regular group policies from being applied to these administrators, you could block inheritance at the ITAdmins OU.

A key point is that you block policy inheritance at the OU level and you block all policies except those that are enforced.

Enforced   You can set the Enforced attribute on any GPO. When set, the settings on the GPO can not be blocked and can not be overridden by lower level GPOs.

For example, you may deploy a script at the domain level that displays a welcome screen when a user logs on and describe the terms of use of the computer. You would want that script to run on all computers without exception. By setting the Enforced attribute on the GPO, the GPO would not be blocked even if a lower level OU has Block Policy Inheritance set.

If a lower level GPO had a conflict with a higher level GPO that was set as Enforced, the GPO with the Enforced attribute set would win.

When Group Policy Is Applied

Group Policy is applied to a computer when the computer turns on and authenticates with Active Directory. Group Policy is applied to a user when the user logs on. When a computer starts or a user logs on, Active Directory is queried for a list of Group Policy objects. These policies are retrieved and applied to the computer and user, respectively.

Additionally, users and computers have a refresh interval. Every 90 to 120 minutes, Active Directory is queried to determine whether there have been any changes to their group policies, and if so, the changes are applied. The refresh interval is 90 minutes by default with an offset of 30 minutes, but both the interval and the offset can be changed with a Group Policy setting.

For domain controllers, the refresh interval is five minutes by default. This setting can also be changed by default. Additionally, group policies are reapplied every 16 hours with a 30-minute offset even if there are no changes. This is done as a security precaution.

So, imagine you change a Group Policy for an OU and you want to see whether it's applying to a user in that OU. How long will have to wait? Up to 2 hours (120 minutes). If you're a consultant and that's billable time, perhaps you don't care. However, you're probably thinking there must be a better way. You are correct.

You can use the command-line tool `gpupdate` to force a computer to query Active Directory and reapply settings. By entering `gpupdate`, the system will query Active Directory to retrieve any changes. This is similar to the 90- to 120-minute refresh interval. It will check for changes to GPOs that apply, and if any are found, it will apply the Group Policy changes.

If you want to reapply all Group Policy settings without checking for changes, you can use the `gpupdate /force` command.

Loopback Processing

Occasionally you may have a need to reverse the order of processing for a GPO when users log onto computers. You can reverse the order of processing of GPOs with loopback processing. Before getting into loopback processing, consider the normal order of processing for Group Policy objects.

When you have a GPO that applies to a user (granting access to Control Panel) and another GPO that applies to a computer (removing access to Control Panel), which one takes precedence? Remember, if there is a conflict (such as granting and removing access to Control Panel), the last GPO applied wins.

To answer the question, consider the following two OUs, each with a GPO linked to it:

Library Computers OU: Lockdown GPO; removes access to Control Panel

ITAdmins OU: GrantAll GPO; grants access to Control Panel

The Lockdown GPO is designed to severely restrict access to computers in the library, including removing access to Control Panel. Users can run a single program for library purposes, but that's all.

On the other hand, the GrantAll GPO is designed to reverse any type of restrictions allowing an IT administrator to do anything, including accessing Control Panel.

Which GPO takes precedence? The answer lies in the phrase "the last GPO applied wins."

Consider an obvious question. What happens last—the computer starts up or the user logs on? Obviously, you can't log onto a computer until it starts up, so the user logs on last. If there is a conflict between two GPOs where one GPO applies to a user and another GPO applies to the computer, the one that applies to the user wins.

In other words, if a user whose user account is in the ITAdmins OU logs into a computer whose computer account is in the Library Computers OU, any conflicts between the GPOs would be won by the user account. Just considering the Control Panel setting, the user would have access to Control Panel.

If you manage the computer in the library, you may not be happy about this situation. What can you do?

The Loopback Processing GPO setting allows you to change the order of the processing. Instead of the user account setting taking precedence, you enable Loopback Processing. This will cause the computer's Group Policy settings to take precedence.

Loopback Processing has two settings:

Replace When Replace is selected, all GPO settings are replaced with the settings in the computer's GPO. This includes the setting of Not Configured. In other words, all other GPOs are ignored.

Merge When Merge is selected, other GPOs are still applied. However, any time there is a conflict, the computer's GPO takes precedence.

Group Policy Management Console

The primary tool you'll use to create and manage GPOs is the Group Policy Management Console (GPMC). The GPMC is installed by default on domain controllers.

Figure 5.15 shows the GPMC with the default domain policy selected.

FIGURE 5.15   The Group Policy Management Console

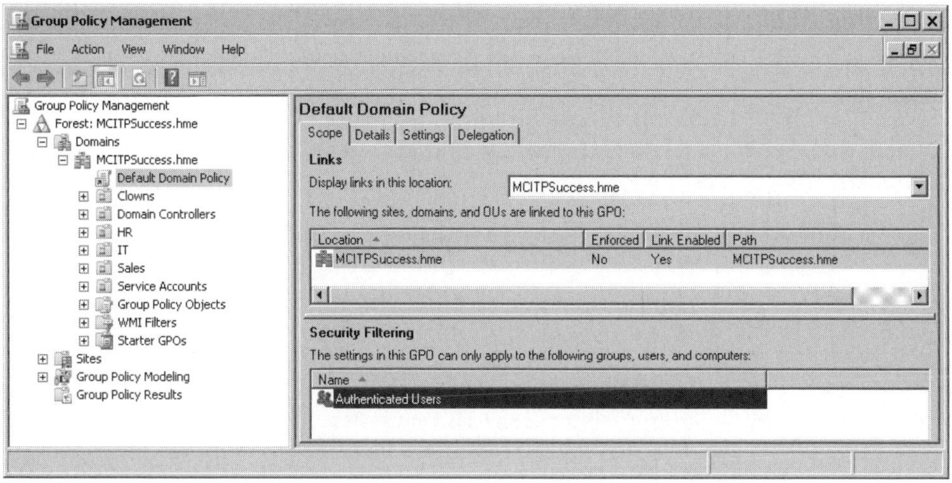

You can use the GPMC to do the following:

- Create GPOs.
- Link GPOs to a site, domain, or OU.
- Disable GPOs.
- Delegate permissions to GPOs.
- Back up and restore GPOs.
- Troubleshoot GPOs.

The following sections will cover these tasks including some exercises that will show you step-by-step how to perform the tasks.

Creating and Linking GPOs

Exercise 5.5 shows you how to launch GPMC, create a GPO, link it, and disable the link.

EXERCISE 5.5

Creating and Linking GPOs in the GPMC

1. Start the GPMC by clicking Start ➢ Administrative Tools ➢ Group Policy Management Console. If the GPMC tree pane is collapsed, open the Domains container and your domain container by clicking the plus sign.

2. Right-click the Group Policy Objects container, and select New.

3. In the New GPO dialog box, enter **EnableRemoveControlPanel as the name. Click OK.**

    Although you have successfully created the GPO, it is empty and is not linked anywhere.

4. Right-click the domain, and select Link an Existing GPO, as shown here.

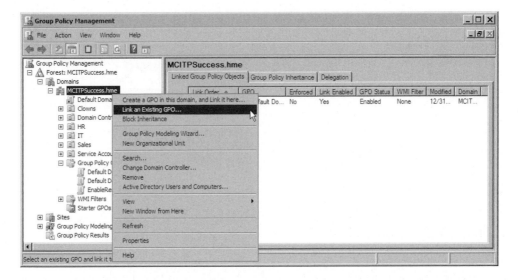

5. In the Select GPO dialog box, select the EnableRemoveControlPanel GPO, and click OK. The GPO is now linked to the domain and will apply to all users and computers in the domain. Remember, though, that the GPO still doesn't have any settings.

6. Select the EnableRemoveControlPanel GPO. If a Group Policy Management Console dialog box appears, read the information, and click OK.

EXERCISE 5.5 *(continued)*

7. Right-click the EnableRemoveControlPanel GPO, and click Edit.

8. In the Group Policy Management Editor page, browse to the User Configuration ➢ Policies ➢ Administrative Templates ➢ Control Panel container.

9. Select the Prohibit Access to the Control Panel setting, as shown here.

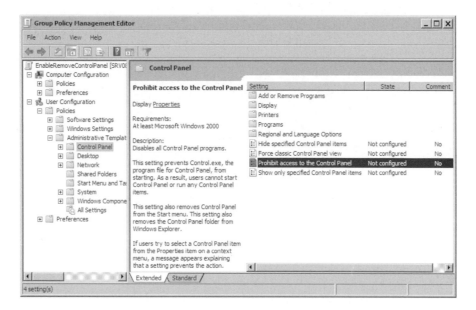

10. Double-click the Prohibit Access to the Control Panel setting to access the properties page.

11. On the Prohibit Access to the Control Panel setting, select Enabled, and click OK.

   At this point, all users and computers within the domain will have access to the Control Panel restricted.

12. Return to the GPMC, and right-click the EnableRemoveControlPanel GPO. Click the Link Enabled setting to remove the check mark. If you right-click the GPO again, it should look like this.

EXERCISE 5.5 *(continued)*

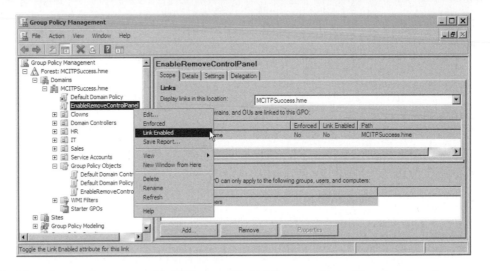

At this point, you have created a GPO named EnableRemoveControlPanel, and you've linked it to the domain. For troubleshooting purposes, you may occasionally want to stop the GPO settings from applying. You don't have to delete the GPO or even delete the link. Instead, you can simply disable the GPO's link.

Disabling Computer or User Configuration Settings

When a group policy is read, all of the settings are scanned even if they aren't set. It's possible that when you create a GPO, you configure settings only in the User Configuration node or in the Computer Configuration node.

However, even if you haven't configured any settings in one of the nodes, each node is still scanned. If you want to optimize the GPO, you can disable the node. Figure 5.16 shows the properties page of a GPO with the computer configuration settings disabled.

To access this property page, you need to be in the Group Policy Management Editor. Right-click the name of the GPO (above the Computer Configuration node, and select Properties).

An alternate way of disabling the User node or the Computer node is through the GPMC. Select the GPO in the tree pane. In the pane on the right, click the Details tab. You can then select one of the following four settings:

- All Settings Disabled
- Computer Configuration Settings Disabled
- Enabled
- User Configuration Settings Disabled

FIGURE 5.16   Disabling a GPO link

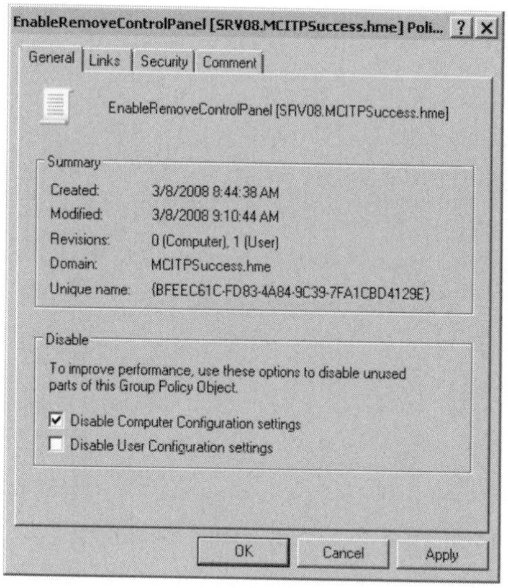

   This can also be used for troubleshooting purposes. For example, if you want to disable the computer configuration settings but not the entire GPO, you can disable just the settings in the computer configuration node. Of course, you could just as easily disable the user configuration settings by checking the second box.

Delegating Permissions to a GPO in GPMC

The GPMC allows you to easily manage who has permissions to GPOs. By changing the permissions, you can modify who the GPO applies to and also delegate who can modify GPOs.

   First it's important to understand the permissions needed for a GPO to apply to a group or user. When a GPO is first created, the Authenticated Users group is assigned the following permissions:

- Read

- Apply Group Policy

   These two permissions are required for the group policy to apply to a user or group. Users become members of the Authenticated Users group when they log on, so by default each GPO will apply to all users that fall within the GPOs scope (site, domain, or OU).

   Just as with any other permissions (NTFS permissions, Share permissions, printer permissions, and so on), the permissions are cumulative. In other words, if a member is a member of multiple groups, the permissions combine. Additionally, just as with other permissions, if Deny is selected, Deny takes precedence.

   If you decided you didn't want this policy to apply to a specific group such as the ITAdmins group, you can select Deny for Apply Group Policy. Figure 5.17 shows Apply Group Policy set to Deny for the ITAdmins group. The ITAdmins group can read the policy, but it cannot apply to them. This is referred to as *filtering Group Policy*.

FIGURE 5.17   Filtering Group Policy

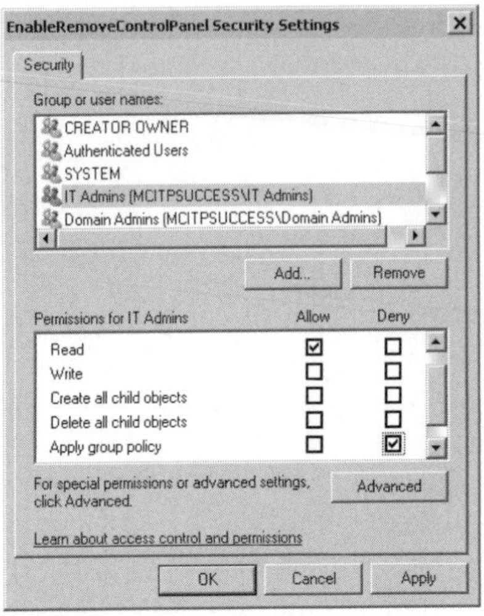

You can access this screen within GPMC by selecting a GPO, selecting the Delegation tab, and clicking the Advanced button. Although you can set advanced permissions, GPOs have three standard permissions that can be assigned or delegated:

Read   Users can read the Group Policy objects, but not modify them.

Edit Settings   Users can read and modify Group Policy settings.

Edit Settings, Delete, Modify Security   Users can read and modify the Group Policy objects. They can also delete the GPO and modify permissions on the GPO. Think of this as full control. The Domain Admins and Enterprise Admins groups are granted these permissions when a GPO is created.

Exercise 5.6 shows you how to delegate permissions to a GPO. It assumes you have created the EnableRemoveControlPanel GPO in Exercise 5.5.

EXERCISE 5.6

Delegating Permissions on a GPO

1. Start the GPMC by clicking Start ➢ Administrative Tools ➢ Group Policy Management Console.

2. Select the EnableRemoveControlPanel GPO created in the previous exercise. If the Group Policy Management Console information box appears, review the information, and click OK.

    In the pane on the right of the Scope tab, notice the Security Filtering area includes the Authenticated Users group. This group is assigned both Read and Apply Group Policy, but you can't really tell that from here.

3. Click the Delegation tab. On the Delegation tab display, you can see that many groups have already been added and assigned specific permissions.

4. Click the Add button.

5. In the Select User, Computer, or Group dialog box, enter **Account**, and click the Check Names button. Account will be replaced with Account Operators. Click OK to select the Account Operators group.

6. On the Add Group or User page, change the permissions from Read to Edit Settings from the drop-down box. Your display will look similar to the one shown here.

7. Click OK to assign the permissions to the Account Operators group.

8. Click the Advanced button.

9. On the EnableRemoveControlPanel Security Settings page, select the Authenticated Users group. Note that both Read and Apply Group Policy is set to Allow.

10. Click the Advanced button.

11. In the Advanced Security Settings dialog box, select Account Operators, and click Edit.

12. On the Permission Entry page, notice the many different permissions that have been assigned. By using the standard permission of Edit Settings, you have added all of these permissions for this group.

13. Click Cancel on the Permission Entry page. Click Cancel on the Advanced Security Settings page. Click Cancel on the EnableRemoveControlPanel Security Settings page.

Using the Group Policy Creator Owners Group to Delegate Permissions

In addition to the permissions available to individual GPOs, you can also delegate permissions to allow a user or group to manage GPOs they create.

By default, only members of the Domain Admins, Enterprise Admins, and Group Policy Creator Owners groups can create GPOs in a domain. If you want delegate permission to create GPOs to users who are not in the Domain Admins or Enterprise Admins group, you should add them to the Group Policy Creator Owners group. Members of the Group Policy Creator Owners group can modify any GPOs they create, but they cannot modify any other GPOs.

For example, you may choose to delegate control of the Sales OU to the SalesITAdmins group (as was done in Exercise 5.1). By adding the SalesITAdmins group to the Group Policy Creator Owners group, you grant them the ability to manipulate the GPOs they create within the OU.

Exercise 5.7 shows you how to add a group to the Creator Owners group and grant them the ability to manage GPOs. It assumes you have created the Sales OU and the SalesITAdmins group in Exercise 5.1.

Adding a User to the Group Policy Creator Owners Group

1. Open Active Directory Users and Computers by clicking Start ➢ Administrative Tools ➢ Active Directory Users and Computers.

2. Browse to the SalesITAdmins group in the Sales OU.

3. Right-click the SalesITAdmins group, and select Properties.

4. On the SalesITAdmins properties page, select the Members tab.

5. Click the Add button.

6. On the Select Users, Contacts, Computers, or Groups page, click the Advanced button. Click the Find Now button.

7. Scroll down until you locate the Group Policy Creator Owners group. Groups are listed in alphabetical order by default. When the group is selected, click OK.

8. On the Select Users, Contacts, Computers or Groups page, click OK.

9. On the SalesITAdmins properties page, click OK.

In addition to granting users the ability to manage GPOs they create, you can also grant them the ability to link GPOs to an OU. You can do this within the GPMC by selecting an OU and selecting the Delegation tab.

Figure 5.18 shows the users and groups granted permissions to link GPOs to the Sales OU. By selecting Perform Group Policy Modeling Analyses or Read Group Policy Results Data, you can also view who has been granted these permissions.

FIGURE 5.18 Permissions delegated to an OU

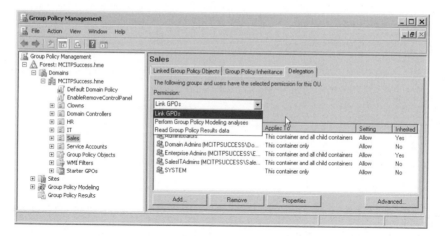

With any of the three permissions selected, you can click the Add button and add users or groups, granting them the appropriate permission.

Exploring a Few Specific Group Policy Settings

Although it's not possible to cover every possible Group Policy setting within this chapter, I do want to cover a few. In this section, you'll learn how to do the following:

- Assign password policies.

- Assign folder redirection.

- Provision applications.

- Restrict device installations.

Assigning Password Policies

Using Group Policy, you can assign password policies. Password policy settings include the following:

- Enforce Password History prevents users from reusing the same password.

- Maximum Password Age forces users to change their password regularly.

- Minimum Password Age prevents users from changing their password back right away.

- Minimum Password Length requires passwords to be a minimum number of characters to make them harder to crack.

- Password Must Meet Complexity Requirements requires passwords to include at least three of the following four requirements: uppercase, lowercase, numbers, and characters. Passwords must also be at least six characters and not include the user's account name or parts of the user's full name.

- Store Password Using Reversible Encryption is used for backward compatibility for some systems. It is not recommended.

A domain will have one password policy that is assigned to all users. This is in the default domain policy by default, as shown in Figure 5.19.

FIGURE 5.19   Password policy in the default domain policy

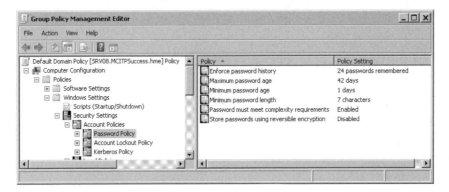

However, you may have a need for a special group of users to have a different password policy enforced. For example, you may create special administrator accounts and want these administrators to have more stringent password requirements than regular users.

In Windows Server 2003–based domains, if you needed a new password policy assigned to users, you were required to create a new domain. This was the only way you could have a different password policy assigned to different users.

In Windows Server 2008, you can create a password policy and have it apply to an individual OU. This is done by creating a password settings object (PSO) and linking it a user or group.

For example, if you wanted the ITAdmins group to have a more stringent password policy, you would create a PSO and link it to the ITAdmins group.

PSOs are created using the Active Directory Service Interfaces Editor (ADSIEdit) tool. ADSIEdit allows you to query, view, and edit all Active Directory Domain Services objects and attributes. You can also use the ADSIEdit tool to set the Applies To property of the PSO.

Assigning Folder Redirection

You can use Group Policy to cause some users folders to be redirected to another location. By default, several users' folders are stored in their profile. In Windows XP and previous versions, this has been in the C:\Documents and Settings folder. In Windows Vista and Server 2008, this is in the C:\Users folder. However, the key is that they are stored on the C:\ drive by default.

You may want to move these folders to a different drive. This could be a second hard drive on users' individual systems (such as the D:\ drive) or on a share on a server. One of the primary benefits of storing the data on a server is that data on a single server can be easily backed up. However, data stored on 50 (or 5,000) individual systems can't be easily backed up.

Folders in the profile include the following:

- AppData (Roaming)
- Desktop
- Start Menu
- Documents
- Pictures
- Music
- Videos
- Favorites
- Contacts
- Downloads
- Links
- Searches
- Saved Games

As an example, you may want to move users' Documents folder (this has previously been called My Documents) to a central share.

Figure 5.20 shows the Group Policy setting to accomplish this. Folder Redirection settings are located in the User Configuration ➤ Policies ➤ Windows Settings ➤ Folder Redirection. By right-clicking the Documents folder and selecting Properties, you can access the Document Properties page and set the policy. Figure 5.20 shows a UNC path of \\MCITP1\Users indicating a share named Users on the server named MCITP1.

FIGURE 5.20   Redirecting documents to a share on a server

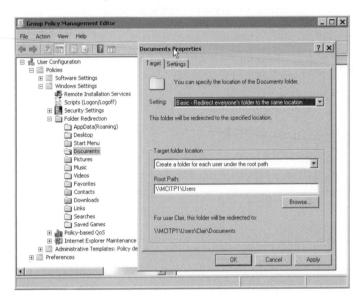

Imagine a user named Sally. If this policy applies to her, her Documents folder will be redirected to a folder named Sally\Documents within the Users share on the MCITP1 server.

Two settings are possible:

Basic—Redirect Everyone's Folder to the Same Location   You would use this in a smaller domain where all users documents and folders can be stored on a single server.

Advanced—Specify Locations for Various User Groups   This is for larger domains or when user's documents and folders cannot be easily stored on a single server. You can add groups and cause a user's data to redirected to different locations based on the user's group membership.

Provisioning Applications

Although in a large environment you may have the luxury of pushing out applications with sophisticated server applications such as Systems Management Server (SMS) or System Center Configuration Manager (SCCM), many smaller companies don't have these tools.

However, you can use Group Policy to deploy applications. You can use Group Policy to either publish or assign an application.

When assigning or publishing applications, document activation is sometimes used. Document activation simply means that when a document is opened, the program associated with the document's extension will be used. For example, the extension .xls is associated with Microsoft Excel. If you received a document named Financial.xls and you double-clicked it, Microsoft Excel would launch, and the file would be displayed.

Publishing applications   Applications can be published to users only. When an application is published to a user, it will be available through the Control Panel by selecting Programs ➢ Get Programs ➢ Install a Program from the Network, as shown in Figure 5.21. After clicking this link, published programs will appear in the list. Published programs will also install through document activation. When published to the user, the user will have access to the application on any computer where they log on.

FIGURE 5.21   Accessing published programs through Control Panel

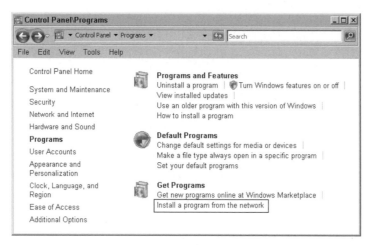

 In Windows XP and Windows Server 2003, you need to access the Add/ Remove Programs applet in the Control Panel to access and install published applications.

Assigning applications   Applications can be assigned to users or computers.

When an application is assigned to a user, it will be available from the Start menu but will not be installed right away. Two actions can cause the application to be installed: the user clicks the application from the Start menu, or the user opens a document associated with the application causing document activation. When assigned to the user, the user will have access to the application on any computer where they log on.

When an application is assigned to a computer, it will be installed on that computer the next time the computer is rebooted. In some situations, the computer will have to be rebooted twice to receive the installation. When assigned to the computer, the application will be available on the computer no matter who logs onto the computer.

When using Group Policy to deploy an application, you need to decide whether you want to deploy to a user or to a computer. To assign an application to all users in your domain, you could use the default domain policy or create another one. From the GPMC, you right-click the policy, click Edit, and then browse to the User Configuration ➢ Policies ➢ Software Settings ➢ Software Installation setting. Right-click the Software Installation setting, and select New ➢ Package. Browse to the location of your .msi file (this should be in a UNC path as in *serverName**ShareName* format). You can then choose Published or Assigned (or Advanced to manipulate the properties before deploying the package), as shown in Figure 5.22. Click OK, and you're done.

FIGURE 5.22   Assigning an application to users

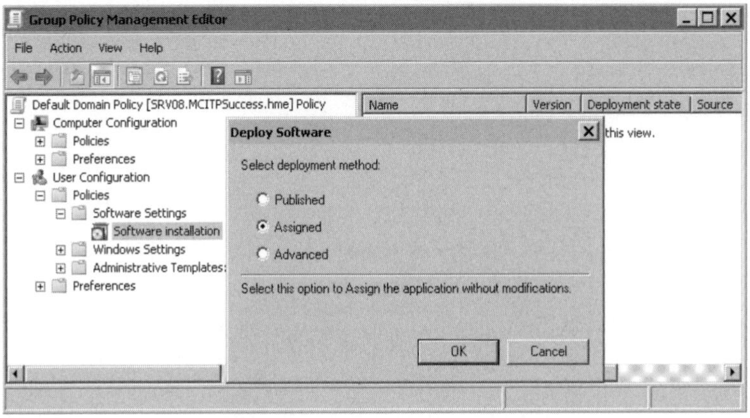

Remember, when assigning or publishing to users, the software is not installed right away. It's available to be installed, but it's waiting for user interaction before it's actually deployed. This can be useful in some environments where you want the software to be available but you know that all users won't install it.

In contrast, if you assign the application to a computer, the software will be assigned to the computer on the next reboot.

Device Installation Restrictions

While USB drives are very valuable to many users, they also represent a security risk within networks. I remember hearing of a security expert who was hired to perform a vulnerability assessment for a bank. He loaded malware on several USB thumb drives and dropped them around the bank and even in the parking lot. Eventually one was installed on a system and a key logger captured the employee's keystrokes and sent all the pertinent information to the security expert.

Unfortunately, there are other stories where the person planting the USB thumb drives aren't security experts doing vulnerability assessments. Instead, attackers are gathering valuable information just for the cost of just a few thumb drives.

Understanding this, it's not uncommon for security conscious administrators to want to prevent USB drives from being installed. You have a full node of settings that can be configured to restrict device installations. You can find these settings in the Computer Configuration, Policies, Administrative Templates, System, Device Installation, Device Installation Restrictions.

You can use these settings to prevent the installation of removable devices, and even allow administrators to override the Device Installation Restriction policies.

Backup and Recovery of GPOs

A lot of time and effort goes into creating and managing GPOs. You never want to experience a disaster where all your GPOs become corrupt, but you do want to plan for it. By keeping backups of your GPOs, if disaster strikes, you are prepared.

Exercise 5.8 shows how to back up and restore GPOs.

EXERCISE 5.8

Backing Up and Restoring GPOs

1. Launch the GPMC by selecting Start ➢ Administrative Tools ➢ Group Policy Management Console.

2. Open the GPMC to show the Forest ➢ Domains ➢ MCITPSuccess.hme ➢ Group Policy Objects container.

3. Right-click the Group Policy Objects container, and select Back Up All.

4. In the Back Up Group Policy Object dialog box, click Browse.

5. In the Browse for Folder dialog box, select the C:\ drive, and click Make New Folder. Rename the folder GPOBackups, and click OK.

6. Back in the Back Up Group Policy Objects dialog box, click Back Up. All of your GPOs will now be backed up. The Backup Progress page shows the progress and indicates success. Click OK.

7. Back in the Group Policy Objects container, right-click the EnableRemoveControlPanel GPO created in an earlier exercise, and select Delete. In the Group Policy Management confirmation dialog box, review the information, and click Yes.

8. Right-click the Group Policy Objects container, and select Manage Backups.

9. On the Manage Backups page, select the EnableRemoveControlPanel GPO, and click the Restore button.

10. In the Group Policy Management confirmation dialog box, click OK to verify you want to restore the GPO. The Restore Progress will appear and indicate success. Click OK.

11. On the Manage Backups page, click Close. Your GPO is restored.

Although the previous exercise showed you how to back up and restore the GPOs, remember that the backup is stored on whatever hard drive you choose. If that drive goes down, you've lost your backup. As a best practice, you should also include the GPO backup folder in your regular backup plan for this server.

Language Specific Administrative Templates

The administrative templates in Group Policy are used to modify registry settings via Group Policy. These were originally released as .adm files, but with Windows Vista they are XML based files. Two types of XML based files exist:

Language Neutral (.admx).   These files are the same in any language.

Language Specific (.adml).   These files are different for different languages.

In the past, there was only one language for these settings. That worked fine if you were in the U.S. and speaking English. However, for other countries speaking other languages, it wasn't so good. With the addition of the .admx and .adml files, Group Policy can be deployed in multiple languages side by side in the same environment.

Summary

In this chapter, you learned many of the specifics related to day-to-day Active Directory tasks that a server administrator would be expected to perform.

You first learned about Active Directory server roles with an emphasis on the important roles and tasks for the 70-646 exam. These included the Active Directory Domain Services (AD DS) role, the Read-Only Domain Controller (RODC) role, and the Active Directory Certificate Services (AD CS) role. You also learned about the common built-in groups available in a domain and how to add users to these groups.

Then, you learned the difference between authoritative and nonauthoritative restores and had an opportunity to actually back up and recover Active Directory. Remember, to do any type of restore, you always start with a restore in Directory Services Restore Mode from the Advanced Options menu.

Group Policy was covered extensively. You learned the purpose of Group Policy, the order of precedence when applying Group Policy objects (site, domain, OU), and about the different settings that can be used within Group Policy.

The primary tool used to manage GPOs is the Group Policy Management Console, and you learned how to use it to create and link GPOs, disable GPOs, delegate permissions to GPOs, and back up and restore GPOs.

Exam Essentials

Know the different Active Directory server roles.   You should have a solid understanding of the different Active Directory roles available. The primary role is Active Directory Domain Services (AD DS), and it is chiefly managed with Active Directory Users and Computers

(ADUC). Other important roles are the Read-Only Domain Controller (RODC) and Active Directory Certificate Services (AD CS).

Understand the RODC password-caching capabilities.   Passwords cached on the RODC are affected by the Password Replication Policy (on the properties of the RODC server object in ADUC) and by the two groups: Denied RODC Password Replication Group and Allowed RODC Password Replication Group.

Know how to delegate control to a user or group.   The Delegation of Control Wizard within Active Directory Users and Computers allows you to easily delegate control to users or groups for specific purposes. Exercise 5.1 in this chapter led you through the steps to do this.

Understand the terms and basic functionality of PKI.   You should understand the basic terms of a public key infrastructure (PKI) including certificates, certification authority (CA), certificate revocation list (CRL), online responders, and the Online Certificate Status Protocol (OCSP). You should know how certificates are shared in a typical SSL session and how their status can be verified using either a CRL or an OCSP.

Understand the different types of certification authorities.   You should know the differences between a root certification authority (CA) and a subordinate CA. Additionally, you should understand that a CA created within a domain is an enterprise CA and that external CAs (such as VeriSign) are known as stand-alone CAs.

Know the basic purposes, rights, and permissions of Active Directory groups.   Expect to be given a scenario identifying required permissions and then pick the group that most closely matches the required rights and permissions. You'll need to know all of the admin groups (Enterprise Admins, Domain Admins, Administrators on a domain controller, local administrators, and so on) and the other groups mentioned in this chapter. You should also remember that use of the Power Users group is no longer recommended.

Know how to back up and restore Active Directory.   You should be able to install the Windows Backup program and back up and restore Active Directory. You should know how to access Directory Services Restore Mode, and you should understand the difference between authoritative and nonauthoritative restores.

Know the purpose of Group Policy and how it is applied.   Group Policy allows you to set any setting (or group of settings) once and have these settings apply to many computers. The order of precedence is site, domain, OU, and the last setting applied wins. You should also understand how Block Policy Inheritance (applied at the OU level) and Enforced (applied at the GPO level) affect the order of precedence.

Be able to delegate permissions for a user to modify GPOs they create.   This one is simple. Remember that for a user to modify GPOs they create, you add that user to the Group Policy Creator Owners group.

Know some of the settings of Group Policy.   Be familiar with a few key Group Policy settings such as password policies, folder redirection, restricting device installations, and deploying applications. Understand the difference between assigning and publishing applications.

Review Questions

1. You manage a domain of 500 users, and you've decided to allow Sally to manage all the users and computers in the Sales organizational unit. How should you grant her the appropriate permissions?

    A. Right-click the domain, and select Delegation of Control Wizard.

    B. Right-click the Sales OU, and select Delegation of Control Wizard.

    C. Right-click Sally's user account, and select Delegation of Control Wizard.

    D. Add Sally's user account to the Domain Admins group.

2. You manage a domain with a remote office. Users in the remote office need to be able to log on to access file and print resources on a server in the local office. However, the WAN link is not reliable, and several times they have logged on using cached credentials, denying them access to the local file and print server. There is very little physical security in this office and little money to add resources. What can you implement to resolve this problem?

    A. Upgrade the file and printer server to a domain controller at the remote office.

    B. Upgrade the file and printer server to an RODC at the remote office.

    C. Upgrade the WAN link.

    D. Upgrade the physical security at the remote office.

3. IT administrators are added to the ITAdmins group, which has been granted significant permissions in your domain. Occasionally members of this group travel to remote offices to provide support and perform maintenance. One of the remote offices hosts an RODC, and you learn that passwords of administrators in the ITAdmins group are being cached on this server. The ITAdmins group should be allowed to log onto the RODC. What can you do to prevent this in the future?

    A. Add the ITAdmins group to the Denied RODC Password Replication Group.

    B. Add the ITAdmins group to the Allowed RODC Password Replication Group.

    C. Change the Password Replication Policy of the remote RODC to Allow for the ITAdmins group.

    D. Create a GPO, and link it to the Default Domain policy to ensure passwords are strong for the ITAdmins group.

4. You manage a large domain with multiple remote offices. Each of the remote offices has RODCs. At the Virginia Beach office, you want members of the VBAdmins group to be cached on the Virginia Beach RODC, but not at RODCs at other offices. What should you do?

    A. Add the VBAdmins group to the Denied RODC Password Replication Group.

    B. Add the VBAdmins group to the Allowed RODC Password Replication Group.

    C. Add the VBAdmins group to the Password Replication Policy of the Virginia Beach RODC, and set it to Deny.

    D. Add the VBAdmins group to the Password Replication Policy of the Virginia Beach RODC, and set it to Allow.

5. You are trying to promote a member server at a remote site to an RODC. However, the choice of RODC does not appear. Which of the following options could cause this problem?

A. The domain functional level is Windows Server 2003 and not Windows Server 2008.

B. The forest functional level is Windows Server 2000 and not Windows Server 2008.

C. The PDC Emulator is not running on a global catalog server.

D. This is normal behavior. You can convert a DC to an RODC only after it has been promoted.

6. Your company has deployed a public key infrastructure (PKI) and issues certificates for a variety of purposes. Because of a security breach in the past, several certificates were revoked and the CRL has become quite large. You are tasked with standing up a server that will use the Online Certificate Status Protocol (OCSP) to answer certificate status requests. What do you recommend?

A. Root CA

B. Subordinate CA

C. Enterprise CA

D. Online responder

7. Your company is planning on making Outlook Web Access (OWA) available so that users can check their email from anywhere on the Internet. This requires a certificate, and management has stated they will not purchase a certificate. What should you use to obtain the certificate?

A. A root stand-alone CA

B. A subordinate stand-alone CA

C. An enterprise CA

D. A self-signed certificate

8. You have modified GPO settings for a test GPO assigned to a test OU. You are logged onto a test system, but the new settings are not applied. What can you do to see the results of the settings?

A. Wait 90 to 120 minutes.

B. Run the GPResults /Force command.

C. Run the GPUpdate /Force command.

D. Launch ADSIEdit, and refresh the screen.

9. You need to delegate permissions to a junior administrator to a local file and print server. Occasionally, he needs to modify TCP/IP settings on this server. What group can you add him to in order to grant him the minimum permissions required to do this job?

A. Administrators

B. Power Users

C. Network Configuration Operators

D. DNSAdmins

10. A junior administrator manages a domain controller at a remote site. You want him to be able to fully manage the domain controller including doing backups, creating shares, and creating files on the server. However, you don't want to give him any access to the domain. What group can you add him to on the DC?

   A. Administrators

   B. Power Users

   C. Server Operators

   D. Network Configuration Operators

11. You manage two domain controllers in your domain. You perform backups of critical volumes on the servers every Sunday. On Wednesday, you learn that one of the vice president's accounts was accidentally deleted. What should you do?

   A. Re-create an account using the VP's original account name.

   B. Perform a nonauthoritative restore to retrieve the VP's account.

   C. Perform an authoritative restore to retrieve the VP's account.

   D. Restore the system state data on a domain controller.

12. You manage a domain and have created several GPOs. You want to create backups of these GPOs. What tool would you use?

   A. ADSIEdit

   B. GPMC

   C. Windows Server Backup

   D. Wbadmin

13. You want to backup critical volumes on your domain controller, but you find that the Windows Server Backup tool is not available. What is the problem?

   A. You can't back up critical volumes on domain controllers.

   B. The Windows Server Backup role has not been added to the DC.

   C. The Windows Server Backup feature has not been added to the DC.

   D. Critical volumes must be backed up using the Wbadmin tool.

14. You manage a Windows Server 2008 domain. You have created a linked GPO named LockdownGPO to an OU named KioskComputers. The GPO is intended to lock down computers in this OU. However, when some users log on, they have significantly more permissions than should be allowed from the GPO. What should you do to ensure the kiosk computers are locked down?

   A. Link the LockdownGPO to the domain.

   B. Link the LockdownGPO to the domain controller OU.

   C. Set the Lockdown GPO to disable user configuration settings.

   D. Set Loopback Processing on the LockdownGPO

15. You manage a large Windows Server 2008 domain of more than 1,000 users. The R&D department has been working on significant new products. If their accounts are compromised, the monetary loss is huge, so management wants to protect these accounts. All users in the R&D department are in a group named RnD and in an OU named RnD. They have asked you to implement a policy requiring all users in the RnD department to use stronger passwords of 15 characters. How should you do this?

A. Create a new domain with a stronger password policy, and place all the RnD users in this domain.

B. Create a GPO, and link it to the RnD users requiring them to use stronger passwords.

C. Create a password settings object, and link it the RnD group.

D. Create a password settings object, and link it the RnD OU.

16. An administrator manages the Marketing OU within your domain. She has created a GPO within her OU but finds that she can't change of any of the settings. What group should you add her to so that she can change settings in the GPO?

A. Domain Admins

B. Administrators

C. Server Operators

D. Group Policy Creator Owners

17. While testing a GPO that has several settings applied, you are having trouble separating all of the settings. The GPO has settings in both the computer configuration and the user configuration. You want to see what the impact would be if the settings of only the computer configuration were applied. How you do this?

A. Disable the User Configuration node in the GPO.

B. Disable the Computer Configuration node in the GPO.

C. Disable the GPO and create a new GPO with only the computer settings.

D. Disable the GPO and create a new GPO with only the user settings.

18. You administer a domain of several hundred users. Your company wants users to store data on a central file and print server. Home folders have been created, but you've learned that Vista users are storing much of their data in the Documents folder instead of in the Home folder. How can you easily have all users store their Documents data on a central server?

A. Reiterate company policy in an email to all employees.

B. Use Group Policy with the Home Folders setting.

C. Use Group Policy with the Redirect Folders setting.

D. Right-click the Documents folder on each user's computer, and change the location.

19. All members of the ITAdmins group need to have the Acme Network Administration tools (used to administer the Acme Network Monitor application) available to them on any machine that they log onto in the domain. The ITAdmins group is in the ITAdmins OU. The Acme Network Administration tools should be available from the Start menu. How should you accomplish this?

  A. Use Group Policy to run DCPromo on each computer within the domain.

  B. Use Group Policy to assign the AcmeNetworkMonitor.msi package to users. Link the GPO to the domain.

  C. Use Group Policy to assign the AcmeNetworkMonitor.msi package to users. Link the GPO to the ITAdmins OU.

  D. Use Group Policy to publish the AcmeNetworkMonitor.msi package to users. Link the GPO to the ITAdmins OU.

20. You want to deploy a line-of-business application needed by personnel in the sales department. You want it installed in all 100 computers used within the sales department. How should you accomplish this?

  A. Use Group Policy, and publish the application to the computers in the sales department.

  B. Use Group Policy, and assign the application to the computers in the sales department.

  C. Use Group Policy, and assign the application to the users in the sales department.

  D. Manually install the application on each computer in the sales department.

Answers to Review Questions

1. **B.**   The Delegation of Control Wizard can be used to assign the correct permissions. You must launch the wizard by right-clicking the Sales OU to grant the permissions to the Sales OU. Launching it at the domain level will grant permissions for the entire domain. The wizard can't be launched from a user account. Adding Sally's account to the Domain Admins group would grant her significantly more permissions than necessary.

2. **B.**   You can upgrade the file and print server to an RODC at no additional cost. Additionally, an RODC presents less risk since passwords that are cached at the server can be limited. Adding a domain controller would present a significant security risk since if it was stolen (and it could be since there is little physical security), the entire domain would be compromised. There isn't money to add resources, and both an upgrade to the WAN link or physical security will cost money.

3. **A.**   The Denied RODC Password Replication group can be used to prevent user's passwords from being cached on an RODC. Adding the ITAdmins group to the Allowed RODC Password Replication group would cause their passwords to be cached. Adding the ITAdmins group to the Password Replication Policy and setting it to Allow will cause their passwords to be cached. There isn't a GPO setting for this purpose.

4. **D.**   If you add a group to the Password Replication Policy of an RODC and set it to Allow, members of this group's passwords will be cached on this RODC only. Setting it to Deny will prevent passwords from being cached. Adding members to the Denied RODC Password Replication Group or Allowed RODC Password Replication Group will affect all RODCs, not just the Virginia Beach RODC.

5. **B.**   Both the forest functional level and domain functional level must be at least Windows Server 2003, not Windows Server 2000. Although the PDC Emulator must be running on a Windows Server 2008 server, it does not need to be running on the same server as a global catalog server. The RODC choice is available when promoting a server from a member server to a domain controller.

6. **D.**   An online responder will answer OCSP requests. OCSP provides the status certificates based on requests (instead of sending the entire CRL). Certificate authorities (root, subordinate, stand-alone, and enterprise) are used to issue and manage certificates. Although they can answer OCSP requests, they do much more.

7. **C.**   Stand-alone CAs are typically commercial (such as VeriSign) and charge for certificates. An enterprise CA is private to a company and can be used to issue certificates at no charge. A self-signed certificate would not meet the needs of OWA.

8. **C.**   The `GPUpdate /Force` command will cause the system to retrieve and reapply all group policies that apply to the system with the current user. Although a normal refresh will take 90 to 120 minutes, you don't need to wait that long. There's no such command as GPResults (plural), but `GPResult` will allow you to view the current GPO settings; `GPResult` does not have a `/force` switch. ADSIEdit can be used to create password settings objects, but it wouldn't be useful in refreshing a GPO.

9. C.   Members of the Network Configuration Operators group can manage the configuration of network features. The Administrators and Power Users groups would grant more permissions than necessary. The DNSAdmins group would grant permissions to manage DNS, but not TCP/IP settings.

10. C.   By adding the user to the Server Operators group, you give the user full access to administer the server without granting permissions to the domain. The Administrators group grants significant permissions to the domain (there is no local Administrators group on a DC, only the domain Administrators group). There is no Power Users group on a DC. The Network Configuration Operators group will grant permissions to make network changes only.

11. C.   By performing an authoritative restore, you can authoritatively restore the vice president's account. If you re-create the account with the same name, it will have a different SID, and the VP won't have access to resources with this new account. If you do a nonauthoritative restore, the account will be deleted as soon as the restored domain controller replicates with an online domain controller. A nonauthoritative restore restores the system state data, but an authoritative restore is needed.

12. B.   You can use the Group Policy Management Console (GPMC) to back up GPOs. The ADSIEdit tool can be used to view and modify Active Directory. Both Windows Server Backup and the Wbadmin command-line tool can be used to back up volumes, but not GPOs individually.

13. C.   The Windows Server Backup feature is not added by default. After adding it, you will be able to do backups. Critical volumes can be backed up on DCs. Windows Server Backup is a feature, not a role. Once the feature is installed, the Wbadmin tool and the Windows Server Backup tool are both available.

14. D.   By setting Loopback Processing, you cause the computer settings to take precedence. Linking the LockdownGPO to the domain or Domain Controller OU will change who the GPO applies to but won't change the order of precedence. Disabling the user configuration settings in the GPO will disable user configuration settings in the GPO but won't change the order of precedence.

15. C.   A password settings object (PSO) can be created and linked to specific users by using the ADSIEdit tool. PSO objects are linked to groups or users, not OUs. Although you needed to create a new domain in Windows Server 2003 domains, PSOs can be used in a Windows Server 2008 domain. GPOs can be linked only to sites, domains, and OUs, not to users or groups.

16. D.   By adding her to the Group Policy Creator Owners group, she will be able to modify settings in GPOs she creates. Both the Domain Admins and Administrators groups will grant her significantly more permissions than necessary. The Server Operators group will allow her to manage a domain controller, but this is not needed.

17. A.   By disabling the User Configuration node of the GPO, only the computer configuration settings will apply. If you disable the computer configuration, only the user settings will apply, not the computer settings. There is no need to disable the entire GPO and re-create another one.

18. C.   The Redirect Folders Group Policy setting can be used to redirect the Documents folder to a UNC path—a share on a server. Relying on users to accomplish the task with an email isn't as reliable as enforcing the policy with a GPO. Home folders have already been created, so home folders don't need to be adjusted. Manually doing this on several hundred computers is too much work.

19. C.   By assigning an application package, you cause it to appear on the Start menu for users who receive the package. Since you want it to be assigned to users in the ITAdmins OU, you would link the GPO to the ITAdmins OU. Running DCPromo promotes servers to domain controllers, and this is neither necessary nor desirable for all computers in the domain. Linking the GPO to the domain would cause all users to receive the GPO, instead of just the users in the ITAdmins OU. Publishing the GPO would cause it to be available through Control Panel, but not on the Start menu.

20. B.   Since the application is needed on the computers, it must be deployed to the computers. You can only assign applications to computers using a GPO. You cannot publish to a computer. Assigning it to users wouldn't guarantee it was on all computers. Manually installing the application would be too much work.

Chapter

6

Monitoring and Maintaining Print and File Servers

MICROSOFT EXAM OBJECTIVES COVERED IN THIS CHAPTER:

✓ **Planning for Server Deployment**

- Plan File and Print Server Roles. May include but is not limited to: virtualization server planning, availability, resilience, and accessibility.

✓ **Planning Application and Data Provisioning**

- Provisioning Data. May include but is not limited to: shared resources, offline data access.

File and print servers are common in any network. One of the great benefits of creating a network is the ability to share resources such as files and printers. By sharing the resources centrally on servers, it becomes easier to manage them.

You can add both a File Services role and a Print Services role to most editions of Windows Server 2008. You can't add the roles to Web or Itanium editions. By adding these roles, you can share both folders and printers, making them accessible to users in the network.

When you add the File Services role, you can also add features and services. For example, you can add the File Server Resource Manager (FSRM) that provides extra tools you can use to create quotas and quota templates, screen for certain files or file types, and create reports. You can also add the Distributed File System (DFS) services. The DFS Namespaces service allows you to organize shares from multiple servers into a single namespace. DFS replication can be used to replicate data to different servers for both redundancy and fault tolerance purposes.

You'll notice in the list of objectives that virtualization server planning, availability, resilience, and accessibility are listed for file and print server roles. Chapter 2, "Planning Server Deployments," covers virtualization. Chapter 9, "Planning Business Continuity and High Availability," covers availability and resilience in more depth.

File Servers

File servers are commonly used in corporate environments. Simply put, file servers are used to hold files that can be shared among users in the environment.

You can create home folders that allow users to store their data centrally on a server instead of on a local system. With home folders, users have access to their data no matter where they log on in the network. One of the great benefits of having users store their data on a central file server is the ability to do backups. It's relatively easy to do backups on a single file server, but if you need to back up the data on 50 individual user systems, you're going to have some problems.

Shares allow users to store and access data on a server. On the server itself, the files and folders will be held on an NTFS partition. When working with file servers, you should understand what shares are, how to create and access a share, and how to restrict access by manipulating both NTFS and share permissions.

A significant new feature in Windows Server 2008 is the FSRM. It includes several tools you can use to control and manage data stored on a file server.

File Server Resource Manager

When you designate a server as a file server, you should add the File Services role using Server Manager. Adding this role means you can add services that allow you to manage your file server.

For example, before you can create shares, your server must have the File Services role added. Once you add the role and the FSRM service, you'll have access to the FSRM tool. Exercise 6.1 shows you the steps to add the File Services role and add the FSRM service.

EXERCISE 6.1

Installing the File Services Role

1. Launch Server Manager by clicking Start ➤ Administrative Tools ➤ Server Manager.

2. Click the Add Roles link to launch the Add Roles Wizard.

3. On the Before You Begin page, review the information, and click Next.

4. On the Server Roles page, select the Files Services role, and click Next.

5. On the File Services page, review the information, and click Next.

6. On the Select Role Services page, select the check box next to the following services:

    ▪   File Server (this should already be checked)

    ▪   Distributed File System (including DFS Namespaces and DFS Replication)

    ▪   File Server Resource Manager

    ▪   Windows Search Service

7. Click Next.

8. On the DFS Namespace page, select Create a Namespace Later Using the DFS Manager. Click Next. Distributed File System (DFS) will be covered later in this chapter.

9. On the Configure Storage Usage Monitoring page, ensure that none of the volumes on your system are selected, and click Next. (Quotas will be covered later in this chapter.)

10. On the Select Volumes to Index for Windows Search Service page, ensure that none of the volumes on your system are selected, and click Next.

EXERCISE 6.1 *(continued)*

11. On the Confirm Installation Selections page, review the information. Your display should look similar to the following image. Click Install.

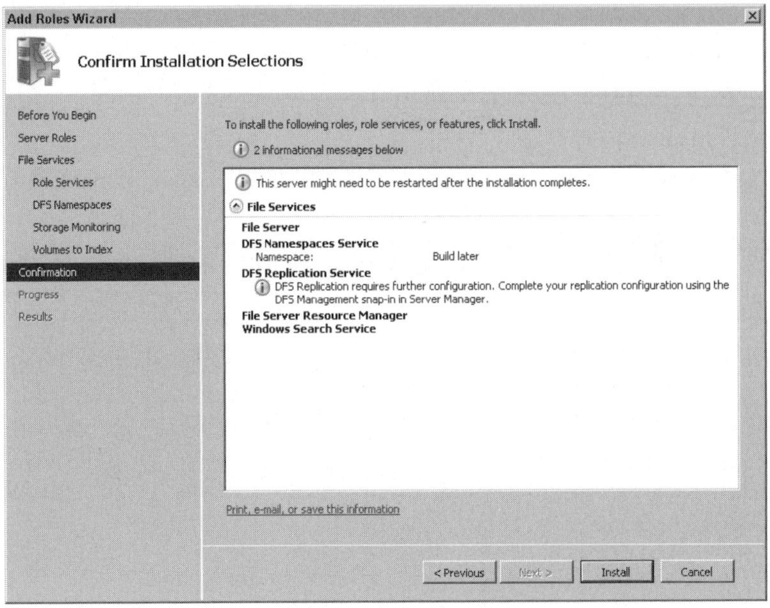

12. Once the installation completes, review the results, and click Close.

You'll now have access to the FSRM tool in Administrative Tools. To launch the FSRM, click Start ➢ Administrative Tools ➢ File Server Resource Manager.

Figure 6.1 shows the FSRM. Notice that you can do quota management, file-screening management, and storage reports management in the FSRM. Each of these management options has its own node, as shown in Figure 6.1.

FIGURE 6.1 File Server Resource Manager

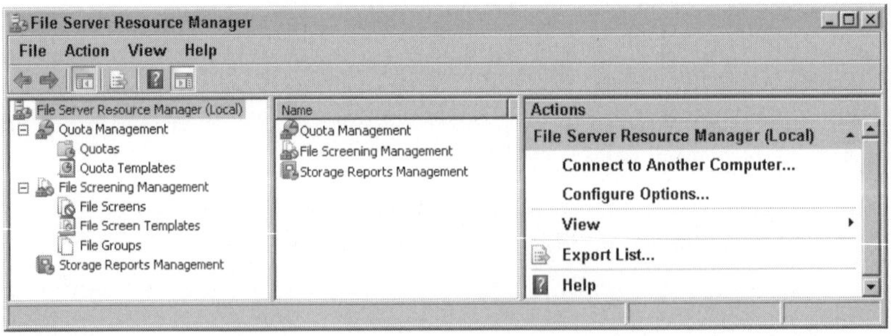

Of course, this begs the question, what the heck are these nodes doing?

Quota Management You can configure quotas to limit how much data a user or group of users can store on individual drives or folders. Quotas can be *soft limits* (meaning warnings are issued and notifications sent) or *hard limits* (where users are restricted from adding any more data). I'll discuss quota management later in this chapter.

File Screening Management File screens allow you to control the types of files that users can save and allow you to generate notifications when users attempt to save unauthorized files. For example, you can create a file screen to prevent any MP3 files or any scripting files from being saved on a server.

Storage Reports Management You can create storage reports to allow you to identify trends in disk usage and monitor any attempts to save unauthorized files. You can create reports based on a schedule (such as every Friday night) or as needed.

While Figure 6.1 shows the FSRM connected to the local computer, you can also use it to connect to remote computers. This can be useful if you are managing multiple file servers. You can use one tool to manage all the servers remotely. To connect to a different server, you simply right-click File Server Resource Manager (Local) and then select Connect to Another Computer.

The FSRM includes several configurable options that apply to each of the nodes. These options are in four property pages. You can access the property pages by right-clicking File Server Resource Manager (Local) and selecting Configure Options.

Figure 6.2 shows the Email Notifications tab of the options.

FIGURE 6.2 Configuring the FSRM options

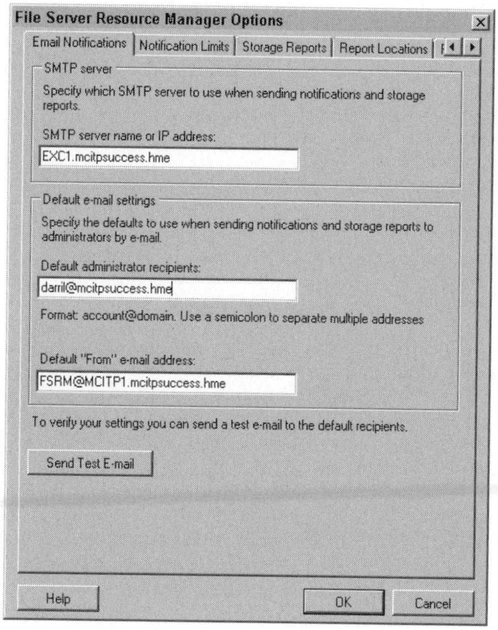

The tabs are as follows:

Email Notifications   You can configure the settings in this page to send email notifications to a specific user on a specific Simple Mail Transfer Protocol (SMTP) server such as Microsoft Exchange. None of the other settings can be configured until you configure at least a default administrator recipient address. Although these settings should point to actual servers and recipients, it's not tested until you click Send Test E-mail. In other words, you can enter an imaginary recipient address so that you can access the other property pages.

Notification Limits   On the notification page, you can configure how often notifications are sent. The default is 60 minutes. For example, when a quota is exceeded, an email will be sent to the email address configured on the Email Notifications tab. If that were your email address, how often would you want to be notified of the same event? It could be that once an hour is just what you want. Or, you may want to change it to once every 8 hours (or 480 minutes).

Times can be set for the following notifications:

- Email notifications (how often an email is sent)
- Event log notifications (how often an event log entry is logged)
- Command notifications (how often an associated command should be generated in response to the event)
- Report notifications (how often a report should be generated)

Storage Reports   The Storage Reports tab allows you to configure different parameters for different reports that can be generated. The different reports that can be generated (and configured in this tab) are as follows:

- Duplicate Files
- File Screening Audit
- Files by File Group
- Files by Owner
- Large Files
- Least Recently Accessed Files
- Most Recently Accessed Files
- Quota Usage

Report Locations   Reports have default locations where they are stored. This is in the system drive (usually C:\) by default in the StorageReports folder. However, you can change the location to another drive if storage space is a problem or to reduce contention with the operating system on the system drive.

When preparing for the 70-646 exam, you should know what the FSRM tool is, its capabilities, and how to access the FSRM.

Shares

A share in Windows Server 2008 is simply a folder that has been configured to be accessible over the network. Any folder can be shared. The purpose of creating a share is so that users can access the data over the network. You can create shares using Computer Management or Windows Explorer.

Once a folder is shared, it can be accessed using a universal naming convention (UNC) of *serverName**shareName*.

Creating Shares

Creating shares is relatively easy. If you know exactly what you want to do and how to do it, you can use Windows Explorer. If you want to use a wizard to create a share, you can use Server Manager or Computer Management.

Not everyone can create shares. On a local computer, you must be in one of the following groups:

- Local Administrators
- Power Users

On a domain controller, you must be in one of the following groups:

- Server Operators
- Administrators
- Domain Admins

Remember, you'll find the Server Operators group only on a domain controller. Users added to this group are granted permissions and rights to manage the domain controller, but not the domain. In other words, they can perform tasks such as create shares on the domain controller, but they cannot create accounts or groups in Active Directory Domain Services.

Exercise 6.2 shows you the steps you can follow to create a share using the Provision Share Wizard within Server Manager. The Provision Share Wizard allows you to view all the capabilities and options available. This exercise assumes you have completed Exercise 6.1.

EXERCISE 6.2

Creating a Share with the Provision Share Wizard

1. Launch Server Manager by clicking Start ➢ Administrative Tools ➢ Server Manager.

2. Within Server Manager, browse to Roles ➢ File Services ➢ Share and Storage Management.

3. Right-click Share and Storage Management, and select Provision Share.

EXERCISE 6.2 *(continued)*

4. On the Shared Folder Location page, click Browse.

5. On the Browse for Folder page, select C:\, and click the New Folder button. Name the folder ServerManagerShare. Click OK.

6. Back on the Shared Folder Location page, click Next.

7. On the NTFS Permissions page, you have the opportunity to change the NTFS permissions. Click Next to accept the defaults.

8. On the Share Protocols page, ensure that the check box for SMB is checked. Notice that NFS is dimmed and you can't select it. If you had installed the Services for Network File System (NFS) when you installed the File Services Role, this would be selectable. Accept the default share name, and click Next.

9. On the SMB Settings page, review the settings, and click Next.

10. On the SMB Permissions page, verify that All Users and Groups Have Only Read Access is selected. Click Next.

11. On the Quota Policy page, verify that Apply Quota is not checked. Click Next.

12. On the File Screen Policy page, ensure that Apply File Screen is not checked. Click Next.

13. On the DFS Namespace Publishing page, ensure that nothing is selected, and click Next.

14. On the Review Settings and Create Share page, click Create.

15. On the Confirmation page, click Close.

Exercise 6.3 shows you the steps you can follow to create a share using both Computer Management and Windows Explorer tools. Notice that you have significantly fewer choices when using these tools. This exercise also assumes you have completed Exercise 6.1.

EXERCISE 6.3

Creating Shares with Computer Management and Windows Explorer

1. Launch Computer Management by clicking Start ➢ Administrative Tools ➢ Computer Management.

2. In Computer Management, browse to System Tools ➢ Shared Folders ➢ Shares. Right-click Shares, and select New Share. This launches the Create a Shared Folder Wizard.

3. On the Welcome to the Create a Shared Folder Wizard page, click Next.

4. On the Folder Path page, click the Browse button.

5. In the Browse for Folder dialog box, select the C:\ disk drive, and click the Make New Folder button. Rename the folder by entering **MyShare**. Select the MyShare folder, and click OK.

6. Back on the Folder Path page, click Next.

7. On the Name, Description, and Settings page, accept the default of MyShare for the share name. Enter the description of **Share created for testing**. Your display should look like the following image.

Notice that the share path is identified using the UNC path of *serverName**shareName* or \\MCITP1\MyShare. Click Next.

8. On the Shared Folder Permissions page, accept the default of All Users Have Read-Only Access. Click Finish.

9. On the Sharing Was Successful page, click Finish.

10. Open Windows Explorer. You can do this on some keyboards by pressing the Windows logo key+E.

11. In Windows Explorer, browse to the root of C:\. In the right pane, right-click an empty area, and select New ➢ Folder. Rename the folder by typing **MyShare2.**

12. Right-click the MyShare2 folder, and select Share.

13. Select the drop-down box, and select Everyone. Click the Add button. Select the drop-down arrow next to the Reader Permission Level for Everyone. Your display should look similar to the following image. Notice that the Everyone group is granted Reader access, but you can change this to Contributor or Co-owner, or you can remove the group. These permissions will be explained in the "Permissions" section.

14. Click the Share button. Your share will be created with the correct permissions.

15. On the Your Folder is Shared page, click Done.

Accessing Shares

Once you've created shares, you'll want to access them. The key to understanding how shares are accessed is in the UNC path described earlier. The UNC path is in the format of *serverName**shareName*. For example, if you created a share named MyShare on a server named MCITP1, you could access the share using the UNC of \\MCITP1\MyShare.

You can do this in most Windows operating systems from the Run line. Press Windows log key+R to access the Run line. In Windows Server 2008 and Windows Vista, it's a little easier. You can click Start and then start typing in the Start Search text box right below the All Programs menu. As you start typing, the system helps you find what is available. For example, if you type just the two backslashes (\\), the search menu will show the computers it is aware of in your network. You can then click any of the computers to connect and browse the available shares.

If you type the name of one of these computers followed by another backslash (such as \\mcitp1\), then the system will connect to that computer and show you what shares are available. You can see this in Figure 6.3. By selecting any of the shares, you will automatically connect to that share.

FIGURE 6.3 Connecting to a share using the Start Search text box

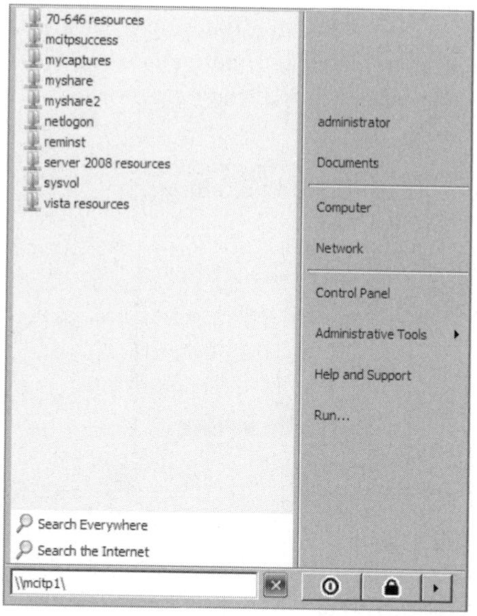

It's also possible to map drives to a UNC path. This is commonly done in networks to give users consistent access to data held on a share. With Windows Explorer open, you can select Tools ➤ Map Network Drive. The Map Network Drive window will appear as shown in Figure 6.4. You can then select a drive letter and enter the UNC path.

FIGURE 6.4 Mapping a network drive

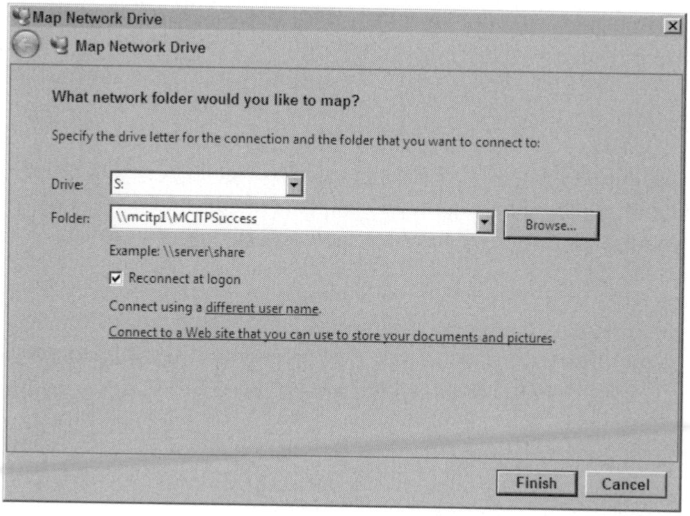

By selecting the Reconnect at Logon check box, you can ensure that users have this drive available to them each time they log on.

While drives can be mapped manually using the Map Network Drive selection in Windows Explorer, it's common to map drives automatically using Group Policy in a corporate environment. Once the drive is mapped, it will show up as a selectable drive in Windows Explorer, as shown in Figure 6.5.

FIGURE 6.5 A mapped drive in Windows Explorer

It's possible that you want to restrict access to a share. If everyone has Full Control access to the share, then it's possible that the data can accidentally be erased or modified. Or, if the infamous disgruntled employee has unrestricted access, it may not be accidental. You can restrict access to shares via permissions.

Permissions

Permissions are used to allow or deny users access to resources. In general, permissions within Microsoft products use the Discretionary Access Control (DAC) model.

In the DAC model, every resource has an owner, and the owner can modify the permissions to the resource. In this context, a resource could be an NTFS file or folder, a share, a printer, or an Active Directory Domain Services object such as an organizational unit.

Every resource has a Discretionary Access Control List (DACL). This sounds more complex than it is. It's just a list of users or groups that are granted access along with the type of access they are granted. Figure 6.6 shows a DACL for the NTFS folder named Users.

Notice in the figure that you have a list of users and groups. The Everyone group is selected, and the permissions for everyone are shown in the permissions pane.

 When looking at users and groups in a permission list, you can easily tell a user entry from a group entry by the icon. A user would have one head in the icon, and a group would have two heads.

While the groups are shown in user-friendly names, the DACL actually stores the security identifier (SID) of the user or group. The system does a lookup for the SID and then shows the user-friendly name.

FIGURE 6.6   NTFS permissions for the MCITPSuccess Users folder

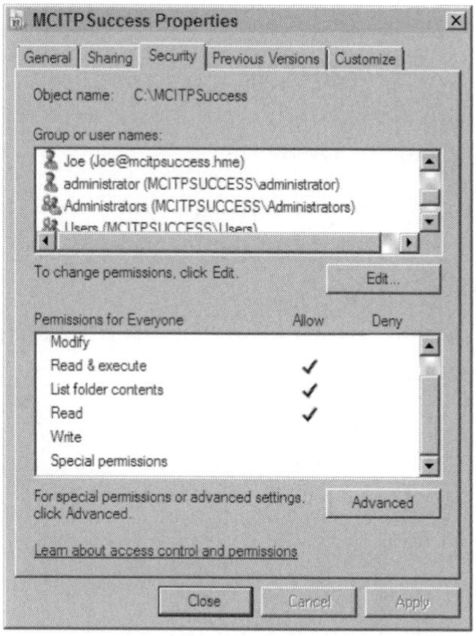

You should remember three important rules with permissions:

Permissions are inherited.   Child containers inherit permissions from parents. For example, if you have a folder named Sales in the `C:\` drive (`C:\Sales`), then any files or folders placed in the Sales folder would inherit the permissions from the Sales folder.

For example, if the Everyone group was granted Full Control to the Sales folder, then the Everyone group would have Full Control to a new document named FY08 sales in this folder.

It is possible to remove permission inheritance, but inheritance is turned on by default.

Permissions are cumulative.   If you are in multiple groups (and this is common) and these different groups are assigned different permissions to a resource, then your permissions are a combination of all the permissions assigned. Your permissions accumulate.

As an example, imagine that you are a member of both the Sales group and the Marketing group. If the Sales group is granted Read permission to a folder and the Marketing group is granted Write permission to the same folder, then your effective permissions are Read and Write—the accumulated permissions from both groups.

Deny takes precedence.   Any time a user or group is assigned the Deny permission to any resource, then Deny takes precedence. It doesn't matter how many other groups grant the user permission; if Deny is selected, the user is denied that permission.

For example, if Joe was specifically denied Write permission on a folder named Sales, but Joe was a member of the Sales group that was granted Full Control to the folder, Joe would *not* be able to write to this folder.

These three rules apply to any resource you'll come across in Windows. This includes NTFS files and folders, shares, and Active Directory Domain Services resources.

NTFS Permissions

NTFS permissions limit who can view and manipulate files and folders on an NTFS drive. The available NTFS permissions are as follows:

Read   A user or group with Read permission can obviously read the data. However, there's more. Read includes the four underlying permissions of: Read Data, Read Attributes, Read Extended Attributes, and Read permissions.

Read & Execute   Some files can be run, or executed. To run an executable file, a user must have the Read & Execute permission.

List Folder Contents   If granted List Folder Contents permission, a user can read the contents of a folder. This permission is granted only to a folder and not a file.

Write   A user who is granted Write permission can make changes to a file. This includes the special permissions of create files/write data, create folders/append data, write attributes, write extended attributes, and read permissions. It does not include the ability to change permissions or delete a file or folder. Typically a user would be granted Read permissions with Write permissions.

Modify   When you grant Modify, it includes Read, Read & Execute, List Folder Contents, and Write. A significant difference between Write and Modify is that with Modify you can delete a file or a folder.

Full Control   Full Control grants the ability to do anything and everything with a file or folder. In addition to all the special permissions listed previously, this includes the three special permissions of Delete Subfolders and Files, Change Permissions, and Take Ownership.

Share Permissions

Share permissions apply to anyone accessing the share over the network. This is an important point. If you access a folder using Windows Explorer locally (even via a terminal server hosting Terminal Services), the share permissions don't apply. However, if you access the share with the UNC path, the share permissions do apply.

If you've used shares in previous versions of Windows (such as Windows XP or Server 2003), you'll notice a slight change in how share permissions are presented. Instead of just presenting the permissions, users and groups can be assigned to roles that have predefined permission levels assigned.

Three permissions are available with shares. You can see each of these permissions in Figure 6.7, where the Administrators group has been granted the Full Control permission.

Read   With Read share permissions granted, users can read the files in the share, but they cannot make any modifications. It is possible for users to copy the files to a local folder on their system and make changes to the copy, but they can't make changes to the original files. When creating a share, Read permission is the default.

FIGURE 6.7 Share permissions

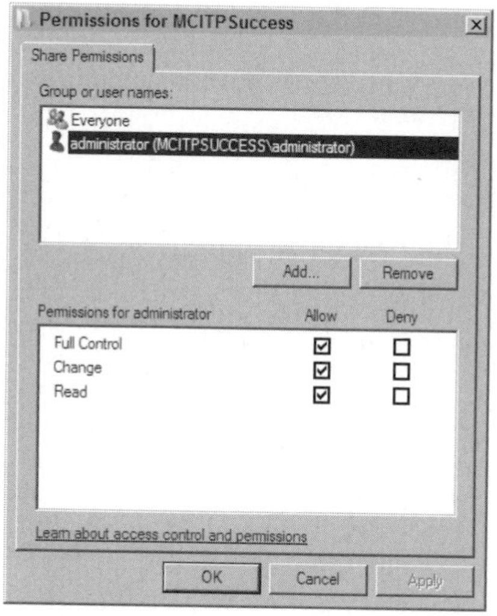

Change Change permission grants a user the ability to modify data within the share. In addition to reading data, files can be added, modified, and deleted.

Full Control Full Control allows a user to do anything with a file or folder contained within a share. A significant difference between Change and Full Control is that a user can modify the underlying NTFS permissions if they are granted the Full Control permission. This assumes, of course, that the underlying file or folder is on an NTFS drive and the user has the proper NTFS permissions.

In Windows Server 2008 and Windows Vista, you typically don't assign the share permissions directly. Instead, wizards guide you through adding users or groups to one of four permission levels. You can think of the permission levels as roles. If a user is in a role, they have the permissions of the role.

You can still access the individual permissions (Read, Change, Full Control), though it takes more clicks than accessing the permission levels.

The permission levels are as follows:

Reader The underlying permission is Read.

Contributor The underlying permissions are Change and Read.

Co-owner The underlying permission is Full Control. Only one user or group is identified as the owner, but additional users can or groups can be added as co-owners.

Owner The Owner role identifies the owner of the share. This is typically the Administrators group since an administrator usually creates the share. If a user not in the Administrators group (such as a user in the Server Operators group or the Power Users group) creates the share, that user will be designated as the owner. Interestingly, if the owner is not in the Administrators group, the owner is not automatically granted any permission and would need to be added to one of the other three roles or manually granted appropriate permissions.

When creating a share with the New Share Wizard in Computer Management, you are given the following choices:

All Users Have Read-Only Access   The Everyone group is added to the Reader role and granted read permission.

Administrators Have Full Access; Other Users Have Read-Only Access   The Administrators group is added to the Owner role and is granted Full Control permissions. The Everyone group is added to the Reader role and granted Read permission.

Administrators Have Full Access; Other Users Have No Access   The Administrators group is added to the Owner role and is granted Full Control permissions. No other access is granted.

Customize Permissions   This starts with the Everyone group having Read permission, but you can add any other permissions as desired.

Everyone used to mean everyone. However, this was recognized as a security risk, and Everyone no longer means everyone. Specifically, the Everyone group no longer includes any users who may have accessed the network with anonymous access.

Combining NTFS and Share Permissions

One of the challenges that many people new to Microsoft technologies have is in understanding how permissions function and applying them. Consider the permissions shown in Table 6.1 for a folder on an NTFS drive. Sally is a user in both the Sales and Marketing groups. What are her NTFS permissions to the folder?

TABLE 6.1   Sally's NTFS Permissions

Group	Permissions
Sales	Read
Marketing	Modify

Remember, permissions are cumulative. In other words, Sally's permissions are a combination of Read and Modify. Since Modify includes Read, Sally is granted Modify permission to the folder.

Share permissions work the same way. If you want to identify the share permissions that apply to a user, you combine them. Looking at Table 6.2, if Sally is in both the Sales and Marketing groups, what share permissions does she have?

TABLE 6.2   Sally's Share Permissions

Group	Permissions
Sales	Read
Marketing	Change

Since the permissions are cumulative, Sally has both Read and Change permissions to the share.

When combining NTFS and share permissions, the effective permissions are the more restrictive of the two. That sounds harder than it is. When determining how to combine NTFS and share permissions, follow these three steps:

1. Identify the cumulative NTFS share permission.
2. Identify the cumulative share permission.
3. Identify which of these two permissions restricts use the most.

For example, consider the scenario shown in Table 6.3. Joe is in both the Sales and Marketing groups.

TABLE 6.3   Combining Joe's NTFS and Share Permissions

Group	NTFS Permissions	Share Permissions
Sales	Read	Change
Marketing	Full Control	Read

Can you tell what Joe's permissions are when he accesses the share over the network? Follow these three steps:

1. **Identify the cumulative NTFS share permission.** The NTFS permissions are Read for the Sales group and Full Control for the Marketing group. The NTFS permissions are cumulative. Since Joe is in both groups, his NTFS permission is Full Control.
2. **Identify the cumulative share permission.** The share permissions are Change for the Sales group and Read for the Marketing group. The share permissions are cumulative. Since Joe is in both groups, his share permission is Change (which includes Read).
3. **Identify which of these two permissions restricts the user the most.** What restricts a user more: Change or Full Control? Since Full Control has no restrictions, Change is more restrictive. Joe's permission when accessing the share over the network is Change.

Offline Data Access

Often users want access to their data when they are disconnected from the network. Mobile users often have a laptop that they use both at work and on the road. By configuring offline files, you can ensure users have access to their data while on the road.

Once offline files are configured, users can access their data files whether they are connected or not. Consider a user named Bob who regularly accesses a share called SalesData on a server named MCITP1. Bob's laptop is also configured to use offline files.

When Bob is logged onto the network, he connects to the share and accesses the data. Later, when Bob logs off the network, the files between his system and the share are synchronized. Any files that have changed on the server are downloaded to his system. While offline, Bob can work with any of the files. He can be on the road, working from home or anywhere else the file server isn't available. Changes made to these files are stored on his system. When Bob returns to work, he logs on, and the offline files are synchronized. Any changes he has made to the files are uploaded to the server.

A common question pops up with this. What happens if Bob made changes to an offline file, and someone else made changes to the same file on the server? When Bob logs on and synchronizes, he will be informed of the issue and prompted to save his file with a different name. He could choose to overwrite the other file and cause someone else's changes to be lost, but someone else would likely be a little upset.

Options for Offline Files

While the scenario with Bob using his own files offline is the most common scenario, you can set up offline files for different purposes. The available options with offline files are as follows:

Only the Files and Programs That Users Specify Will Be Available Offline   This is the default setting. When a user's system is configured for offline files, they can right-click a file on a share and select Make Available Offline, as shown in Figure 6.8. This is also referred to as *manual caching*. Once a user chooses this option for a file, it will be synchronized each time the user logs on or off.

All Files and Programs That Users Open from the Share Will Be Automatically Available Offline   With this choice, any files that a user opens will automatically be marked to be available offline. Each time a user logs on or off, the files will be checked for changes and synchronized.

> **Optimized for Performance**   This setting can be selected or deselected only with the All Files and Programs That Users Open from the Share will be Automatically Available Offline setting, as shown in Figure 6.9.
>
> When this option is selected, files are downloaded to the client, but any changes on the client are *not* uploaded back to the server. It is most commonly used for executable files or files that you don't want users to change.

If an executable file was modified on the client, most likely this modification was from a virus. You wouldn't want to propagate the virus through your network. Additionally, a share could hold company documents such as the policy manual or the details on the 401k plan. You wouldn't want users modifying these documents (for instance, changing the 401k matching amount), so you should select this option. If a user does modify the files, those files would not be uploaded during the synchronization process.

FIGURE 6.8   File choice of Make Available Offline

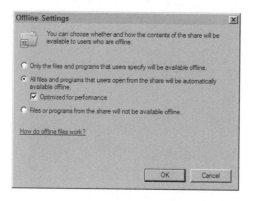

FIGURE 6.9   Enabling automatic one-way caching (Optimized for Performance)

The Optimized for Performance selection is the most misunderstood. Think of it as setting offline files for one-way synchronization. They are synchronized down to the client but never up to the server.

Files or Programs from the Share Will Not Be Available Offline   When this choice is selected, offline files are not available for this share.

Once you determine the options you need, you'll need to configure offline files. Offline files need to be configured in two places—on the server by configuring the share and on the client.

Configuring a Share for Offline Files

You can configure the settings for offline files using either Computer Management or Windows Explorer. Exercise 6.4 shows you the steps to enable offline files on a share using both tools.

EXERCISE 6.4

Enabling Offline Files

1. Launch Computer Management by clicking Start ➢ Administrative Tools ➢ Computer Management.

2. Access the Shares folder by opening System Tools ➢ Shared Folders.

3. Right-click the MyShare share you created in Exercise 6.3, and select Properties. Your display will look similar to the following graphic.

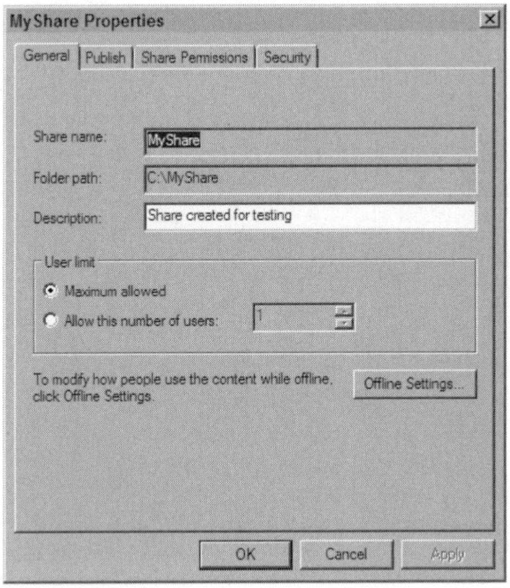

4. Click the Offline Settings button.

5. On the Offline Settings page, notice that the default is set to Only the Files and Programs That Users Specify Will Be Available Offline.

6. Click the Optimized for Performance check box. This automatically chooses the second option.

7. Click Cancel in the Offline Settings dialog box. Click Cancel on the property page.

8. Click Start, right-click Computer, and select Explore to launch Windows Explorer. Browse to the C:\MyShare folder.

9. Right-click the MyShare folder, and select Properties. Click the Sharing tab.

10. On the Sharing tab, click the Advanced Sharing button. Your display will look similar to the following image. Notice that this display has a Caching button instead of an Offline Settings button.

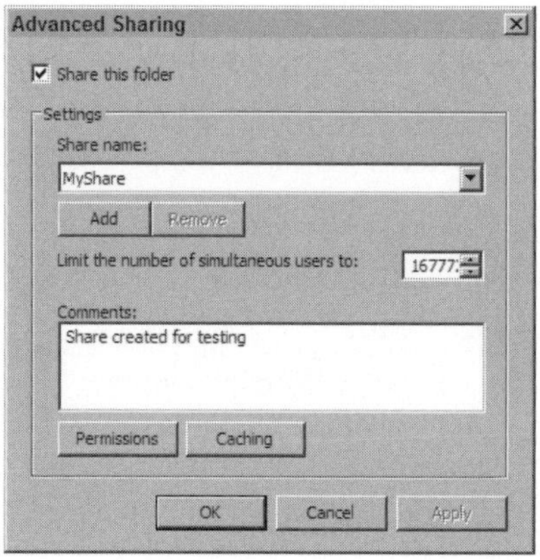

11. Click the Caching button. The Offline Settings page appears, giving the same choices you saw when accessing this page from Computer Management.

Configuring the Client for Offline Files

When pursuing the 70-646 exam, you'll be expected to understand how to configure the server more than the client. However, to fill in the holes, this section explains what you'd do to enable offline files on the client. The procedure to enable offline files is a little different between Windows XP and Windows Vista.

For Windows XP, you launch Windows Explorer and select Tools ≻ Options ≻ Folder Options. Select the Offline Files tab, and your display will look similar to Figure 6.10.

For Windows Vista, you can access the offline-files configuration page by selecting Control Panel ≻ Network and Internet ≻ Offline Files. Figure 6.11 shows the Offline Files dialog box available on Windows Vista after offline files have been enabled.

FIGURE 6.10 Enabling offline files in Windows XP

FIGURE 6.11 Enabling offline files in Windows Vista

Figure 6.10 also includes the Encrypt Offline Files to Secure Data option. Notice that this is not checked by default. If the files are encrypted on the server, they are decrypted before being sent across the wire, and by default they will be stored on the client's computer in a decrypted format. If the files need to be protected beyond the NTFS permissions, you should check the box to encrypt the offline files.

Disk Quotas

Sometimes when users realize they can store data on your server, they get carried away. You might expect that 500GB of storage space is more than enough on your server to support 100 users, but you come in one day and learn that the disk space is full. This is exactly the problem that *disk quotas* were created to solve. Disk quotas allow you to track and/or restrict the amount of space users can consume. You can create disk quotas by using the FSRM or by using basic NTFS capabilities.

Creating Disk Quotas with FSRM

The Quota Management node of the FSRM tool allows you to manage the amount of disk space users are using. Using the FSRM, you can do the following:

- Create limits to limit space allowed for a volume or a folder.
- Generate notifications when quota limits are approached or exceeded.
- Define quota templates that can easily be applied to volumes or folders.

Several quota templates already exist that you can use to apply quota limits to volumes or folders. Figure 6.12 shows the default templates available. The two quota types are hard and soft. A *soft* quota limit will log when quotas are exceeded but won't prevent the limits from being exceeded. *Hard* quota limits prevent the limits from being exceeded.

Exercise 6.5 shows you the steps you can follow to apply a quota from a template. You'll also explore some of the properties of quota templates.

FIGURE 6.12   Quota templates in the FSRM

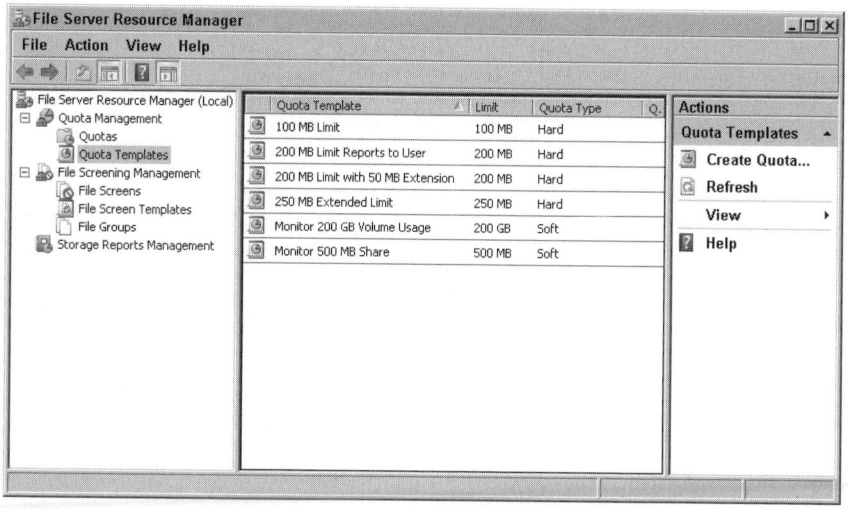

EXERCISE 6.5

Enabling Quotas

1. Launch the FSRM by clicking Start ➤ Administrative Tools ➤ File System Resource Manager.

2. Open the Quotas node, and select Quotas.

3. Right-click Quotas, and select Create Quota.

4. On the Create Quota page, click the Browse button.

5. In the Browse for Folder dialog box, select the C:\ drive. Click the Make New Folder button, and rename the folder to Quota. Click OK.

6. Back on the Create Quota page, ensure that Create Quota on Path and Derive Properties from This Quota Template are selected. Your display should look similar to the following image.

7. With 100 MB Limit selected in the drop-down box, review the settings in the Summary of Quota Properties area. Notice that the limit is set as 100 MB (Hard) and several notifications are configured. All of these settings are derived from the quota template.

8. Change the 100 MB Limit setting to Monitor 500 MB Share. Notice that the limit is changed to 500 MB (Soft) and different notifications are configured.

9. Select the Define Custom Quota Properties option, and click the Custom Properties button.

10. On the Quota Properties of C:\Quota page, review the settings and then click the Copy button. This will copy the settings from the 100 MB Limit quota template to this page. Notice that several notification thresholds have been added. Your display should look similar to the following image.

11. Notice the Hard Quota setting is selected. A hard quota will prevent the limits from being exceeded. A soft quota will provide notifications but won't prevent the quota from being exceeded.

12. Click the Add button to add a notification. The Add Threshold page will appear. On this page, you can define what happens when a threshold is reached. The default is 85%, meaning usage has reached 85 percent. When this threshold is reached, you can configure the following actions:

- Email Message. You can modify the contents of the email and select the option to send a copy of the email to both an administrator and the user.

- Event Log. You can modify the text of the log entry and add variables that can be added to the text.

- Command. You can select a command or script to run in response to a threshold being reached.

- Report. You can select a report to be generated in response to the event.

13. The following graphic shows the Add Threshold page with the Report tab selected. Select and review each of the tabs. After reviewing the tabs, click Cancel.

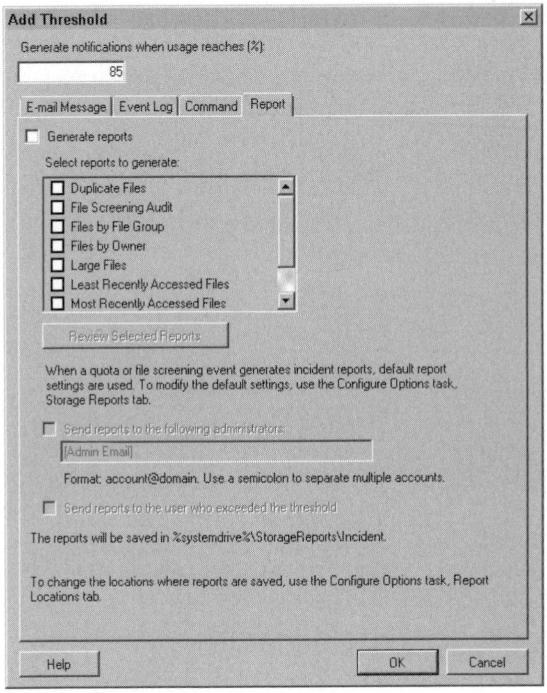

14. Back on the Quota Properties of C:\Quota page, click OK.

15. On the Create Quota page, click Create.

16. On the Save Custom Properties as a Template page, select Save the Custom Quota Without Creating a Template, and click OK.

Creating Disk Quotas with NTFS

Although you have much more flexibility by using disk quotas with the FSRM, you can also set quotas on an individual disk using NTFS capabilities. Using NTFS, disk quotas are set on individual partitions. In other words, you can configure quotas for the C:\ drive, the D:\ drive, and so on. You can access the disk quota configuration page from Windows Explorer or Disk Management within Computer Management.

Using either of these tools, right-click the disk, select Properties, and then select the Quota tab. You'll see a display similar to Figure 6.13.

FIGURE 6.13 Enabling quotas on a disk

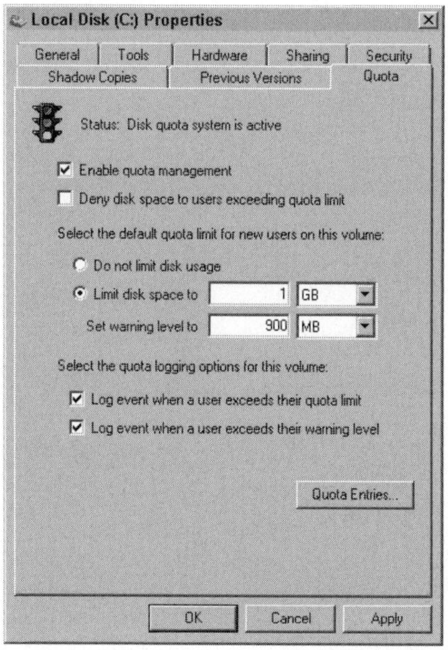

The various settings available on this page are as follows:

Enable Quota Management   Checking this box will enable quota management on the selected disk drive. This doesn't necessarily indicate users will be denied how much space they can use if they exceed the quota. It indicates only that space is being tracked.

Deny Disk Space to Users Exceeding Quota Limit   Checking this box will deny disk space to any users who exceed the limit. If this box is not checked, users can exceed their limits.

Limit Disk Space To   When the choice of Limit Disk Space To is selected, you can set both warning and limit levels. This setting is dependent on the Deny Disk Space to Users Exceeding Quota Limit. If the Deny Disk Space setting is selected, users will be prevented from exceeding their limits. If the check box is not selected, only entries in the log will be entered.

Log Event When a User Exceeds Their Quota Limit   When checked, a log entry is added to the application log when the quota limit is exceeded.

Log Event When a User Exceeds Their Warning Level   When checked, a log entry is added to the application log when the warning limit is exceeded.

It's important to understand that quotas are calculated based on file ownership and based on uncompressed size. Once a user reaches their quota limit, the only way to get under the limit is by taking files off the disk. There aren't any shortcuts or workarounds that a user can try to escape the quota limit.

Quota limits are calculated based on file ownership.   A user is not able to move files to a different location on the same drive to change their allocation. If they own the files, the files are calculated as part of their quote no matter where they are located on the drive.

Quota limits are calculated based on uncompressed size.   Users can't compress the files to gain more space. Disk quotas use only the files' uncompressed size in their calculations.

Indexing and Searching

Two services provide search capabilities on a file server: the Windows search service and indexing. Both services provide users with the capability to easily find data based on keywords searches.

You can install only one of the search services on any server. These services are added as additional services of the File Services role. Figure 6.14 shows the screen you'll see when you click the Add Role Services link with the File Services role selected.

FIGURE 6.14   Adding role services to the File Services role

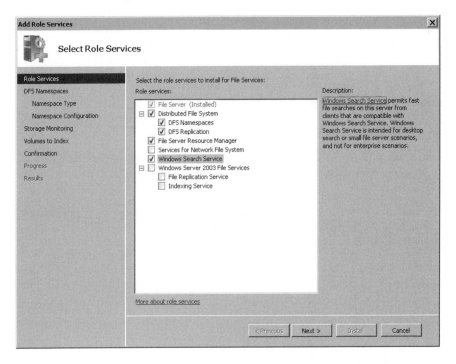

Both the Windows search and indexing services are extremely resource intensive when first started. Since each service needs to search all the files on the system, it can take an extraordinarily long time. During this time, your system will be much slower than normal. If implementing it on a server, do so during nonpeak times.

Each service is based on the creation of an index similar to the index in the back of this book. If you were looking for information on the FSRM, you could turn to the back of the book and find it in the index. It would then tell you exactly which pages contain information on the FSRM.

Additionally, the index in the back of the book is organized in alphabetical order, making it much easier to locate keywords. You don't have to search through the entire book, or even the entire index, to locate what you want.

Similarly, when indexing is enabled, an index is created based on words from files. Many noise terms (such as *the*, *and*, *as*, and *so on*) are not indexed. Depending on how many files are indexed, an index can be quite large. Neither service is intended for large enterprise scenarios, but they can be quite useful on smaller file servers.

Files that are indexed by both services include the following:

- Email
- Contacts
- Calendar appointments
- Documents
- Photos
- Multimedia

Windows Search Service

Microsoft touts the Windows search service as having several enhancements over the indexing service. Although both services are resource intensive, the Windows search service is more efficient.

Windows Vista includes a version of the Windows search service that allows it to easily search a Windows Vista system or a server running the Windows search service. This service can also be installed on computers running Windows XP.

Indexing Service

The indexing service is the same legacy service included with Windows Server 2003. It is included for backward compatibility. If choosing a new indexing service for a Windows Server 2008 file server, Microsoft recommends using the Windows search service.

Print Servers

Print servers are used in many environments to accept print jobs and send them to print devices. Any computer can act as a print server simply by sharing a printer. However, in the context of this book, a print server will primarily be a server running Windows Server 2008.

When running a Windows Server 2008 server as a print server, you must first add the Print Services role through Server Manager. Figure 6.15 shows the Print Management console that is available after installing the Print Services role on a server.

FIGURE 6.15   Print Management console

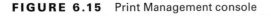

You can launch the Print Management console by clicking Start ≻ Administrative Tools ≻ Print Management. This is the same Print Management console you would see in Vista Business and Vista Enterprise products.

Using the Print Management console, you can install, view, and manage all the printers in your organization. Notice that one server (MCITP1) is selected in Figure 6.15, but you can add as many servers as desired to the console.

Understanding Shared Printers

Take a look at Figure 6.16 to see how a print server could be configured. Both PrinterA and PrinterB are on the network with their own IP address. PrinterB is connected directly to the print server using a cable such as USB or FireWire. PS1 is the print server, and it is sharing PrinterA and PrinterB.

FIGURE 6.16   A print server sharing printers

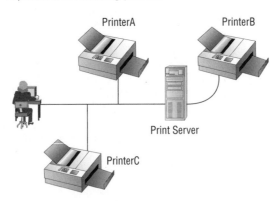

This may not make sense at first. Looking at the diagram, there's no difference between PrinterA and PrinterC. However, there is a difference in how the print server is configured. In the opening paragraph, I stated that PrinterA was being shared from PS1 (the print server). This means that users send print jobs destined to PrinterA through PS1. PS1 manages the jobs and then sends them to PrinterA. In contrast, users send print jobs directly to PrinterC.

Why is PS1 sharing PrinterA and not sharing PrinterC? It's just a matter of choice. The purpose of the diagram is to show it can be done both ways.

Just because we have printers on the network doesn't mean they must be managed by a print server. Users can manually configure and send print jobs directly to PrinterC. However, more work is required.

As a simple example, the driver would need to be manually added to the client in order to print to PrinterC. This can sometimes be a time-consuming task. If the driver isn't automatically installed on the end user's computer, an administrator must manually install it on each system that needs to use the printer.

On the other hand, PrinterB is connected directly to PS1. PrinterB can be shared, and PS1 will act as the print server for this printer. If a user connects to the printer share, the driver will automatically be downloaded to the client. You, as the administrator, need to ensure only that the correct driver is located on the server, instead of manually installing it on each desktop computer that wants to use the printer.

Printer A can also be shared off PS1. However, instead of using the USB or FireWire port on the server, you'd create a TCP/IP port. The port would have the address of the printer and could connect directly to the printer when sending print jobs.

The Print Process

When managing printers and print servers, it makes things a little easier if you understand how the print process works.

Consider Figure 6.17. The user sends a print job that ultimately should be printed on PrinterA. The client's computer must have the correct driver to properly format the job. Once the print job is formatted correctly, it is sent to the server (PS1) as shown in step 1.

FIGURE 6.17 Sending a print job through a print server

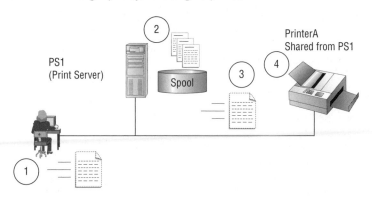

The server could have other jobs waiting to be printed. Since computers work much more quickly than printers, print jobs are often *spooled* to the hard drive. Or in simpler terms, the print jobs are stored in files on the hard drive in a folder named Spooler. In step 2, the server spools the print job onto the hard drive. This file will wait its turn. When it's time for the file to be sent to the printer, the file will be retrieved from the spooler and sent to the printer as shown in step 3. The file is printed on the printer in step 4.

If you have the spooler on the C:\ drive (the default), you need to ensure you have enough space on the C:\ drive to spool all the print jobs. It's not uncommon to run out of space. If that occurs, you need to move the spooler.

To move the spooler to a different disk, launch Print Management. Right-click the print server, and select Properties. Figure 6.18 shows the properties page available from the Print Management console. You can simply change the location of the spool folder.

FIGURE 6.18   Changing the spooler

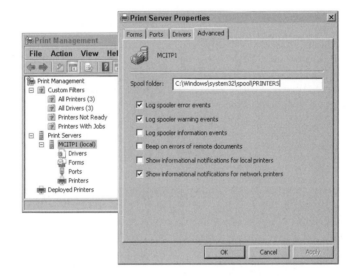

 Any print jobs held in the spool folder will be lost when you change the location. You should do this only when you're sure that the spooler doesn't have any jobs within it.

Installing a Printer

It's relatively easy to install a printer. The biggest challenge is finding the correct driver. If it's a new printer, you can install the driver from the CD that came with the system. If it's an older printer, you can usually find a driver on the manufacturer's website.

Exercise 6.6 shows you how to install a printer. The exercise will install a nonexistent printer, so you won't be able to print to it. However, the procedure will show you the process of installing a printer and give you a printer that you can publish to Active Directory Domain Services in the next exercise.

EXERCISE 6.6

Add the Print Services Role and Install a Printer

1. Launch Server Manager by clicking Start ➤ Administrative Tools ➤ Server Manager.

2. Click the Roles node, and select Add Roles. Review the information on the Before You Begin page, and click Next.

3. On the Select Server Roles page, select the Print Services role, and click Next.

4. Review the information on the Print Services page, and click Next.

5. On the Select Role Services page, ensure the Print Server service is selected, and click Next.

6. On the Confirm Installation Selections page, click Install. The Print Services role will be added. When complete, click Close. You will now have the Print Management tool available from the Administrative Tools menu.

7. Launch Print Management by clicking Start ➤ Administrative Tools ➤ Print Management.

8. Within Print Management, browse to your Print Servers ➤ your server name ➤ Printers.

9. Right-click Printers, and select Add Printers.

10. On the Printer Installation page, select Add a New Printer Using an Existing Port. Select LPT1 (or LPT2 if LPT1 is being used). Click Next.

11. On the Printer Driver page, select Install a New Driver, and click Next.

12. On the Printer Installation page, select Xerox in the Manufacturer pane, and select Tektronix Phaser 860B by Xerox in the Printers pane. You could also select your actual printer from this page. If you need to install the driver with the wizard, you can click the Have Disk button to do so. Click Next.

13. On the Printer Name and Sharing Settings page, ensure the Share This Printer box is checked. Accept the default printer name. Change the share name to Phaser. Click Next.

14. On the Printer Found page, click Next.

15. When the wizard completes, click the Finish button on the completion page.

At this point, your printer is shared and can be located using the UNC path name. If the printer server is named PS1, the UNC path would be \\PS1\Phaser.

Users can connect to the printer using the wizard on their machines. When prompted by the wizard, they would enter the UNC path, and the correct driver would automatically be downloaded.

Printer Pooling

Printer pooling allows you to add print devices to the same printer configuration on a print server. This can be useful when you have a print device that is overloaded or you simply want to add fault tolerance to a print device.

When printer pooling is enabled, users still submit their jobs to the printer as normal. However, the server now checks to see which print device is available to determine which print device receives the print job.

For example, imagine you have enabled printer pooling for two printers (named PTR1 and PTR2) connected to your print server. Sally sends a print job to the print server. The print server checks to see whether PTR1 is available. Since PTR1 is available, the print job is sent to PTR1. Seconds later, Joe sends a print job to the print server. The print servers checks to see whether PTR1 is available. It isn't, so the server then checks PTR2. Since PTR2 is available, Joe's print job is sent to PTR2.

If PTR1 develops a fault, then the print server will recognize that PTR1 is not available and automatically send print jobs to PTR2. Figure 6.19 shows printer pooling enabled for two printers using two separate TCP/IP ports.

Printer pooling works only if the print devices are identical and use the same print drivers. To enable printer pooling, follow these steps:

1. Select the properties of the printer in Print Management.

2. Select the Ports tab.

3. Select the Enable Printer Pooling check box.

4. Select the port for the second physical device.

Printer Publishing

Often, you'll want users to be able to locate printers by searching Active Directory Domain Services. Installing and sharing the printer is the first step, but you must also publish the printer in Active Directory Domain Services in order for users to find it.

FIGURE 6.19   Enabling printer pooling

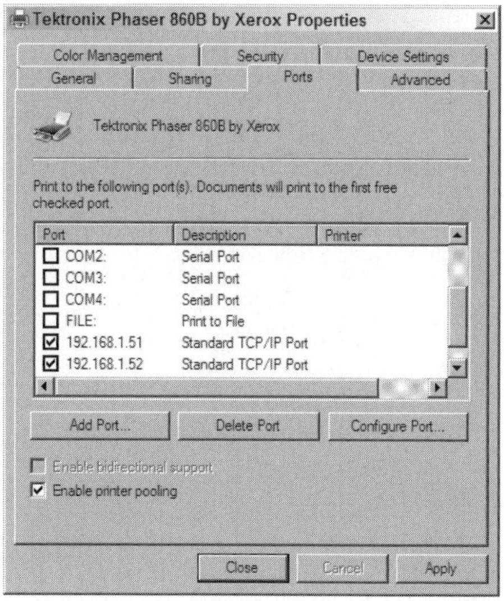

Using Active Directory search tools, users can search for printers with the following characteristics:

- Can print double-sided
- Can print color
- Can staple
- In certain locations
- With specific names

However, before any of this is possible, the printer must be listed in Active Directory Domain Services. If you have shared a printer, you can easily cause it to be listed in Active Directory Domain Services.

Right-click the shared printer from within Print Management, and select List in Directory, as shown in Figure 6.20.

You can now use one of the tools available to search Active Directory Domain Services and locate the printer.

As an example, you can launch Active Directory Users and Computers by clicking Start ➢ Administrative Tools ➢ Active Directory Users and Computers. Click your domain object in the left pane, and select Action ➢ Find to launch the search feature. You can see this in Figure 6.21.

Change the Find box from Users, Contacts, and Groups to Printers. Click the Features tab, and select Can Print Color. Click the Find Now button, and you'll see the Tektronix Phaser 860B by Xerox printer that was installed in the previous exercise.

FIGURE 6.20   Publishing a printer in Active Directory Domain Services

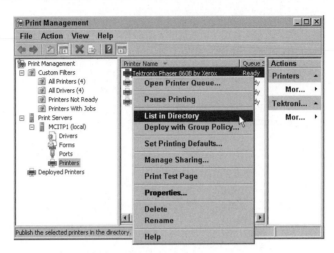

FIGURE 6.21   Launching search from within Active Directory Users and Computers

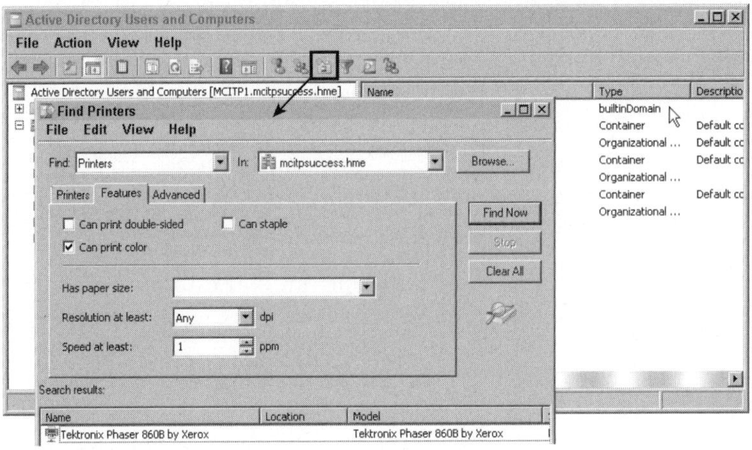

Distributed File System

The Distributed File System is one of the services available within the File Services role. With DFS, you have two distinct capabilities. First, you can use DFS to organize multiple folders from multiple servers in a single namespace. This makes it easy for users to find data without having to remember multiple UNC path names. Second, you can use DFS to replicate content among multiple servers and ensure the data is highly available. This can be done for data used by end users and is also being used to replace the File Replication Service to replicate Active Directory Domain Services content.

Using DFS Namespaces to Organize Content

When using DFS to organize content, you must create a DFS namespace to group shared folders from different servers into a single namespace.

The primary goal of creating a DFS namespace is to make it easy for end users to find data on the network. Consider Figure 6.22. In this figure, you can see that sales data is held on four different servers in four different shares.

FIGURE 6.22   Multiple servers, multiple shares, and multiple UNC paths

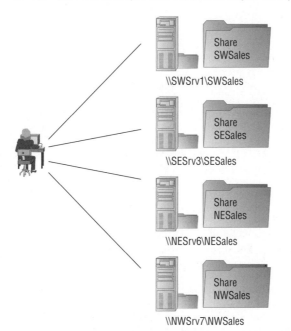

If a user was interested in southwest sales data, he'd have to connect to the SWSales share on the SWSrv1 server. If he then wants information on northeast sales, he'd connect to the NESales share on the NESrv6 server.

For some users this is hard to understand. As an example, when something goes wrong in a network, some users often say "The server is down" as if there is only one single server hidden away somewhere doing everything. Trying to get users to comprehend there are different servers and that they need to learn multiple UNC paths to reach each one is challenging, to say the least.

Instead, you could create a DFS namespace as shown in Figure 6.23. All users have to connect to is a domain path (\\mcitpsuccess.com\Sales). Even though the actual data is on different shares on different servers, the DFS namespace presents itself as a single UNC path.

FIGURE 6.23   Single namespace for multiple servers and shares

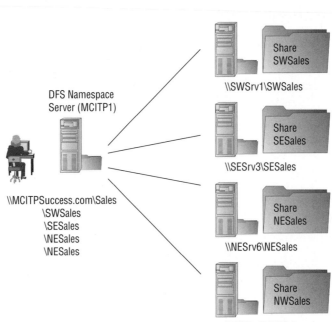

In other words, when the user connects to the \\mcitpsuccess.com\Sales path, he will see the \SWSales, \SESales, \NESales, and \NWSales folders. The data is actually retrieved from the back-end servers, but this is transparent to the user.

The following are some terms associated with DFS namespaces:

Namespace server   The namespace server is the server that hosts the namespace. In Figure 6.23, MCITP1 is the namespace server.

Namespace root   The namespace root is the starting point of the namespace. In Figure 6.23 the namespace root is \\mcitpsuccess.com\Sales.

Folder target   A folder target is any folder that is derived from another UNC path. In Figure 6.23, each of the folders under the \Sales folder would be considered folder targets since the data is actually coming from different servers.

Folder   A folder can be used to organize folder targets. For example, a South folder could be created under the \\mcitpsuccess.com\Sales namespace. You could then place the two folder targets in this folder as \\mcitpsuccess.com\Sales\South\SESales and \mcitpsuccess.com\Sales\South\SWSales.

DFS Replication

You can also use DFS to replicate data. DFS Replication performs as a multimaster replication service that can be used to keep data folders synchronized.

Multimaster replication means that the changes can occur anywhere. Consider two servers in two different cities. Your goal is to have identical data on both servers so users in both cities can modify the data. With DFS replication, it will track all the changes made to the data and ensure that all changes are replicated to each server. DFS replication can be used with DFS namespaces or by itself.

Here are some terms associated with DFS replication:

Replication group   A set of servers that participates in the replication of one or more replicated folders.

Replicated folder   A folder that is replicated between servers in a replication group. Any data change in the folder is replicated to all members in the replication group.

Member   Any server that is in a DFS replication group is known as a member.

Consider Figure 6.24, which illustrates a replication group. It has two members (two servers) in the replication group.

FIGURE 6.24   DFS replication group

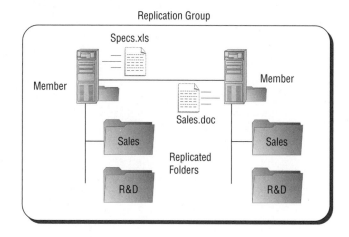

Each server hosts the same two replicated folders: Sales and R&D. Whenever a change occurs in a file in one of the folders, the change is replicated to the replicated folder on the other member.

In the figure, it looks like all the files (`specs.xls` and `sales.doc`) are being replicated. However, DFS uses the Remote Differential Compression (RDC) protocol to replicate only what has changed in the file instead of the entire files. Since the entire file isn't being replicated, DFS scales well, even when data is traversing slower WAN links.

Although using DFS to replicate data folders in Windows Server 2008 is similar to how it worked in Windows Server 2003 R2, there are significant differences in how DFS can be implemented to replicate Active Directory Domain Service's sysvol folder. These differences are described in the next section, "FRS and sysvol."

However, when you use DFS in Windows Server 2008 for data replication, you do have some significant improvements:

- Improved command-line tools
- Improved search capabilities within a namespace
- Increased scalability
- Better response to unexpected shutdowns
- Improvements in replication performance
- Support for read-only domain controllers

DFS is replacing the FRS used in previous editions of Windows.

FRS and sysvol

FRS has historically been used to replicate the sysvol contents. You may remember when you promoted a server to a domain controller, the DCPromo tool asked you where you wanted to install the sysvol folder.

By default, the sysvol folder is stored in C:\Windows\sysvol. The sysvol folder holds Group Policy data files and scripts (such as logon and logoff scripts).

It's important that these files are replicated between domain controllers accurately. When a user logs onto a computer within a domain, they may hit one domain controller today and another domain controller tomorrow. Which domain controller they log on to can be affected by where they're logging on from, but it's completely transparent to the user. However, no matter which domain controller a user authenticates with, they must still have the same group policies apply and have the same scripts run. The only way this can happen is if group policies and scripts are replicated to each domain controller.

Enter FRS. Before Windows Server 2008, FRS was the only method of replicating and synchronizing the sysvol folder between domain controllers when the content changed. As long as your domain functional level is less than Windows Server 2008 domain functional level, you are using FRS for sysvol replication. You can view your domain functional level by using Active Directory Users and Computers, as shown in Figure 6.25.

You can access the screen in Figure 6.25 by launching Active Directory Users and Computers, right-clicking the domain, and selecting Raise Domain Functional Level.

FIGURE 6.25 Viewing the domain functional level

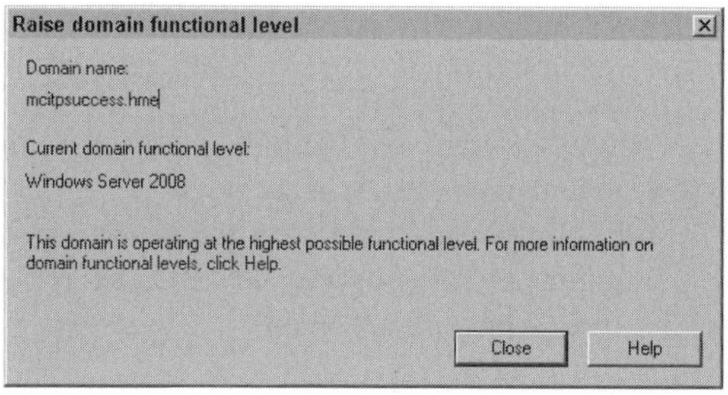

Raise domain functional level ☒

Domain name:
mcitpsuccess.hme|

Current domain functional level:
Windows Server 2008

This domain is operating at the highest possible functional level. For more information on domain functional levels, click Help.

[Close]   [Help]

Do you remember what it means if your *domain functional level* is set to Windows Server 2008 as discussed in Chapter 1? Can you support Windows Server 2003 servers in this domain functional level?

Yes, you can. If you are in Windows Server 2008 domain functional level, it means that all your **DOMAIN CONTROLLERS** are running a Windows Server 2008 operating system. Other servers could be running Windows Server 2000, 2003, or even NT 4.0. The domain functional level is related only to the **DOMAIN CONTROLLERS**.

Just because the domain is shown to be in Windows Server 2008 domain function level doesn't mean that it is using DFS for sysvol replication.

The choice between FRS and DFS for sysvol replication is made automatically when DCPromo is run:

- If the domain functional level is Windows Server 2008 when DCPromo is run, then DFS is used for replication.

- If the domain functional level is less than Windows Server 2008 when DCPromo is run, then FRS is used for replication.

You can switch from FRS to DFS after promoting a domain to Windows Server 2008 domain functional level. However, the procedure is rather complex. You would use a command-line tool called dfsrmig.exe which allows you to migrate the sysvol replication from FRS to DFS.

There is a subtle difference here when DFS is supported for replicating the Active Directory Domain Services sysvol folder and when DFS is supported to replicate regular data content. You cannot use DFS to replicate the sysvol folder until the domain functional level is raised to Windows Server 2008. However, DFS is used to replicate data between member servers in a replication group if the servers are running at least Windows Server 2003 R2.

DFS and WSUS

You can replicate any content you desire using DFS. While typically you'll be replicating files and folders that users will use directly, you can also replicate data needed for servers.

For example, in a large organization you may have multiple Windows Server Update Services (WSUS) servers. A single WSUS server would be used to download all the updates and then downstream WSUS servers would retrieve the updates from the first WSUS server.

To ensure these updates are highly available, you could store the updates on a DFS link and replicate the updates to multiple targets. This would ensure that the updates are available to the WSUS servers even if the first WSUS server failed.

Domain-Based vs. Stand-Alone Namespaces

When choosing namespaces, you need to decide whether you'll use a domain-based namespace or a stand-alone namespace:

Stand-alone DFS namespace This is a single server acting as a DFS server. A server can have multiple stand-alone namespaces; however, each stand-alone namespace is stored on only one server.

Similar to a domain-based DFS namespace, each namespace can have multiple folders, and each folder can have multiple folder targets configured.

The DFS namespace configuration information is stored locally in the registry of the host server so it provides no fault tolerance within itself. However, a stand-alone DFS namespace can be created on a clustered file server.

The path to the namespace includes the server name, for example, \\MCITP1\Sales.

Domain-based DFS namespace A domain-based DFS namespace can be hosted on one or more servers acting as DFS servers. Multiple DFS namespace servers are recommended for fault tolerance. DFS can include multiple DFS namespace roots and multiple folder targets on different servers. In other words, other DFS domain-based DFS namespaces can be added to a domain-based DFS server and appear as though they are all accessible through the single server.

The DFS namespace configuration information is stored in Active Directory Domain Services, providing a significant level of fault tolerance. The namespace configuration information is also stored in a memory cache on each namespace server. A server hosting a domain-based DFS namespace cannot be added to a cluster.

The path to the namespace includes the DNS or NetBIOS domain name, for example, \\mcitpsuccess.com\Sales and \\mcitpsuccess\Sales. An added feature in a domain-based DFS namespace is the ability for clients to have preferred targets—this a DFS server a client will use as long as it is operational. If the preferred target fails, the client will automatically be referred to another server in the namespace. Once the preferred DFS server is restored, the client will fail back to a preferred target.

Client failback is supported on Windows XP SP2 (with a hotfix) and newer clients including Windows Vista.

Any time you want to ensure your data is highly available, consider implementing a domain-based DFS namespace.

In general, you'll use a domain-based namespace unless one of the following conditions exists:

- You're not using a domain (Active Directory Domain Services).

- You want to use a failover cluster. Domain-based namespaces will not support cluster
  configurations.

Two modes are available if you choose a domain-based namespace:

Windows Server 2008 mode   This mode includes additional features and is much more
scalable than Windows Server 2000 mode. Whenever possible, it's recommended to choose
this mode.

Windows Server 2008 mode supports access-based enumeration. In other words, users are
able to see only the folders they have access to based on permissions.

To choose this mode, the domain must be in the Windows Server 2008 functional level,
and all DFS namespace servers must be running Windows Server 2008.

Windows 2000 Server mode   For backward compatibility, you can choose Windows 2000
Server mode. Once the conditions for Windows Server 2008 mode are met, you can migrate
to Windows Server 2008 mode.

Replication Topology

When configuring replication among servers in a replication group, you have three choices
of how to configure it. You will see these choices available in Exercise 6.7 (in the following
section).

Hub and spoke   The hub and spoke topology has a central server that replicates to other
servers. This topology is ideal for environments where you have a central office location
(such as a headquarters) and remote offices connected with slower connections.

For example, consider Figure 6.26. The HQ server is the hub, and it replicates the changes
to each of the spokes (the remote offices). With this topology, you don't need to have connections between each of the remote offices.

Full mesh   In a full mesh topology, each of the DFS servers replicates to all the other DFS
servers. If any of the servers or any of the connections develops a problem, the topology
continues to operate. You would use a full mesh topology in a well-connected network; you
wouldn't typically use it across WAN connections.

No topology   When you choose no topology, you are given the opportunity to design your
own topology. This is useful if you have several DFS servers in one well-connected location
and some servers located across a WAN connection. In this scenario, you can configure a
hybrid of the hub and spoke and the full mesh topologies.

FIGURE 6.26   Hub and spoke topology

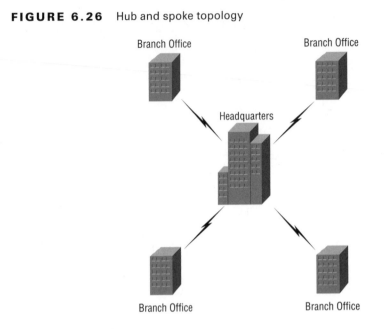

Creating a DFS Replication Group

Exercise 6.7 shows you how to create a DFS-based replication group using two member servers. You will need at least two member servers to complete this exercise. Remember, though, that they don't have to be real servers. You can use Virtual PC to create two servers in two separate instances of Virtual PC. Additionally, the File Services role with both the Distributed File System services (DFS Namespaces and DFS Replication) must be installed on both servers.

This exercise assumes you have completed Exercise 6.1 where you installed the File Services role and Exercise 6.3 where you created the MyShare share.

EXERCISE 6.7

Replicating Data with DFS

1. Launch the DFS Management snap-in by clicking Start ➢ Administrative Tools ➢ DFS Management.

2. Right-click Replication, and select New Replication Group.

3. On the Replication Group Type page, ensure Multipurpose Replication Group is selected, and click Next.

4. On the Name and Domain page, enter **MCITPStudy** as the name of replication group. Accept the default domain name. Click Next.

5. On the Replication Group Members page, add your server and two other servers. (If you are using a test environment and don't have three physical servers, you can create computer accounts in Active Directory Users and Computers and add the three computer accounts as your three servers. You won't be able to see the data transfer, but you will be able to view the configuration of the hub and spoke topology configuration.) Your display will look similar to the following graphic. Click Next.

6. On the Topology Selection page, ensure Hub and Spoke is selected. This topology is ideal when you have a headquarters location and branch office locations. Each branch office will replicate only to the headquarters location and will conserve bandwidth. Click Next.

7. On the Hub Members page, select your server as the hub, and click Add. This simulates your server as the server at headquarters. Click Next.

8. On the Hub and Spoke Connections page, you'll see the other two servers with your server selected as the required hub. Click Next.

9. On the Replication Group Schedule and Bandwidth page, click the Replicate During the Specified Days and Times, and click Edit Schedule. Notice that you can specify exactly when replication will occur and throttle the bandwidth usage from this page. Click Cancel.

10. Back on the Replication Group Schedule and Bandwidth page, select Replicate Continuously Using the Specified Bandwidth. Click Next.

11. On the Primary Member page, select the server you are currently working on as the primary member. Content will be replicated from here to the other member in your replication group. Click Next.

12. On the Folders to Replicate page, click Add.

13. On the Add Folder to Replicate page, click Browse. Select the MyShare folder you created in an earlier exercise, and click OK. On the Add Folder to Replicate page, click OK. If desired, you can add content to this folder to verify it is being replicated to your second server.

14. Back on the Folders to Replicate page, you can select as many folders to replicate as you desire. Click Next when you are done.

15. On the Local Path of MyShare on Other Members page, select your second server, and click Edit.

16. On the Edit page, click Enabled. Click Browse.

17. On the Browse for Folder page, click Make New Folder. Rename the folder MyShare. Click OK. Your display will look similar to the following image. On the Edit page, click OK.

18. Back on the Local Path of MyShare on Other Members page, click Next.

19. On the Review Settings and Create Replication Group page, review your settings, and click Create. The wizard will run. Your display should look like the following image indicating success.

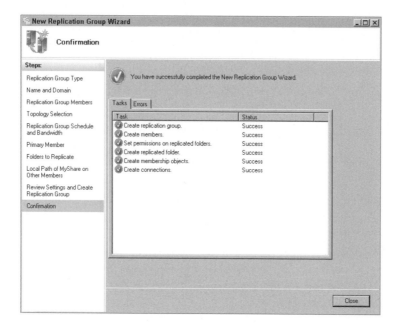

20. On the Confirmation page, click Close.

21. In the Replication Delay message box, click OK.

22. Access your second computer, and verify that data from the first computer has replicated to the second computer. If you don't have any data in the source folder, add a file to the folder and then verify it has been replicated.

If desired, you can play with adding and deleting data from the two folders on the two servers. For example, if you add a file in the MyShare folder on MCITP1, you can then look at the folder on MCITP2 and verify the file appears as soon as you press F5 to refresh the screen.

On MCITP2, you can add a file and verify the file appears on MCITP1 as soon as you press F5.

Last, you can verify that file deletions are also replicated. If you delete a file on MCITP1, it is almost immediately deleted from MCITP2. If you delete a file on MCITP2, it is almost immediately deleted from MCITP1.

Pretty darn cool!

SharePoint Services

Another way files are frequently shared in networks today is with SharePoint services. SharePoint services provides document storage and management capabilities with search, management, administration and deployment features.

With SharePoint, users are able to access files and resources via a web browser. One of the significant benefits with SharePoint is the ability for multiple users to easily share and collaborate files from a central location.

SharePoint services comes in two primary flavors:

Windows SharePoint Services (WSS)   WSS is a free download for Windows Server 2008. The current version is WSS 3.0. WSS is the base service for SharePoint Server products

SharePoint Server products   The current SharePoint server is Microsoft Office SharePoint Server 2007. It is available at an additional cost, similar to how Microsoft SQL Server or Microsoft Exchange Server can be purchased and installed on Windows Server 2008.

Microsoft Office SharePoint Server 2007 includes all the base capabilities of WSS 3.0 but you can think of it as a superset of WSS. It includes significant additional features and capabilities. Microsoft Office SharePoint Server 2007 is typically utilized in larger organizations and enterprises where better scalability is desired.

Both Windows SharePoint Services and Microsoft Office SharePoint Server 2007. Both products offer the same base features while SharePoint server offers many additional features and better scalability. Features supported on both platforms include:

- **Document collaboration.** Collaboration tools include the ability to check out documents of multiple types, track major and minor versions, track workflow and more.
- **Real-time Presence and Communication.** Tells users when a user in online.
- **Standard Site Templates.** Templates are included to streamline the process of getting websites up and operational with supported features and services as quick as possible.
- **Blogs.** Users can easily create and maintain their own web logs (blogs) once configured.
- **Search.** Indexing can be enabled on the content to allow users to easily locate any documents.
- **Calendars.** Calendars can be included within pages allowing users to schedule events.
- **Task and issue coordination.** Basic project management capabilities are available. Gantt charts can be used to show task relationships and status. Additionally you can utilize issue tracking capabilities.
- **Surveys.** Developers can easily add surveys to their websites. Surveys can be simple single page surveys or complex multiple page surveys are even surveys that include conditional branching (asking additional questions based on the response to another question).

If you want users to be able to easily share files and access them via a web browser, consider either Windows SharePoint services or Microsoft Office SharePoint Server. The hardest part is deciding which one meets your needs best.

Application Pools

SharePoint uses Internet Information Services (IIS) to host the websites. In early versions of IIS multiple websites all shared the same application space. The result was that when one Web application failed, they all failed.

Today, Web applications are easily isolated from each other by using application pools. Each Web application is contained within its own application pool and runs as an isolated worker process.

The primary benefit is that when a single Web application fails, none of the other applications are affected. You can also control the amount of resources any single website uses.

SharePoint and WSRM

Since a SharePoint server can host multiple web sites, you may want to ensure that any single site doesn't take too many resources. Windows System Resource Manager (WSRM) can be used to restrict resources to specific application pools.

For example, you may notice that occasionally your SharePoint server experiences very high usage. You can create a WSRM policy so that if the server does get exceptionally busy (say over 80 percent utilization), all individual application pools will be restricted to no more than 10 percent of the resources.

WSRM was discussed in more depth in Chapter 3, "Using Windows Server 2003 Management Tools." WSRM can be used to manage multiple sites in SharePoint.

Summary

In this chapter, you learned how to configure file and print servers within Windows Server 2008. Windows Server 2008 includes two roles (the File Services role and the Print Services role) to support this functionality.

Once you add the roles through Server Manager, you can add more role services. You learned how to add the File Server Resource Manager and use it to provision shares on a file server.

You also learned how to add the Print Services role, add and share printers, and publish these printers to Active Directory. You learned about Distributed File System and how it can be used to organize data in a single namespace. You also learned how DFS can be used to replicate data.

Last, you learned about SharePoint services and how it can be used to allow users to easily share files accessible via a web browser.

Exam Essentials

Know how to install File Services and Print Services.   You should be familiar with the process of using Server Manager to add these roles. Additionally, you should know what services are available under the File Services role.

Know what the FSRM is and what it does.   The File Server Resource Manager allows you to manage shares. It includes three management tools: quota management, file-screening management, and storage reports management.

Understand permissions related to shares.   You should know who can create shares (Server Operators, Power Users, and greater) and the available permissions. This includes both NTFS permissions and share permissions. You should also understand the roles (such as Reader, Contributor, and Co-owner) for shares and how they relate to permissions.

Understand offline files.   You should understand the purpose of offline files, how they work, and how to configure them on a share. For example, you should know that users can access offline files when disconnected, and changes will automatically be synchronized when they log on and reconnect to the network.

Know the difference between Windows search and indexing.   You should understand that both services are used for searching. Indexing is the legacy service included for backward compatibility. The Windows search service is the current version of indexing recommended on a Windows Server 2008 server.

Know how to publish shared printers to Active Directory.   Users may need the capability to search the network for printers with specific capabilities such as print in color or print double-sided. By listing a shared printer in Active Directory (publishing to Active Directory), you can enable this feature.

Know the purposes and capabilities of DFS   You should know that DFS can be used to ensure data is highly available by replicating content between multiple servers. Know the differences between stand-alone and domain-based namespaces. In environments with limited bandwidth, you can configure DFS servers in a hub and spoke configuration.

Understand the differences between DFS and FRS related to the sysvol folder.   You should know when FRS is used to replicate the sysvol folder and when DFS is used. DFS is much more efficient and less susceptible to problems when replicating sysvol so should be used whenever possible. DFS can be used only when your domain is in Windows Server 2008 domain functional level. If the domain was originally in a lesser domain functional level, you must migrate FRS to DFS to change how the sysvol folder is replicated.

Review Questions

1. Joe is an administrator in a remote office. The remote office holds an RODC. Joe needs to be able to create shares on the domain controller. What group should you add him to so that he can create the shares?

    A. Power Users

    B. Server Operators

    C. Domain Administrators

    D. Local Administrators

2. You have created a share named Sales on a server named MCITP1. You want Sally to be able to modify permissions to files within this share. What role would you add her to?

    A. Full Control

    B. Owner

    C. Co-owner

    D. Contributor

3. You have created a share named Sales on a server named MCITP1. You want Sally to be able to create files within the share. What role would you add her to?

    A. Reader

    B. Creator-Owner

    C. Modifier

    D. Contributor

4. You have created a share named Sales on a server named MCITP1. You want all the users in the global group named G_Sales to be able to read files within the share. What role would you add the group to?

    A. DL_Reader

    B. Read permissions

    C. Reader

    D. Contributor

5. Sally is the CEO of MCITPSuccess.com. She uses a laptop with a docking station at work and takes the laptop with her when traveling. When traveling, she needs access to her data files that are normally held on a share on the server. What can you do to give Sally access to her files no matter where she is located?

    A. Configure offline files.

    B. Share Sally's data on the server.

    C. Post Sally's data to an IIS server to make it available.

    D. Create a VPN.

6. You have implemented offline files on a server share. You want to ensure that files are synchronized down to the clients but changes are not synchronized back to the share. What should you do?

    A. On the share permissions, assign the Everyone group Deny Write.

    B. On the NTFS permissions, assign the Everyone group Deny Write.

    C. On the Offline Settings page, select One-Way Caching.

    D. On the Offline Settings page, select Optimized for Performance.

7. You manage a file server named FS1. You want to restrict the amount of space that users can take within a share named Sales on the server. What tool can you use?

    A. WSRM

    B. DFS

    C. WDS

    D. FSRM

8. You have configured disk quotas on a volume on the MCITP1 server with soft limits. You want to be notified by email if a user exceeds a limit. What tool can you use?

    A. Server Manager

    B. Computer Management

    C. Windows Explorer

    D. FSRM

9. You have shared a printer as clrLaser on a print server named PS1. You want users to be able to search for the printer in Active Directory Domain Services. What should you do?

    A. Create a GPO, and apply it to the Printers container.

    B. Right-click the printer in Active Directory, and select Enable Searching.

    C. Right-click the printer in Print Management, and select Enable Searching.

    D. Right-click the printer in Print Management, and select List in Directory.

10. You have shared a printer as clrLaser on a printer server named PS1. You notice that the print jobs are quite large, and you're concerned the space isn't large enough for the spooler. You want to move the spooler from the C:\ drive to the D:\ drive, which has more than 80GB of free space. How can you do this?

    A. In Print Management, right-click the clrLaser printer, and select Properties. Change the location of the spool folder.

    B. In Print Management, right-click the PS1 server, and select Properties. Change the location of the spool folder.

    C. Reinstall the clrLaser printer, and change the location when prompted by the wizard.

    D. This can't be done. The spooler must stay on the C:\ drive.

11. You manage a domain named mcitpsuccess.com. It includes several domain controllers that are running Windows Server 2008. One of the DCs was originally running on Windows Server 2003 but was upgraded to Windows Server 2008 this week. No other changes to the domain were done. You want to use Distributed File System (DFS) for replication of the sysvol folder. What should you do? Choose two.

   A. Raise the domain functional level to Windows Server 2008.

   B. Raise the forest functional level to Windows Server 2008.

   C. Migrate FRS to DFS.

   D. Install the file DFS role.

12. You want to install Distributed File System (DFS) on a server to create a domain-based DFS namespace. What must be installed before you can install the DFS service?

   A. WSRM

   B. WSUS

   C. WDS

   D. File Services

13. You manage a file server running Windows Server 2008 with the File Services role installed. Users run Windows XP and Windows Vista. The file server hosts research data that about 100 researchers often search when creating scientific papers. However, the searches are frequently slow. You are asked whether there's anything that can be done to improve the searches. What should you suggest?

   A. Implement the Windows search service on the server.

   B. Implement indexing on the server.

   C. Copy the research data onto the client systems.

   D. Ask users to limit their searches.

14. You have just run DCPromo on a Windows Server 2008 server within a domain with other domain controllers. Some of the domain controllers are running Windows Server 2003, and some are running Windows Server 2008. What is being used for replication of group policies and scripts?

   A. DFS

   B. FRS

   C. WDS

   D. WSUS

15. You manage two Windows Server 2008 servers in a medium-sized domain. You want to configure the servers so that data folders on one member server are identical to the data folders on another member server. What should you configure?

   A. DFS replication

   B. DFS namespace

   C. FRS replication

   D. FRS namespace

16. You manage two Windows Server 2008 servers in a medium-sized domain. The domain functional level is Windows Server 2003. You want to configure a replication group so that data folders on one member server are identical to the data folders on another member server. What service will accomplish this?

    A. DFS

    B. FRS

    C. WDS

    D. DNS

17. You are an administrator in a domain running several Windows Server 2008 file servers. You want to stand up a DFS server to organize the shares on all the servers onto a single DFS namespace. Further, you want to place this DFS server into a cluster for fault tolerance. What type of DFS should you configure?

    A. Stand-alone

    B. Domain-based

    C. FRS-based

    D. Windows Server 2008 mode–based

18. You are an administrator in a domain running several Windows Server 2008 file servers. You have two DFS servers in your organization, and you want to create a single DFS namespace that is stored on each of the DFS servers. What type of DFS should you configure?

    A. Stand-alone

    B. Domain-based

    C. FRS-based

    D. Multiple root–based

19. You administer a Windows Server 2008 file server that hosts multiple shares. You have learned that some users are storing copyrighted files (such as pirated MP3s) on some of the shares. You want to prevent the storage of these types of files and also have access to reports that can show information on your shares. What should you add?

    A. DFS

    B. FRS

    C. FSRM

    D. WSRM

20. Your company has a headquarters located in Virginia Beach and three branch offices located in surrounding cities. The branch offices are connected to the main office via WAN links. Each office has a Windows Server 2008 file server, and each office needs access to an up-to-date Projects folder. The Projects folder must remain available even if a single server fails and even if one of the WAN links fails. Network traffic over the WAN links must be minimized. What should you do?

A. Create a stand-alone DFS namespace using the full mesh topology for DFS replication.

B. Create a stand-alone DFS namespace using the hub and spoke topology for DFS replication.

C. Create a domain-based DFS namespace using the full mesh topology for DFS replication.

D. Create a domain-based DFS namespace using the hub and spoke topology for DFS replication.

Answers to Review Questions

1. **B.** You should add Joe to the Server Operators group. This will allow him to create shares and do other administrative tasks on the domain controller without granting him administrative rights to the domain. Neither the Power Users group nor the Local Administrators groups exists on a domain controller. Adding Joe to the Domain Administrators group would grant him significant privileges and violate a basic security tenet of least privilege.

2. **C.** The Co-owner role is granted Full Control permissions and Modify permissions. There isn't such a thing as a Full Control role, but Full Control permissions can be granted. You can't add someone to the Owner role. Instead, someone is an owner if she created an object or she took ownership of an object. The Contributor role would not grant the ability to modify permissions.

3. **D.** The Contributor role is granted permissions necessary to create files within a share. The Reader role would allow users to only read files, not make any changes. The Creator-Owner isn't a role, but a Windows group used to identify the user who created an object. Owners can modify permissions. There is no such role as Modifier.

4. **C.** The Reader role is granted permissions necessary to read files within a share. There is no such role as a DL_Reader or Read permissions. The Contributor role would allow users to make modifications to the files, but only read permissions should be granted.

5. **A.** With offline files, Sally's data will be synchronized to her laptop when she logs on and logs off. This will give her access to her data files no matter where she is located. For Sally to access the data on the server, it must already be shared. Posting a CEO's data on a web server (Internet Information Services) wouldn't be very safe and wouldn't necessarily give her access to her data from anywhere. A virtual private network connection is a possibility but would be much more complex and expensive to implement. Using offline files is a simpler solution.

6. **D.** By selecting Optimized for Performance, you ensure that data changes are synchronized down to the client but not synchronized back up to the server. The Offline Settings page does not have a One-Way Caching selection, but Optimized for Performance works as one-way caching. If you selected Deny Write for either NTFS or share permissions, users wouldn't be able to create files or make changes to files on the share. Although that may or may not be desirable, the question only wanted to stop synchronization.

7. **D.** The File Server Resource Manger (FSRM) allows you to implement quotas on a volume or folder basis. Since a share is created from a folder, you could implement a quota restriction on the folder that is used for the Sales share. The Windows System Resource Manager (WSRM) is used to limit the amount of CPU and memory resources that an application is using. Distributed File System (DFS) is used to replicate data or create a virtual folder namespace. Windows Deployment Services (WDS) is used to automate deployments of operating systems.

8. D.   The File Server Resource Manger (FSRM) allows you to implement quotas on a volume or folder basis. Once a quota is reached, you can configure the response to send an email, log an entry in the application log, run a command, or run a report. You can't create quotas from Server Manager. Although you can create quotas in Computer Management and Windows Explorer, you can't create events (such as sending an email, running a command, or running a report) in response to the threshold being reached. You can configure it only to log an entry in the application log.

9. D.   To cause shared printers to be listed in Active Directory, you'd right-click the printer in Print Management and select List in Directory. A GPO is not needed, and there is no such thing as a Printers container. If the printer isn't published to Active Directory Domain Services, you won't be able to locate it in Active Directory Domain Services. Print Management doesn't have an Enable Searching selection for printers.

10. B.   A print server has one print spooler for all printers. To change it, you'd select the properties of the print server, not the printer. There is no way to change the spooler from the printer's property page or via the installation wizard. Since you can move the spooler, saying it can't be moved is incorrect.

11. A, C.   To use DFS, you must be in Windows Server 2008 domain functional level. If replication was originally done with File Replication Service (FRS), then you must migrate FRS to DFS. Since one of the servers was just upgraded from Windows Server 2003 and no other changes were done to the domain, the domain functional level could not be Windows Server 2008. This also means that replication is currently being done with FRS. You would need to raise the domain functional level to Windows Server 2008 and migrate FRS to DFS. The forest functional level does not matter. There is no DFS role.

12. D.   The File Services role needs to be installed in order to add the DFS service. The Windows System Resource Manager (WSRM) is used to limit the amount of CPU and memory resources that an application is using. Windows Software Update Services (WSUS) is used to deploy updates to computers, and Windows Deployment Services (WDS) is used to automate deployments of operating systems.

13. A.   The Windows search service is a File Services role service that can be added to increase performance of searches on a file server. Indexing is an older Windows Server 2003 search service that could be added, but the Windows search service performs better. It would not make sense to copy the centralized data to 100 different systems. Asking users to limit searches isn't a reasonable request when there's a technical method to improve searches.

14. B.   File Replication Service (FRS) is being used for replication of the sysvol folder (Group Policy files and scripts). Distributed File System (DFS) replication of sysvol is supported only when the domain functional level is Windows Server 2008. Since some domain controllers are running Windows Server 2003, the domain functional level cannot be Windows Server 2008. Windows Deployment Services (WDS) is used to automate deployments of operating systems. Windows Software Update Services (WSUS) is used to deploy updates to computers.

15. A.   You should configure Distributed File System (DFS) replication. Specifically, you'd create a replication group including both servers as member servers with replicated folders. A DFS namespaces doesn't necessarily replicate data but instead provides a method of organizing content in a single namespace to make it easier for the user. File Replication Service (FRS) was the file replication service used for data prior to Windows Server 2003 R2. As a side note, FRS is still used for replication of the Active Directory sysvol folder on domain controllers in domains where the domain functional level is less than Windows Server 2008 domain functional level and even on some domains where the level has been raised to Windows Server 2008 domain functional level.

16. A.   The Distributed File Service (DFS) can be used to replicate data in a replication group on servers running Windows Server 2008. The File Replication Services (FRS) was used to replicate data in DFS on operating systems earlier than Windows Server 2003 R2. The sentence "The domain functional level is Windows Server 2003" is meaningless in this context; it matters only when discussing the replication of Active Directory's sysvol folder, but the question specified data folders. Windows Deployment Services (WDS) is used to automate the deployment of operating systems. Dynamic Naming Service (DNS) is used to provide name resolution of host names.

17. A.   To support a cluster, you must use a stand-alone Distributed File System (DFS) server. Domain-based DFS does not support clusters. File Replication Service (FRS) is considered legacy and wouldn't be used for Windows Server 2008 file servers. You can choose either Windows Server 2000 mode or Windows Server 2008 mode with domain-based DFS servers, but these choices are not available with a stand-alone DFS server.

18. B.   A domain-based Distributed File System (DFS) namespace can be stored on one or more DFS servers. A stand-alone DFS namespace can be stored on only one DFS server. File Replication Service (FRS) is considered legacy and wouldn't be used for Windows Server 2008 file servers. There is no such thing as a multiple-root DFS server.

19. C.   The File Server Resource Manager (FSRM) gives you access to several tools, including the ability to screen files and view reports. The Distributed File System (DFS) allows you to create DFS namespaces and use DFS replication but doesn't include the capability of screening files. The File Replication Service (FRS) is considered legacy and only replicates files. The Windows System Resource Manager (WSRM) is used to limit the amount of CPU and memory resources that an application is using.

20. D.   A domain-based Distributed File System (DFS) namespace can be used to easily replicate content from one server to other servers by using DFS replication. The hub and spoke topology will minimize network traffic over the WAN links since the remote offices won't need to replicate to each other. A stand-alone DFS namespace can be stored on only one DFS server, so it wouldn't work. A full mesh topology would require each branch office to be connected to every other branch office so network traffic would not be minimized.

Chapter

7

Planning Terminal Services Servers

MICROSOFT EXAM OBJECTIVES COVERED IN THIS CHAPTER:

✓ **Planning for Server Deployment**

- Plan Infrastructure Services Server Roles. May include but is not limited to: address assignment, name resolution, network access control, directory services, application services, certificate services.

✓ **Planning Application and Data Provisioning**

- Provision Applications. May include but is not limited to: presentation virtualization, terminal server infrastructure, resource allocation, application virtualization alternatives, application deployment, System Center Configuration Manager.

- Provision Data. May include but is not limited to: shared resources, offline data access.

Terminal Services (TS) is a key application server role you should understand. It includes several TS services that allow you to host full desktops or single applications.

Although Terminal Services is most often hosted on a server within your network specifically for internal users, you can also use some of the TS technologies to provide access to internal resources via the Internet.

Using services such as TS Web Access, you can allow users to remotely run TS RemoteApp applications via the Internet. TS Gateway allows users to access internal resources via the Internet. When providing access to resources via the Internet, you'll also use Internet Information Services 7.0 (IIS 7.0).

In this chapter, you'll learn about the different TS server services and IIS 7.0.

You'll notice in the list of objectives that address assignment, name resolution, directory services, and certificate services are listed in the Planning for Server Deployment section, and presentation virtualization, resource allocation, System Center Configuration Manager, and offline data access are listed in Planning Application and Data Provisioning. Chapter 2, "Planning Server Deployments," covers presentation virtualization. Chapter 3, "Using Windows Server 2008 Management Tools," covers resource allocation and System Center Configuration Manager. Chapter 4, "Monitoring and Maintaining Network Infrastructure Servers," covers address assignment and name resolution. Chapter 5, "Monitoring and Maintaining Active Directory," covers directory services and Certificate Services. Chapter 6, "Monitoring and Maintaining Print and File Servers," covers offline data access.

Terminal Services Servers

Terminal Services is a server role in Windows Server 2008. It provides users with access to either Windows-based programs or a full Windows desktop located on a server.

The full features of TS are experienced only on computers running Windows Vista or Windows Server 2008, but Terminal Services does support Windows XP and Windows Server 2003 products.

Figure 7.1 shows the big picture of how Terminal Services runs. The terminal server would be heavy on resources such as memory, processing power, disk space, and network capacity. Multiple clients can connect to the server, and their session will run completely within the server.

FIGURE 7.1   Running Terminal Services on a server

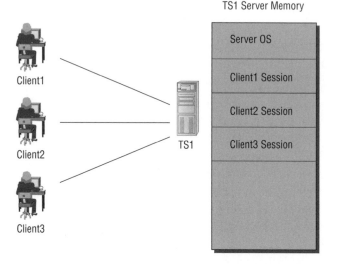

In the figure, you can see that each client is running a session on the server. This session could be an individual application or a complete desktop session.

Why would you want to do such as thing?

Imagine a large insurance company. I envision dozens of operators (maybe more) in a huge room just sitting and waiting for you to call for an insurance quote. Once you call and ask your questions, they begin typing information into a computer program so they can give you an accurate quote.

This computer program is highly specialized for that insurance company only, otherwise known as a *line-of-business* application. You could deploy the application to the computers for each person answering phones. However, if you needed to make a change, you'd need to change each system.

On the other hand, if you deployed the application to a terminal server, you would need to make the change in only one location.

Terminal Services can be used by administrators to remotely administer servers and also by end users. Except for TS Web Access, the Terminal Services role does not need to be installed to remotely administer a server. For a review of how this is done, take a look at Chapter 3.

Another reason to use Terminal Services is when users need to run separate versions of an application. Some applications can't run two versions side by side on the same operating system.

As an example, Outlook 2003 and Outlook 2007 can't be installed on the same system. However, a user may want to run Outlook 2007 on their system but occasionally use Outlook

2003. By using Terminal Services, Outlook 2003 can be installed for users, allowing them to run both versions.

When looking at Terminal Services, you should be aware of the following terms and services:

Terminal server   This is the server that hosts the Terminal Services role. You can host full Windows desktops on this server or individual applications.

TS RemoteApp   Any application that has been configured to run within a Terminal Services session is referred to as a RemoteApp program. TS RemoteApp programs can be configured with or without TS Web Access. When configured without TS Web Access, a TS RemoteApp program will run in its own window on the user's desktop (as long as the user is running Windows Vista or Server 2008).

TS Gateway   TS Gateway is a role service available after the TS role has been installed. It allows authorized remote users to connect to resources on an internal network via the Internet. In other words, the TS Gateway is the gateway to other computers. Remote users can connect to terminal servers, terminal servers running RemoteApp programs, or computers with Remote Desktop enabled.

TS Session Broker   The TS Session Broker is used in larger implementations of Terminal Services where multiple terminal servers are configured in a load-balanced terminal server farm. TS Session Broker stores session state information allowing a user who disconnects to reconnect to the same server. Disconnected users will be able to reconnect to the same session without any loss of data.

TS Web Access   TS Web Access is a role service within the Terminal Services role. With TS Web Access configured, users can connect from a web browser to the remote desktop of a server or a client computer. Programs that can run in the browser via TS Web Access are known as TS RemoteApp applications. TS RemoteApp programs are accessible over the Internet or over an intranet using Internet technologies.

TS Licensing   Terminal Services client access licenses (TS CALs) are required for devices and clients that will access a TS server. TS Licensing is a management system used to manage TS CALs. TS Licensing can be used to install, issue, and monitor the availability of TS CALs on a TS server. When Terminal Services is first installed, you are granted a 120-day grace period for licensing. During that grace period you can determine how many licenses you'll need and purchase them. After the grace period expires, users will no longer be able to access the terminal server.

Users are able to access a Terminal Services server from within a network or over the Internet.

Terminal Services Role

The first step in configuring a terminal server is to add the Terminal Services role. You can add all the supporting services at the same time or install Terminal Services first and then add the supporting services later.

If you want to install Terminal Services specifically to allow users to run specific applications from within your network, you should take the following steps:

1. Add the Terminal Services role. (No additional role services are required.)

2. Change the installation mode to install applications.

3. Install an application.

4. Change the installation mode to execute applications.

> When using a terminal server for applications, it's highly recommended that you install the terminal server services first before installing the applications. If you install a terminal server after applications are installed, it's possible the applications won't work in a multiuser environment.

At this point, users will be able to access the terminal server, and each user can have their own desktop. However, if you want users to be able to launch an application within their own desktop, you can configure the application as a TS RemoteApp.

The steps required to configure an application as a RemoteApp are as follows:

1. Add the application as a RemoteApp using the TS RemoteApp Manager.

2. Create a remote desktop configuration file (.rdp file) or a Windows Installer package within the TS RemoteApp Manager.

3. Use the .rdp file or the Windows Installer package to deploy the application to users.

> A remote desktop file (.rdp) holds custom settings used to launch a remote desktop session. A user could double-click the .rdp file to launch the Remote Desktop Connection application, and it will be launched with the settings in the .rdp file.

At this point, users will have access to the remote applications either from the desktop or from the Start menu: Start ➤ All Programs ➤ Remote Programs.

The first time the program is launched, it is installed for the user. After it is installed, it looks like it's running on the end user's system.

Network Level Authentication

Before adding the Terminal Services role, you should understand the basics of Network Level Authentication (NLA). NLA is new to Windows Server 2008. It provides enhanced security for the terminal server by authenticating the client before a TS session begins.

Although it's still possible to enable connections without NLA, it exposes the TS server to increased risk from malicious users and malicious software.

The requirements to use NLA are as follows:

- The terminal server must be running Windows Server 2008.

- The client computer must be using at least Remote Desktop Connection 6.0 (RDC 6.0).

- The client computer must be able to support the Credential Security Support Provider (CredSSP) protocol.

Windows Vista and Windows Server 2008 clients use RDC 6.0 and support the CredSSP protocol by default. If you're supporting down-level clients (such as Windows XP and Windows Server 2003), you need to do some checks:

- Windows XP needs to have at least SP2 installed.
- Windows Server 2003 needs to have at least SP1 installed.

With the proper service packs, Windows XP and Windows Server 2003 can support NLA.

 For more information on the Remote Desktop Client 6.0 and how it can run on down-level clients, check out Knowledge Base article 925876 on Microsoft's website. The easiest way to get there is to enter **KB 925876** in your favorite search engine.

You can tell whether your version of Remote Desktop Connection supports NLA by clicking the icon at the top left of the window and selecting About. Your display will look similar to Figure 7.2. If NLA is supported, the About box will include the phrase "Network Level Authentication Supported."

FIGURE 7.2   Verifying NLA support in RDC

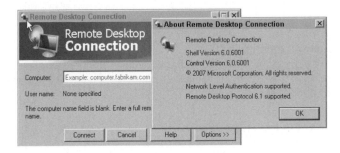

When installing the Terminal Services role, you will be able to choose from the following two authentication methods:

Require Network Level Authentication   Choose this if all your clients can support NLA.

Do Not Require Network Level Authentication   This choice allows computers running any version of Remote Desktop Connection to connect to the terminal server.

Installing the Terminal Services Role

It is not recommended that you install Terminal Services on a domain controller in a production environment. Regular users are not allowed to log onto a domain controller by default, so permissions will need to be weakened to allow users to access a terminal server that is installed on a domain controller.

However, you may not have that many servers in your test environment. If you install Terminal Services on your domain controller, you will receive a warning, but it will still install.

Exercise 7.1 shows you the steps to follow to add the Terminal Services role to your server.

EXERCISE 7.1

Installing the Terminal Services Role

1. Launch Server Manager by clicking Start ➤ Administrative Tools ➤ Server Manager.

2. Click the Add Roles link to launch the Add Roles Wizard.

3. On the Before You Begin page, review the information, and click Next.

4. On the Server Roles, select the Terminal Services check box. You display will look similar to the following image. Click Next.

5. On the Terminal Services page, review the information, and click Next.

6. On the Select Role Services page, select the Terminal Server check box. If a warning box appears saying you shouldn't install Terminal Server on a server running Active Directory Domain Services, review the information, and select Install Terminal Server Anyway. Although this is not recommended for a production server, it is acceptable for a learning environment.

7. You can add other role services to provide more Terminal Services functionality. For this exercise, only the Terminal Server service is added. Click Next.

8. Review the information on application compatibility issues. Click Next.

9. On the Specify Authentication Method for Terminal Server page, select Require Network Level Authentication, and click Next.

10. On the Specify Licensing Mode page, select Configure Later, and click Next.

11. On the Select User Groups Allowed Access to This Terminal Server page, verify that the Administrators group is added, and click Next. For a production server, you would also add the group that contains users to whom you want to grant access. As an example, you may have a global group named G_TelephoneOperators that includes all the users answering the phones. You could add the G_TelephoneOperators group on this page to grant these users access to the terminal server.

12. On the Confirm Installation Selections page, review the information, and click Install.

13. When the installation completes, the Installation Results page will appear letting you know you must restart the server. Click Close.

14. On the Add Roles Wizard page prompting you to restart, click Yes to restart your server.

15. After you reboot and log back on, the Installation Results page will appear. It should look similar to the following image. Click Close.

At this point, the terminal server will accept remote sessions by users. However, since you haven't added any RemoteApp applications, users will be able to access only the desktop on the terminal server and launch applications from there.

Installing Applications on a Terminal Server

When installing applications on a terminal server, you need to take a couple of extra steps to ensure the application can work in multiuser mode.

Before installing the application, you must put the terminal server in a special installation mode. After installing the application, you need to return the terminal server to execution mode.

You can use the Control Panel's Programs and Features page to install an application. It includes a link that will automatically place the terminal server into the install mode, install the application, and then return the terminal server to execute mode.

To use the Control Panel Wizard, launch the Control Panel, and click the Install Application on Terminal Server link, as shown in Figure 7.3.

FIGURE 7.3   Using Control Panel to change the terminal server installation mode

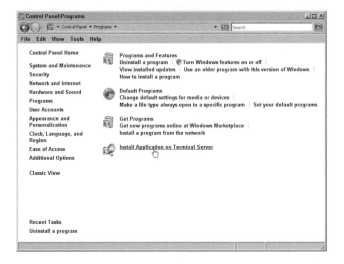

    The Install Application on Terminal Server link appears only after you have added the Terminal Services role. If it doesn't appear, verify you have added the Terminal Services role.

Follow the wizard to install the application. After the install is done, click Close in the Control Panel Wizard to complete the process.

You can also use the command line to enter installation mode and execute mode. The process is as follows:

1. From the command line, enter **Change user /install**.

2. Install the application.

3. From the command line, enter **Change user /execute**.

Vista Desktop Experience

When users connect to a terminal server on Windows Server 2008, the look and feel is that of a Windows Server 2008 server. For users who connect with Windows Vista, it is possible for the Windows Server 2008 Terminal Services session to emulate a Windows Vista desktop experience.

To support this, you must add the Desktop Experience feature to the terminal server via the Add Features link in Server Manager. Once the Desktop Experience feature is installed, Windows Vista applications (such as Windows Media Player and Windows Calendar) will appear on the All Programs menu.

Terminal Services and the Firewall

When Terminal Services is installed, the Windows Firewall settings on the server are automatically configured with the following exceptions:

- Remote Desktop
- Terminal Services

If you need to provide access to Terminal Services through a firewall external to your terminal server, you need to ensure that port 3389 is open. In other words, if users are accessing your terminal server through the Internet, you'd open port 3389 at the company firewall between the network and the Internet.

The exception to opening port 3389 is to stand up a TS Gateway and provide access via port 443 (using RDP over SSL) as discussed later in this chapter.

Terminal Services and WSRM

The Windows System Resource Manager (WSRM) was explained in more depth in Chapter 3. You can use WSRM to control how much CPU and memory resources are allocated to individual users or individual sessions within Terminal Services.

 WSRM is a new feature available in Windows Server 2008. Its ability to throttle the CPU and memory resource usage on a per-user or per-session basis can be very valuable on a high-capacity terminal server.

The following are the two primary resource-allocation policies that would be used for a terminal server:

- Equal_per_user
- Equal_per_session

The only real difference between the two is when a user creates two different sessions. In the equal_per_user setting, users would have as many resources in each session as they would if they created only one session. In the equal_per_session, users would have the same amount of memory and processor resources in each session.

TS RemoteApp

TS RemoteApp programs appear to run on a user's desktop but actually run on the Terminal Services server. Applications can be configured to run as a RemoteApp application in the TS RemoteApp Manager.

Once an application is configured as a RemoteApp, users can access the application via several methods:

- Double-click a Remote Desktop Protocol (.rdp) file.
- Double-click a program icon that has been created and distributed as a Windows Installer package.
- If the Windows Installer package has been distributed via Group Policy, the program will be available on the Start menu or the desktop.
- Double-click a program where the filename extension is associated with a RemoteApp program.
- Click a link on a website by using TS Web Access.

Exercise 7.2 shows you the steps to follow to add a RemoteApp program to your Terminal Services server and how to make it accessible from another system.

These exercise assumes you can find a Windows Installer file (*.msi) to use. If this is not possible, you can skip the steps of installing an application and instead make an installed application available as a RemoteApp program. Not all applications will work if they weren't installed when the terminal server was in install mode. However, the Server Manager application will work for this exercise.

EXERCISE 7.2

Installing a RemoteApp Program

1. Launch a command prompt by clicking Start and entering **CMD** in the Search line.

2. On the command line, enter `change user /install`.

   The command should respond with the text "User Session is Ready to Install Applications."

3. Launch an application's Windows Installer file (.msi file). The program you install isn't as important as the process of installing an application from the Windows Installer file. For example, you could download the Windows Automated Installation Kit (WAIK), burn it to a CD, and launch the WAIK installation program by clicking StartCD and then clicking the Windows AIK Setup link.

If you don't have access to an .msi file, you can skip this step and step 4.

4. The Windows Installer program should run. Follow the wizard to complete the installation.

5. Once the installation completes, return to the command line, and enter the following command to return the server to execution mode:

```
change user /execute
```

The command should respond with the text "User Session Is Ready to Execute Applications."

6. Launch Server Manager by clicking Start ➤ Administrative Tools ➤ Server Manager.

7. Open the TS RemoteApp Manager by selecting Server Manager ➤ Roles ➤ Terminal Services ➤ TS RemoteApp Manager.

8. In the Actions pane on the right side, select Add RemoteApp Programs.

9. On the Wizard Welcome page, click Next.

10. On the Choose Programs to Add to the RemoteApp Programs List page, select the program you installed. Your display will look similar to the following graphic. There are many programs that could be selected, but the program you just installed is what you want to select for this exercise. In the graphic, the Windows PE Tools Command Prompt and Windows System Image Manager programs (installed from the Windows Automated Installation Kit) are selected. Click Next.

If you didn't install an application using a Windows Installer file, you can select the Server Manager application from this menu. For any application that isn't installed while the terminal server is in install mode, there is no guarantee it will work in a multiuser environment.

11. On the Review Settings page, review the information, and click Finish.

12. Back in Server Manager, ensure the TS RemoteApp Manager is still selected. Select the application you installed in the RemoteApp Programs pane at the bottom. Right-click your application to reveal the context menu, as shown in the following image.

13. Select Create .rdp File.

14. On the Wizard Welcome page, click Next.

15. On the Specify Package Settings page, review the settings. Notice that the default location is the C:\Program Files\Packaged Programs folder. Click Next.

16. On the Review Settings page, click Finish. Windows Explorer is opened to the folder you specified, and the .rdp file is available there.

17. Return to Server Manager, right-click your application in the RemoteApp Programs pane, and select Create Windows Installer Package.

18. On the Wizard Welcome page, click Next.

19. On the Specify Package Settings page, review the settings. Notice that the default location is the C:\Program Files\Packaged Programs folder. Click Next.

20. Review the information on the Configure Distribution Package page, as shown in the following image. Notice that you can select the shortcut to appear on the desktop or in a folder that you specify. The default folder is Remote Programs, but you could just as easily change the folder to the name of the application, so there is no real indication that it is a remote application. Click Next.

21. On the Review settings page, click Finish. Windows Explorer is opened to the folder you specified, and the Windows Installer file is available there.

At this point, you could deploy the Windows Installer file to users with Group Policy. Or, you could manually copy both the .rdp and .msi files to a system and run them there.

Just to see how it works, you could copy the files to a Windows Vista system and double-click them to install them. If you double-click the Windows Installer file, the application will install a shortcut on your Start menu as specified when you created the application. The first time you launch it, it will take some time to install. After the first time, the program launches quickly.

Similarly, you could double-click the .rdp file on a Windows Vista system. If the program were already installed, the application would launch in its own window. If it weren't already installed, it would install and then launch.

In both instances (running from the Start menu or running from the .rdp file), the application will launch in its own window just as if it is an application installed on the Windows Vista system.

From the user's perspective, it looks almost just like a regular Window in Windows Vista. Almost. The window actually looks more like a Windows Server 2008 window with squared edges rather than a Windows Vista window using Aero and soft edges.

Terminal Services Gateway

TS Gateway is used to allow clients running Remote Desktop Connection to access internal resources via the Internet. The following are the different resources that can be accessed through a TS Gateway:

A terminal server   Users will have access to a full desktop on the terminal server. For example, you may want users to have access to a range of applications accessible via thin clients through the Internet.

TS RemoteApp programs   The application will run on the server but appear in its own window on the client's desktop. For example, you may want users to have access to only a single application instead of a full desktop.

Remote Desktop–enabled servers and clients   Any server or client that has Remote Desktop enabled can be accessible via TS Gateway. Administrators can use this to remotely administer servers. Clients can use this to remotely access their desktops.

For a big picture overview of TS Gateway, take a look at Figure 7.4.

FIGURE 7.4   Using TS Gateway to access Terminal Services resources

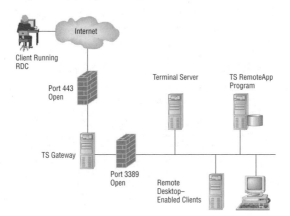

In the figure, you can see that an external client running Remote Desktop Connection is able to access internal resources from the Internet via TS Gateway. Although Terminal Services traditionally uses port 3389 at the firewall, opening port 3389 is often frowned upon by security-conscious firewall administrators.

TS Gateway instead uses the HTTPS port (port 443) that is typically open anyway. TS Gateway uses the Remote Desktop Protocol over Secure Sockets Layer (SSL) for encryption (commonly referred to as RDP over SSL).

Notice that port 443 is open in the external firewall of the DMZ in the figure. This allows RDP over SSL to access the TS Gateway server. The TS Gateway server then decrypts the traffic and uses port 3389 on the internal firewall of the DMZ.

A two-host firewall is commonly referred to as a *demilitarized zone* (DMZ). The Internet is completely insecure, so placing a host directly on the Internet presents many risks. Additionally, the internal network needs to have a high level of security. Some servers (such as servers running IIS) need a certain level of protection but also need to be accessed via the Internet. Placing these servers in the DMZ provides a layer of protection but also allows access via the Internet.

🌐 Real World Scenario

Opening Firewall Ports

Just as a firewall in a car is designed to protect what's inside (the occupants of the car) from what's outside (an engine if it starts on fire), firewalls in networks are designed to protect the internal network from the Internet.

A network firewall protects the internal network by blocking all traffic except for what is specifically allowed in. One of the ways to allow traffic in is to open ports. Each port represents a potential vulnerability, so to reduce vulnerabilities, you reduce the number of open ports to the absolute minimum.

Although remote administration has been available for a long time through port 3389, it was unused in many networks. Asking a firewall administrator to open another port is like asking a bank security manager to put covers over their cameras. You could insist that putting the covers on the cameras "will keep the dust off them so they'll last 10 years longer."

Of course, putting covers on cameras to increase their longevity sounds insane. But that's what the security-conscious firewall admin hears when you ask him to open a port on the firewall. Expect to spend a lot of time and energy justifying the action.

On the other hand, if an application uses a port that's already open, you don't have to ask for any changes. Since port 80 and port 443 are often already open for HTTP and HTTPS, respectively, using these ports for other purposes (such as RDP over SSL) makes sense.

One of the benefits of using TS Gateway is that access can be granted without needing to create a virtual private network (VPN) using a remote access server. A VPN grants access to an entire network, while TS Gateway can be used to provide access to a specific server or a specific application.

In addition to the Terminal Services role, the following role services should also be installed on the server hosting the TS Gateway server:

Web Server (IIS)   The Web Server (IIS) service includes the Web Server services and the Management Tools services. The web server accepts the HTTPS requests from the Internet and allows predefined connections through to internal resources.

Network Policy and Access Services   This service includes the Network Policy Server (NPS) service. The NPS service can be used to inspect clients for specific health issues (such as the existence of up-to-date antivirus tools) before access is granted.

Network Access Protection (NAP) can be used to protect the internal network. For example, you can use NAP to ensure that TS clients have antivirus software installed, or the Windows Firewall is enabled. NAP was covered in more detail in Chapter 4.

RPC over HTTP Proxy   The Remote Procedure Call (RPC) over HTTP Proxy service performs the intermediary role for RPC clients to connect across the Internet to RPC server programs.

Windows Process Activation Service   This includes the Process Model service. The Windows Process Activation Service is used to generalize the IIS process model and eliminate the dependency on HTTP. This allows non-HTTP applications to be hosted on IIS.

The TS Gateway server must be running Windows Server 2008. Clients accessing the network via TS Gateway must be one of the following:

- Windows Vista SP1
- Windows XP SP3
- Windows XP SP2 with RDC 6.0 installed
- Windows Server 2008
- Windows Server 2003 (with SP 1 or SP2) and RDC 6.0

Microsoft has created a video and a "test-drive" experience that show TS Web Access, TS Gateway, and TS RemoteApp applications. If you want to gain a deeper insight into these services, you can access the links from here:

http://www.microsoft.com/heroeshappenhere/testdrive/windows-server-2008/default.mspx

You can configure authorization polices to control who is granted access to your TS Gateway server and then which resources they can access once they are connected. The two types of resource policies available are resource authorization policies (TS RAP) and connection authorization policies (TS CAP).

Both a TS CAP and a TS RAP must be created before users can connect.

Terminal Services Connection Authorization Policy (TS CAP)   The TS CAP is used to specify which users can connect. TS CAP policies use groups to define who can connect, and by specifying a group, you restrict access to only users in this group.

For example, if you want only members of the ITAdmins group to be able to access to the TS Gateway, you can create a TS CAP with the ITAdmins group. When creating a TS Cap, you specify how users will authenticate. Users can authenticate with a username and password or with a smart card.

Terminal Services Resource Authorization Policy (TS RAP)   A TS RAP is used to specify which internal resources a user can access once they connect to a TS Gateway server. By specifying the servers, you are restricting which servers clients can access.

When you create a TS RAP, you specify that users can connect to any computer on the network or that users can connect only to computers within a group. For example, you may want users to connect to only three servers, named TS1, TS2, and TS3. You can create a group named TSServers; add TS1, TS2, and TS2 to the group; and then add the TSServers group to the Terminal Services resource authorization policy.

> The difference between the TS CAP and the TS RAP is that the TS CAP is used to define who can connect (by restricting users) and the TS RAP identifies the servers they can connect with (by restricting servers).

You can also use TS Network Access Protection (TS NAP) to restrict access to a terminal server. Network Access Protection was explained in more detail in Chapter 4, "Monitoring and Maintaining Network Infrastructure Servers, but in short you can use TS NAP to restrict clients based on their health or configuration.

For example, a NAP policy can inspect a client to ensure anti-malware software is installed and up-to-date or the Windows Firewall is enabled. If the client doesn't meet the requirements, a health certificate will not be issued and the client will be prevented from accessing the network.

Terminal Services Session Broker

TS Session Broker is needed only when you are running multiple TS servers. TS Session Broker provides two primary functions:

Load balancing   With load balancing, you can distribute the load between multiple servers in a load-balanced terminal server farm. Once installed and configured, the TS Session Broker will automatically send new sessions to the server with the fewest sessions.

Session state management   Sessions state is information about a user's session when connected to a TS server. If a user disconnects and reconnects, you would want them to be reconnected to the same session on the same server. The TS Session Broker stores the session state information to ensure users connect to the same server.

Each time you log onto a terminal server, you create a session on that system. The session could be a full desktop where you're able to launch several applications, or it could be a single application launched as a TS RemoteApp session. If you get disconnected, the session remains available on the terminal server. Users could get disconnected because of network problems, a computer crash, or any number of other reasons. However, since the session is held on the server with session state information, once users authenticate, they are immediately reconnected to their session. Session state information includes the following:

- Session IDs
- Usernames
- Name of the server where the session is located

You need to install the TS Session Broker service on only one terminal server. Each of the other terminal servers will be configured with the identity of the server running the TS Session Broker service.

Take a look at Figure 7.5 and then follow the steps listed next for an idea of how the TS Session Broker service works when a user connects.

FIGURE 7.5   Connecting with TS Session Broker

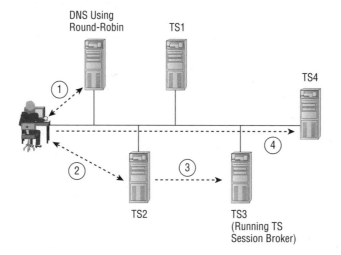

1. In step 1, the user queries DNS for the IP address of a terminal server.
   - Round-robin DNS could be used.
   - With round-robin, DNS gives the IP address of TS1 first. For the next request, DNS gives the IP address of TS2, and so on, until all terminal servers have been included. DNS then starts back on TS1.
2. In step 2, the user authenticates with the terminal server identified by DNS. In the figure, the user has been referred to TS2 by DNS and authenticates with TS2.
3. In step 3, the authenticating terminal server queries the terminal server running TS Session Broker (TS3). The TS Session Broker identifies the TS server that has the fewest connections (TS4 in the figure). The authenticating terminal server redirects the client to TS4.
4. The client connects to TS4 in step 4.

Of course, all of this is transparent to the user. The user starts the session, authenticates, and then connects to the session.

Terminal Services Web Access

TS Web Access is used to provide access to Terminal Services RemoteApp programs via a web browser. Additionally, users can connect to computers where they have Remote Desktop access.

 Although TS Web Access and TS Gateway may sound similar, the difference is in how they connect. Users connect via TS Gateway using Remote Desktop Connection, while users connect via TS Web Access via a web browser.

TS RemoteApp applications can be accessed via TS Web Access on the Internet or via an intranet. A user simply accesses the web page hosting the links for the TS RemoteApp and clicks the link.

Since TS Web Access includes Remote Desktop Web connection, users can use the same web browser to remotely connect to hosts where they have Remote Desktop access.

When designing a TS Web Access solution, you would add a TS Web Access web part to your custom-built web page, or you would add the web page to a Windows SharePoint Services website.

If a user launches several programs using TS Web Access, they will appear as separate programs on their desktop but will all be in a single session on the terminal server.

To run TS Web Access, the following requirements must be met:

- TS Web Access must run on a server running Windows Server 2008.

- Internet Information Services 7.0 must be installed on the same Windows Server 2008 server.

Client computers that access TS Web Access must support Remote Desktop Connection 6.1. RDC 6.1 includes an ActiveX control that is required to launch TS RemoteApp applications. RDC 6.1 is included with the following operating systems:

- Windows XP SP3

- Windows Vista SP1

- Windows Server 2008

Interestingly, the TS Web Access server does not need to be a Terminal Services server. It can be an Internet-facing server to accept connections but have access to an internal terminal server hosting TS RemoteApp programs.

As mentioned earlier in this chapter, you can access a test-drive of the TS Web Access at the following link:

`http://www.microsoft.com/heroeshappenhere/testdrive/windows-server-2008/default.mspx`

Terminal Services Licensing

When using Terminal Services (TS) to allow users to remotely create desktops or run TS RemoteApp applications, you often need a TS Client Access License (TS CAL) for the connection. Creating, tracking, and maintaining these licenses can be quite challenging.

TS Licensing is an additional role service you can add after installing the Terminal Services role for the management of TS licenses. You must have at least one license.

When you first install the Terminal Services role, you are granted a grace period of 120 days on Windows Server 2008 servers. During the grace period, a terminal server can accept connections without licenses. The grace period begins the first time a terminal server accepts a client connection. When a permanent TS Cal is issued by a license server to a client connecting to a terminal server, the grace period ends even if the 120-day grace period hasn't been reached.

If you're using Remote Desktop for administrative purposes, you are allowed two concurrent connections to remotely administer any server. You don't need additional licenses for remote administration.

Two types of TS CALs can be issued. When configuring CAL licensing, you need to configure the terminal servers using the same licensing mode as the TS Licensing server.

TS Per Device CAL   The first time a computer or device connects, it is issued a temporary license by default. If the computer connects again, the license server is checked to determine whether there are any available TS CALs to issue. If so, the computer or device is issued a permanent CAL. Any user can connect to a terminal server using a computer that has been issued a TS Per Device CAL.

Once all the available CALs are issued, computers or devices will be denied access the second time they try to connect.

TS Per User CAL   A TS Per User CAL gives a user the right to access a terminal server on any number of computers or devices. Unlike TS Per Device CALs, TS Per User CALs are not enforced by the Licensing server. Administrators still have a responsibility to track the licenses and ensure adequate licenses are purchased.

You can configure the TS Licensing mode from the Terminal Services Configuration Manager, as shown in Figure 7.6.

FIGURE 7.6   Configuring the licensing mode

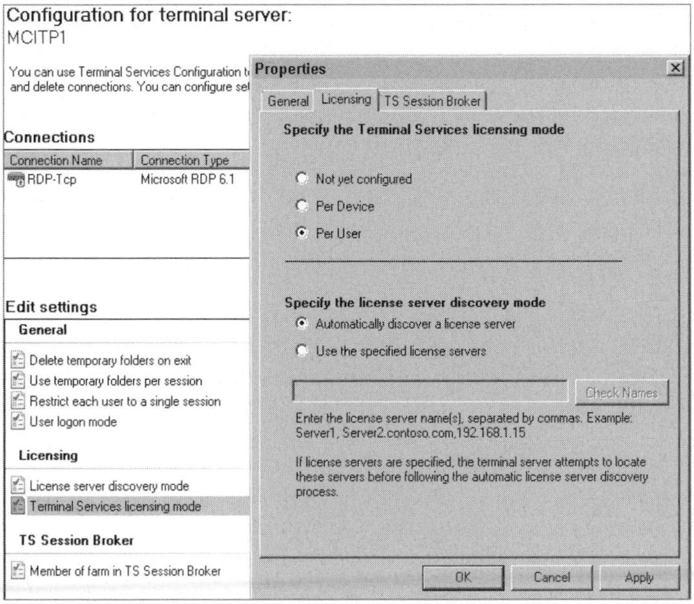

To access the licensing mode page, follow these steps:

1. Launch Terminal Services Configuration Manager by clicking Start ➤ Administrative Tools ➤ Terminal Services ➤ Terminal Services Configuration,

2. In the Edit Settings section, double-click Terminal Services Licensing Mode.

3. On the Licensing tab of the Properties dialog box of the terminal server, you can specify Per Device or Per User as the licensing mode.

Internet Information Services

Internet Information Services 7.0 is included as a role you can add within Windows Server 2008. IIS is used as a web server; in other words, it is used to serve web pages to clients.

A client can be any system (Microsoft or non-Microsoft) running a web browser such as Internet Explorer. A page is requested, IIS creates HTML-formatted pages, and the client receives the HTML page and displays it in the browser.

Earlier in this chapter, I discussed both TS Web Access and TS Gateway. Both of these Terminal Services role services require IIS. Even if you aren't hosting a specific website, you will need to add the Web Server (IIS) role to support these services.

Web Servers on the Internet

The most popular web server on the Internet is Apache. It often runs on Unix (or Unix derivatives such as Linux) but can be run on other platforms, including Windows. One of the big draws to Linux and Apache is that they're free.

In addition to Linux and Apache, web developers often use MySQL as the database and Perl, Python, or PHP as the programming language. This combination is often referred to as LAMP, or the LAMP solution stack. All the components of LAMP are free.

Microsoft has long been trying to increase its marketing share with web servers. One of the things it has done is improve the capabilities and the usefulness of web applications by using ASP.NET and the .NET Framework. Additionally, ASP.NET applications can easily tie into Microsoft's SQL Server.

Over the years, it has become increasingly easy for web developers to create sophisticated applications using these tools. Microsoft has even made it easy for hobbyists to create their own websites using free tools such as Web Developer Express (available as a free download). Since these applications run on IIS and IIS runs on Windows, as the popularity of IIS increases, more and more Windows Servers are being deployed specifically to host IIS both on the Internet and within intranets.

IIS and ASP.NET

IIS 7.0 uses Active Server Pages .NET (ASP.NET) to create web applications. One of the benefits of ASP.NET is that web pages can be quite dynamic through the creation of web applications. As an administrator, you won't be expected to build web applications, but you do need a little background information.

In the past, websites were created within individual, static Hypertext Markup Language (HTML) pages. Today, static HTML pages just aren't enough to draw an audience to a site and keep them there. Instead, sites must be much more dynamic and sophisticated.

ASP.NET gives web developers access to Microsoft's .NET Framework, which allows them to create sophisticated pages quite quickly. Additionally, the pages within a site aren't created as separate entities but rather as part of an integrated web application.

Take a look at Figure 7.7. A user could click a link that sends an HTTP (or HTTPS) request. The IIS server receives the request, processes it, and then returns an HTML-formatted page.

FIGURE 7.7   IIS 7.0 and an ASP.NET web application

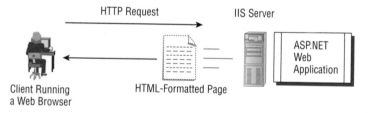

Once the server sends the HTML page to the client, the page is destroyed. However, the client's session data is maintained on the server, allowing information about the user to be maintained and presented in each page.

For example, if you purchase something on the Internet, you enter your contact information on one page, credit card information on another page, and so on. Information from one page is maintained as session data on the server so you don't have to repeatedly enter this information on each page.

You can tell whether the web server serving your web pages is using an ASP.NET application by the extension of the request. IIS 7.0 web applications use the .aspx extension. For example, if you go to the IIS home page, you'll see this address:

```
http://www.iis.net/default.aspx?tabid=1
```

To support ASP.NET applications, you also need to select the Application Development role services when installing IIS. This will include the Windows Process Activation Service and the .NET environment.

IIS and the Windows Process Activation Service

IIS 7.0 requires the installation of the Windows Process Activation Service (WAS). The primary purpose of WAS is to manage application pool configuration and the creation and lifetime of worker processes.

> It looks like a typo seeing Windows Process Activation Service abbreviated as WAS. A logical question is "Where'd the P go?" WAS is accurate. The Windows *Process* Activation Service is different from Microsoft's Windows *Product* Activation service, which is used to deter privacy and abbreviating it this way helps to differentiate the two.

In other words, when an ASP.NET application begins on an IIS server, WAS manages the resources used within the application (such as memory and variables). When a user's session begins, WAS manages the resources used within the session.

WAS also removes IIS's dependency on the Hypertext Transfer Protocol (HTTP) as the only method of communication. This allows the IIS server to support Windows Communication Foundation (WCF) services using non-HTTP protocols.

You should use WAS only if you are supporting a .NET Framework 3.0 (or greater) application or running IIS 7.0. When adding the IIS 7.0 role, you will be prompted to install WAS since it's required.

IIS and WSRM

You can use the Windows System Resource Manager to ensure that resources are allocated equally among processes and users. (I covered WSRM in more depth in Chapter 3. I mention it here only as it relates to IIS 7.0.)

You can use WSRM on a server running IIS to manage processor and memory resources. Specifically, you can configure policies to allocate resources on a per-process, per-user, or per-IIS-application-pool basis.

One of the features available with WSRM is to create calendar rules so that different policies can be applied automatically at different times. This can be valuable on an IIS server when managing peak and nonpeak times.

If you're running a Windows Server 2008 server with only the IIS role, you typically wouldn't need WSRM. However, if you're running another server application (such as SQL Server), you can use WSRM to ensure neither one of the applications tries to hog all the resources.

URL Authorization Rules

A new feature available with IIS 7.0 is the ability to grant or deny access to specific websites, applications, directories, or files on your server. You can do this with ULR authorization rules.

In the past, authorization was done only on individual files and folders using the underling access control lists (NTFS permissions). By using an authorization rule, you can now control access based on the URL. As an example, you could be hosting an intranet server that has content available for all users and that has other content that you want to restrict to only web developers. You can create URL authorization rules to restrict the access.

The URL Authorization service is not installed by default when IIS is installed. You'll need to add the URL Authorization service, and the feature will appear within the IIS Manager console.

Installing IIS

You can install IIS as a role within Windows Server 2008. Exercise 7.3 shows you the steps to follow to add the IIS role to your server. It's not recommended to install IIS on a domain controller in a production environment, but this is acceptable for a practice environment.

EXERCISE 7.3

Installing the IIS Role

1. Launch Server Manager by clicking Start ➤ Administrative Tools ➤ Server Manager.

2. Right-click Roles in the menu, and select Add Roles.

3. On the Before You Begin page, review the information, and click Next.

4. On the Select Server Roles page, click the Web Server (IIS) check box, and click Next.

5. The Add Roles Wizard will display a dialog box indicating additional features are required. This will look similar to the following graphic. Click the Add Required Features button.

6. On the Select Server Roles page, click Next.

7. On the Web Server (IIS) page, review the information, and click Next.

8. On the Select Roles Services page, select the Application Development check box.

9. In the Add Roles Wizard dialog box, you'll be prompted to include the Windows Process Activation Service (including the .NET environment). Click the Add Required Features button. Your display will look similar to the following graphic. Click Next.

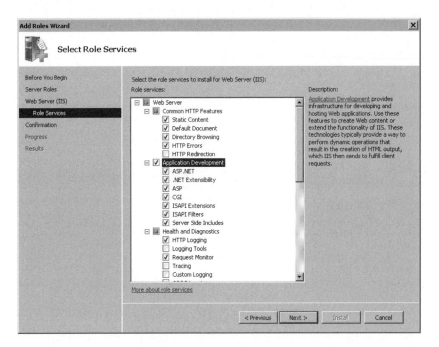

10. On the Confirm Installation Selections page, review your choices, and click Install.

11. When the installation completes, click Close.

Ports Used by IIS

IIS uses well-known ports identified by the Internet Assigned Numbers Authority (IANA). The first 1,024 ports (ports 0 through 1023) are known as *well-known* ports.

Within the TCP/IP protocol suite, the IP protocol uses IP addresses to get packets to the computer. Once a packet makes it to the computer, the port is used to identify which service to pass the packet to for processing. Both TCP and UDP ports can be used, but IIS uses only TCP ports. The two well-known ports used by IIS are as follows:

- Port 80 is used for HTTP requests. Data is transmitted in an unencrypted format.

- Port 443 is used for HTTPS requests. Data is encrypted using Secure Sockets Layer (SSL) and transmitted in an encrypted format.

Summary

In this chapter, you learned the different Terminal Services (TS) capabilities associated with the Terminal Services role. You had an opportunity to install the Terminal Services role and install a RemoteApp program on the server.

You learned how you can use TS Web Access to provide access to internal RemoteApp applications via the Internet and how you can use TS Gateway to provide access to internal resources via the Internet.

You can use Session Broker in a TS farm to balance the load across several terminal servers and also ensure that users always return to the same session if they become disconnected.

When using Terminal Services, TS Client Access Licenses (TS CALs) are needed. You learned about the requirements and how Terminal Services Licensing is used to track your licenses.

Last, you learned about Information Services 7.0 (IIS 7.0) and the different features and services available with it.

Exam Essentials

Understand the purposes of Terminal Services.   You should understand that Terminal Services can be used to allow users to run full desktop sessions or single applications. Terminal Services includes several underlying services that provide specific features.

Understand TS RemoteApp.   You should know that a TS RemoteApp is an application that can be run remotely from a terminal server, but it appears as another application on the end user's desktop. Recognize that TS RemoteApp can allow incompatible applications to appear to run side by side. One version of an application can be run on the local system and another incompatible version can be run on the terminal server, yet both appear to be running on the local system.

Know the purpose of TS Gateway.   You should know that TS Gateway is used to provide access to internal resources via the Internet. It makes use of Terminal Services and requires IIS. Since it uses ports 80 and 443 (which are often opened anyway), it minimizes the need to open additional ports. You should also know that a TS CAP is used to specify which users can connect, and a TS RAP is used to restrict the servers to which the authorized users can connect.

Know the purpose of TS Web Access.   You should know that TS Web Access is used to provide access to TS RemoteApp applications via the Internet. It uses Terminal Services and requires IIS.

Know the purpose of TS Session Broker.   You should know that TS Session Broker is used for load balancing among several terminal servers and also allows disconnected users to reconnect with the same session.

Understand TS CALs and TS Licensing.   You should know that TS CALs are required for terminal server connections when used for nonadministrative purposes and that a 120-day grace period is allowed after a Terminal Services role is added. Terminal Services Licensing is a role service added to create, track, and maintain TS CALs.

Know what IIS is and what ports it uses.   You should know that Internet Information Services 7.0 (IIS 7.0) is a web server that is used to host applications and also supports TS Web Access and TS Gateway. The two well-known ports used by IIS are port 80 and port 443. You should also be aware that specific content can be restricted by using URL authorization rules.

Review Questions

1. Which of the following is a valid reason to create a terminal server running Terminal Services?

   A. To prevent users from launching applications on their desktop

   B. To ensure users are using RDC 6.0

   C. To allow users to run different versions of an application

   D. To give users access to other users' desktops for remote control

2. Sally is running Outlook 2003. Because of an add-in that she's using, she does not want to upgrade to Outlook 2007 since the add-in is not compatible. What can be done?

   A. Install Outlook 2007 on a terminal server, and grant Sally access to the terminal server to run Outlook 2007.

   B. Install Outlook 2007 on a separate system, and have Sally use both systems.

   C. Uninstall Outlook 2003. Install Outlook 2007; then reinstall Outlook 2003 so that both can run together.

   D. Install Outlook 2007 to run side by side with Outlook 2003.

3. A new company policy is being considered to allow administrators in your company to work from home one day a week. The management of your company objects to this because administrators won't be able to administer the servers from home if a problem occurs. Company policy states that port 3389 is not to be opened, and VPNs are not authorized. What could you recommend?

   A. Use a third-party tool to remotely administer the servers.

   B. Place the servers on the Internet to make them accessible.

   C. Use a WSS server to provide access to the servers.

   D. Use a Terminal Services server to provide access to the servers.

4. You are using a Terminal Services (TS) server to allow users to run TS RemoteApp applications from their desktop. In-house developers have created a line-of-business application named SalesTracking. You install SalesTracking on the terminal server and add it as a RemoteApp application. However, whenever two or more users connect, they experience intermittent errors. What should you do? Choose two.

   A. Uninstall the application; then reinstall it using the Control Panel link to install an application on a terminal server.

   B. Uninstall the application; then reinstall it using the Change User command before and after the installation.

   C. Have the developers rewrite the application in multiuser mode.

   D. Right-click the application in the TS RemoteApp Manager, and select the Allow Multi-User setting.

5. You manage a Terminal Services server. Users typically access it to launch a desktop on the server and run applications within the server. You want to enable a specific application to run within a window on the user's desktop. What should you use?

   A. TS Gateway

   B. TS RemoteApp

   C. TS Session Broker

   D. TS with WSRM

6. You have configured a Terminal Services server to run a TS RemoteApp using the default settings. You then deploy the application via Group Policy. How can a user launch the TS RemoteApp program?

   A. By accessing the Remote Programs menu available from the Start menu

   B. By double-clicking an `.rdp` file from their desktop

   C. By launching RDC and selecting Start the Following Program on Connection on the Programs tab

   D. By launching RDC and launching the program within the Terminal Services session

7. You are managing a Terminal Services (TS) server. Several users complain that their TS sessions slow down significantly about midmorning almost every day. After investigating, you discover that another user is running a resource-intensive report that is slowing everything down. What can you do?

   A. Have the user schedule his report to run at night.

   B. Use FSRM to equally allocate resources.

   C. Use WDS to equally allocate resources.

   D. Use WSRM to equally allocate resources.

8. You manage a Terminal Services server that is used by more than 100 clients. After doing some performance testing, you realize that the server needs to be beefed up. You have ordered a new server and plan on migrating the clients to the new server once it arrives. In the interim, you want to want to ensure each user has an equal amount of resources. What should you do?

   A. Select the equal_per_user allocation policy in WSRM.

   B. Select the equal_per_session allocation policy in WSRM.

   C. Select the equal_per_user allocation policy in FSRM.

   D. Select the equal_per_session allocation policy in FSRM.

9. You want administrators to be able to remotely administer internal servers via the Internet. You also want to ensure that only administrators can connect. What should you use?

   A. TS Gateway with TS CAP

   B. TS Gateway with TS RAP

   C. TS RemoteApp

   D. TS with WSRM

10. You want to enable users to remotely access TS RemoteApp programs over the Internet using TS Gateway. Which operating systems would support this functionality? (Choose all that apply.)

   A. Windows XP SP1

   B. Windows Vista SP1

   C. Windows Server 2003 SP1

   D. Windows Server 2008

11. You manage a Terminal Services server farm that includes five terminal servers. You need to ensure that if a user's session is disconnected before they log off, they are able to reconnect to the same session. What should you ensure is included in the server farm?

   A. TS Gateway

   B. TS RemoteApp

   C. TS Session Broker

   D. TS with WSRM

12. You manage a Terminal Services server farm that includes five terminal servers. You've found that one terminal server is extremely busy with the most sessions. What should you add to the server farm to provide load balancing?

   A. TS Load Balancing

   B. TS RemoteApp

   C. TS Session Broker

   D. TS with WSRM

13. Developers have created a TS RemoteApp application that your company wants to make available to sales people on the road. What should you configure within your network to support this?

   A. TS Web Access

   B. TS Gateway

   C. IIS 7.0

   D. WSRM

14. You are managing a Windows Server 2008 server named SRV1 that is running both SQL Server and IIS 7.0. You've found that during SQL Server peak times, IIS is frequently slow. What can you use to ensure resources are divided equally between IIS and SQL?

   A. FSRM

   B. WSRM

   C. TS Gateway

   D. TS Web Access

15. You started testing Terminal Services in your network about four months ago. It has been working very well, and several pilot users have been reporting positive results. Today, all the users report that Terminal Services is no longer working. You verify the server is still running. What's the likely problem?

    A. The TS RemoteApp grace period has expired.

    B. The TS Licensing grace period has expired.

    C. The IIS grace period has expired.

    D. The Terminal Services grace period has expired.

16. Internal developers want to host an ASP.NET application within the intranet. They ask you to enable a server role to support the application. What server role should you enable?

    A. TS

    B. WSRM

    C. FSRM

    D. IIS

17. What's the primary difference between TS Web Access and TS Gateway?

    A. TS Web Access uses IIS 7.0, but TS Gateway does not.

    B. TS Gateway Web Access uses IIS 7.0, but TS Web Access does not.

    C. TS Web Access provides access to TS RemoteApp applications, while TS Gateway provides access to internal resources.

    D. TS Gateway provides access to TS RemoteApp applications, while TS Web Access provides access to internal resources.

18. Choose the correct statements concerning TS Gateway and TS Web Access. (Choose all that apply.)

    A. TS Web Access uses the Remote Desktop Connection tool.

    B. TS Gateway uses the Remote Desktop Connection tool.

    C. TS Web Access uses a web browser.

    D. TS Gateway uses a web browser.

19. You are implementing a solution using TS Gateway. What port needs to be open on the firewall to support TS Gateway?

    A. 80

    B. 389

    C. 443

    D. 3389

20. You want administrators to be able to remotely administer internal servers via the Internet. You need to minimize the number of open ports on the company's firewall server, and you also want to ensure the administrator's client system has the Windows Firewall enabled. What should you use?

A. TS Gateway with TS CAP

B. TS Gateway with TS RAP

C. TS Gateway with TS NAP

D. TS RemoteApp

Answers to Review Questions

1. C.   One of the reasons to create a Terminal Services (TS) server is to allow users to run different versions of applications that can't be installed on the same system. For example, Outlook 2003 and Outlook 2007 aren't compatible on the same system but could be run by the same users if one is in a TS session and one is on the local system. TS wouldn't prevent users from launching applications on their desktop. Remote Desktop Connection 6.0 is the newer version of the application used to connect to TS sessions but isn't a reason to create a terminal server. A TS server is not required to allow either Remote Desktop Connection or Remote Assistance when used for administrative purposes such as remote control.

2. A.   Outlook 2003 and Outlook 2007 aren't compatible on the same system. However, if one application is run in a Terminal Services session and the other application is run on the client's computer, both applications can run. It's not necessary to create two separate client systems. Uninstalling and reinstalling the different versions of Outlook won't make them compatible because they will not work side by side on the same computer.

3. D.   Terminal Services can be used to provide remote access. Using Terminal Services (TS) Gateway, administrators can be granted access to internal servers via the Internet. TS Gateway uses IIS to accept RDP over SSL connections (using port 443) and translates them into Terminal Services connections. Although a third-party tool may be available, don't expect this to be a valid answer on a Microsoft exam. Placing the servers on the Internet would make them susceptible to unacceptable risks. Windows SharePoint Services (WSS) is used for file management and sharing. WSS doesn't have a method available for remote administration.

4. A, B.   To ensure applications work in multiuser mode, you must change the terminal server to installation mode before installing it and then change it back to execution mode after installing it. You can do this automatically via the Control Panel link called Install an Application on Terminal Server. You can do this with the `Change User /Install` and `Change User /Execute` commands. Applications don't need to be developed in a special multiuser mode, and there is no such setting in TS RemoteApp Manager as Allow Multi-User.

5. B.   Terminal Services (TS) RemoteApp applications can be deployed to users' computers and, once launched, will open in a window on the user's desktop just as if they were any other application on their computer. The fact that a RemoteApp application is running remotely on a server is transparent to the user. TS Gateway is used to allow users to remotely access internal terminal services resources from the Internet. TS Session Broker is used to manage sessions between multiple terminal servers. Windows Server Resource Manager (WSRM) is used to distribute resources equally between users or sessions.

6. A.   Terminal Services (TS) RemoteApp applications can be deployed to users' computers using either `.rdp` files or Windows Installer files. Group Policy can be used to deploy the Windows Installer file. Once installed, the application is accessible via the Start menu or the desktop. The default Start menu folder is Remote Programs, but this can be modified. It would be much harder to deploy an `.rdp` file to a user's desktop (though it could be done with a scripting file to copy the `.rdp` file to each user's desktop). Remote Desktop Connection (RDC) wouldn't be launched separately to access a TS RemoteApp program.

7. D.   The Windows Server Resource Manager (WSRM) can be used to equally allocate resources and prevent any single user or user session from slowing down all other sessions. It's not necessary to have the user change how they are running their reports. The File Server Resource Manager (FSRM) allows you to implement and manage quotas on drives, but not memory and CPU usage. Windows Deployment Services (WDS) is used to automate deployments.

8. A.   If you use the Windows System Resource Manager (WSRM) equal_per_user resource allocation policy, each user will be granted the same amount of resources (CPU and memory). If you use the equal_per_session, then each session will have the same amount of resources, but the question stated that you want to ensure each *user* has the same amount of resources. The File System Resource Manager (FSRM) can be used to set file quotas on a folder or drive, but it cannot allocate system resources.

9. A.   Terminals Services (TS) Gateway will allow users to access internal resources via the Internet. A Terminal Services connection authorization policy (TS CAP) is used to restrict access to specific users. TS Gateway uses IIS to accept RDP over SSL connections and translates them into Terminal Services connections. A TS resource authorization policy (TS RAP) is used to restrict access to specific servers, not the users. TS RemoteApp would run only a single program, but you'd need to run more than one program to administer a server. Windows Server Resource Manager (WSRM) is used to allocate CPU and memory resources equally.

10. B, D.   From the options, only Windows Vista SP1 Windows Server 2008 will support the use of TS RemoteApp. Windows Server 2003 with SP1 will need RDC 6.0 installed. RDC 6.0 is installed by default in Windows Vista and Windows Server 2008. Windows XP SP2 will support TS Gateway if RDC 6.0 is installed.

11. C.   Terminal Services (TS) Session Broker is a service that provides session state management (and load balancing). If a user disconnects from a session before logging off, they can log back on to reconnect to the same session. In a TS server farm, the TS Session Broker ensures the user connects to the same server. Terminal Services (TS) Gateway will allow users to access internal resources via the Internet. TS RemoteApp allows users to run a single program via a terminal server. Windows Server Resource Manager (WSRM) is used to equally allocate CPU and memory resources.

12. C.   TS Session Broker provides load balancing (and session state management). Each new session is directed to the terminal server with the fewest connections. There isn't a service known as TS Load Balancing. TS RemoteApp allows users to run a single program via a terminal server. Windows Server Resource Manager (WSRM) is used to equally allocate CPU and memory resources.

13. A.   Terminal Services (TS) Web Access is used to provide TS RemoteApp applications to users via a web browser. TS Gateway is used to provide access to internal resources via the Internet. IIS is a web server, and WSRM is used to ensure resources are equally distributed.

14. B.   Windows System Resource Manager (WSRM) can be used to allocate CPU and memory resources equally between two different applications on the same server. The File Server Resource Manager (FSRM) allows you to implement and manage quotas on drives, but not memory and CPU usage. Terminals Services (TS) Gateway will allow users to access internal resources via the Internet. TS Web Access is used to provide access to a TS RemoteApp program.

15. B.   When you first install Terminal Services (TS), you are granted a grace period of 120 days. During this time, the terminal server will accept connections without licenses. After the grace period is over, the terminal server will not accept connections without licenses. There is no grace period for TS RemoteApp, IIS, or Terminal Services.

16. D.   Internet Information Services (IIS) is a web server and will host ASP.NET applications. Terminal Services is used to provide remote access. Windows System Resource Manager (WSRM) is used to ensure resources are allocated equally. The File Server Resource Manager (FSRM) allows you to implement and manage quotas on drives.

17. C.   TS Web Access provides access to TS RemoteApp applications. TS Gateway provides access to internal resources. Both require the use of IIS 7.0.

18. B, C.   Terminal Services (TS) Gateway allows a user running Remote Desktop Connection (RDC) to access internal resources via port 443. A web browser cannot be used for TS Gateway. TS Web Access is used to provide access to TS RemoteApp programs via a web browser. TS Web Access includes Remote Desktop Web connection, but users cannot use Remote Desktop Connection alone to connect to a TS Web Access session.

19. C.   Terminal Services (TS) Gateway uses port 443 to traverse the firewall using the Remote Desktop Protocol (RDP) over Secure Sockets Layer (SSL) for encryption. Port 80 is commonly used for HTTP. Port 389 is used for LDAP and port 3389 is used for remote administration.

20. C.   Terminals Services (TS) Gateway will allow users to access internal resources via the Internet and since it uses port 443 (commonly used for HTTPS) it minimizes the number of ports needed to be opened on the firewall. TS Gateway can be used with TS Network Access Protection (NAP) to inspect the clients and only allow access if they are healthy. Health is determined by a NAP policy created by an administrator and could be configured to ensure the client's firewall is enabled. A Terminal Services connection authorization policy (TS CAP) is used to restrict access to specific users. A TS resource authorization policy (TS RAP) is used to restrict access to specific servers. TS RemoteApp would run only a single program, but you'd need to run more than one program to administer a server.

Chapter
8

Planning Windows Server 2008 Security

MICROSOFT EXAM OBJECTIVES COVERED IN THIS CHAPTER:

✓ **Planning for Server Deployment**

- Plan Server Installations and Upgrades. May include but is not limited to: Windows Server 2008 edition selection, roll-back planning, BitLocker implementation requirements.

✓ **Monitoring and Maintaining Servers**

- Monitor and Maintain Security and Policies. May include but is not limited to: remote access, monitor and maintain NPAS, network access, server security, firewall rules and policies, authentication and authorization, data security, auditing.

You can't manage any network today without thinking about security. Security needs to be implemented at each layer of your network, and if you wait until the network is fully implemented before thinking about security, you're too late. This chapter starts with a micro view of security, covering what you can do at the disk level. You can implement NTFS permissions to control data access as was presented in Chapter 6, "Monitoring and Maintaining Print and File Servers." Taking disk security up a notch, you can use BitLocker Drive Encryption and/or NTFS's Encrypting File System (EFS) to provide an extra layer of data protection.

At the server level, you can use auditing to monitor activities. Finally, you'll learn about some security issues to be aware of at the network level, including firewalls, remote access methods, and encryption techniques used to protect data as it is transferred between computers.

You'll notice in the list of objectives that Windows Server 2008 edition selection and rollback planning are listed. Windows Server 2008 edition selection is actually discussed in Chapter 1, "Introducing Windows Server 2008," and rollback planning was covered in Chapter 2, "Planning Server Deployments. Additionally, Chapter 4, "Monitoring and Maintaining Network Infrastructure Servers," provided complementary information for Network Protection and Access Services (NPAS) related to authentication and authorization.

Disk-Level Security with BitLocker

You can protect your data on your disks by using New Technology File System (NTFS) and/or BitLocker Drive Encryption. NTFS permissions were covered in Chapter 6, but for some systems, you may want better protection.

BitLocker Drive Encryption (BitLocker for short) is relatively new. It is available in Windows Vista (Ultimate and Enterprise editions) and Windows Server 2008. (If you learned about BitLocker in Windows Vista, you'll be happy to know that the same knowledge applies to all editions of Windows Server 2008.)

The primary purpose of BitLocker is to prevent the loss of data on a hard drive in case the entire computer is lost or stolen. Admittedly, it's not as common to lose a server as it is to lose a laptop, but servers can be stolen. The greatest risk is with servers deployed to remote offices without adequate physical security.

If your server is stolen but is protected with BitLocker, it's unlikely that the thief will gain access to the protected data. A hacker will typically have to make changes to the system to gain access.

When changes are detected on your system, such as disk errors, changes to the BIOS, or changes to startup files, your system becomes locked, and data within the hard drive is no longer accessible. Instead, the system enters the BitLocker Recovery Console. You must either provide a complex recovery password or have access to a recovery key on a USB flash drive to unlock the system from the BitLocker Recovery Console.

BitLocker Requirements

To enable BitLocker, you'll need to meet one of the following two requirements:

Trusted Platform Module 1.2   The Trusted Platform Module (TPM) is a special microchip built into your computer. TPM 1.2 and newer support storing the BitLocker key within the TPM. The BitLocker key is used to unlock the system. When the computer starts, the system is inspected for any suspicious changes. If changes aren't noticed, the BitLocker key within the TPM is used to unlock the system.

Support for USB flash drive on computer startup   For systems that don't have TPM 1.2 built in, you can use a removable USB flash drive. The computer startup works the same way. If BitLocker detects any suspicious changes, the system will remain locked. Otherwise, Bit-Locker will retrieve the BitLocker startup key from the USB flash drive and unlock the drive.

In addition to having either TPM or USB support on startup, your hard drives have to meet some specific requirements:

Must have at least two partitions   One partition will contain the Windows operating system (the Windows folder). This partition will be encrypted. The other partition will be unencrypted and is used to start the computer.

BitLocker partition must be the active partition   The second partition (the one that does not hold the Windows folder) must be marked as active. When the system boots, it will boot to this partition, and after the system is verified to be safe (not modified), the first partition will be unlocked.

BitLocker partition must be at least 1.5GB   The Windows Recovery Environment (WinRE) is installed on this partition. You can also add recovery applications on this partition if desired.

Must be formatted with NTFS   Both partitions must be formatted with NTFS.

Must have compatible BIOS   The BIOS must be compatible with TPM and must support USB devices during computer startup. If your BIOS does not meet these requirements, you can probably download an update and flash your BIOS.

Adding the BitLocker Feature

BitLocker Drive Encryption is not available by default. You must first add the BitLocker Drive Encryption feature using Server Manager. Exercise 8.1 shows the steps to add the BitLocker feature to your server.

EXERCISE 8.1

Adding the BitLocker Feature

1. Launch Server Manager by clicking Start ➢ Administrative Tools ➢ Server Manager.

2. In the left pane, select Features. In the main pane, click the Add Features link.

3. On the Select Features page, select the BitLocker Drive Encryption check box. Click Next.

4. On the Confirm Installation Selections page, click Install.

5. On the Installation Results page, review the information, and click Close. You will need to restart the system to complete the installation of the BitLocker feature.

6. After rebooting, the BitLocker installation will complete. Click Close on the Installation Results page.

Once the BitLocker feature is installed, the BitLocker menu selection will be available via Control Panel. Figure 8.1 shows how you can access the BitLocker menu once the feature is installed. You can access this by selecting Control Panel ➢ Security and then clicking BitLocker Drive Encryption. If Control Panel is set to classic view, you can launch the BitLocker Drive Encryption applet directly from Control Panel. More than likely, you won't be able to enable BitLocker yet, though.

Figure 8.2 shows a system that has the BitLocker feature installed but does not have the partitions configured properly or the TPM hardware. In the following sections, you'll solve both of these problems.

FIGURE 8.1   Security menu showing BitLocker Drive Encryption

FIGURE 8.2　BitLocker menu

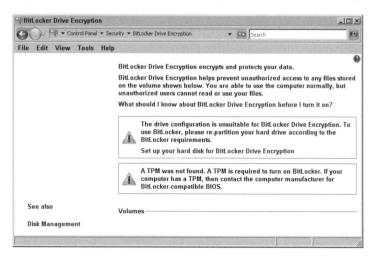

Configuring the Partitions

If you want to enable BitLocker, you'll need to configure the partitions (or volumes). You can use Disk Management to do this, as detailed in Exercise 8.2.

Volumes and Partitions

Since the release of Windows Vista, the terms *volumes* and *partitions* have become almost synonymous. The only exception is with dynamic disks.

As you work with tools and wizards, you may notice that sometimes the details indicate you're working on a partition, and other times (even within the same tool) the details indicate you're working on a volume. When you're working with basic disks, the terms *partition* and *volume* are completely interchangeable.

Any drive letter (such as C:\, D:\, and so on) could be one of the following:

- A complete disk (that has only one partition or volume).

- Part of a partitioned disk. Basic disks can be divided into four partitions. Any primary partition is represented by a single drive letter. This single drive letter could be called a *partition* or a *volume*.

- Part of a set of physical disks. This occurs only with dynamic disks. For example, your C:\ drive could be protected with a RAID-1 (mirror). C:\ would be referred to only as a *volume* and would include two physical disks.

EXERCISE 8.2

Configuring Partitions for BitLocker

1. Launch Server Manager by clicking Start ➢ Administrative Tools ➢ Computer Management.

2. Select Disk Management in the Storage section.

3. If you have only one partition on your system, right-click the existing partition, and select Shrink Volume.

4. In the Shrink dialog box, enter **2000** in the Enter the Amount of Space to Shrink in MB text box. Your display will look similar to the following graphic. Remember, the BitLocker partition must be at least 1.5GB in size. Click Shrink.

Shrink C:	☒
Total size before shrink in MB:	152625
Size of available shrink space in MB:	122546
Enter the amount of space to shrink in MB:	2000
Total size after shrink in MB:	150625

Size of available shrink space can be restricted if snapshots or pagefiles are enabled on the volume.

[Shrink]   [Cancel]

5. After the shrink operation completes, you will have your original partition and unallocated space about 2GB in size.

6. Right-click the unallocated space, and select New Simple Volume.

7. On the Welcome to the Wizard page, click Next.

8. On the new Simple Volume Wizard page, accept the size of 2000, and click Next.

9. On the Assign Drive Letter or Path page, accept the default, and click Next.

10. On the Format Partition page, ensure that File System is set as NTFS. Change the volume label to BitLocker. Click the Perform a Quick Format and Enable File and Folder Compression check boxes. Your display will look similar to the following graphic.

New Simple Volume Wizard [x]

Format Partition
To store data on this partition, you must format it first.

Choose whether you want to format this volume, and if so, what settings you want to use.

○ Do not format this volume

● Format this volume with the following settings:

File system:	NTFS ▼
Allocation unit size:	Default ▼
Volume label:	Bitlocker

☑ Perform a quick format
☑ Enable file and folder compression

[< Back] [Next >]   [Cancel]

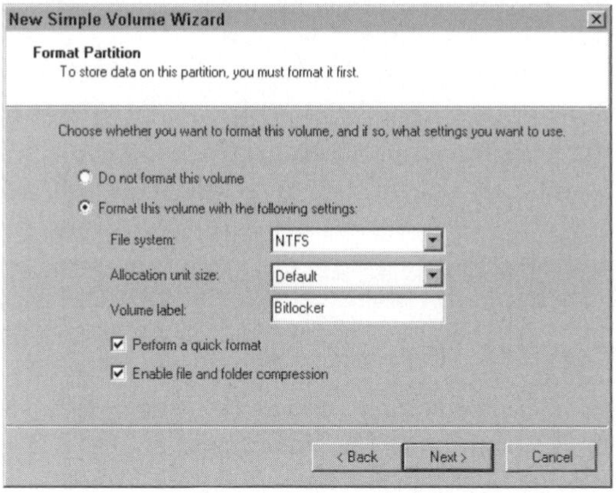

Remember that BitLocker requires the partitions to be NTFS. A quick format will allow the system to format the disk partition without performing complete checks on each sector of the disk. If doing this on a production server, you should leave the Perform a Quick Format box unchecked. Click Next.

11. On the Completing the New Simple Volume Wizard page, click Finish.

Once you have created your BitLocker partition, you'll need to mark it as Active. Figure 8.3 shows how to mark the partition as active. Be careful with this, though. You want to mark the partition as active only when you're ready to actually add the BitLocker feature.

FIGURE 8.3   Marking a partition as active

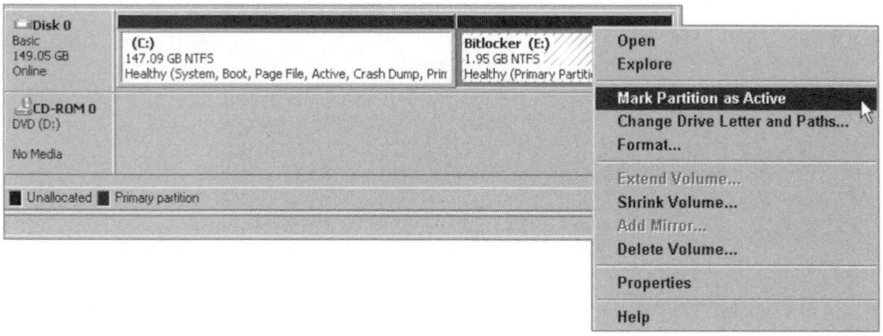

Disk 0		
Basic 149.05 GB Online	**(C:)** 147.09 GB NTFS Healthy (System, Boot, Page File, Active, Crash Dump, Prin	**Bitlocker (E:)** 1.95 GB NTFS Healthy (Primary Partiti

CD-ROM 0
DVD (D:)

No Media

■ Unallocated ■ Primary partition

Open
Explore
Mark Partition as Active
Change Drive Letter and Paths...
Format...
Extend Volume...
Shrink Volume...
Add Mirror...
Delete Volume...
Properties
Help

WARNING   If you mark the partition as active before you're ready to add the BitLocker feature, you could render your system inoperable. The system will try to boot to the active partition, but if the active partition doesn't have an operating system, nothing will happen.

Enabling BitLocker on Non-TPM Systems

If your system doesn't have TPM 1.2, you can enable your system to use a USB flash drive instead. This involves modifying Group Policy.

Exercise 8.3 shows the steps involved in creating a Group Policy object (GPO) to enable BitLocker for non-TPM. After creating the GPO, you need to link it to a site, domain, or OU where you want it applied. You can also modify local computer Group Policy to do the same thing for a single computer.

EXERCISE 8.3

Enabling BitLocker on Non-TPM Systems

1. Launch the Group Policy Management Console (GPMC) Manager by clicking Start ➤ Administrative Tools ➤ Group Policy Management.

2. Select the Group Policy Objects container. Right-click it, and select New.

3. In the New GPO dialog box, enter **Enable BitLocker** as the name. Click OK.

4. Right-click the Enable BitLocker GPO, and click Edit.

5. Browse to the Computer Configuration ➤ Policies ➤ Administrative Templates ➤ Windows Components ➤ BitLocker Drive Encryption container.

6. In the right pane, double-click Control Panel Setup: Enable Advanced Startup Options. Your display will look similar to the following graphic.

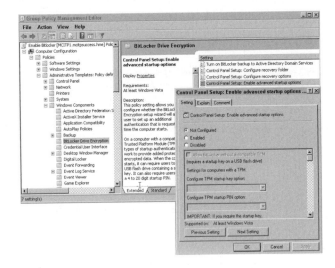

7. Select the Enabled radio button. When you do, the Allow BitLocker Without a Compatible TPM check box will be selected. Click OK.

Since this GPO is not linked anywhere, it won't be applied. If you link it (for example, if you link it to an OU), then the computers within that OU can enable BitLocker using a startup key on a USB flash drive instead of the TPM hardware.

Starting a System with BitLocker

When a system has BitLocker Drive Encryption fully enabled, the drive must be unlocked before the system starts. There are two possibilities for this process:

With TPM 1.2   If the system has TPM 1.2, the process is automatic. TPM checks the integrity of boot components and the boot configuration data on the system. If the boot components appear unaltered and the encrypted disk is in the original computer, TPM unlocks the disk.

Without TPM1.2 (using a USB flash drive)   If BitLocker has been enabled on a system without TPM, then the encrypted drive will remain locked until the volume master key is read from the USB flash drive. You don't have the benefit of system integrity verification process if you don't have TPM. If the USB flash drive holding the volume master key is available, the system can be booted.

Multifactor Authentication with BitLocker

BitLocker Drive Encryption supports multifactor authentication on systems that include support for TPM 1.2. You can't use multifactor authentication on systems that start with a USB flash drive instead of TPM.

Multifactor authentication can be enabled with a personal identification number (PIN) or with a USB flash drive. Once enabled, the system requires either the PIN to be entered or the USB flash drive to be inserted whenever the system starts or resumes from hibernation.

Multifactor authentication with a PIN   After TPM has completed the system verification process, the user is prompted to enter a PIN. The PIN can be from 4 to 20 characters.

Multifactor authentication with a USB drive   After TPM has completed the system verification process, the system looks for a USB flash drive. If it's not found, the user will be prompted to insert the USB flash drive. The USB flash drive holds the startup key, and without it, the system will not continue.

Multifactor authentication is optional on systems with TPM. However, the startup key held on the USB flash drive is required on systems using Bit-Locker without TPM.

Multifactor authentication is optional. You can enable BitLocker Drive Encryption without needing an additional PIN or USB flash drive.

BitLocker Recovery

When the system starts, the TPM module performs several integrity checks. If any of these integrity checks fail, the system will remain locked, and BitLocker will enter recovery mode. The following system changes will be detected:

- Moving the BitLocker-encrypted drive to a new computer
- Installing a new motherboard with a new TPM
- Turning off, disabling, or clearing the TPM
- Making certain changes to the BIOS
- Making changes to the master boot record or boot sector
- Making changes to the boot manager, early boot components, or boot configuration data

> If you need to make changes to any of these components, you can disable BitLocker before making your changes. After making the changes, you can reenable BitLocker.

Once your system enters recovery mode, you will be required to either enter the recovery password or insert the USB flash drive holding the recovery key. Without the recovery password or the USB flash drive holding the recovery key, you won't be able to access the encrypted drive.

Recovery password   The recovery password is 48 digits divided into 8 groups. The BitLocker Recovery Console is entered very early in the boot process, and it's likely you won't have full access to the keyboard but will be able to use only the function keys. The password is numerical only. Function keys F1 through F9 are used for numbers 1 through 9, respectively. F10 is used for 0.

Recovery key   A recovery key is a file stored on a USB flash drive. The benefit of using the recovery key instead of a recovery password is that you don't have to enter the 48 numbers using the function keys. To use the recovery key, your system needs to support USB flash drives early in the boot process.

Encrypting File System

The NTFS file system includes the ability to individually encrypt files using the Encrypting File System. Users can use EFS to individually encrypt files or folders. Files are then stored on the drive in an encrypted format. Unauthorized users are prevented from accessing the files.

Once enabled for files or folders, EFS works automatically without any additional user intervention. When an authorized user opens an encrypted file, it is decrypted and opened. When the user saves the file, it is automatically decrypted and saved in the decrypted format.

To utilize EFS, the partition must be formatted with NTFS. It's highly unlikely you'll come across a server formatted as FAT or FAT32, but if you do, you'll probably want to convert it to NTFS. You can use the following command:

```
CONVERT X: /FS:NTFS
```

In the command, *X*: is the volume or partition you want to convert.

EFS and BitLocker

EFS and BitLocker are completely different technologies. They work differently and have different goals, but it is possible to utilize both BitLocker and EFS on the same drive.

Some of the differences between BitLocker and EFS are as follows:

Files encrypted   BitLocker encrypts all files (including system files) on the drive where it's implemented. EFS encrypts only individual files based on the user's preference.

Requirements   BitLocker requires the Trusted Platform Module for full functionality. EFS requires the drive to be formatted with NTFS.

Permissions required   BitLocker can be implemented only by an administrator. Any regular user can employ EFS to encrypt their files.

Encrypting Files and Folders

It's relatively easy to use EFS on any file or folder. In general, it's recommended you encrypt folders instead of individual files. When a folder is encrypted, all files within the folder will automatically be encrypted.

To encrypt a folder, follow these high-level steps:

1. Launch Windows Explorer.
2. Right-click the folder you want to encrypt.
3. Click the Advanced button (from the General tab).
4. Click the Encrypt Contents to Secure Data check box, as shown in Figure 8.4.
5. Click OK in the Advanced Attributes dialog box.
6. Click OK in the folder properties box.

Usually files and folders are displayed in black text within Windows Explorer. Files and folders that are encrypted are displayed in green text by default.

It's also possible to encrypt and decrypt files from the command line using the `cipher` command.

FIGURE 8.4   Enabling encryption on a folder

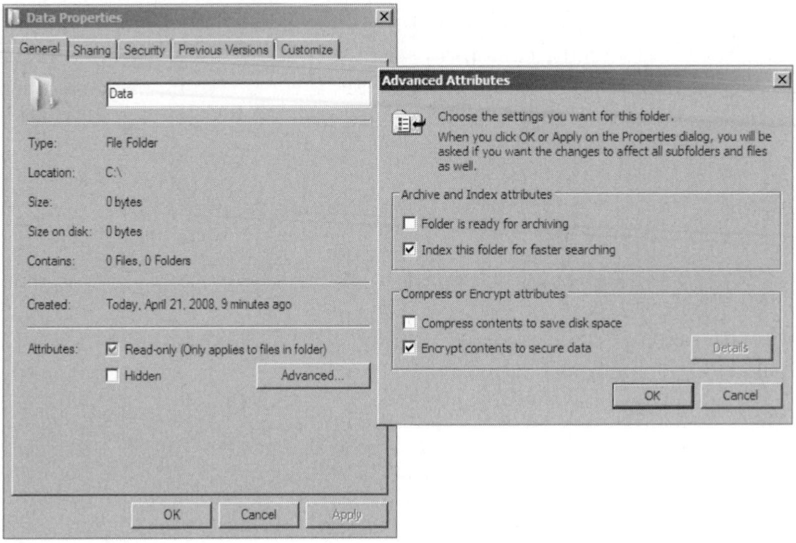

EFS Certificates and Keys

Both symmetric and asymmetric methods of encryption are used with EFS. Knowing how these two encryption types work will give you a greater understanding of EFS encryption.

Symmetric encryption   Symmetric encryption uses a single key to both encrypt and decrypt data. Symmetric encryption is quicker than asymmetric encryption. EFS encrypts the data using a symmetric key. The symmetric key is stored in an encrypted format in each encrypted file in the data decryption field (DDF).

Asymmetric encryption   Asymmetric encryption uses one key for encryption and one key for decryption. These keys are referred to as the *public key* and the *private key*. When using a public/private key pair, one key can encrypt (but not decrypt), and the other key can decrypt (but not encrypt). In other words, if the public key encrypts something, only the private key can decrypt it; similarly, if the private key encrypts something, only the public key can decrypt it.

In EFS, the user's public key is used to encrypt the symmetric key. When the user attempts to open an EFS file, the user's private key is used to decrypt the symmetric key. The symmetric key is then used to decrypt the data.

Figure 8.5 shows how EFS uses both symmetric and asymmetric encryption. When EFS needs to encrypt a file, it first creates a symmetric key (step 1) and then encrypts the data with this symmetric key (step 2). When needed, the data will be decrypted with this symmetric key.

FIGURE 8.5   Encrypting a file with EFS

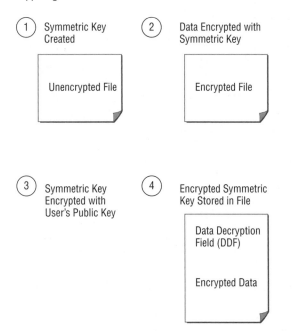

The symmetric key is stored with the file so that the file can be decrypted when necessary. Since it is stored with the file, it needs to be protected. The symmetric key is encrypted with the user's public key (step 3) and then stored in the data decryption field of the file (step 4).

Figure 8.6 shows the process when a file is opened and decrypted. When the user attempts to open the file, the user's EFS certificate (which holds the user's private key) is accessed (step 1). The encrypted symmetric key is retrieved from the DDF (step 2). Note that the data is still encrypted at this point.

The user's private key is then used to decrypt the symmetric key (step 3). With the symmetric key decrypted, it can then be used to decrypt the data (step 4).

At the core of this process is the user's private key, which is kept in the user's EFS certificate. Once a user logs on, she will have automatic access to the certificate. If another user attempts to open the file, he won't have access to the first user's certificate and the private key. Without the private key, the data can't be decrypted.

Although you may occasionally read that EFS-protected data is compromised, it's not because the EFS encryption is hacked. Instead, a user's password is guessed or hacked. Once the user's password is known, anyone can log on as that user and gain automatic access to EFS-protected files. Using strong passwords can go a long way toward protecting users' accounts and EFS-protected data.

FIGURE 8.6   Decrypting a file with EFS

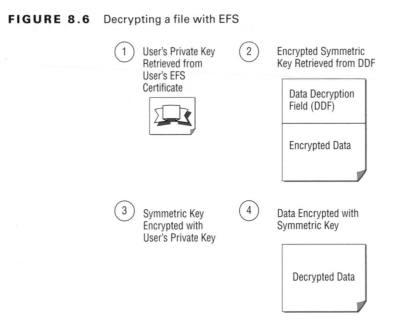

Recovering EFS-Encrypted Files

Since the EFS keys are stored as part of the operating system, you can lose access to the keys if you install a new operating system after a failure. The primary protection against this data loss is to ensure you have a backup of your certificate and encryption keys.

If you have a backup of your certificate, then you can import your certificate into the new operating system and use it to decrypt the files encrypted in the previous operating system.

Backing Up Your EFS Certificate

You can export your certificate and then store the certificate on removable media such as a USB flash drive or CD-ROM. When you need to recover EFS files (such as after a server's operating system is rebuilt), you can import the certificate into the certificate store.

Exercise 8.4 shows the steps involved in exporting your EFS certificate. These steps assume there is a certificate to export. Remember, the certificate is created the first time you encrypt a file or folder. If you haven't done so with your current account, do so now.

EXERCISE 8.4

Exporting Your EFS Certificate

1.   Launch a Microsoft Management Console (MMC) by clicking Start and entering **MMC** in the Start Search box.

2.   Press Ctrl+M to add a snap-in.

3. In the Available Snap-ins section, select Certificates, and click Add.

4. On the Certificates Snap-in page, ensure My User Account is selected, and click Finish.

5. In the Add or Remove Snap-Ins page, click OK.

6. In Certificates console, browse to Certificates ➢ Personal ➢ Certificates. Select the certificate with the Intended Purpose of Encrypting File System setting. Right-click the certificate, and view the All Tasks selections. Your view will look similar to the following graphic.

7. Select Export from the All Tasks menu. On the Welcome to the Wizard page, click Next.

8. On the Export Private Key page, select Yes, Export the Private Key and then click Next.

9. On the Export File Format page, Personal Information Exchange -PKCS #12 (.PFX) will be selected. Select the Export All Extended Properties check box. Leave all the other check boxes unchecked. Click Next.

10. On the Password page, enter the password of **P@ssw0rd** in the Password and Confirm Password boxes. You can also choose your own password. Click Next.

11. On the File to Export page, click the Browse button. In the Save As dialog box, select Browse Folders (on the bottom left) if the folders aren't visible. Browse to the root of C:\ (or another folder of your choosing). Enter **EFSExportCert** in the File Name text box, and click Save.

12. Back on the File to Export page, click Next.

13. On the Completing the Wizard page, review the information, and click Finish. A Certificate Export Wizard dialog box will appear indicating the export was successful.

You can now copy the certificate to a floppy, USB flash drive, or CD so that it can be stored in a safe place.

Importing Your EFS Certificate

If you have to rebuild your server's operating system, you won't have access to the files that were encrypted in the original operating system unless you have access to the original key. If you have a backup of your EFS certificate, you can import the certificate, and you will then have access to your EFS files.

Exercise 8.5 shows the steps involved in importing your EFS certificate. These steps assume you have completed Exercise 8.4.

EXERCISE 8.5

Importing Your EFS Certificate

1. Launch the Certificate Manager by clicking Start and entering **certmgr.msc** in the Start Search box.

2. In the Certificates console, browse to Certificates ≻ Personal. Right-click the Certificates container, and view the All Tasks selections. Your display will look similar to the following figure.

3. Select Import to launch the Import Certificate Wizard.

4. On the Welcome to the Wizard page, click Next.

5. On the File to Import page, browse to the file location where you exported the certificate in Exercise 8.4.

6. Change the extension that the system is looking for by selecting the drop-down box above the Open button. Select the Personal Information Exchange (*.pfx, *p12), as shown in the following graphic.

EXERCISE 8.5 *(continued)*

7. Select your certificate, and click Open.

8. Back on the File to Import page, click Next.

9. On the Password page, enter **P@ssw0rd** (or the alternate password you may have chosen). Select the Mark This Key as Exportable check box. Notice that you can also enable strong private key protection from this page. Click Next.

10. On the Certificate Store page, accept the default to place all certificates in the following store (with the Personal Certificate Store shown). Click Next.

11. On the Completing the Wizard page, click Finish.

12. A dialog box will appear indicating that the import was successful.

Data Recovery Agent

Imagine this: I work at your company, and I've been working on some research and development projects. All the data is stored on a server and protected using EFS, and I'm the only user who has access to the data. Then, a wonderful thing happens. I win the lottery! Woo hoo! Somehow I forget about these project files and start a vacation that ultimately lasts several months. In the meantime, you're trying to access these files that can be accessed using only my private key. But since you don't have my private key, you can't access the files.

For many companies, this is unacceptable. A back door to the data is needed. The data recovery agent (DRA) is the back door. A data recovery agent is a designated person who has the ability to open encrypted files.

Figure 8.7 shows an EFS-protected file with a data recovery field (DRF). The data recovery field is similar to the data decryption field. It holds an encrypted version of the symmetric key used to encrypt the data. The difference is that the symmetric is encrypted with the DRA's public key and can be decrypted only with the DRA's public key.

FIGURE 8.7   DRF within an EFS-protected file

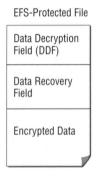

EFS-Protected File

Data Decryption Field (DDF)

Data Recovery Field

Encrypted Data

Someone responsible is designated as the data recovery agent. From then on, any files that are encrypted include a DRF. The DRA is then able to access any files using the key available in the DRA's certificate.

A new feature available within Windows Server 2008 is the ability to embed a DRA's certificate onto a smart card.

Key Recovery Agent

A key recovery agent (KRA) is similar to a data recovery agent. The difference is that the KRA can recover private keys, while the DRA is used to recover data.

When key recovery is implemented, private keys are stored in a key archival data store. If a user's private key becomes lost or damaged, the KRA can retrieve the private key from the store and return it to the user. Recovered keys can also be issued to other users who will act on behalf of the original user.

KRA vs. DRA

In any organization, you can implement a key recovery agent, a data recovery agent, both, or neither. What is done is largely subjective.

The existence of either a DRA or a KRA creates a back door to retrieve data. However, both also present a security risk. If attackers gain access to the DRA or KRA keys, they can then retrieve data that was intended to be protected. For some companies, the risks outweigh the benefits, and neither a DRA nor a KRA is implemented.

Auditing for Server Security

One of the primary things you can do when implementing server security is to watch what's happening on the server by implementing an auditing policy. With Windows Server 2008 you can do regular auditing or specialized Active Directory auditing.

Regular auditing is the same type of auditing that has been available on Windows Server products since Windows Server 2000. Windows Server 2008 has introduced more detailed auditing capabilities with Active Directory. When enabled, directory service access events can be logged with more detailed information.

Auditing can watch for certain events, and when these events occur, it will log the event in the Security log. You can configure auditing of both success and failure events. You can view the Security log using Event Viewer.

With auditing, you can monitor several types of events. Figure 8.8 shows the Group Policy settings for these settings, and the following text explains each category. Once enabled, events will be logged in the Security log and can be viewed using Event Viewer.

FIGURE 8.8   Enabling auditing via Group Policy

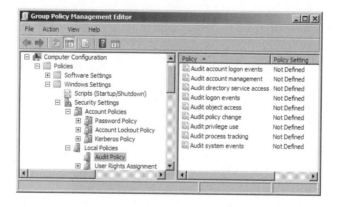

Account logon events   Account logon events are generated when a user attempts to authenticate against a domain controller. Failure events are logged when authentication isn't successful, and success events are logged when the user enters the correct credentials.

Account management   Account management events are generated when a user, group, or computer account is created, modified, or deleted. Both success and failure events can be audited.

Directory service access   Auditing can be enabled on any individual directory service object. It's important to note that there is a two-step process for enabling directory service access. You would first enable directory service access auditing. Then you would go to the individual object where you want to audit.

Each directory service object (users, computers, groups, OUs, and so on) has a security access control lists (SACLs). Each SACL lists users or groups by security identifier (SID) and the auditing requirement.

Logon events   Logon events are generated when a user attempts to authenticate against a local computer (not a domain controller).

Object access   Object access enables auditing for objects. For example, you may want to know when a file, folder, or registry key is accessed, modified, or deleted. By enabling object access auditing via Group Policy, you can then enable auditing at individual objects. Just as enabling directory service access auditing is a two-step process, enabling object access auditing is a two-step process. Each object has a security access control lists. Each SACL lists users or groups by security identifier and the auditing requirement.

Policy change   Policy change can audit any changes to user rights assignment policies, audit policies, and trust policies.

Privilege use   Privilege use auditing can track each time a user exercises a user right. In general, a *right* is something a user is allowed to do, such as change the system time. (Rights and permissions are sometimes confused; *permissions* grant you a specific type of access to an object.)

Not all privileges are audited by default. To enable auditing of the following user rights, you need to modify the FullPrivilegeAuditing registry key:

- Bypass traverse checking
- Debug programs
- Create a token object
- Replace process-level token
- Generate security audits
- Back up and restore operations

Process tracking   Process tracking auditing is used to log events in response to specific applications (or individual process) events. These include events such as program activation, process exit, and indirect object access.

System events   System events auditing is used to log specific events from a computer. Some common events that are logged include when a computer is restarted or shut down.

Auditing Detailed Active Directory Events

If desired, you can enable the logging of more detailed Active Directory events. You first must enable the logging of directory service access success and failure events. Once enabled, you can then enable the logging of the following subcategories:

- Directory Service Access
- Directory Service Changes

- Directory Service Replication
- Detailed Directory Service Replication

 You can enable the Directory Service Access auditing policy on the Default Domain Controllers GPO, which is linked to the Domain Controllers OU. It has meaning only on domain controllers, so it wouldn't be set at a site level, at the domain level, or at OUs that hold other servers or workstations.

The Directory Service Access subcategory logs additional details when Active Directory objects are accessed.

The Directory Service Changes subcategory logs information that many administrators want on a regular basis. For example, when a change is made, both the old and new values are logged so an administrator can see what the value was both before and after the change. If an object is moved, both the old and new locations will be logged.

Information on replication is useful when troubleshooting replication problems.

To enable any of these subcategories, you would use the auditpol command-line tool. The basic syntax of auditpol when enabling the detailed Active Directory auditing is shown in the following commands:

- Enable success for the subcategory:

```
auditpol /set /subcategory:"subcategory name" /success:enable
```

- Enable failure for the subcategory:

```
auditpol /set /subcategory:"subcategory name" /failure:enable
```

- Disable success for the subcategory:

```
auditpol /set /subcategory:"subcategory name" /success:disable
```

- Disable failure for the subcategory:

```
auditpol /set /subcategory:"subcategory name" /failure:disable
```

All the subcategory names are entered just as they've been described previously but are listed here for clarity. Note that since each of the subcategories has spaces, you must include the quotes in the command. As an example, when enabling detailed success auditing for directory service changes, you would enter the following command:

```
auditpol /set /subcategory:"directory service access" /success:enable
```

Enabling Directory Service Access Auditing

- sEnable Audit Directory Service Access via Group Policy.
- Enable auditing at the object level.

The following high-level steps identify how to enable auditing for directory service access events:

1. Enable Audit Directory Service Access via Group Policy as shown in the previous section.

2. In Active Directory Users and Computers, enable the viewing of advanced features by selecting Advanced Features from the View menu.

3. Right-click an object that you want to audit (such as an OU).

4. Click the Security tab. Click the Advanced button. Figure 8.9 shows the current auditing enabled on the Domain Controllers OU.

FIGURE 8.9 Enabling auditing on a directory service object

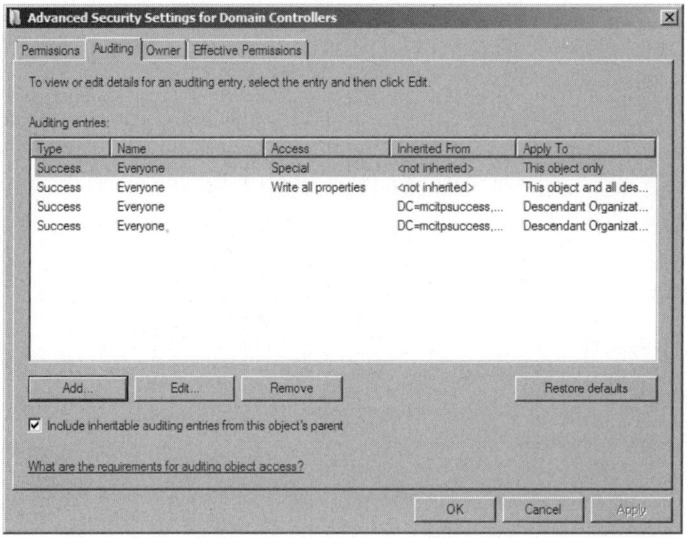

Advanced Security Settings for Domain Controllers				☒

Permissions | Auditing | Owner | Effective Permissions |

To view or edit details for an auditing entry, select the entry and then click Edit.

Auditing entries:

Type	Name	Access	Inherited From	Apply To
Success	Everyone	Special	<not inherited>	This object only
Success	Everyone	Write all properties	<not inherited>	This object and all des...
Success	Everyone		DC=mcitpsuccess,...	Descendant Organizat...
Success	Everyone		DC=mcitpsuccess,...	Descendant Organizat...

| Add... | Edit... | Remove | | Restore defaults |

☑ Include inheritable auditing entries from this object's parent

What are the requirements for auditing object access?

| | OK | Cancel | Apply |

The entries on the Auditing tab are referred to as the object's *security access control list* (SACL). Each entry has a security identifier that is converted to a friendly name and the specific access that will be audited. You can compare this to the *discretionary access control list* (DACL), which is an access control list that includes the SIDs and permissions for individual objects.

5. Click the Add button, and add the user or group you want to audit. You can choose Everyone to audit access for any user.

6. Pick the individual actions that you want to audit. If you want to audit all possible access, select Full Control for the Successful and Failed columns, as shown in Figure 8.10.

FIGURE 8.10   Enabling Full Control access auditing on an OU for the Everyone group

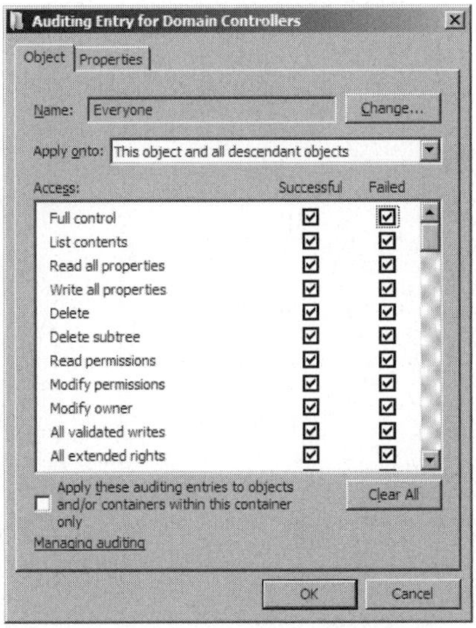

If you want to enable more detailed auditing for the directory service subcategories, use the auditpol command-line tool as described previously.

Enabling Object Access

Similar to how Active Directory Access is a two-step process, it's also a two-step process to enable object access auditing for any regular objects. In this context, an object would be items such as a file, folder, registry key, or printer.

The two distinctive steps required to enable directory service auditing are as follows:

- Enable object access via Group Policy.
- Enable auditing at the object level.

The following high-level steps identify how to enable auditing for object access:

1. Enable object access via Group Policy as shown earlier.

2. Access the properties page of the object you want to audit. For example, if you wanted to audit access to the C:\Data directory, you'd access the properties page of C:\Data.

3. Access the Security tab of the object, and click the Advanced button.

4. Select the Auditing tab. This will show you the security access control list.

5. Add a user by clicking Edit and clicking Add.

6. After you've added a user, identify the access you want to audit. For example, if you want to know whether a user ever attempts or succeeds in deleting data, select the Delete for Successful and Failed check box, as shown in the Figure 8.11.

FIGURE 8.11   Auditing deletes in the data folder by the Everyone group

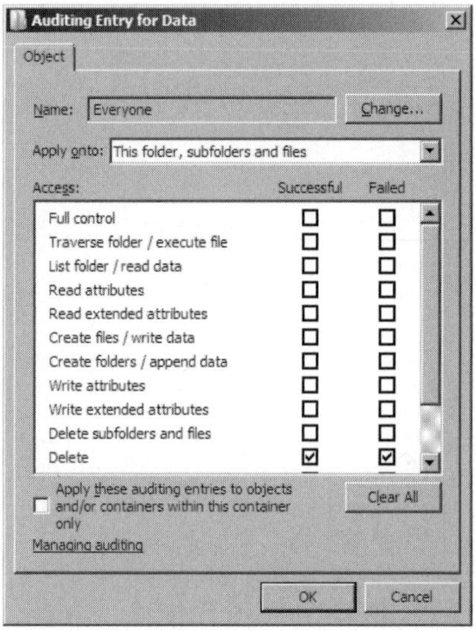

If you enable only object access auditing via Group Policy, nothing will be audited by default. Similarly, if you enable object access auditing at individual objects but don't enable object access auditing via Group Policy, nothing will be audited.

Network Security

You can also implement security at the network level. The three primary network security elements discussed in this section are as follows:

Firewalls   Used to protect the network from Internet attacks and internal clients from emerging threats (such as viruses or worms released internally).

Remote access   When providing access to your internal network from an external network (such as the Internet), you need to implement security measures to protect your network. This includes using Network Policy Access Services to ensure the health of remote clients and deciding which tunneling protocol to use with VPNs (PPTP, L2TP, or SSTP).

Network Encryption with IPSec   Data being transmitted is vulnerable to sniffing attacks. Data can be protected by encrypting it prior to transmission.

Firewalls

Firewalls are placed at the edge of your network, primarily to block out unwanted Internet traffic, and are also enabled on internal hosts (servers and client computers) to protect them from internal threats such as viruses or worms that may have been inadvertently brought in by a user.

The basic premise of a firewall is to block all traffic except what is specifically authorized. Exceptions are added in the form of rules that specify what traffic is allowed. If a rule is met, the traffic is allowed. Otherwise, the traffic is blocked.

Figure 8.12 shows how firewalls can be placed at the edge of a network (between the internal network and the Internet) and also enabled on hosts in the network. The figure also shows a common configuration of a demilitarized zone (DMZ).

FIGURE 8.12   Firewalls in a network

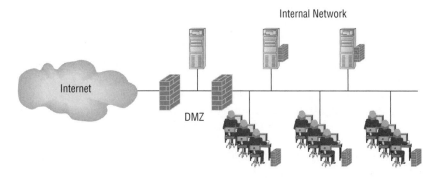

A DMZ is used to provide a safer environment for servers that need to be accessible from the Internet. For example, you may have a web server that needs to be accessible on the Internet, but instead of placing it directly on the Internet, you place it in the DMZ. You can then use the Internet-facing firewall to filter out unwanted traffic and allow only what is desire.

Packet Filtering

Packet filtering is the basic method used by firewalls to allow or disallow traffic. Packet filters can filter traffic based on the following:

- IP addresses
- Ports
- Some protocols

In general, packet filtering starts by blocking all traffic. Then, one by one, you create rules to allow the specific traffic you want to allow.

It's worthwhile to review some basic networking concepts here. Within a network, the IP address is used to get a data packet to a host (such as a server). When the packet reaches the server, the server then needs to process it. The server looks within the packet to determine the port or the protocol that is being addressed. Once determined, the server then passes the packet information to the appropriate service to process the packet.

Ports are divided into three ranges by the Internet Assigned Numbers Authority (IANA). The first two ranges have specific services defined that run on specific ports:

Well-known ports   These are the first 1,024 ports (port 0 through 1023). Some common ports you should be familiar with from this book are 80 (HTTP), 443 (HTTPS), and 389 (Lightweight Directory Access Protocol). Well-known ports are used by system processes or by programs executed by privileged users.

Registered ports   These are ports 1024 through 49151. These are less commonly known but have many ports that are reserved. On most systems, these ports can be used by user processes or programs executed by ordinary users.

Dynamic (or private) ports   These ports can be dynamically assigned by services. Typically these ports are used by clients as source ports so that the returning packet can be processed. Dynamic ports are in the range of 49152 to 65,535.

Figure 8.13 shows the process of port. In step 1, the user submits an HTTP request to the web server to retrieve a web page. The destination port is port 80, which is the well-known port for HTTP. Additionally, the client would designate a source port in the dynamic range so the system knows where to send the returning packet. For this example, I've chosen port number 57575, but it could be any port in the dynamic range.

FIGURE 8.13   Packet filtering in a firewall

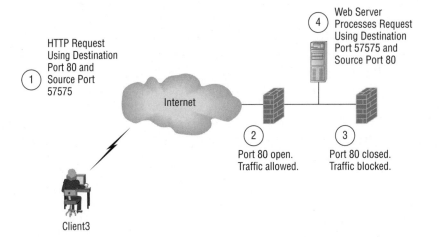

In step 2, the Internet-facing firewall receives the packet. Since the packet has a destination of port 80, the packet would be allowed. The packet filter could also specify that only packets addressed to the specific IP address of the web server and using port 80 would be allowed.

To protect the internal network, port 80 would be closed on the internal firewall as shown in step 3. Traffic that is allowed through the external firewall would be blocked internally.

Step 4 shows the web server processing the request. The traffic is coming from a web server, so the source port is port 80. Since the client chose port 57575 as its source port, this same port must be used as the destination port.

Firewalls are typically programmed to allow returning traffic, so since it allowed the traffic to the web server, it would allow the returning traffic. When the client receives the packet, it knows that it used port 57575, so it would pass the information to process that initiated the request.

Server Internal Firewall

In addition to implementing a firewall at the edge of your network, you can also enable the firewall on each of your individual hosts. Windows XP, Windows Vista, Windows Server 2003, and Windows Server 2008 all have firewall technologies that can be implemented.

These host-based firewalls are basic packet-filtering firewalls. However, they can be significant in increasing the protection of your systems, especially if a virus or worm makes its way into your network.

For stand-alone Windows Server 2008 computers, you can configure the firewall using the Windows Firewall with Advanced Security console. You can access this by clicking Start and typing **Firewall** in the Start Search box.

Figure 8.14 shows the Windows Firewall console. In the figure, the Firewall console was launched on a server in a domain, and it indicates that the domain profile is Active.

FIGURE 8.14 Windows Firewall console

The Windows Firewall on Windows Server 2008 supports three different profiles. These different profiles are used to group firewall rules and connection security rules into common settings. Only one profile is applied at a time.

Domain profile If a computer is connected to the same network where it has a computer account, the domain profile is applied. When set to the domain profile, only firewall rules set to the domain profile through Group Policy apply.

Private profile   If a computer is connected to network where its domain account is not located (in other words, it doesn't authenticate with a domain controller), the private profile is applied. These settings are more restrictive than the domain profile.

Public profile   The public profile is applied for a computer not connected to a domain and located in a public place such as an airport or a coffee shop. This is the most restrictive set of rules for the firewall.

Although the private and public profiles make sense for end users running desktop operating systems, they don't make much sense for servers. I can't imagine carrying a server through an airport and firing it up while waiting for my next flight. With this in mind, when studying Windows Server 2008, you should concentrate on understanding the domain profile.

Within a domain, the firewall settings can be manipulated via Group Policy. The path to the firewall settings is Computer Configuration ➤ Policies ➤ Administrative Templates ➤ Network ➤ Network Connections ➤ Windows Firewall. Figure 8.15 shows the Group Policy Management Console opened to the Windows Firewall settings.

FIGURE 8.15   Group Policy firewall settings

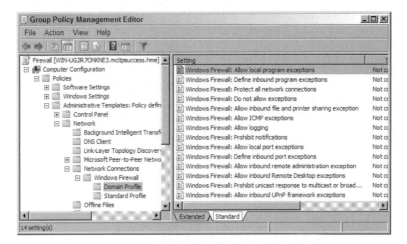

The domain profile in Group Policy is the profile you will manipulate for systems within your domain. It has the following settings, all of which start with Windows Firewall:

- Allow Local Program Exceptions
- Define Inbound Program Exceptions
- Protect All Network Connections
- Do Not Allow Exceptions
- Allow Inbound File and Printer Sharing Exceptions
- Allow ICMP Exceptions

- Allow Logging
- Prohibit Notifications
- Allow Local Port Exceptions
- Define Inbound Port Exceptions
- Allow Inbound Remote Administration Exception
- Allow Inbound Remote Desktop Exceptions
- Prohibit Unicast Response to Multicast or Broadcast Requests
- Allow Inbound UPnP Framework Exceptions

 All the firewall settings have detailed explanations in the Group Policy Management Editor. For more information about any of these settings, double-click the setting within the editor, and click the Explain tab.

One of the neat features of the Windows Firewall on Windows Server 2008 is that each time you add a new feature or role, the firewall is automatically configured to support the new functionality. This prevents some needless hair pulling as you try to figure out why the new feature or role isn't working. However, if you add third-party applications, you may need to configure the server to support the application.

Internet Security and Acceleration

The Internet Security and Acceleration (ISA) server is Microsoft's firewall product. It is a full-featured server product similar to SQL Server or Exchange. In other words, it's not a free role or service that you can add to Windows Server 2008 but instead a server application available for purchase.

ISA has long been respected among firewall-evaluation agencies. It was approved for certification of Common Criteria Evaluation Assurance Level 4+ (EAL 4+), which is the highest level possible recognized by all countries participating in the Common Criteria certification.

Typically, you would deploy ISA as the only application running on the server. One of the core security principles is to reduce the attack surface of any server, so running additional services with ISA presents additional security risks.

In addition to doing traditional packet filtering, ISA can do more advanced inspection of traffic. Microsoft has announced that the next generation of ISA will be known as the Forefront Threat Management Gateway (Forefront TMG).

Remote Access

Remote access is the process of providing access to your internal network from an external source. You can do this via direct-dial methods (using phone lines) or via a public network such as the Internet. When using a public network, tunneling protocols are used to create a virtual private network (VPN).

In Windows Server 2008, the server role that performs this function is the Network Policy role.

Figure 8.16 shows a diagram using a remote access server. In the diagram, both dial-up remote access and a VPN are shown. For dial-up remote access, the client has a modem and phone line and directly dials the remote access server (which also has a modem and phone line). The remote access server then provides access to the internal network.

FIGURE 8.16   Remote access

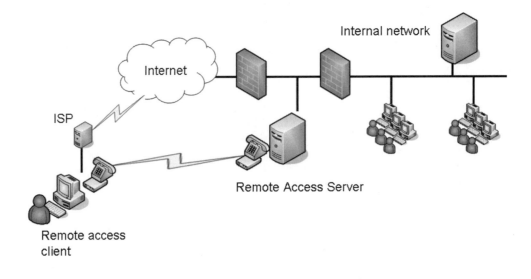

Internal network

Internet

ISP

Remote Access Server

Remote access client

 The VPN server and the remote access server are one and the same, just as a car and a race car could be the same thing. A race car is more descriptive. A race car is always a car, but a car is not always a race car. Similarly, *VPN server* is more descriptive than *remote access server*; it describes the connection type of remote access. Although a VPN server could always be referred to as a remote access server, a remote access server wouldn't always be a VPN server. A remote access server could use dial-up or VPN connections.

A VPN differs in the connectivity to the remote access server. Instead of connecting directly to the remote access server via a telephone line, the client tunnels through the Internet. Any time the client connects via a phone line, the Point-to-Point Protocol (PPP) is used.

First, the client gains access to the Internet through a local Internet service provider (ISP). If it's dial-up, the client uses PPP to connect, but it's also possible the client has a broadband connection to the Internet.

Once connected to the Internet, the client then uses the tunneling protocols to reach the VPN server. Once the server is reached, the client is granted access to the internal network.

Understanding Confidentiality, Integrity, and Authentication.

When discussing information technology security, three terms are commonly used. They are often referred to as CIA: confidentiality, integrity, and authentication.

Confidentiality means that if the data is intercepted, it can't be read. Confidentiality is achieved through the use of encryption. Different tunneling protocols utilize different methods of encrypting data.

Integrity ensures that the data has not been modified in transit. Integrity is achieved by using hashing or checksums. A hash is calculated before the data is sent, and then the data is sent with the hash. When the data is received, the hash is calculated again and compared to the original hash. If the two hashes are different, the data has been modified. Not all tunneling protocols verify data integrity.

Authentication verifies that a user or host is who they claim to be. Authentication is achieved through the use of credentials such as usernames and passwords or certificates. Both user-level authentication and machine-level authentication are possible. Not all tunneling protocols provide machine-level authentication.

When planning for a VPN server, you'll need to decide on which tunneling protocol to use. The following tunneling protocols can be used with a Microsoft VPN server:

PPTP   The Point-to-Point Tunneling Protocol (PPTP) is the oldest of the three. It is supported by Windows 2000 and newer operating systems. It can be used with IP-based connections. Data is encrypted using Microsoft Point to Point Encryption (MPPE), providing data confidentiality. PPTP does not provide data integrity or machine-level authentication.

L2TP   The Layer 2 Tunneling Protocol (L2TP) is supported by clients running Windows 2000 or newer operating systems. L2TP is commonly used with IPSec, and you'll often see it as L2TP/IPSec. IPSec provides data confidentiality and integrity to L2TP. Machine-level authentication can be achieved through the use of a preshared key or computer certificates.

One of the drawbacks to L2TP when used with IPSec is that it can't pass through a Network Access Translation (NAT) server. If a NAT was needed, administrators often had to move backward to a PPTP solution that sacrificed security.

SSTP   The Secure Socket Tunneling Protocol (SSTP) is the newest tunneling protocol. It is supported only on clients running Windows Vista SP1 or newer operating systems. SSTP uses Secure Sockets Layer (SSL) to encrypt the data and provide data confidentiality. Further, it uses HTTPS over TCP port 443 to pass traffic through firewalls, making it an easier solution to implement without requiring modifications to firewalls. Port 443 is often already open on firewalls. Unlike L2TP/IPsec, SSTP can pass through a NAT. SSL within SSTP also provides data integrity and machine-level authentication.

Network Policy and Access Services

Windows Server 2008 includes the role of the Network Policy and Access Services (NPAS) to support remote access. NPAS provides the following services:

- Routing and Remote Access
- Network Policy Server (NPS)
- Health Registration Authority (HRA)
- Host Credential Authorization Protocol

This section is addressing only the Routing and Remote service of NPAS. In Chapter 4, the topic of Network Access Protection was presented, which included the other elements of NPAS.

Network Access Protection (NAP) is a significant addition to Windows Server 2008. As a reminder, it can be used to examine the health of clients such as ensuring that certain service packs or hotfixes are installed, antivirus software is running and up-to-date, and much more. The health requirements are determined by the administrator and enforced in a health policy. Healthy clients are issued a health certificate and granted access to the network, while unhealthy clients are quarantined and allowed access only to a restricted area of the network.

Since remote access clients are accessing the network from external locations, the ability to examine their health is very important. Expect any remote access solution to include network access elements today.

To add remote access services, you would add the Network Policy and Access Services role. Exercise 8.6 shows the steps to add this role to your server.

EXERCISE 8.6

Adding the Network Policy and Access Services Role

1. Launch Server Manager by clicking Start ➤ Administrative Tools ➤ Server Manager.

2. In the left pane, right-click Server Manager, and select Add Roles.

3. Review the information on the Before You Begin page, and click Next.

4. On the Select Server Roles page, select the Network Policy and Access Services check box, and click Next.

5. On the Network Policy and Access Services page, review the information, and click Next.

6. On the Select Role Services page, select Remote Access Service. Your display will look similar to the following graphic. Click Next.

7. On the Confirm Installation Selections page, click Install.

8. Once the installation is complete, click the Close button.

To successfully configure the remote access service, you will need either two NICs or one NIC and one modem. One NIC would be used to connect to your back-end network, and the other NIC (or the modem) would be used to accept connections from remote clients.

RADIUS

You can also create a Network Policy Server to perform as a Remote Authentication Dial-In User Service (RADIUS) server. A RADIUS server performs centralized authentication, authorization, and accounting for remote access (dial-up and VPN) servers and even wireless access points.

For example, you could have multiple VPN servers. Instead of having each VPN server handle all the authentication and logging activities, you could create a RADIUS server to perform these functions. Each VPN server can then pass the authentication requests to the RADIUS server. It will handle the details of the authentication and can also be configured to log details such as accounting and period status information about the session.

When configuring a RADIUS server, one of the things you'll need to plan for is how to do logging. You have two choices:

Local file logging With local file logging, the data is logged into comma-separated text files. Although all the information is available, it isn't easy to view and manipulate the data in its native format. These text files are sometimes imported into Microsoft Excel spreadsheets for better viewing. Use local file logging when you need to minimize costs.

SQL Server logging Using a SQL Server to store the logged data provides you with much more capabilities. Since the data is stored in a database, it's easy to query and manipulate the information. The drawback is that SQL Server costs additional money. Use SQL Server logging when you need to easily query the data and your budget can afford it.

Network Encryption with IPSec

Earlier in this chapter, you learned about BitLocker Drive Encryption and Encrypting File System. Both of these technologies allow data to be encrypted on the hard drive. However, when BitLocker or EFS protected data is sent over the network, it is sent in an unencrypted format.

Sniffers can be used to capture, analyze, and exploit traffic sent in an unencrypted format. One of the core methods to ensure against unauthorized disclosure of information sent over a network is to encrypt it.

A *sniffer* (such as the freeware Wireshark or Microsoft's Network Monitor) is used to capture packets on the network. If data is sent in unencrypted format, a sniffer is able to capture and read the data.

If you want to encrypt data on the network, you can use IPSec. IPSec is a set of protocols used to protect data at the IP layer. Because it works at the IP layer, it will work with a broad range of applications.

IPSec provides two layers of protection: authentication and encryption. The Authentication Header (AH) in an IPSec packet can be used to authenticate both hosts in a session. If AH is used alone, the data is not encrypted. The Encapsulating Security Protocol (ESP) can be used to encrypt data. If ESP is used, AH must also be used.

When you implement IPSec, you can use one of the three default policies or create your own policy. Each of the policies can be assigned either locally or via Group Policy. Figure 8.17 shows the Group Policy settings. You can find these settings in the Computer Configuration ➤ Policies ➤ Windows Settings ➤ Security Settings ➤ IP Security Policies on Active Directory.

FIGURE 8.17   Group Policy IPSec policy settings

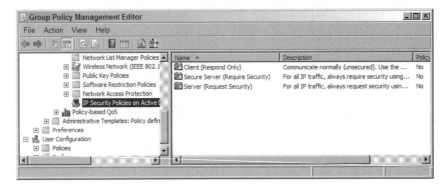

The three default policies are as follows:

Client (Respond Only)   Clients with this policy can communicate with other servers that request or require IPSec. However, these clients will never initiate an IPSec session.

As an example, you could set the Client (Respond Only) policy at the domain level via Group Policy so that it would apply to all clients within the domain. This would ensure that all clients would be able to communicate via IPSec with any other hosts that request an IPSec session.

Server (Request Security)   Servers (or any host) with the Server (Request Security) policy will try to initiate an IPSec session with any other hosts that try to connect. However, if the other host cannot communicate with IPSec, the server will still communicate using unsecure methods.

For example, you could have some servers that you want to use IPSec whenever possible, but you also have some clients that cannot communicate with IPSec. By placing all the servers in an OU and creating a Group Policy object and linking it to the OU, you can assign this policy. It will use IPSec with most clients (assuming they have an IPSec policy assigned) but will still communicate with clients even if they can't communicate with IPSec.

Secure Server (Require Security)   Servers that have the Secure Server (Require Security) policy will try to initiate an IPSec session with any other hosts that try to connect. If the other host cannot communicate with IPSec, the connection will be terminated.

For example, if you have some servers with highly confidential data that you never wanted to be transmitted on the network in an unencrypted format, you could assign this policy to it. Clients could connect only if they were able to talk via IPSec.

The three default policies are generic and refer to all types of traffic. However, you can modify these policies (or create your own) to encrypt specific traffic. For example, if you want to ensure that zone transfer traffic between two DNS servers is encrypted, you can set the policy encrypt all traffic on TCP port 53 between the two servers. Since DNS queries occur on UDP port 53, this rule would not affect DNS queries, but only zone transfer traffic.

Summary

In this chapter, you learned about security aspects at the disk level, the server level, and the network level, including some information on VPN protocols.

You learned that entire volumes can be protected with BitLocker Drive Encryption and about the requirements to enable and recover BitLocker. You also learned about EFS, including how to recover EFS files with a DRA and recover keys with a KRA.

For server security, you learned the basics of auditing and how to enable more detailed auditing for directory services.

When implementing a VPN, you learned about the different tunneling protocols that are available including the newer SSTP. Although SSTP works with only Windows Vista SP1 or newer clients, it has the significant benefit of using port 443, which is often open on the firewall for HTTPS. You also learned how IPSec can be used to encrypt traffic as it travels on the network.

Exam Essentials

Know the requirements for BitLocker Drive Encryption.   You should know that BitLocker requires Trusted Platform Module (TPM) 1.2 to fully implement the features. You should also know that it requires two partitions, both NTFS, and that the BitLocker partition (the unencrypted partition) must be at least 1.5GB in size.

Understand BitLocker Recovery requirements.   You should know what's required to recover a BitLocker drive if it becomes locked. This includes using either the recovery password or a USB flash drive with the recovery key.

Know how to implement multifactor authentication with BitLocker.   Multifactor authentication can be implemented by requiring users to take extra steps on computer startup or when resuming from hibernation. You should know the two multifactor authentication methods supported by BitLocker: requiring a user to enter a PIN or requiring a user to insert a USB flash drive with the startup key.

Understand the Encrypting File System (EFS).   You should have a basic understanding of EFS, how it works, and what it can protect. This includes knowing how to encrypt files and knowing that it can be used in conjunction with BitLocker.

Know how to recover EFS data.   You should know how to recover both EFS files and EFS keys. This includes an understanding of the data recovery agent (DRA) and the key recovery agent (KRA).

Understand auditing and how to implement auditing.   You should know the basics of auditing on any server and how to do more advanced auditing on a domain controller. Be familiar with the procedures of enabling auditing via Group Policy and using the auditpol command.

Understand firewalls.   You should know the basics of firewalls and how packet filtering is used to block or allow traffic. You should also be aware of the built-in firewall available in Windows Server 2008 products, Group Policy settings that can apply to all clients, and Microsoft's dedicated firewall product Internet Security Accelerator (ISA).

Know the available tunneling protocols.   You should know the different tunneling protocols and their strengths and weaknesses. This includes PPTP, L2TP, and SSTP. PPTP is the oldest and provides the least protection. SSTP is the newest protocol and uses port 443 to easily traverse firewalls. SSTP works only with Windows Vista SP1 or newer operating systems.

Understand encryption techniques when transmitting data.   You should know that data can be encrypted on the wire within a network with IPSec. IPSec has three default rules that can be implemented: Client, Server, and Secure Server.

Review Questions

1. You are deploying a Windows Server 2008 server to a remote office. The server will hold files that you want to protect, but the remote office doesn't have adequate physical security. How should you protect the files?

    A. Use NTFS permissions.

    B. Use a RODC.

    C. Use BitLocker.

    D. Encrypt the data with SSL.

2. You are considering enabling BitLocker on a Windows Server 2008 server. Of the following, what are the minimum requirements? (Choose all that apply.)

    A. TPM 1.2

    B. One partition

    C. Two partitions

    D. USB flash drive using a PIN

3. You manage a Windows Server 2008 server that has been protected with BitLocker. After the system experienced a failure and was repaired, it enters only the BitLocker Recovery Console. What can you insert into the system to get past the BitLocker Recovery Console?

    A. A USB flash drive with the startup PIN

    B. A USB flash drive with a recovery password

    C. A USB flash drive with a recovery key

    D. A USB flash drive with a startup key

4. You manage a Windows Server 2008 server that has been protected with BitLocker. The recovery password was stored on a USB flash drive. After the system experienced a failure and was repaired, it enters only the BitLocker Recovery Console. How can you unlock the disk?

    A. Enter the password using the function keys.

    B. Insert the USB flash drive when prompted.

    C. Insert the USB flash drive with the recovery key.

    D. Boot into the system and disable BitLocker. Enter the recovery password when prompted.

5. You are deploying a Windows Server 2008 server to a remote office. You decide to deploy Bit-Locker Drive Encryption with the system and verify the server meets all the hardware requirements. You also want to add multifactor authentication to unlock the drive. Of the following, what can be used to add multifactor authentication to BitLocker? Choose all that apply.

A. Require the user to enter a password when the computer starts or resumes from hibernation.

B. Require the user to enter a PIN when the computer starts or resumes from hibernation.

C. Require the user to use a smart card when the computer starts or resumes from hibernation.

D. Require the user to insert the USB flash drive holding the startup key when the computer starts or resumes from hibernation.

6. You are considering creating a RADIUS server to handle authentication and accounting for several VPN servers. You expect to have a high volume of accounting data, and you want to be able easily query the data. What would you do?

A. Configure RADIUS accounting using local logging.

B. Configure RADIUS accounting using SQL Server.

C. Enable directory service access auditing.

D. Enable object access auditing.

7. You want to deploy BitLocker on a server you manage at a remote site. Unfortunately, the server doesn't meet the minimum hardware requirements. Can you still protect the hard drive with BitLocker, and if so, how?

A. No. If the minimum requirements aren't met, you can't enable BitLocker.

B. Yes. Users will need to start the server with a USB flash drive that has an embedded startup key.

C. Yes. Users will need to start the server with a USB flash drive that has an embedded recovery key.

D. Yes. Users will need to start the server by entering a PIN.

8. Users within your organization encrypt files using EFS. The company policy states that if a user leaves the company for any reason, someone must be able to open and retrieve the user's encrypted data. What should you implement to allow someone to open another user's encrypted data?

A. DRA

B. KRA

C. Robocopy

D. ERA

9. Users within your organization encrypt files using EFS. The company policy states that private keys used to encrypt EFS data must be archived. If a key becomes lost or corrupt, a designated person must be able to retrieve the key. What should you implement to allow lost keys used for EFS to be restored?

   A. DRA

   B. KRA

   C. Robocopy

   D. ERA

10. You manage a domain controller, and you want to ensure that any changes to any active directory objects are logged. You also want to ensure that the most possible details are included. Directory Service auditing has been enabled via a Group Policy object at the domain level. What else should you do? (Choose two.)

    A. Use ADUC to enable auditing of objects at the domain level.

    B. Use the `auditpol` command-line tool to enable auditing of objects at the domain level.

    C. Use the GPMC to enable verbose logging.

    D. Use the `auditpol` command-line tool to enable auditing of the subcategory Directory Service Access.

11. You are troubleshooting replication problems and want to ensure that detailed replication events are logged. You have modified the default domain controller policy to enable auditing of directory service access events, but you aren't seeing the level of detail you need. What else should you do?

    A. Modify the default domain policy to enable auditing of directory service access events.

    B. Enable auditing of object access events for the domain controllers.

    C. Remove the default domain controller policy, and replace it with the default domain policy.

    D. Enable auditing of subcategories using the `auditpol` command-line tool.

12. You want to audit all failed attempts of domain logon. What should you enable?

    A. Account logon auditing

    B. Logon auditing

    C. Object access auditing

    D. Directory Service Access auditing

13. Management is considering purchasing a full-featured firewall product for your network, and they ask you for a recommendation. What Microsoft product could you recommend?

    A. Sidewinder

    B. ISA

    C. SQL Server

    D. Exchange

14. You want to allow SSL traffic into your network. You need to create a rule on the firewall to support this. What port needs to be opened?

    A. 80

    B. 443

    C. 1701

    D. 1723

15. You manage a network of more than 500 clients, including both Windows XP and Windows Vista clients. Management wants you to enable the Windows Firewall on all the clients. How would you accomplish this?

    A. Launch the Windows client firewall on each of the clients and configure it.

    B. Write a script to enable the firewall on logon.

    C. Write a script to enable the firewall on computer startup.

    D. Use Group Policy.

16. You want to ensure that Internet NNTP traffic is not on your network. How can you achieve this?

    A. Create a VPN with SSTP, and require all Internet access to use this VPN.

    B. Create a firewall rule to block the well-known ports.

    C. Create a firewall rule to block the NNTP port.

    D. Create a firewall rule to block the NNTP IP addresses.

17. Which of the following protocols can be used for a VPN server in Windows Server 2008? (Choose all that apply.)

    A. LT2P

    B. PPTP

    C. SSTP

    D. VPTP

18. You are considering deploying a VPN solution in your network. Clients will connect using Windows XP and Windows Vista. What tunneling protocol could you implement that would provide the highest level of protection?

    A. LT2P

    B. PPTP

    C. SSTP

    D. PPP

19. You are considering deploying an SSTP VPN solution in your network. What port must be opened on the firewall to support this solution?

   A. 80

   B. 443

   C. 1701

   D. 1723

20. You are considering deploying an SSTP VPN solution in your network. What are the oldest clients that can support this?

   A. Windows NT 4.0

   B. Windows 2000

   C. Windows XP

   D. Windows Vista SP1

Answers to Review Questions

1. **C.** BitLocker Drive Encryption can be used to protect entire volumes and is useful on servers when you don't have adequate security. NTFS permissions can be hacked if the server is stolen. If the server was a domain controller, making it a Read-Only Domain Controller (RODC) would be appropriate, but the question doesn't indicate it is a domain controller. SSL is used to encrypt data over the wire (typically when using Internet technologies) but couldn't protect the server if stolen.

2. **A, C.** The basic requirements for BitLocker are Trusted Platform Module TPM 1.2, two partitions (with the BitLocker partition at least 1.5GB), both partitions formatted with NTFS, and compatible BIOS. If TPM 1.2 is not available, you can use a USB flash drive with a recovery key, but a USB flash drive with a PIN would not work.

3. **C.** Of the choices, only a USB flash drive with a recovery key can be used. You can also manually enter the recovery password, but the system won't read the recovery password from the USB flash drive. A startup PIN can be used for multifactor authentication. A USB flash drive with a startup key can be used for multifactor authentication (or on systems without TPM support in place of TPM).

4. **A.** The password is a 48-digit (numbers-only) password. Since the keyboard may not be fully functional in the BitLocker Recovery Console, the password is entered using the function keys. The recovery password won't be read by inserting the USB flash drive, and the question indicates only the recovery password was stored, not the recovery key. If BitLocker has locked the system, you won't be able to boot into the system.

5. **B, D.** Multifactor authentication can be enabled by requiring the user to enter a PIN on startup or insert a USB flash drive that holds the startup key. The recovery password is used for recovery. There is no BitLocker setting to require a user to enter a password when the computer starts or resumes from hibernation. Smart cards aren't integrated with BitLocker. The recovery key is used for recovery.

6. **B.** A Remote Authentication Dial-In User Service (RADIUS) server configured with SQL Server for accounting would be easy to query. Local logging would create comma-separated text files that wouldn't be easy to query; if you needed to minimize costs, you would use local logging. Neither Directory Service Access auditing nor object access auditing would log accounting data collected from a RADIUS server.

7. **B.** On systems without Trusted Platform Module (TPM) 1.2, you can enable BitLocker to use a USB flash drive with an embedded startup key. The startup key is different from the recovery key used for recovery purposes. You can enable the use of a PIN for multifactor authentication on systems that have TPM, but a PIN can't be used in place of a TPM.

8. **A.** A designated recovery agent (DRA) can retrieve user's data when the user is unavailable to do so. The key recovery agent (KRA) can recover keys, but not data. Robust Copy (Robocopy) is a command-line tool that can be used to copy files. EFS doesn't have an ERA.

9. B.   A key recovery agent (KRA) is used to recover lost or damaged keys. A data recovery agent (DRA) is used to recover data, but not keys. Robust Copy (Robocopy) is a command-line tool that can be used to copy files. EFS doesn't have an ERA.

10. A, D.   Two steps are required to enable auditing. First, you must enable auditing using Group Policy (which the question indicates has already been done), and second, you must enable auditing of the object from within Active Directory Users and Computers (ADUC). To enable detailed logging, you need to enable auditing of one of the Directory Service sub-categories using the `auditpol` command-line tool. You can't use `auditpol` to enable auditing at any specific level (such as at the domain level), and the Group Policy Management Console (GPMC) doesn't have a setting for "verbose logging."

11. D.   You can use the `auditpol` command-line tool to enable detailed logging for directory service replication events. Since directory service events apply only to domain controllers, there is no need to modify the default domain policy. Object access events are logged when objects (such as files or folders) are accessed but wouldn't help with replication events. Removing the default domain controller policy would significantly weaken security for the domain controllers and wouldn't help log events for replication.

12. A.   Account logon events are recorded when a user attempts to log on to a domain. Logon events are recorded when a user attempts to log on to a local computer. Object access events record when objects (such as files, folders, registry, and so on) are accessed. Directory service access is used to audit changes to Active Directory.

13. B.   Internet Security and Acceleration (ISA) server is Microsoft's firewall product. The next generation will be Forefront Threat Management Gateway (Forefront TMG). Sidewinder is Secure Computing's firewall product, not Microsoft's. Microsoft SQL Server is database engine, and Microsoft Exchange is an email server.

14. B.   Port 443 is used for Secure Sockets Layer (SSL). Port 80 is used for HTTP. Port 1701 is used for L2TP. Port 1723 is used for PPTP.

15. D.   By using Group Policy, you can set the firewall settings once, and have the settings applied to many (or all) the clients. It isn't reasonable to set the firewall manually on 500 clients. Writing a script isn't necessary since you have Group Policy settings.

16. C.   You can create a firewall rule to block NNTP traffic (port 119) to ensure that Internet NNTP traffic isn't on your network. A VPN is used to access an internal network from an external source but wouldn't be used to access the Internet internally and couldn't be used to block NNTP traffic. Blocking all well-known ports (0 to 1024) would eliminate NNTP, but it would also eliminate all other traffic using the other 1023 ports. Since there's an unknown number of NNTP servers on the Internet, it wouldn't be feasible to block all possible IP addresses.

17. A, B, C.   The Layer 2 Tunneling Protocol (L2TP), Point to Point Tunneling Protocol (PPTP), and Secure Socket Tunneling Protocol (SSTP) can all be used to support a VPN server in Windows Server 2008. There is no such thing as VPTP.

18. A.   The Layer 2 Tunneling Protocol (L2TP) provides the highest level of protection for these clients. The Point to Point Tunneling Protocol (PPTP) doesn't provide data integrity of machine-level authentication. SSTP can't be used with Windows XP; it is supported with only Windows Vista SP1 or newer clients. The Point-to-Point Protocol (PPP) is dial-up protocol, not a VPN protocol.

19. B.   Port 443 is used for Secure Sockets Layer (SSL), and the Secure Socket Tunneling Protocol (SSTP) uses SSL. Port 80 is used for HTTP but does not support a VPN solution. Port 1701 is used for L2TP. Port 1723 is used for PPTP.

20. D.   SSTP can be used only with clients running at least Windows Vista SP1. It is not supported on older clients.

Chapter 9

Planning Business Continuity and High Availability

MICROSOFT EXAM OBJECTIVES COVERED IN THIS CHAPTER:

✓ **Planning for Server Deployment**

- Plan Application Servers and Services. May include but is not limited to: virtualization server planning, availability, resilience, and accessibility.

✓ **Planning for Business Continuity and High Availability**

- Plan Storage. May include but is not limited to: storage solutions, storage management.

- Plan High Availability. May include but is not limited to: service redundancy, service availability.

- Plan for Backup and Recovery. May include but is not limited to: data recovery strategy, server recovery strategy, directory service recovery strategy, object level recovery.

Business continuity planning is becoming more and more important in businesses today. Disasters happen, and the ability to ensure the business continues to operate no matter what happens is important.

From a user's perspective, the loss of a single file could be disastrous. High-availability planning includes taking steps to ensure that users' files, hard drives, and even servers are protected. If any component (files, drives, or servers) is deemed so important that it needs to be available to ensure smooth business continuity, you as the administrator need to know how it can be protected.

In this chapter, I'll cover Shadow Copies, RAID disks, failover clusters, network load balancing (NLB) clusters, backup and recovery methods, and the Windows Recovery Environment (WinRE). You can use these strategies individually or together for any business continuity plan or high-availability strategy you're involved with.

You'll notice in the list of objectives that virtualization server planning, directory service recovery strategy, and object-level recovery topics are listed. Chapter 2, "Planning Server Deployments," covers virtualization, and Chapter 5, "Monitoring and Maintaining Active Directory," covers directory service strategy and object-level recovery.

Shadow Copies

Shadow Copies is a capability that can easily be enabled that allows users to restore files on their own without the intervention of an administrator. When enabled, a user is able to restore deleted files or restore a file to its previous version.

You can enable Shadow Copies only on NTFS drives. When you are configuring Shadow Copies, you can choose where to store the previous versions and how often to create previous versions. Be careful, though. Once you enable Shadow Copies, you can't change the location without losing all your previous versions, so it's a good idea to pay attention to where the previous versions will be stored.

As a general practice, it's recommended you store the data from Shadow Copies on a separate physical drive whenever possible. Having the data on a separate drive reduces the I/O load on the drive and provides better performance.

The default schedule for previous versions to be created is every weekday at 7 a.m. and 12 p.m. (noon). You can add and remove schedules at any time without impacting previous versions currently stored on your system.

Files and folders have a Previous Versions tab on their properties pages. By selecting the Previous Versions tab, users can access and restore previous versions of the files. As an example, you may regularly use a Microsoft Excel spreadsheet as a template. Normally, you would open the template, save it with another name, and start modifying the file. If one day you forgot to save the file with another name and instead overwrote the template, you could access the previous versions to restore the original file.

When you select a previous version of a file, you have three choices:

Open   Clicking the Open button opens the previous version of the file. You can then decide what you want to do with the file. For example, you can choose to save it to a different location, save it with a different name, or close it and then click the Restore button to restore the original file to this version.

Copy   Clicking the Copy button allows you to copy the file to a new location or with a new name.

Restore   Clicking the Restore button restores the original file to this version.

Exercise 9.1 shows the steps to enable Shadow Copies and access a previous version of a file.

EXERCISE 9.1

Enabling Shadow Copies

1. Launch Windows Explorer.

2. Browse to the C:\ drive. Right-click the C:\ drive, and select New ➢ Folder. Name the folder StudyNotes.

3. Browse to the C:\StudyNotes folder. Right-click within the empty folder, and select New ➢ Text Document. Rename the document to 70-646 Study Notes.

4. Double-click the document, and enter the following text: **Remember to use the flash cards and do the practice test questions on the CD before taking the exam.**

5. Press Ctrl+S to save the file; then close it. Leave Windows Explorer open.

6. Launch Computer Management by clicking Start ➢ Administrative Tools ➢ Computer Management.

7. Right-click Shared Folders, and select All Tasks ➢ Configure Shadow Copies. Your display will look similar to the following graphic (though you may have only one volume).

EXERCISE 9.1 *(continued)*

8. Select the C:\ volume, and click Settings.

9. In the Storage Area section, select the D:\ drive to store the previous version copies (if you have a D:\ drive). If you don't have a D:\ drive, it's OK to store the previous version copies on the C:\ drive; however, you should be aware that it's considered a best practice to store them on a separate drive.

10. Click the Schedule button. Your display will look similar to the following graphic. Notice that the schedule currently has two schedules. The first one (the one that is visible in the graphic) makes a copy of changed files every weekday at 7 a.m. The second schedule makes a copy of changed files every weekday at 12 p.m.

11. After viewing the schedule, click OK.

12. On the Settings page, click OK.

13. To create shadow copies on the C:\ volume, click the Create Now button. Once it is done, click OK.

14. Return to Windows Explorer, and open the text file you created earlier in this exercise.

15. With the file open, delete all the text. Press Ctrl+S to save the file; then close it.

16. Within Windows Explorer, right-click the file, and select Restore Previous Versions. Your display will look similar to the following graphic.

17. Select the previous version of the file, and click Open. Notice this allows you to view the file; next you can choose to save the file in the same location or somewhere else. Close the file.

18. Click the Copy button. The Copy Items dialog box allows you to copy the previous version of the file to wherever you like. Click Cancel.

19. Click the Restore button. In the Are You Sure? dialog box, click Restore, and then click OK. Notice you no longer have a previous version of your file. Click OK.

20. Open your file, and verify the original text has been restored.

Disks

When configuring fault tolerance for a server, you will often consider fault tolerance on your disks first. Fault tolerance on disks comes in the form of Redundant Array of Independent Disks (or Redundant Array of Inexpensive Disks), or RAID.

When deciding on RAID, one of the first decisions you'll face is whether to use software RAID or hardware RAID:

Software RAID   Software RAID is supported by the operating system only. Windows Server 2008 supports RAID-0, RAID-1, and RAID-5. However, you must first convert your disks to dynamic disks to support RAID configurations. When you install Windows Server 2008, your disks will be basic. You can convert them using Disk Management.

If cost is a major consideration, you can implement software RAID without the added expense of additional hardware.

Hardware RAID   Hardware RAID is more expensive but generally performs much better than software RAID. Many servers have hardware support built right into the motherboard for hardware RAID.

If performance is a major consideration, hardware RAID is a better choice than software RAID.

RAID arrays can be internal or external. An array appears to the operating system as a single logical drive (such as D:\) but has many physical drives. It's common to have external arrays for RAID-5 and RAID-10.

RAID Configurations

Multiple configurations of RAID are possible, but many have fallen out of use. The four RAID configurations you should know are RAID-0, RAID-1, RAID-5, and RAID-10. RAID-0 does not provide any fault tolerance. RAID-1, RAID-5, and RAID-10 all provide fault tolerance.

I fully expect that this is not the first time you've come across RAID, so I'm not spending a lot of time describing the details of how RAID works internally. Instead, the focus is where each RAID would be used. If you need a refresher or just want to know how the different RAID configurations work internally, I suggest you check out www.RAID.com. That site has descriptions with some good animations for RAID-0 (www.raid.com/04_01_00.html), RAID-1 (www.raid.com/04_01_01.html), RAID-5 (www.raid.com/04_01_05.html), and RAID-10 (www.raid.com/04_01_10.html).

RAID-0   RAID-0 is also known as *striping*. You can use RAID-0 to increase the read and write speeds of your disks. Files are divided into stripes, and the stripes are placed on the different drives. Data can be read from (or written to) each of the disks simultaneously, significantly improving the performance.

Figure 9.1 shows a RAID-0. Since data is stored equally on each of the disks, no data space is lost.

FIGURE 9.1   RAID-0

Three physical disks configured
as a striped array (RAID-0).
This provides 1.5 TB of usable
storage space.

RAID-0 cannot be used for the boot or system partition (the volume holding the operating system) but could be used for any drives holding data if you want to increase performance.

The name of RAID-0 is somewhat of a misnomer since it is not redundant. In other words, RAID-0 does not provide any fault tolerance.

RAID-0 includes at least two disks but would often use more disks depending on the hardware supporting it. If used on dynamic volumes (software RAID), the maximum is 32 volumes.

RAID-1   RAID-1 is also known as *mirroring*. It includes two disks and two disks only. RAID-1 is used to provide fault tolerance to the operating system (the boot and system partitions). Additionally, some server applications use RAID-1 to protect some elements of the data. For example, to protect the transaction logs in SQL Server, you would use RAID-1.

Figure 9.2 illustrates RAID-1. In RAID-1, whatever is written to one disk is written to the other disk. If one of the disks develops a fault, the system can tolerate it because the other disk has a full copy of the data.

FIGURE 9.2   RAID-1

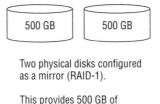

Two physical disks configured
as a mirror (RAID-1).

This provides 500 GB of
usable storage.

RAID-1 doesn't provide any increased write performance, but many controllers are configured so that the data can be read off the two drives, simultaneously increasing read performance.

RAID-5   RAID-5 is also known as *striping with parity*. A minimum of three disks is required for RAID-5. For software RAID-5, Microsoft supports as many as 32 separate disks.

Figure 9.3 shows RAID-5 with three disks. Data is striped across each of the drives with each stripe including a parity stripe. For example, you could have a file named 70–646 Study Notes, and it could be contained within the first stripe. In this example, disk 1 and disk 2 would hold the data, while disk 3 would hold the parity bits used for fault tolerance.

FIGURE 9.3   RAID-5

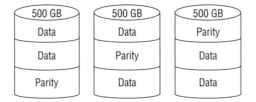

Three physical disks configured
as a stripe with parity (RAID-5).

This provides 1 TB of usable storage.

If one of the disks develops a fault, the RAID-5 can use the parity bits to determine the contents of the faulty drive. It can tolerate the fault and continue to operate. If two drives fail in a RAID-5, the data is lost.

You can use RAID-5 to provide fault tolerance for data. RAID-5 cannot be used to provide protection to the operating system (the boot and system partitions).

A RAID-5 provides significant improvements in both read and write performance compared to a regular disk. It also provides better performance over a RAID-1.

RAID-10   RAID-10 starts as a mirror (RAID-1) of two disks. Additional mirrors are added and striped (RAID-0), as shown in Figure 9.4. Each part of the RAID-10 includes two disks configured as a RAID-1.

Just as a regular RAID-0 could include many additional disks configured as a stripe, you can configure many additional disk pairs on your RAID-10 configuration. The only requirement is that for each additional stripe you add, it must be a pair of disks configured as a mirror.

FIGURE 9.4   RAID-10

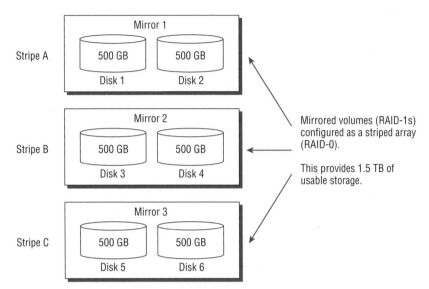

A RAID-10 provides two primary benefits:

- It provides significant fault tolerance. You would have to lose two drives of any specific mirror (such as disk 1 and disk 2 or such as disk 3 and disk 4) to actually lose data. If you lost one drive in each of the mirrors (such as disk 1, disk 4, and disk 5), the RAID-10 would still operate.

- A RAID-10 provides performance gains. Since the data is spread across multiple drives, you'll enjoy improvements in reads and writes (similar to how a RAID-0 provides improvements in reads and writes).

Disk Storage Solutions

Data can be stored either internally or externally in relation to the server. When stored internally, the server could have hardware-implemented RAID built into the motherboard or available through additional adapter cards.

External data could be available on serial attached SCSI (SAS) or a storage area network (SAN). I'll discuss SAS and SAN later in this section.

Data on the disks can be accessed using different architectures. The two primary architectures used to access storage are the Virtual Disk Service (VDS) and Multipath I/O (MPIO):

Virtual Disk Service   The VDS architecture includes the underlying components used to access disks. Before VDS (developed after Windows 2000 was released), if a company built a storage device, they would have to create their own application to manage the device. Administrators had to contend with different applications used to access different disks on different servers.

Disks, Partitions, and Volumes

When discussing disks, you should know the different terms, especially since they can be used interchangeably.

A physical disk can be divided into partitions (though it's not often done on a server). When divided, the each partition is referred to by a drive letter (C:\, D:\, and so on). If the disk is a single partition, the entire disk could be referenced with a single drive letter (such as C:\).

In past versions of Windows, the term *volume* meant that the disk was converted to a dynamic volume. However, you'll frequently see the term *volume* used interchangeably with *partition* and *disk*. The actual meaning depends on the context of how the term is used. For example, you could have a single disk divided into different partitions. Each of the partitions could be referred to as *volumes*. Similarly, a single disk with a single partition could be referred to as a *volume.*

The big difference with volumes (as opposed to partitions and disks) is that when multiple disks are combined (as is done with RAID), the combined disks are referred to as a single *volume.* As an example, you could have two physical drives in a RAID-1 (mirror) providing fault tolerance for the operating system, and it would be referred to as the C:\ volume. On the same system you could have three more drives configured in a RAID-5 providing fault tolerance for data, and it would be referred to as the C:\ volume.

With VDS, the manufacturer needs to provide only the hardware provider. Common commands and tools (such as DiskPart and Disk Manager) can be used for each disk.

VDS can be used for both internal and external storage, and it is commonly used with RAID arrays.

Multipath I/O   MPIO is a group of technologies used to allow servers with multiple host bus adapters to access multiple disks simultaneously. MPIO is used to provide a high level of redundancy and availability for the disks.

If using multipath I/O for clusters, it's important to ensure that the hardware and software are matched to each other. Both host bus adapters and multipath I/O software can be very version sensitive.

Multipath I/O can be used with serial attached SCSI, iSCSI, and Fibre Channel. MPIO establishes multiple sessions or connections to the storage array.

When data is stored externally, you will typically choose from either SAS or a SAN. These choices can be used when implementing a regular server, a failover cluster, or network load balancing. Failover clusters and network load balancing topics are presented later in this chapter.

Serial attached SCSI   SAS is a SCSI array directly attached to the server via a serial SCSI connection. The attached storage device could be configured as RAID-0, RAID-1, RAID-5, or RAID-10 depending on the design goals. (For example, if you wanted to provide fault tolerance and have the best throughput, you'd use a RAID-10.) Although SAS is also used for tape devices, our interest for this chapter is only for disk devices.

Storage area network   A SAN is a specialized network that provides a centralized pool of disk storage that can be accessed by multiple computers. The difference between network attached storage (NAS) and a SAN is that NAS refers to a single device dedicated to storage, while a SAN is an entire network dedicated to storage. Disks within a SAN are typically shared among multiple computers.

 Although NAS is also possible, I'm giving it less emphasis here because it can't be used with failover clusters or network load balancing. NAS refers to storage that is available on the network (as opposed to direct attached storage such as serial attached SCSI), which is directly attached to the computer.

In addition to the different types of storage, there are also different types of access methods. You should be aware of the following technologies:

iSCSI   Internet Small Computer System Interface (iSCSI) allows a computer to connect to a storage network using TCP/IP commands. The computer is referred to as the *initiator*, and the network storage device is referred to as a *target*. Since TCP/IP is used, it doesn't require any specialized hardware or connections. iSCSI does require a dedicated network adapter, and gigabit network interface cards are recommended when used with clusters.

iSCSI is often viewed as a low-cost alternative to Fibre Channel because it doesn't require specialized hardware and uses technology (TCP/IP) that most network administrators already know.

One drawback to iSCSI is that you cannot use teamed network adapter cards with iSCSI. They are not supported.

Fibre Channel   Fibre Channel (FC) is a high-speed connection often used for storage networking. Fibre Channel uses dedicated hardware (Fibre Channel switches and host-bus adapters) and dedicated connections to create access to the storage network.

One reason to use Fibre Channel instead of iSCSI is if you want to isolate the disk traffic from the network. Since Fibre Channel uses dedicated connections to the storage network, it won't interfere with regular network traffic.

 When deciding between iSCSI and Fibre Channel, two of the biggest considerations are cost and network impact. If you need to minimize costs, use iSCSI since it uses the existing network infrastructure and reduces costs in both hardware purchases and training. If you need to minimize the impact on the network, use Fibre Channel since it uses dedicated hardware and connections for traffic.

Failover Clustering

Failover clustering is used to provide redundancy at the server level. In other words, if you want to ensure that services remain running on a server even if the server fails, you can implement failover clustering. Failover clustering is often used in situations where you can't afford any outage for a particular service or you need to ensure the service is highly available.

> In previous versions of Windows, failover clusters were known as *server clusters.* In Windows Server 2008, the terminology is failover clusters or failover clustering.

Some of the common uses of failover clusters include the following:

- Database servers (such as Microsoft SQL Server)
- Email servers (such as Microsoft Exchange)
- File servers
- Custom or line-of-business applications

A failover cluster includes two or more servers that are referred to as *nodes*. When one of the nodes fails, another node server in the failover cluster is able to pick up the load. In Windows Server 2008, you can implement clustering on servers by adding the failover cluster feature through the Server Manager.

As an example of a failover cluster, consider Figure 9.5. It shows Microsoft SQL Server configured in a failover cluster. From the perspective of the clients, there is only one server—the server labeled as the virtual SQL server. However, the configuration includes two physical servers configured as nodes in the cluster.

FIGURE 9.5   Clustering solution

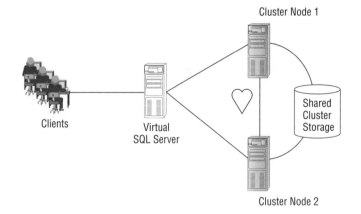

In this configuration, both nodes (node 1 and node 2) would be running Windows Server 2008. One node (cluster node 1, for example) would be running Microsoft SQL Server and provide all the responses to SQL queries. Cluster node 2 would not answer queries but instead would monitor the health of cluster node 1 by monitoring the "heartbeat" on a separate connection. If cluster node 1 fails, cluster node 2 would learn of the failure through the loss of the heartbeat. If cluster node 1 can't be restarted, cluster node 2 would take over. From the perspective of the clients, there may be a momentary delay, but overall there would no interruption in service.

Notice that both cluster nodes have a connection to the shared cluster storage. This shared cluster storage could be a serial attached SCSI or a SAN (connected using either iSCSI or Fibre Channel). Each node in the cluster needs access to the same data in order to be able to take over the load at a moment's notice.

Each node in the cluster will have three separate connections: one for network access (by the clients), one for monitoring the other node, and one for access to the shared cluster storage.

Requirements

Failover clusters have both hardware and software requirements. Additionally, Windows Server 2008 includes a Validate tool you can use to assist with the installation of a cluster and verify proper installation.

Software

The software requirements are related to the operating systems. The following versions of Windows Server 2008 support failover clusters:

- Windows Server 2008 Enterprise

- Windows Server 2008 Data Center

- Server Core installation of Windows Server 2008 Enterprise

- Server Core installation of Windows Server 2008 Datacenter

> **NOTE**   Although servers with only a Server Core installation can be part of a failover cluster, Server Core supports only the DHCP, DNS, Active Directory Domain Services, Active Directory Lightweight Services, Streaming Media Services, File Services, and Print Services server roles. Server Core does not support Microsoft SQL Server or Microsoft Exchange. If you want to use a failover cluster to protect Microsoft SQL Server or Microsoft Exchange applications, you must use a full installation of the operating system.

Each node within the cluster must be running the same version of Windows Server 2008. Additionally, all servers within the cluster should be patched identically.

Hardware

When configuring failover clusters, you should use matched servers. In other words, each node should have identical hardware (or at least as close as possible).

When planning the number of nodes, you need to pay close attention to the basic resources (CPU, memory, and NIC) used by each node. For a node to take over the load of other nodes, it must have enough resources. For example, imagine a two-node cluster where each of the nodes is actively running a server application (such as SQL Server) and each node is utilizing 20 percent of the basic resources. If one of the nodes fails, the other node could pick up the load, and the maximum load you could expect with both nodes is 40 percent. However, imagine the same two-node cluster with each node having a 70 percent load. If one of the nodes fails, the other node won't have enough resources to handle the additional load. Either the node will slow down to a crawl or, worse, the node could crash as it tries to keep up.

Additionally, the type of data storage you use will dictate other hardware requirements. For example, if you're using Fibre Channel, you'll need to include Fibre Channel host adapters. If using iSCSI, you'll need to include dedicated adapters for the iSCSI connection.

Failover clusters in Windows Server 2008 now support GUID Partition Table (GPT) disks that can have capacities larger than 2 terabytes (TB). You would use either GPT disks or master boot record (MBR) disks, but if you need more than 2TB, you'd use GPT-based disks.

Validate Tool

Microsoft Windows Server 2008 includes a built-in cluster Validate tool (previously known as ClusPrep). The Validate tool runs a series of tests to ensure the hardware and software meets the minimum requirements and also helps to configure the cluster with best practices settings.

Configuring a cluster can be very complex. You go very far by first ensuring that you're running the same operating system and your hardware is identical on each of the nodes. Once that's verified, you can run the Validate tool.

Although you may be able to get a cluster to work even if it fails the Validate tool, it won't be supported by Microsoft if you have a problem.

Nodes and Quorums

Any failover cluster will have at least two nodes. Up to 16 nodes are supported with x64-based failover clusters, though failover clusters with 16 nodes will be rare.

In generic terms, a *quorum* identifies the minimum number of members needed to make decisions. For example, a business entity may have five officers, but business rules dictate that at least three officers must be present to vote on issues. In other words, it takes three officers to make a quorum.

Similarly, a failover cluster uses a quorum to identify the minimum number of nodes needed to keep the cluster operational. If one node fails, certainly you want to keep operating. But what if two or more clusters fail? Based on the quorum model you choose, you can have different numbers of failures and continue to operate.

An important part of the voting process is the witness disk.

Witness Disk and Witness File Share

You are able configure a witness disk in a Windows Server 2008 cluster. The witness disk replaces the quorum disk that was used in previous operating system cluster configurations and holds a copy of the cluster configuration database.

The witness disk is given a vote as if it is a cluster node. In other words, if you have a two-node cluster and one node fails, you still have a majority that is operational as long as the witness disk is still operational. The node that is still up and the witness disk form a quorum.

Instead of a witness disk, it's also possible to have a witness file share. The same rules apply when using a witness file share instead of a witness disk. The witness file share is given an equal vote when determining whether quorum exists. If one node in a two-node cluster fails, the cluster will stay operational as long as the witness file share is up and reachable.

Quorum Configuration Choices

When configuring your cluster, you'll need to specify the quorum configuration. The quorum configuration specifies how many votes are needed to keep the cluster operational. Votes are tied to the nodes and/or the witness disk or the files share witness.

The following four quorum configuration choices are available within Windows Server 2008 failover clusters:

Node Majority   A Node Majority quorum configuration requires a simple majority of nodes to be online to maintain a quorum and stay online. A Node Majority is recommended for clusters with an odd number of nodes (such as three or five nodes). The witness disk (or witness file share) is not given a vote in the Node Majority quorum.

For example, if you have three nodes and one node fails, you'd still have two nodes up (which is a majority). The cluster will still have a quorum and still stay operational. If two nodes failed in your three-node cluster, you would no longer have quorum, and the cluster would stop functioning.

Node and Disk Majority   In the Node and Disk Majority quorum, a disk is labeled as the witness disk, and it has a vote in the quorum. A Node and Disk Majority is recommended for clusters with an even number of nodes (such as two, four, or six). With the witness disk included as member of the quorum, you would have an odd number of members (such as three, five, or seven).

For example, if you have two nodes and one node failed (but the witness disk was still up), you'd still have a majority (the one operational node and the witness disk). The cluster will still have a quorum and still stay operational. If one node failed in your two-node cluster and the witness disk also failed, you would no longer have a quorum, and the cluster would no longer function.

Node and File Share Majority   The Node and File Share Majority quorum configuration is similar to the Node and Disk Majority quorum configuration. The difference is that instead of using a witness disk, the cluster uses a witness file share. In other words, a separate physical disk isn't required for the witness disk; instead, a share available on the network can be used.

Using the Node and File Share Majority quorum configuration is especially useful in geographically separated sites. For example, you could have headquarters with one node and a remote site with another node. You could then configure the witness file share so that it's accessible to both sites.

Now, if either of the nodes went down, the other node could still access the witness file share and remain operational. Additionally, if either site lost connectivity with the other site, the cluster nodes could still continue to operate as long as they had access to the witness file share.

No Majority: Disk Only   This is not a recommended choice but is included for backward compatibility. It allows failures of all nodes except one as long as the disk used for storage remains online.

When deciding which quorum configuration to choose, you have to count only the nodes. If you have an odd number of nodes, use the Node Majority quorum configuration. (However, if your clusters are geographically separated, the Node and File Share Majority is the best choice for an odd number of nodes.) If you have an even number of nodes, use either the Node and Disk Majority or Node and File Share Majority. The No Majority: Disk Only configuration is generally not recommended and is included only for backward compatibility with existing clusters.

Network Load Balancing

The primary purpose of a network load balancing cluster is to provide scalability. In other words, network load balancing is used to allow more and more clients to access the same service without impacting performance. Client requests are distributed among the servers, and if a server fails, NLB detects the failure and sends the load to another server.

Figure 9.6 shows an NLB cluster. The NLB cluster presents itself as a single IP address to clients and uses an algorithm based on the IP address of the clients to map the clients to one of the nodes in the NLB cluster.

In the event of a failure of one of the nodes, clients are automatically redirected to another node. If a node fails while a user is connected, the client will typically retry the connection, and one of the other nodes in the NLB cluster will sense the outage and answer the request.

Although an NLB cluster provides high availability, it does so differently than failover clustering. A failover cluster concentrates on fault tolerance strategies to allow a separate server to take over the load if a single server fails. In contrast, an NLB cluster doesn't use fault tolerance strategies but instead just makes more servers available.

FIGURE 9.6   NLB cluster

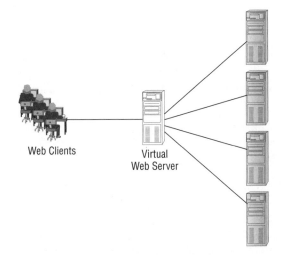

Web Clients   Virtual
                  Web Server

Consider a gas station with one gasoline pump. It can serve only one customer at a time, and if the pump develops a problem, the gas station stops selling gasoline. Newer convenience-store-based gasoline stations have as many as 20 pumps. These stores can serve as many as 20 customers at a time. Even if one of the pumps develops a problem, the store can still serve 19 customers.

Similarly, an NLB cluster can increase availability and scalability by adding servers doing the same function. For example, a single web server can serve pages to a website to a specific number of customers at a time. If the web server developed a problem, the website would go down. If you added multiple web servers in a web farm, all configured with the same website, you could serve more customers simultaneously. Additionally, if one of the web servers went down, the website would still be operational.

One of the key differences between failover clusters and NLB clusters is that nodes in an NLB cluster don't share any resources. Each individual server within an NLB cluster runs independently. Even if a node fails and a user is redirected to another node, there isn't a need to access the same data.

Common uses of NLB include the following:

- Web servers
- FTP servers
- Web services
- VPN servers
- Firewall servers
- Proxy servers
- Other stateless applications

You can support up to 32 nodes on an NLB cluster.

Requirements

Unlike failover clustering, which has several restrictions, there are very few restrictions on an NLB cluster:

All Windows Server 2008 editions   You can install an NLB cluster on servers running any edition of Windows Server 2008, including the Web edition. Since web servers are commonly run on Windows Server 2008 Web edition, additional upgrades aren't required on the operating system.

This is different from a failover cluster that is supported only on Windows Server 2008 Enterprise and Datacenter editions.

No extra hardware   NLB works "out of the box." You don't need to purchase additional hardware to make it work. NLB can even work with just a single NIC. This is significantly different from a failover cluster that requires matching servers and additional hardware to support each node in the cluster.

NLB is installed as a feature   To install the NLB Windows networking driver component on a server, you simply add network load balancing. Figure 9.7 shows the NLB feature being added through Server Manager. Once it's installed, you can manage the NLB cluster with the Network Load Balancing Manager tool.

FIGURE 9.7   Adding the NLB feature

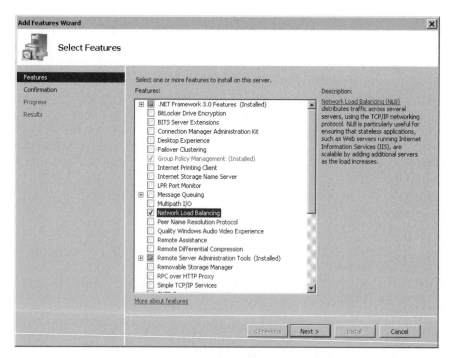

IPv6 is supported   NLB clusters can be configured to support IPv6. Additionally, you can configure the NLB cluster to support both IPv4 and IPv6 simultaneously.

NLB and Server Core Installation

It is possible to configure an NLB cluster on several servers running in Server Core mode. As a reminder, the Server Core installation includes only the minimum services and applications required for the role. There is no GUI—only the command line in the Server Core installation.

Internet Information Services (IIS) is included as one of the roles in a Server Core installation, but since Server Core provides only the command line, you won't have access to the typical IIS GUIs such as IIS Manager and the IIS administration tool. The AppCmd command-line tool is used to perform administration tasks for IIS on a Server Core installation.

However, you may want to remotely manage IIS. For example, you may be running Windows Vista or Windows XP on your desktop but want to remotely administer your IIS servers running on Server Core in the NLB cluster. You can do this by enabling Windows Remote Management (WinRM).

I covered remote administration of Server Core in more depth in Chapter 2 and in Chapter 3, "Using Windows Server 2003 Management Tools," but as a reminder, you can enable WinRM by running the WinRM quickconfig command on the Server Core servers.

In IIS 6.0, remote administration was automatically enabled. Remote administration of IIS 7.0 is disabled by default and must be enabled in addition to enabling WinRM.

Windows Server Backup Features

Windows Server Backup Features is a feature within Windows Server 2008. It isn't added by default but can be added with the Server Manager through the Add Features Wizard. Once it's installed, you can back up data and volumes on your servers. You can use Windows Server Backup Features to perform and manage backups on the local computer or remote computers.

The Windows Server Backup Features feature includes the following:

Windows Server Backup tool   The Windows Server Backup tool is a Microsoft Management Console (MMC) snap-in used to perform backup and restores. As a GUI, it is easy to use for backups and restores by following simple wizards.

Command-line tools   You can use the command-line tools to create and manage backups on your server. Windows PowerShell must be installed to support the Windows Server Backup command-line tools. With the PowerShell cmdlets, you can automate backups through scripting. Additionally, you have the Wbadmin command-line tool that can be used for backups.

⊕ **Real World Scenario**

System State

System state data has been available as a backup (and restore) choice in Windows operating systems since Windows 2000. It includes key data including the registry, boot files (including system files), files that are protected by Windows File Protection (WFP), and other files depending on the role of the server. For example, a domain controller would include Active Directory Domain Services and the Sysvol directory.

In release candidates of Windows Server 2008, system state wasn't available as an option for backup and restore procedures. A lot of users gave feedback to Microsoft that system state was desirable (instead of doing full volume backup and restores). Microsoft listened, and the final release includes the ability to back up and restore system state data if desired.

You may run across some documentation that indicates you can't back up system state data, but that knowledge is based on early release candidates, not the final release of Windows Server 2008. You can back up system state using the Wbadmin command-line tool.

Once you install the Windows Server Backup feature, you have the following choices for backups:

Full server (all volumes)   You can use the Windows Server Backup tool to select all volumes connected to your system from within Windows Backup. Backups created using this option can be used by the Windows Complete PC Restore available in the WinRE covered in the next section.

Selected volumes   This choice allows you to pick and choose which volumes to back up. If you have many volumes, you can use this option to pick only the volumes needed for a system recovery or only the volumes that include your data. You can restore volumes using the Windows Server Backup tool.

System state   System state can be backed up using the Wbadmin tool. You can restore the system state data using the Wbadmin tool. Wbadmin is covered in a little more depth later in this chapter.

After you have backed up volumes, you can use the Windows Server Backup tool to restore volumes or data. Windows Server Backup includes a wizard to pick the volumes you want to restore or to pick individual files and folders.

Figure 9.8 shows the Windows Server Backup tool with the Recovery Wizard launched.

You can choose to restore data to the original location or to another location. You can even choose what action to take if the file still exists in the original location (such as overwrite the existing file or create copies).

FIGURE 9.8   Windows Server Backup Recovery Wizard

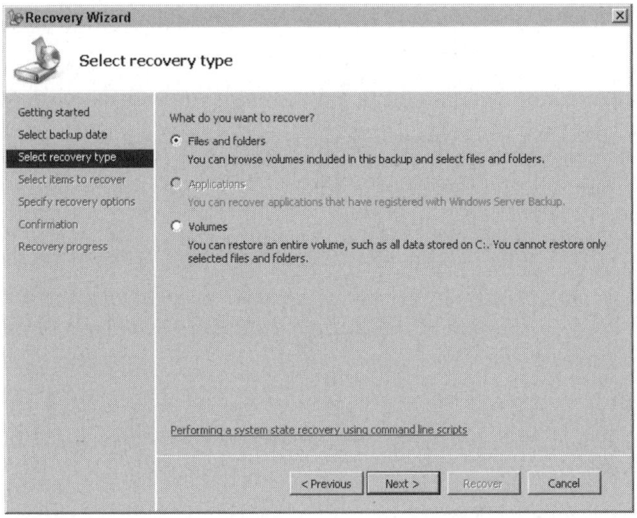

Backup Locations

When doing backups with the Windows Server Backup tool, you can choose multiple locations to store the backup. These include the following:

Disks   You can back up to internal and external disks. External disks can be portable USB-connected disks. These are becoming quite popular, and 500GB USB disks are very affordable. These can be used to back up system volumes for recovery purposes or data volumes to restore user's data.

Optical drives and other removable media   You can back up volumes manually to optical media drives (such as DVDs). You can't pick this option when scheduling backups.

Remote shared folders   You can back up data to a remote path using a Universal Naming Convention (UNC). UNC paths are formatted as \\ServerName\ShareName. For example, you could have a server named MCITP1 and a share named Success. The UNC path would be \\MCITP1\Success.

Interestingly, you cannot back up to tape using the Windows Server Backup or Wbadmin. Of course, you can back up to tape using third-party tools.

Wbadmin

The Wbadmin command-line tool allows you to perform all of the same tasks from the command line that you can perform from the GUI. The benefit of any command-line tool is that you can script the solution and then schedule it to run at any time. Wbadmin allows you to automate your backups through scripting.

Additionally, you can back up and restore system state using the Wbadmin tool. This was covered in more depth in Chapter 5.

Once you install the Windows Backup feature, you have access to the Wbadmin tool. The following commands are available at the command line:

- Enable Backup. You can use this command to enable or modify scheduled backups.

- Disable Backup. You can use this command to disable scheduled backups.

- Start Backup. You can immediately start a backup with this command. You can use this to run a one-time backup.

- Stop Job. This command will stop a backup or recovery that is currently running.

- Get Versions. You can read the version information from available backups with this command. Version information includes the backup time and date stamp, the backup destination, and the version identifier.

- Get Items. This will list information on individual items contained within a backup.

- Start Recovery. You can begin a recovery of volumes, applications, folders, or files with this command.

- Get Status. This reports the status of a currently running job by indicating the volume being backed up and the percentage complete.

- Get Disks. This shows disks that are currently online.

- Start Systemstaterecovery. This will begin a system state recovery from a selected backup. If you are attempting to restore system state for a domain controller, you can do so only from the directory services restore mode (DSRM).

- Start Systemstatebackup. This will begin a backup of system state data.

- Delete Systemstatebackup. You can delete backups of system state data with this command.

- Start Sysrecovery. You can begin a recovery of the full system with volumes that have the operating system's state.

- Restore Catalog. If the backup catalog is corrupted, this command will recover a backup catalog.

- Delete Catalog. This will delete a backup catalog.

Each of the Wbadmin commands has extensive syntax requirements beyond the scope of this book. For the syntax of any of the commands, you can get help at the command line with the following syntax:

Wbadmin command /?

For example, if you want more information on the Start Systemstaterecovery command, you can enter the following command:

Wbadmin Start Systemstaterecovery /?

Using Windows Server Backup

Exercise 9.2 shows the steps to launch Windows Server Backup and run a server recovery backup.

 TIP If you don't have the backup feature installed, you can follow the steps in Exercise 5.2 in Chapter 5.

EXERCISE 9.2

Running Windows Server Backup

1. Click Start ➢ Administrative Tools ➢ Windows Server Backup.

2. In the Windows Server Backup tool, click Backup Once.

3. On the Backup Options page, select Different Options (if it's not already selected), and click Next.

4. On the Select Backup Configuration page, select Custom, and click Next.

5. On the Select Backup Items page, select the check box for only the volume (or volumes) needed for system recovery. Deselect the check boxes for the remaining drives (if there are any). Ensure the check box for Enable System Recovery is selected. Your display will look similar to the following graphic (though your system may not have as many volumes). Click Next.

6. On the Specify Destination Type page, select Local Drives, and click Next. Note that you can choose to store the date on local drives (including locally connected USB drives or remote shared folders using the UNC of \\serverName\shareName).

7. On the Select Backup Destination page, select your destination drive from the drop-down box. Notice that you can't select one of the drives that are included in the system recovery as the destination. Click Next.

8. On the Specify Advanced Option page, ensure that VSS Copy Backup (recommended) is selected. Click Next.

9. On the Confirmation page, review your choices, and click Backup. The backup will start and show you progress. You can close the backup tool and continue to work while the backup tool runs in the background. The amount of time needed for the backup depends on the amount of data being backed up.

10. When the backup is complete, click Close.

Windows Recovery Environment

The Windows Recovery Environment is a partial version of the operating system. It is based on the Windows Preinstallation Environment (WinPE) but has a primary purpose of recovery. It includes several tools you can use in the event of a serious failure on your server to perform operating system or full server recoveries.

The tools included in the WinRE are as follows:

Windows Complete PC Restore If you created a full server backup, you can use the Windows Complete PC Restore tool to fully restore your operating system and server. If you select this option, the system will search for a valid backup location (such as a DVD drive or a portable USB disk drive). You can then restore from the full server backup stored on this location.

Windows Memory Diagnostic tool If you suspect your server has problems with the physical random access memory (RAM), you can use this tool to check the RAM. This tool does require a valid server 2008 installation to function. If you choose this option, you will be prompted to either restart the computer immediately and run the Memory Diagnostic tool or allow it to run on the next boot.

Command prompt   You can access to the command prompt with administrator privileges in the WinRE. This allows you to access the file system if needed. You also have access to Windows Backup Admin (Wbadmin) commands.

Entering WinRE

There are four ways to enter the Windows Recovery Environment:

Boot from the installation CD   When you boot from the installation CD, you can select Repair Your Computer from the installation screen. Exercise 9.3 will walk you through the steps for this process.

Deploy from WDS   You can create a Windows RE image file (.wim) and deploy it using Windows Deployment Services (WDS). WDS was covered in much more depth in Chapter 2.

Create a bootable WinRE disk   It's also possible to create a WinRE bootable disk. To create a WinRE bootable disk (in the format of an .iso file), you could use the Business Desktop Deployment (BDD) tools or the Windows Automated Installation Kit (WAIK). Both tools take some time to master and use, but in time I fully expect completed .iso files to begin appearing.

Create a bootable WinRE partition   It's possible to create a bootable WinRE partition on your hard disk. The partition should be at least 1.5GB in size and preferably be on a different physical disk than the operating system. If the operating system partition fails, you would still be able to boot into the WinRE partition.

If you want to install WinRE on a separate partition, check out this blog entry from the WinRE team: http://blogs.msdn.com/winre/archive/2007/01/12/how-to-install-winre-on-the-hard-disk.aspx. Special thanks to Stuart Ami (this book's technical editor) for finding this valuable blog entry.

The best way to understand WinRE is to launch it and take a look. Exercise 9.3 shows the steps to enter the WinRE environment from the installation DVD.

EXERCISE 9.3

Launching WinRE

1.   Insert your Windows Server 2008 installation DVD, and boot from it.

2.   When prompted to set your language and other preferences, click Next.

3.   On the Install Now page (shown in the following graphic), click the Repair Your Computer link located at the bottom-left corner.

EXERCISE 9.3 *(continued)*

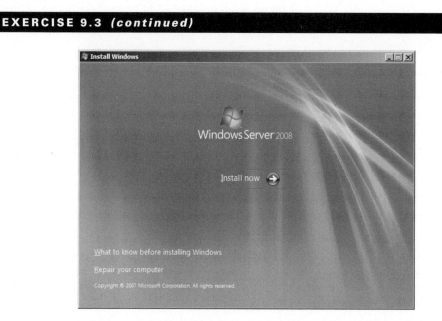

4. On the System Recovery Options page, you can select the operating system that you want to repair. If there aren't any operating systems listed, you can still enter the WinRE environment by clicking Next.

5. On the Choose a Recovery Tool page (shown in the following graphic), you can choose Windows Complete PC Restore, Windows Memory Diagnostic Tool, or Command Prompt. Choose Command Prompt.

6. In the command prompt window, enter `wbadmin /?`. You'll see a list of commands available via the `Wbadmin` tool in WinRE.

Summary

In this chapter, you learned about several different possibilities of ensuring business continuity and making your data highly available.

Any NTFS disk can have Shadow Copies enabled on it, allowing previous versions to be created on a regular schedule. Users can then restore their data on their own.

You learned about many of the RAID disk solutions and what is relevant with Windows Server 2008 such as RAID-0, RAID-1, RAID-5, and RAID-10.

A significant portion of the chapter was dedicated to failover clusters. You learned that failover clusters can be used to provide fault tolerance for a server. A drawback of failover clusters is the added cost due to the hardware and shared storage requirements. Fibre Channel (FC) is significantly more expensive, but iSCSI brings the cost down some by using existing network infrastructure.

Network Load Balancing (NLB) clusters can be used for servers that don't need shared storage (such as IIS, firewalls, and proxy servers). Unlike failover clusters that can be installed only on Windows Server 2008 Enterprise or Datacenter editions, NLB clusters can be installed on any version.

You learned about the capabilities of Windows Server Backup and the Wbadmin command-line tool. Backups can be stored on local disks, DVDs (though only for manual backups), USB disks, and even network shares.

Last, you learned about the Windows Recovery Environment (WinRE) and how it can be accessed.

Exam Essentials

Understand Shadow Copies and previous versions.   You should understand that by enabling Shadow Copies, users will have access to previous versions of their files.

Know the different types of RAID.   You should know which types of RAID provide fault tolerance (RAID-1, RAID-5, and RAID-10) and which doesn't (RAID-0). You also should know which RAID is used for protecting the operating system (RAID-1) and which RAID is used to protect data with the best performance (RAID-5 or RAID-10).

Understand failover clusters and their requirements.   You need to know the purpose of failover clusters (provide fault tolerance for servers). You should also know that you must have Windows Server 2008 Enterprise or Datacenter edition to support failover clusters. You should also know which quorum configuration to select when deploying clusters.

Know the storage strategies available for failover clusters.   You should be aware of the different storage strategies available and when they should be used. Fibre Channel (FC) uses dedicated hardware and dedicated connections so wouldn't affect the network traffic but costs more. iSCSI can use the existing network infrastructure so costs less. GUID Partition Table disks can be used if storage larger than 2TB is needed.

Understand the purpose of network load balancing.   You should know that network load balancing (NLB) is used to provide high availability. NLB doesn't use shared data storage as a failover cluster does. For any server roles that don't need shared storage, NLB can be used for high availability. NLB can be installed on any Windows Server 2008 edition.

Know the backup and restore capabilities of Windows Server 2008.   You should know the capabilities of the Windows Server Backup and Wbadmin tools, such as what can be backed up, where backups can be stored, and what can be restored.

Know about the Windows Recovery Environment.   You should know the capabilities available in the Windows Recovery Environment (WinRE) and how the WinRE can be accessed.

Review Questions

1. You are tasked with recommending a strategy that allows users to retrieve previous versions of files without intervention by an administrator. If a disk fails, you should be able to restore individual files. All servers are running Windows Server 2008. What should you do? (Choose all that apply.)

    A. Perform a daily backup of data.

    B. Enable Shadow Copies, and store them on the same volume.

    C. Enable Shadow Copies, and store them on a different volume.

    D. Enable clustering on the server.

2. Users store their data on a file server running Windows Server 2008. Recently, a junior administrator has spent a lot of time retrieving data files for several users from backups. You'd like to reduce the administrator's need to do this. What can you do?

    A. Install Windows Server Backup on the users' desktops.

    B. Install Windows Complete PC Restore on the users' desktops.

    C. Install the WinRE on the users' desktops.

    D. Enable Shadow Copies.

3. You are preparing to deploy Microsoft SQL Server on a Windows Server 2008 server. You have five disks. You want to provide protection of the operating system and the data in the event a single disk fails. You also want to optimize the performance of the disks. What should you do?

    A. Create a RAID-1 and a RAID-5. Place the operating system and the SQL data files on the RAID-1 and the SQL transaction log on the RAID-5.

    B. Create two RAID-5 volumes. Place the operating system on one RAID-5 and the SQL files on the other RAID-5.

    C. Create a RAID-1 and a RAID-5. Place the operating system and the SQL data files on the RAID-5 and the SQL transaction log on the RAID-1.

    D. Create a RAID-1 and a RAID-5. Place the operating system and the SQL transaction log on the RAID-1 and the SQL data files on the RAID-5.

4. You are tasked with configuring a Windows Server 2008 server that will operate as a file server. You have five SCSI drives, and you need to ensure that the operating system is separated from the data. Additionally, you need to ensure that the server will continue to function completely even if a disk fails. What should you do?

    A. Configure the five disks as a RAID-5 array.

    B. Configure three disks as RAID-0 and two disks as a RAID-1. Put the operating system on the RAID-1 and the data on the RAID-0.

    C. Configure three disks as a RAID-5 and two disks as a RAID-1. Put the operating system on the RAID-5 and the data on the RAID-1.

    D. Configure three disks as a RAID-5 and two disks as a RAID-1. Put the operating system on the RAID-1 and the data on the RAID-5.

5. You are researching the requirements to install Microsoft SQL Server 2005 on a Windows Server 2008 server. Your solution must include redundancy for SQL Server if a single server fails. What should you recommend?

   A. Install Windows Server 2008 Standard edition on two servers, and implement network load balancing.

   B. Install Windows Server 2008 Enterprise edition on two servers, and implement network load balancing.

   C. Install Windows Server 2008 Enterprise edition on two servers, and implement failover clusters.

   D. Install Windows Server 2008 Data Center edition using a Server Core installation on two servers, and implement failover clusters.

6. You are researching the requirements to deploy file server on Windows Server 2008. Your solution must meet the following requirements: maintain access to all data if a single server fails or if a single disk fails. The disks should be configured for optimum disk throughput. What should you do?

   A. Implement a two-node failover cluster with external storage configured as a RAID-10.

   B. Implement a two-node failover cluster with external storage configured as a RAID-0.

   C. Implement a two-node failover cluster with external storage configured as a RAID-1.

   D. Implement a two-node failover cluster with internal storage configured as a RAID-10.

7. Your company is deploying a line-of-business application on Windows Server 2008 servers internal to the network. You are tasked with identifying a method that will ensure the application will continue to run even if a single server fails. What should you recommend?

   A. Deploy a three-node failover cluster using the Node and File Share Majority quorum configuration.

   B. Deploy a three-node failover cluster using the Node and Disk Majority disk only quorum configuration.

   C. Deploy a two-node failover cluster using the Node and File Share Majority quorum configuration.

   D. Deploy a two-node failover cluster using the No Majority: Disk Only quorum configuration.

8. Your company has its headquarters in Virginia Beach and a branch office in Suffolk. The company is planning on deploying a client/server application that will be available to users at the headquarters and the branch office. You are tasked with identifying a method of ensuring the application will remain available even if a single server fails, while minimizing costs. All servers run Windows Server 2008. What should you recommend?

   A. Deploy a one-node failover cluster at headquarters and a one-node failover cluster at the branch office.

   B. Deploy a two-node failover cluster at headquarters and a two-node failover cluster at the branch office.

   C. Deploy a two-node failover cluster including one node at headquarters and one node at the branch office.

   D. Deploy a two-node failover cluster at headquarters and a one-node failover cluster at the branch office.

9. You are preparing to deploy three file servers running Windows Server 2008. All the file servers will connect to Ethernet switches. You want to maximize fault tolerance while using the existing network infrastructure. What should you do?

    A. Install Windows Enterprise edition on each server. Deploy the servers in a failover cluster. Deploy a Fibre Channel storage area network.

    B. Install Windows Enterprise edition on each server. Deploy the servers in a failover cluster. Deploy an iSCSI storage area network.

    C. Install Windows Standard edition on each server. Deploy the servers in a failover cluster. Deploy an iSCSI storage area network.

    D. Install Windows Standard edition on each server. Deploy the servers in an NLB cluster. Deploy a Fibre Channel storage area network.

10. You are planning to deploy two SQL Servers supporting two separate database applications. You want to ensure that if a single server fails, users can still access data from each of the application. You want to ensure that data from the disk volume remains available even if a single disk fails. Last, you need to ensure your solution supports volumes larger than two TB. What should you do?

    A. Deploy a two-node cluster. Configure the external storage as a RAID-0 array. Format the array as a GPT disk.

    B. Deploy a two-node cluster. Configure the external storage as a RAID-10 array.

    C. Deploy a one-node cluster. Configure internal storage as a RAID-10 array. Format the array as a GPT disk.

    D. Deploy a two-node cluster. Configure the external storage as a RAID-5 array. Format the array as a GPT disk.

11. You are preparing to deploy three file servers running Windows Server 2008 in a failover cluster. The storage strategy for the cluster needs to isolate the cluster storage traffic from the existing network and ensure that data is available if one of the storage controllers fails. What should you do?

    A. Use iSCSI with VDS.

    B. Use iSCSI with MPIO.

    C. Use Fibre Channel with VDS.

    D. Use Fibre Channel with MPIO.

12. You are tasked with planning the deployment of a web-based application. You need to provide high availability for the web-based application in the event of a single server failure. Additionally, you must minimize costs. What should you choose?

    A. Install Windows Server 2008 Enterprise edition on two servers, and configure a failover cluster.

    B. Install Windows Server 2008 Datacenter edition on two servers, and configure a failover cluster.

    C. Install Windows Server 2008 Web edition on two servers, and configure an NLB cluster.

    D. Install Windows Server 2008 Standard edition on two servers, and configure an NLB cluster.

13. You have configured two servers running Server Core as part of a network load balancing cluster. You've also installed IIS on both servers to host a website. You want to remotely administer IIS on these servers. Is this possible, and if so how?

    A. No. It's not possible to remotely administer this configuration.

    B. Yes, it's possible. Ensure your desktop computer is running Windows Vista, and run WinRM tool on Windows Vista.

    C. Yes, it's possible. Enable WinRM on both IIS servers in the NLB cluster.

    D. Yes, it's possible. Install RDC 6.0 on both the IIS servers in the NLB cluster.

14. You need to provide input into your company's business continuity plan for the domain controllers that you maintain. You must be able to completely restore any domain controllers in the event of a complete server failure. What would you recommend? (Choose all that apply.)

    A. Use Windows Server to perform a full server backup on an internal disk of each domain controller. Create a bootable WinRE disk available for each domain controller.

    B. Use Windows Server to perform a full server backup on an internal disk of each domain controller. Configure WDS to deploy WinRE when needed.

    C. Use Windows Server to perform a full server backup to a network share for each domain controller. Install WinRE on a partition on the domain controller.

    D. Use Windows Server to perform a full server backup to a network share for each domain controller. Configure WDS to deploy WinRE when needed.

15. You manage a Windows Server 2008–based file server. You need to design a backup strategy that will allow you to schedule backups and allow you to perform a complete server recovery and restore data to the file level if needed. What should you do?

    A. Enable previous versions on the server.

    B. Use Windows Server to perform backups to DVD.

    C. Use Windows Server to perform backups to an internal drive.

    D. Use Windows Server to perform backups to an external USB drive.

16. You manage a Windows Server 2008–based file server. You need to design a backup strategy that will allow you to restore both the operating system and data files in the event of a total server failure. Of the following, what can be used for the restore?

    A. WinRE and Windows Complete PC Restore

    B. WinRE and Windows Server Backup

    C. WDS and Windows Server Backup

    D. Windows Server Backup and previous versions

17. You are asked to recommend a failover cluster storage solution for a Windows Server 2008 server on a TCP/IP network. The solution should minimize costs. What do you recommend?

    A. Basic

    B. Dynamic

    C. FC

    D. iSCSI

18. You are developing a business continuity plan and are considering your domain controllers. You want to be able to perform a complete recovery of each entire domain controller in the event of failure of the server. Each of the domain controllers is installed on Windows Server 2008. Which of the following options will fulfill this goal? (Choose all that apply.)

    A. Create a WinRE partition on each domain controller.

    B. Use WDS to deploy the WinRE.

    C. Install the Complete PC and Restore feature on each domain controller.

    D. Use WDS to deploy the Complete PC and Restore feature.

19. You want to implement a recovery plan for Windows Server 2008 servers you manage. How can the WinRE be launched? (Choose all that apply.)

    A. From the command line

    B. From WDS

    C. From the installation DVD

    D. From a bootable WinRE disk

20. A server you manage has suffered a catastrophic failure. You are considering launching the WinRE to assist. What can be launched from the WinRE? (Choose all that apply.)

    A. The WinRE command prompt

    B. Windows Complete PC Restore

    C. Windows Memory Diagnostic Tool

    D. Windows Server Backup

Answers to Review Questions

1. **A, C.**   Shadow Copies will allow users to retrieve previous versions of their data without an administrator's help. As a best practice, you should store the Shadow Copies on a separate volume (on a separate physical disk). Performing a daily backup of data, you'll be able to restore data if any drive fails. Clustering will allow the services of the server to continue running even if the server fails, but this is not required in the scenario.

2. **D.**   By enabling Shadow Copies, users can retrieve previous versions of their files without administrator user intervention. There is no need to install Windows Server Backup on the user's desktop. You can't install Windows Complete PC Restore or the WinRE on the user's desktops.

3. **D.**   The operating system can be protected only with a RAID-1. For best performance with fault tolerance, data should be protected with a RAID-5. Placing data files on a RAID-1 does not provide the best performance. The operating system cannot be placed on a RAID-5. Although you should protect the SQL transaction log by placing it on a RAID-1 (not a RAID-5), you didn't need this knowledge to answer the question.

4. **D.**   To separate the data from the operating system and provide fault tolerance, you should need to use a RAID-1 and a RAID-5. The operating system cannot be loaded on a RAID-5 but must be protected with RAID-1. RAID-5 would be used to protect the data. RAID-0 does not provide any fault tolerance.

5. **C.**   To provide redundancy for a server in case the server fails, you should use failover clusters. Failover clusters can be installed on Windows Server 2008 Enterprise edition or Datacenter edition. The Server Core installation cannot be used to protect applications (only services such as DHCP, DNS, file servers, or Active Directory Domain Services). Load balancing does not provide fault tolerance.

6. **A.**   A two-node failover cluster will provide fault tolerance if a single server fails. An external RAID-10 will provide fault tolerance to the disk subsystem and provide the best disk throughput. RAID-0 does not provide fault tolerance, and RAID-1 doesn't provide the best throughput. You can't use internal storage with a failover cluster.

7. **C.**   Since you want to protect one server and minimize costs, a two-node cluster would be the best choice. The Node and File Share Majority quorum configuration (or the Node and Disk quorum configuration) is recommended for an even number of nodes. Three nodes would add unnecessary costs. The No Majority: Disk Only quorum configuration is included for backward compatibility and is otherwise not recommended.

8. **C.**   A single two-node cluster can be used. One node would be at each location, and if the node fails, the users would be automatically redirected to the other node. There's no such thing as a one-node failover cluster. It would be much more expensive than necessary to implement two failover clusters (one at each office).

9. B.   A failover cluster will maximize fault tolerance. Windows Server 2008 Enterprise and Datacenter editions support failover clusters. You can use the existing network infrastructure to support iSCSI. A Fibre Channel will not use the existing network infrastructure but require additional hardware. Windows Server 2008 Standard edition does not support failover clusters. A network load balancing (NLB) cluster does not provide fault tolerance.

10. D.   A two-node cluster will support the requirement to keep the services operational if a single server fails. RAID-5 will ensure the data is protected (as will RAID-10). Using GPT disk, you can support volumes larger than two terabytes. RAID-0 won't provide fault tolerance for the disks. Without GPT, there isn't support for volumes larger than 2TB. There is no such thing as a one-node cluster.

11. D.   Fibre Channel will isolate the storage traffic from the existing network by using dedicated hardware and connections. Multipath I/O (MPIO) will provide fault tolerance if a storage controller fails. iSCSI uses existing network infrastructure and the Virtual Disk Service (VDS) does not provide fault tolerance if a controller fails.

12. C.   You can configure two servers in a network load balancing (NLB) cluster on Windows Server 2008 Web edition. An NLB cluster will allow the web application to remain operational even if a single server fails, and it will minimize the costs since an NLB cluster can be installed on Windows Server 2008 Web edition. A failover cluster would require additional hardware, so an NLB cluster would be preferable in this situation. Windows Server 2008 Standard edition costs more than Windows Server 2008 Web edition, so the Web edition would be preferable.

13. B.   If you enable Windows Remote Management (WinRM) on the Server Core servers, you can remotely manage it. WinRM doesn't need to be enabled on the client computer. Remote Desktop Connection 6.0 (RDC 6.0) is not needed for remotely administering a Server Core installation.

14. D.   You can perform a full server backup to a network share for each domain controller to prepare for complete server failure. You can restore this from the Windows Recovery Environment (WinRE). There are four ways to access the WinRE: deployed from Windows Deployment Services (WDS), from the installation DVD, from a created bootable CD, or from an installed WinRE partition. You can't back up a volume to a volume that is being backed up and a full server backup includes all volumes. Further, if you experienced a complete server failure, the backup wouldn't be available if stored locally.

15. D.   You can back up data to an external USB drive. In the event of a server failure, you can restore from the USB drive. Previous versions (available if you enable Shadow Copies) will not allow you to restore the server. You can't schedule backups to DVD. You can't perform a full server backup to an internal disk, so backing up volumes to an internal disk won't meet the requirements.

16. A.   The Windows Recovery Environment (WinRE) includes the Windows Complete PC Restore option. Windows Server Backup is not available in WinRE and can't be deployed with Windows Deployment Services (WDS). Windows Server Backup can't be accessed in the event of a total server failure and previous versions are used by end users, not during a total server failure.

17. D.   An Internet Small Computer Serial Interface (iSCSI) interface minimizes costs by utilizing existing network infrastructure. Fibre Channel (FC) is generally more expensive since it requires dedicated hardware and connections. The cost is not affected if disks are basic or dynamic.

18. A, B.   You can use Windows Deployment Services (WDS) to deploy the Windows Recovery Environment (WinRE) or create a WinRE partition on the domain controller. You can also use the installation DVD to boot into the WinRE or create a bootable CD with the WinRE. You can't install the Complete PC and Restore feature on a server but instead can install only the WinRE, which includes the Complete PC and Restore feature.

19. B, C, D.   The Windows Recovery Environment (WinRE) can be launched from Windows Deployment Services (WDS), from the installation DVD (by selecting Repair Your Computer), or from a bootable WinRE disk. You can't launch WinRE from the command line.

20. A, B, C.   The system recovery options available from the Windows Recovery Environment (WinRE) are Windows Complete PC Restore, Windows Memory Diagnostic Tool, and the WinRE command prompt. You can't access the Windows Server Backup from the WinRE.

About the Companion CD

IN THIS APPENDIX:

- ✓ What you'll find on the CD
- ✓ System requirements
- ✓ Using the CD
- ✓ Troubleshooting

What You'll Find on the CD

The following sections are arranged by category and summarize the software and other goodies you'll find on the CD. If you need help with installing the items provided on the CD, refer to the installation instructions in the "Using the CD" section of this appendix.

Some programs on the CD might fall into one of these categories:

Shareware programs are fully functional, free, trial versions of copyrighted programs. If you like particular programs, register with their authors for a nominal fee and receive licenses, enhanced versions, and technical support.

Freeware programs are free, copyrighted games, applications, and utilities. You can copy them to as many computers as you like—for free—but they offer no technical support.

GNU software is governed by its own license, which is included inside the folder of the GNU software. There are no restrictions on distribution of GNU software. See the GNU license at the root of the CD for more details.

Trial, *demo*, or *evaluation* versions of software are usually limited either by time or by functionality (such as not letting you save a project after you create it).

Sybex Test Engine

For Windows

The CD contains the Sybex test engine, which includes all of the assessment test and chapter review questions in electronic format, as well as two bonus exams located only on the CD.

PDF of the Book

For Windows

We have included an electronic version of the text in `.pdf` format. You can view the electronic version of the book with Adobe Reader.

Adobe Reader

For Windows

We've also included a copy of Adobe Reader so you can view PDF files that accompany the book's content. For more information on Adobe Reader or to check for a newer version, visit Adobe's website at `www.adobe.com/products/reader/`.

Electronic Flashcards

For PC, Pocket PC, and Palm

   These handy electronic flashcards are just what they sound like. One side contains a question or fill-in-the-blank question, and the other side shows the answer.

System Requirements

Make sure your computer meets the minimum system requirements shown in the following list. If your computer doesn't match up to most of these requirements, you may have problems using the software and files on the companion CD. For the latest and greatest information, please refer to the ReadMe file located at the root of the CD-ROM.

- A PC running Microsoft Windows 98, Windows 2000, Windows NT4 (with SP4 or later), Windows Me, Windows XP, or Windows Vista
- An Internet connection
- A CD-ROM drive

Using the CD

To install the items from the CD to your hard drive, follow these steps:

1. Insert the CD into your computer's CD-ROM drive. The license agreement appears.

Windows users: The interface won't launch if you have autorun disabled. In that case, click Start ➤ Run (for Windows Vista, Start ➤ All Programs ➤ Accessories ➤ Run). In the dialog box that appears, type **D:\Start.exe**. (Replace *D* with the proper letter if your CD drive uses a different letter. If you don't know the letter, see how your CD drive is listed under My Computer.) Click OK.

2. Read the license agreement, and then click the Accept button if you want to use the CD.

   The CD interface appears. The interface allows you to access the content with just one or two clicks.

Troubleshooting

Wiley has attempted to provide programs that work on most computers with the minimum system requirements. Alas, your computer may differ, and some programs may not work properly for some reason.

The two likeliest problems are that you don't have enough memory (RAM) for the programs you want to use or you have other programs running that are affecting installation or running of a program. If you get an error message such as "Not enough memory" or "Setup cannot continue," try one or more of the following suggestions and then try using the software again:

Turn off any antivirus software running on your computer. Installation programs sometimes mimic virus activity and may make your computer incorrectly believe that it's being infected by a virus.

Close all running programs. The more programs you have running, the less memory is available to other programs. Installation programs typically update files and programs; so if you keep other programs running, installation may not work properly.

Have your local computer store add more RAM to your computer. This is, admittedly, a drastic and somewhat expensive step. However, adding more memory can really help the speed of your computer and allow more programs to run at the same time.

Customer Care

If you have trouble with the book's companion CD-ROM, please call the Wiley Product Technical Support phone number at (800) 762-2974. Outside the United States, call +1(317) 572-3994. You can also contact Wiley Product Technical Support at http://sybex .custhelp.com. John Wiley & Sons will provide technical support only for installation and other general quality-control items. For technical support on the applications themselves, consult the program's vendor or author.

To place additional orders or to request information about other Wiley products, please call (877) 762-2974.

Glossary

A

Active Directory A directory service included in Active Directory Domain Services that stores information about resources (such as users, computers, and groups). The data is stored in a database and made available to users and computers on the network.

Active Directory Certificate Services (AD CS) A server role used to create certification authorities and issue certificates. Certificates and certification authorities are part of a public key infrastructure (PKI).

Active Directory Domain Services (AD DS) A server role using a distributed database to store and manage information about network resources and application-specific data from directory-enabled applications (such as Active Directory–integrated DNS). A server running AD DS is called a *domain controller.*

Active Directory–integrated (ADI) zone A DNS zone that is stored in Active Directory and replicated by Active Directory. A significant benefit of using ADI zones is that DNS zone transfers are part of Active Directory replication and don't need to be managed separately.

Administrators (domain) A group on the domain that grants members full and complete permissions and rights on computers within the domain. Someone in the Administrators group has full control on domain controllers.

Administrators (local) A group on the local system that grants members full and complete permissions and rights on that system. A user account in the local Administrators group on Server1 can do anything and everything on Server1 but has no permissions on Server2.

B

baseline A beginning point. When monitoring a server, you first create a baseline that shows what the performance is at this moment in time. Later, you can take measurements and compare them against the baseline to determine whether any changes have occurred. Standard computer images can also be a baseline. By using Windows Deployment Services (WDS), you can deploy standard images as a baseline configuration and then use other tools such as Group Policy to fine-tune those images.

basic image An image with the operating system only. It is derived from the install.wim file that can be found on the installation DVD. Basic images can be deployed using Windows Deployment Services (WDS). Basic images can also be modified by installing applications or otherwise modifying the configuration of the system and saving as a custom image.

BitLocker Drive Encryption A set of technologies that encrypts the entire contents of a hard drive. If a computer is lost, the contents of the drive should remain protected. BitLocker requires the use of special hardware (a trusted platform module) to support its full capabilities.

boot image   An image used to boot a system into the Windows Preboot Execution (WinPE) environment. Once booted into a boot image, operating system images can be downloaded and installed onto the computer.

C

capture image   An image captured from a functional computer. You can configure a system with applications and operating system changes and then capture the image. Captured images can then be deployed to other computers using WDS and will have the identical configuration.

certificate   An electronic file. It holds information about the holder of the certificate, the issuer of the certificate (the CA), when it expires, and a key that can be used for encryption. Certificates are used for a wide variety of purposes, but the two primary purposes of a certificate are encryption and authentication.

certificate revocation list   A list of certificates that have been revoked. Certificates are revoked if they have been compromised. When a client receives a certificate, they will often query the certification authority for the certificate revocation list (CRL, pronounced "crill") to verify it is valid. The Online Certificate Status Protocol (OCSP) can also be used to check the status of a certificate.

certification authority   A server that issues, manages, and verifies certificates. A certification authority (CA, commonly pronounced as "cah") can be either public or private.

collector-initiated subscription   An event subscription where the computer receiving the events (the collector) initiates the transfer. This is also known as a *pull subscription*. The collector periodically contacts the source computer and pulls the events.

Cscript.exe   A command-based script host. Cscript.exe allows you to run scripts from the command line. It is the complement to the Windows Script Host, which runs scripts within Windows using dialog boxes.

custom image   An image used to fully deploy a system. Custom images are derived from basic images but are modified to include applications and any other operating system settings as desired.

D

data collector set   A group of data collection points used to review or log the performance of a system. You can access several predefined data collector sets within the Reliability and Performance Monitor that can be used to easily measure the performance of your server. You can also create your own user-defined data collector sets.

data recovery agent (DRA)   A designated person or account that can decrypt files encrypted with the encrypting file system (EFS). This is useful if the original owner's account is unavailable to decrypt the files.

DCPromo   A program run to promote a server to a domain controller or run demotion operations. You run DCPromo from either the command line, the Run line, or the Start Search box.

DFS namespace   A virtual view of shared folders hosted by a Distributed File System (DFS) namespace server. A single DFS namespace is used to make it easy for end users to find data on the network.

DHCPv6 Stateful mode   Indicates that the DHCP server is being used to issue IPv6 addresses to clients.

DHCPv6 Stateless mode   Indicates that the DHCP server is not being used to issue IPv6 addresses to clients. Clients using IPv6 will autoconfigure their own IPv6 address using the prefix from a local router advertisement.

discover image   Used by non-PXE clients to allow them to boot using a CD or DVD. Clients can then connect to a WDS server to select and download an install image.

disk quotas
Used to track and/or restrict the amount of space users can consume on a disk. Disk quotas can be created by using File Server Resource Manager (FSRM) or by using basic NTFS capabilities. FSRM provides significant greater capabilities.

Distributed File System (DFS)   A service within the File Services role. DFS allows you to organize multiple folders from multiple servers in a single namespace to make it easy for users to find data from a single path. DFS can also be used to replicate content between multiple servers for high availability.

DNS zone   A group of resource records associated with a specific namespace. A domain named mcitpsuccess.com would have a DNS server hosting a zone with the same name. All resource records (such as A, AAAA, PTR, NS, MX, CNAME, SRV, and SOA) would be hosted within one of the DNS zone files. The two DNS zone files are forward lookup zone (primarily used to resolve a hostname to an IP address with an A or AAAA record) and reverse lookup zone (primarily used to resolve an IP address to a hostname).

Domain Name System (DNS)   A server role in Windows Server 2008 that provides name resolution of hostnames. DNS includes many types of records (A, AAAA, PTR, NS, MX, CNAME, SRV, and SOA) and is used within a domain to help clients and servers locate resources on the network. DNS is required within an Active Directory Domain Services domain.

Domain Naming Master   One of five FSMO roles. The Domain Naming Master is used to manage the creation of new domains within the forest. Only one Domain Naming Master exists within a forest.

Dynamic Host Configuration Protocol (DHCP)   A server role in Windows Server 2008 used to dynamically provide TCP/IP configuration information to clients. TCP/IP information includes IP address, subnet mask, default gateway, address of DNS server, address of WINS server, domain name, and much more.

dynamic update   Process of dynamically updating DNS records. When a client turns on, it will typically receive TCP/IP configuration information (including an IP address and the IP address of a DNS server) from DHCP. The client will then give the DNS server its name and IP address to update the A record. It's common for the DHCP server to update the client's PTR record.

E

enterprise certification authority (CA)   A certification authority that exists within an Active Directory Domain Services domain. A company can create an enterprise CA to issue certificates within the enterprise instead of purchasing certificates from an external stand-alone CA.

F

failover cluster   A server redundancy feature that allows a service to continue operating even if a server fails. A failover cluster has two or more servers configured as nodes in a failover cluster. Nodes in a failover clusters must share the same data source. If one node fails, another node will access the data source and continue to provide the service.

Fibre Channel (FC)   A high-speed connection used for storage networking. Fibre Channel uses dedicated hardware (Fibre Channel switches and host bus adapters), making it more expensive than iSCSI.

file screens   A tool available within the File Server Resource Manager that allows you to control which types of files users can save. A file screen can specifically restrict certain files and generate notifications to an administrator when users attempt to save unauthorized files. Examples of files that may be screened include .mp3 audio files and .mpg video files.

File Server Resource Manager (FSRM)   A service within the File Server role used to manage resources on a file server. The FSRM includes tools to help you understand, control, and manage the quantity and type of data stored on your servers. This includes quota management, file-screening management, and storage reports management tools.

forest   One or more trees of domains contained within the same logical structure and created off a single root domain. Trees are one or more domains with the same namespace. For example, mcitpsuccess.com and training.mcitpsuccess.com both have the same namespace of mcitpsuccess.com. A single root domain without any child domains or other trees is also accurately called a *tree* and a *forest*.

forward lookup zone   Holds the resource records to provide name to IP address resolution of hosts within a DNS zone. The primary records used within a forward lookup zone are the A (used for IPv4 addresses) and the AAAA (used for IPv6 addresses). DNS clients query the DNS server with a hostname, and DNS responds with an IP address. Other records are also contained within a forward lookup zone, such as NS, MX, CNAME, SRV, and SOA.

FSMO roles   Flexible single master operations roles held by domain controllers within a forest. Domain controllers hold equal roles as peers with the exception of these roles. The FSMO roles perform specific tasks within the forest and individual domains. Two of the roles are unique within the forest (Schema Master and Domain Naming Master), and the other three roles (RID Master, PDC Emulator, and Infrastructure Master) are unique within each domain. In other words, if you had a forest with three domains, you would have one Schema Master, one Domain Naming Master, three RID Masters, three PDC Emulators, and three Infrastructure Masters.

G

global catalog   A listing of all objects in a forest. The global catalog is queried to locate objects (such as users, computers, groups, printers, and so on) within a forest. The global catalog is hosted on a global catalog server.

GlobalNames Zone (GNZ)   A type of DNS zone used to resolve single-label names. Single-label names are referred to as GlobalNames and have been traditionally resolved using WINS. A GNZ zone can be used to aid in the retirement of Windows Internet Name Service (WINS) within a network.

Group Policy   A group of settings that can be used to centrally manage users and computers within an Active Directory Domain Services environment. The great strength of Group Policy is that you can configure a setting once and have it apply to many users and computers within your environment. You can use Group Policy to manipulate hundreds of settings, such as deploying applications, redirecting folders, restricting the installation of removal devices, managing passwords, and much, much more.

Group Policy Management Console (GPMC)   A Microsoft Management Console (MMC) snap-in that can be used to manage Group Policy within a forest. You can create, assign, manipulate, back up, restore, troubleshoot, and manage Group Policy objects from within the GPMC.

Group Policy objects (GPOs)   An object that can be linked to sites, domains, and organizational units for the purpose of managing users and computers. GPOs have two nodes (computers and users) with hundreds of configuration options that can be configured. A linked GPO will apply to all users and computers within the scope of the GPO.

I

Infrastructure Master   One of five FSMO roles. The Infrastructure Master is used in a multiple domain forest to keep track of changes in group membership in other domains for a group in its own domain. The Infrastructure Master is not needed in a single-domain forest. Only one Infrastructure Master exists within any domain.

install images   An image installed on a computer from WDS that includes a full operating system. A basic install image includes just the operating system. A custom install image includes applications, service packs and updates, baseline security settings, configuration settings, and anything else desired on the image. Install images can be deployed to multiple computers using WDS.

Internet Information Services 7.0 (IIS 7.0)   A server hosting the Web Server role running IIS 7.0. IIS is used to host websites and web applications. IIS is also used with Terminal Services and SharePoint sites.

Internet Small Computer System Interface (iSCSI)   A method of connecting a computer to a storage network using existing network infrastructure. iSCSI adds to the overhead of the existing network infrastructure, but if the network can support it, it is significantly less expensive than Fibre Channel.

IPSec   A method of encryption used in networks and with L2TP to connect with a VPN. IPSec provides data confidentiality, integrity, and authentication.

K

key recovery agent (KRA)   A designated account that can recover private keys. This is similar to the data recovery agent (DRA), which can recover data, but it goes a step further and can actually recover keys used to encrypt the data.

L

Layer 2 Tunneling Protocol (L2TP)   A tunneling protocol used to connect with a virtual private network (VPN). L2TP is commonly used with IPSec in a VPN. L2TP/IPSec can't be used if it needs to pass through a Network Address Translation (NAT) server.

loopback processing   A GPO setting causing a policy applying to a computer to take precedence over a policy applying to the user who is logging on. Normally, the policy applying to the user would take precedence since the user logs in after the computer starts up and the last policy applied takes precedence. In some situations (such as a computer in a lab or in a library), you may want the computer policy to take precedence, and you can use loopback processing to configure this.

N

Network Access Protection (NAP)   A group of technologies used to restrict access to a network based on the configuration of a client. NAP can be used to inspect a client to ensure it meets the requirements specified by an administrator, such as having certain updates or services packs, having the firewall enabled, or having anti-malware software installed with up-to-date signatures.

network-level authentication (NLA)   Security used to authenticate the user, the client machine, and the server before a Terminal Services session begins. NLA is supported by default on Windows Vista and Server 2008 but can also be supported on Windows XP with SP2 (or greater) or Windows Server 2003 with SP1 (or greater).

network load balancing (NLB)   A cluster used to provide scalability and high availability. A NLB cluster balances client requests between multiple servers. If one of the nodes in the cluster fails, clients are redirected to other nodes. NLB clusters do not share a data source. If a data source needs to be shared, you must use a failover cluster.

O

Online Certificate Status Protocol (OCSP)   A protocol used to the check the status of certificates issued by a certification authority (CA). When a client receives a certificate, they can query an online responder to verify whether the certificate is valid. OCSP is used as an alternative to checking the certificate revocation list (CRL).

online responder   A server running the Online Responder service that responds to Online Certificate Status Protocol (OCSP) status requests. The online responder receives OCSP status requests from clients querying about the status of a certificate. The online responder returns a response of "good," "revoked," or "unknown."

P

Password Replication Policy   A policy used to define which passwords (if any) will be cached on an RODC. It's common to configure this policy so that regular user accounts are cached but accounts with higher permissions (such as members of the Administrators, Account Operators, Server Operators, and Backup Operators groups) accounts are not cached.

password settings object (PSO)   A tool used to change the password policy for individual users or groups. Historically, you could have only one password policy in a domain. Using a PSO, you can assign a different password policy for a specific group. This is typically done to apply a more stringent password policy for users with elevated privileges.

PDC Emulator   One of five FSMO roles. The PDC Emulator is used for several miscellaneous tasks, such as time synchronization in the domain and managing passwords in the domain. Only one PDC Emulator role exists within any domain.

Point-to-Point Tunneling Protocol (PPTP)   An older tunneling protocol used to connect with a virtual private network (VPN). Data is encrypted with Microsoft Point-to-Point Encryption, which provides data confidentiality. PPTP does not provide data integrity or machine-level authentication. Historically, PPTP was used instead of L2TP when a VPN needed to be created through a Network Address Translation (NAT) server. With Windows Server 2008, SSTP can be considered instead.

PowerShell
A scripting language that extends the command-line interface. It includes more than 130 command-line tools called *cmdlets*.

prestaging   Creating a computer in Active Directory with the computer's GUID. This is sometimes done for PXE clients that will have an image deployed to them via WDS.

primary zone   A zone hosted by a DNS server where the server is authoritative for the zone. A primary zone holds the only read/write copy of the database (unless multiple Active Directory–integrated primary zones are configured). Zone data is transferred to the secondary zone via zone transfers.

processor affinity   Used to link a specific process with a specific processor in a multiple processor system in Windows System Resource Manager (WSRM).

public key infrastructure (PKI)   A group of technologies that work together to allow certificates and keys to be used for authentication and encryption. A PKI includes all the requirements to issue and manage certificates including certificate authorities, certificate revocation lists, the Online Certificate Status Protocol, online responders, and more.

PXE   Preboot Execution. A PXE (pronounced "pixie") client can automatically connect to a WDS server without having any operating system installed. Instead, the client boots, contacts DHCP for TCP/IP configuration information, and then contacts a WDS server to download a boot image.

R

RAID   Redundant Array of Independent (or Inexpensive) Disks.

RAID-0   Two or more disks striped together. RAID-0 is used to increase read and write performance.

RAID-1   Two disks configured as a mirror. RAID-1 is used to provide fault tolerance for the operating system partition and sometimes used to protect application files such as SQL Server transaction logs. A RAID-1 configuration can survive the failure of either one of the disks.

RAID-5   Three or more disks striped together with parity for fault tolerance. RAID-5 is used to provide fault tolerance for data disks and can survive the failure of any single disk.

RAID-10   A more complex RAID configuration that combines RAID-1 and RAID-0. It requires an even number of disks, with each pair of disks created as a mirror and additional pairs used to stripe the mirrors. A RAID-10 configuration provides significant fault tolerance since more than one drive can fail (as long as it's not two drives in the same mirror).

Read-Only Domain Controller (RODC)   A domain controller role that can be configured so that only a minimal number of users' credentials is stored locally. It is designed to be deployed to remote locations where either technical support or physical security is limited. If the domain controller is compromised, only a few user accounts would be compromised instead of the entire Active Directory database.

Reliability and Performance Monitor   A Microsoft Management Console (MMC) designed to allow you to monitor and analyze many system metrics. It includes monitoring tools, data collector sets, and reporting capabilities.

remote access   Process of providing access to an internal network from an external source. Remote access can be provided via dial-up as long as the client and the remote access server have modems and telephone lines. It's more common to configure the server as a VPN server. The VPN server would have a public IP address, and clients would connect using a tunneling protocol such as PPTP, L2TP, or SSTP.

Remote Desktop Connection   An application used to remotely connect to other computers. While connected via Remote Desktop Connection (RDC), you can do just about anything on the remote server that you can do locally. RDC includes additional features including network-level authentication.

reverse lookup zone   Holds the resource records to provide IP address to name resolution of hosts within a DNS zone. The primary record used within a reverse lookup zone is the PTR record. DNS clients can query the DNS server with an IP address, and DNS responds with a hostname. Reverse lookup zones are optional but are typically used for security purposes.

RID Master   One of five FSMO roles. The RID Master is used to create new unique security identifiers (SIDs) within a domain. It issues unique SIDs to other domain controllers in the domain that are used to uniquely identify users, computers, and groups. Only one RID Master exists within any domain.

rollback plan   A plan designed to allow you to get back to where you started if an upgrade or migration goes bad. It's not uncommon for problems to occur during migrations and upgrades. If the worst happens and you can't finish the project, you at least want to get users back to their original states. The rollback plan can include backups that can be restored or enabling another server to take over the role of the original server.

S

schema   The definition of all objects contained within a forest. Objects (such as users, computers, groups, and so on) are defined in the schema with specific attributes. Only objects contained within the schema can be created, and only attributes in the schema can be used to identify an object. Only one schema exists for an entire forest. The schema is typically modified during the lifetime of the forest to support additional objects and/or object attributes.

Schema Master   One of five FSMO roles. The Schema Master holds the only writable copy of the schema. It ensures that if the schema is modified, it is modified in only one location. Only one Schema Master exists within the forest.

Scregedit.wsf   A script file that can be used to modify the registry editor on a Server Core installation.

Secure Socket Tunneling Protocol (SSTP)   A tunneling protocol using Secure Sockets Layer (SSL) to encrypt the data when connecting to a virtual private network (VPN). SSL within SSTP provides data confidentiality, data integrity, and machine-level authentication. It uses HTTPS over TCP on port 443. Unlike L2TP/IPSec, SSTP can pass through a Network Address Translation (NAT) server.

serial attached SCSI (SAS)   A SCSI array directly attached to a server via a serial SCSI connection.

Server Core   A new feature available within Windows Server 2008 with only a minimal amount of services and capabilities enabled. Server Core includes only the command line and can be used for the following server roles: Active Directory Domain Services, Active Directory Lightweight Directory Services, DHCP, DNS, File Services, Print Services, Steaming Media Services, Web Services, and Hyper-V.

Server Manager   The primary applet used to manage Windows Server 2008 roles and features. You can also use Server Manager to run diagnostics, perform configuration tasks, analyze best practices, and manage your storage.

ServerManagerCmd   The command-line equivalent of the Server Manager applet. It allows you to perform many of the same tasks on a server from the command line that you can perform using the Server Manager GUI.

Shadow Copies   A feature that can be enabled to allow users to restore their own files without intervention of an administrator. The Shadow Copies feature can be enabled only on NTFS drives.

share   A folder that has been configured to be accessible over the network. Once a folder has been shared, it is accessible via a UNC path as \\ServerName\ShareName.

source computer–initiated subscription   An event subscription where the computer generating the events (the source computer) sends them to a collector computer. This is also known as a *push subscription*.

stand-alone CA   A certification authority that exists completely separately from an Active Directory Domain Services domain. Public CAs are known as stand-alone CAs.

standard image   A baseline image that includes the operating system, applications, and settings. A standard image is also referred to as a *custom image*.

storage area network (SAN)   A specialized network used to provide a centralized pool of disk storage that can be accessed by multiple computers.

Sysprep   An application that is executed on a computer to remove unique settings prior to capturing the system as an image. Many settings (such as a computer's name and security identifier) must be unique on a computer. Sysprep removes these unique settings so that the image can be deployed to multiple computers from WDS.

System Center Configuration Manager   The newer version of Systems Management Server (SMS). The System Center Configuration Manager (SCCM) allows administrators to easily assess, deploy, and update clients, servers, and mobile devices.

T

Terminal Services   A server role used to host applications and services that can be remotely accessed. Terminal Services can host several different services, including TS RemoteApp, TS Gateway, TS Session Broker, and TS Web Access.

test bed   A computer or group of computers used for testing. Administrators normally test technologies and changes in a protected environment to determine the impact on the production environment before actually moving the technology or changes to the production environment. A test bed could be a single server or a network of multiple servers.

tree   One or more domains that share the same namespace. For example, mcitpsuccess.com and consulting.mcitpsuccess.com both have the same namespace of mcitpsuccess.com. A single domain without any child or parent domains would accurately be called a tree.

trusted platform module (TPM)   A special microchip built into a computer to support BitLocker. TPM senses when a system has been tampered with (perhaps by a thief) and locks a drive protected with BitLocker. The only way to unlock the drive is by using the BitLocker key that the owner would have but a thief would not have.

TS Connection Authorization Policy (TS CAP)   A policy used to specify which users can connect to a TS Gateway. If users aren't identified in a TS CAP (or aren't in a group that is identified in a TS CAP), they are restricted from connecting with TS Gateway. A TS Gateway is configured with a TS CAP, with a TS RAP, and often with NAP.

TS Gateway   A Terminal Services role service that provides users access to internal network resources via the Internet. Access to TS Gateway is controlled through the use of Terminal Services Connection Authorization Policies (TS CAP), Terminal Services Connection Authorization Policies (TS CAP), and Network Access Protection (NAP).

TS Licensing   A management system used to manage Terminal Services client access licenses.

TS RemoteApp   An application configured to run within a Terminal Services session. A TS RemoteApp program can run within its own window on the user's desktop. It can also be configured to run from a web browser when configured with TS Web Access.

TS Resource Authorization Policy (TS RAP)   A policy used to specify which resources users can access when they connect to a TS Gateway server. Connected users can be restricted to accessing only a select group of servers within a network identified by a computer group. A TS Gateway server is configured with a TS CAP, with a TS RAP, and often with NAP.

TS Session Broker   A Terminal Services role service used to balance the load between multiple Terminal Services servers in a server farm. When a user connects, the TS Session Broker service identifies which server is the least busy and directs the client to that server. Additionally, if a client gets disconnected from a session, the TS Session Broker service ensures that the client is redirected to the same server holding their session data.

TS Web Access   A Terminal Services role service used to allow users to connect to a remote desktop over the Internet using a web browser. TS RemoteApp programs can run within the browser when accessed via TS Web Access.

U

universal naming convention (UNC)   A path to a share on a server. The path takes the format of \\ServerName\ShareName in Windows operating systems.

V

virtual private network (VPN)   A method of accessing a private network over a public network (such as the Internet). VPNs are accessed using a tunneling protocol such as PPTP, L2TP, or SSTP.

W

Windows Deployment Services (WDS)   A Windows Server 2008 role that is used to deploy images to computers. WDS can be used to deploy boot, basic, and custom images including the operating system, settings, and applications. It can also be used to capture images from computers. By creating a target computer configured exactly as you need it, you can then capture the image and deploy it to multiple computers simultaneously.

Windows Internet Name Service (WINS)   A Windows Server 2008 feature that provides name resolution for NetBIOS names. The use of and need for WINS servers is significantly decreasing in networks. GlobalNames Zones in DNS may be used to reduce the need for WINS servers in some networks.

Windows Remote Shell   A tool that allows you to remotely execute command-line tools and scripts. Windows Remote Shell is also known as `WinRS.exe`. `WinRS` is commonly used with Windows Server 2008 servers running Server Core. The Server Core computer would be configured to accept remote commands with the `WinRM` command. The `WinRS` command can then be used to remotely execute the commands.

Windows Script Host (WSH)   A Windows scripting language that interfaces with the graphical user interface of Windows. `Cscript.exe` is the command-line version of WSH.

Windows System Resource Manager (WSRM)   A feature on Windows Server 2008 that allows you to limit the amount of resources available to applications, users, or user sessions. WSRM is commonly used with Terminal Services servers but can also be used with any servers that host multiple sessions or users such as a SharePoint server.

Index

Note to the reader: Throughout this index **boldfaced** page numbers indicate primary discussions of a topic. *Italicized* page numbers indicate illustrations.

G

M

N

Wiley Publishing, Inc. End-User License Agreement

The Absolute MCITP: Windows Server 2008 Server Administrator Book/CD Package on the Market!

Get ready for your Microsoft Certified Information Technology Professional: Windows Server 2008, Server Administrator certification with the most comprehensive and challenging sample tests anywhere!

The Sybex Test Engine features:

- All the review questions, as covered in each chapter of the book
- Challenging questions representative of those you'll find on the real exam
- Two full-length bonus exams available only on the CD
- An Assessment Test to narrow your focus to certain objective groups.

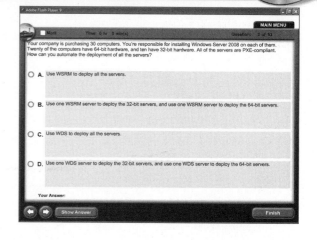

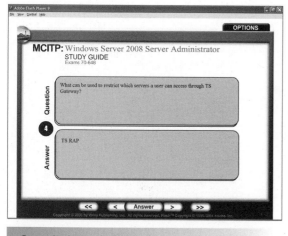

Search through the complete book in PDF!

- Access the entire *MCITP: Microsoft Windows Server 2008 Server Administrator Study Guide* complete with figures and tables, in electronic format.
- Search the *MCITP: Microsoft Windows Server 2008 Server Administrator Study Guide* chapters to find information on any topic in seconds.

Use the Electronic Flashcards for PCs or Palm devices to jog your memory and prep last-minute for the exam!

- Reinforce your understanding of key concepts with these hardcore flashcard-style questions.
- Download the Flashcards to your Palm device and go on the road. Now you can study for the MCITP: Windows Server 2008, Server Administrator (70-646) exam any time, anywhere.

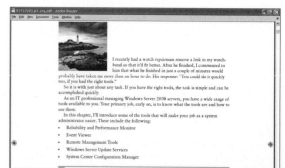